W9-AOK-202

Spell of Desire

Volume 4

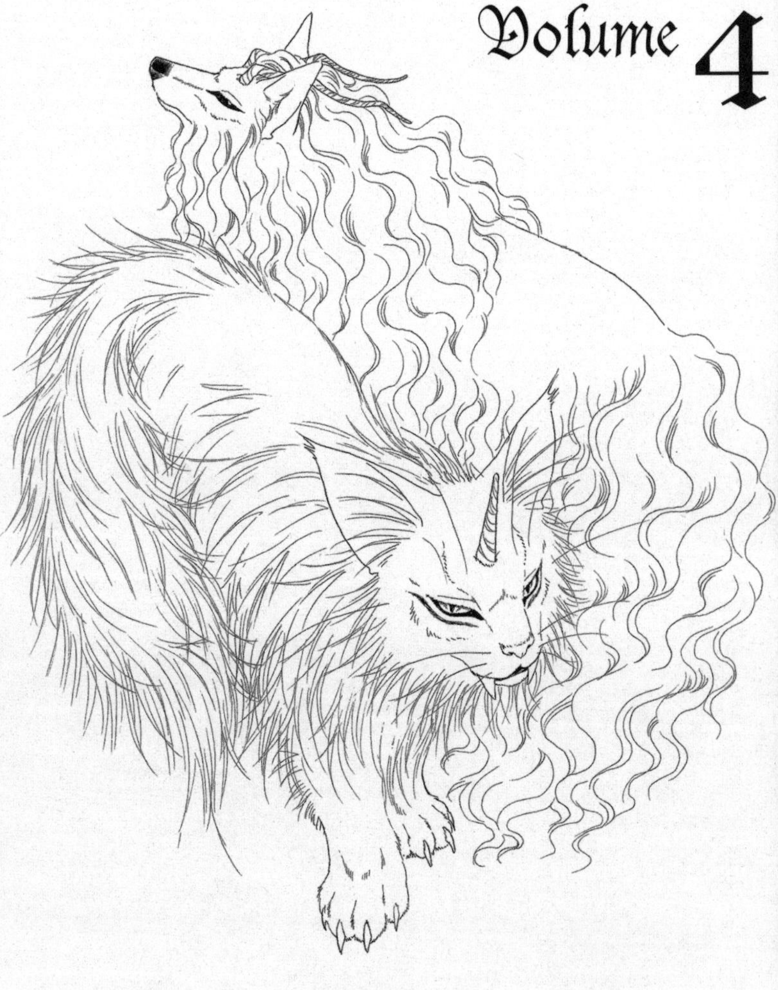

story & art by Tomu Ohmi

Spell of Desire

Contents

Volume 4

story

Kaoruko's peaceful life is changed forever by the arrival of Kaname, a knight charged with protecting her after she is unwillingly entrusted with immense magic belonging to her mother, known as the Witch Queen. The Witch Queen's power is beyond Kaoruko's ability to control—except when Kaname kisses her! Kaname's protection isn't enough to keep Kaoruko from being called before the Black Witches Coven that's ruled by her absent mother. Kaoruko chooses to become a Black Witch herself, but her own power can only be awakened if she loses her virginity in a ritual. Kaname intervenes, and he and Kaoruko consummate their love for each other... As a result, Kaname is branded as a fallen knight!

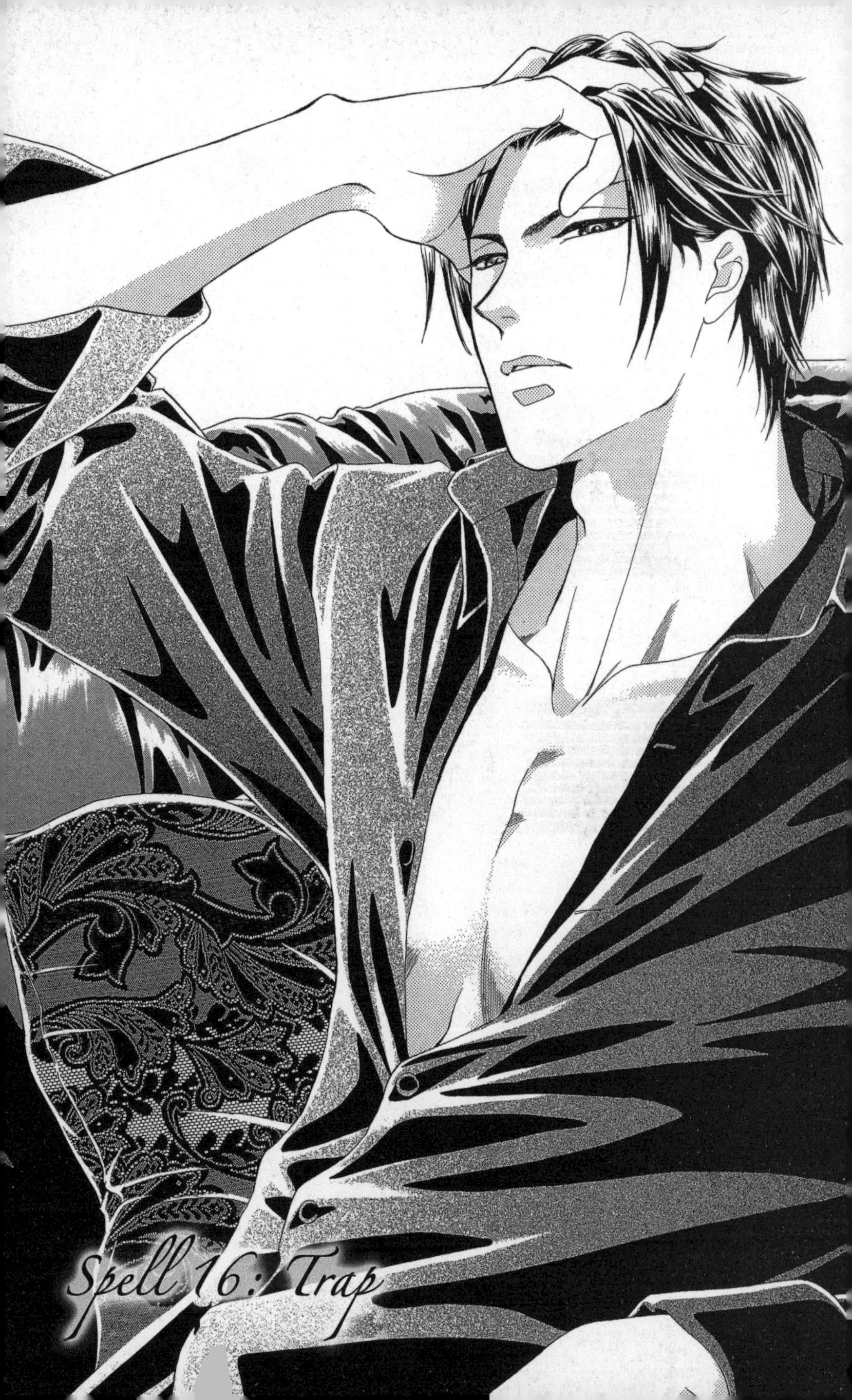
Spell 16: Trap

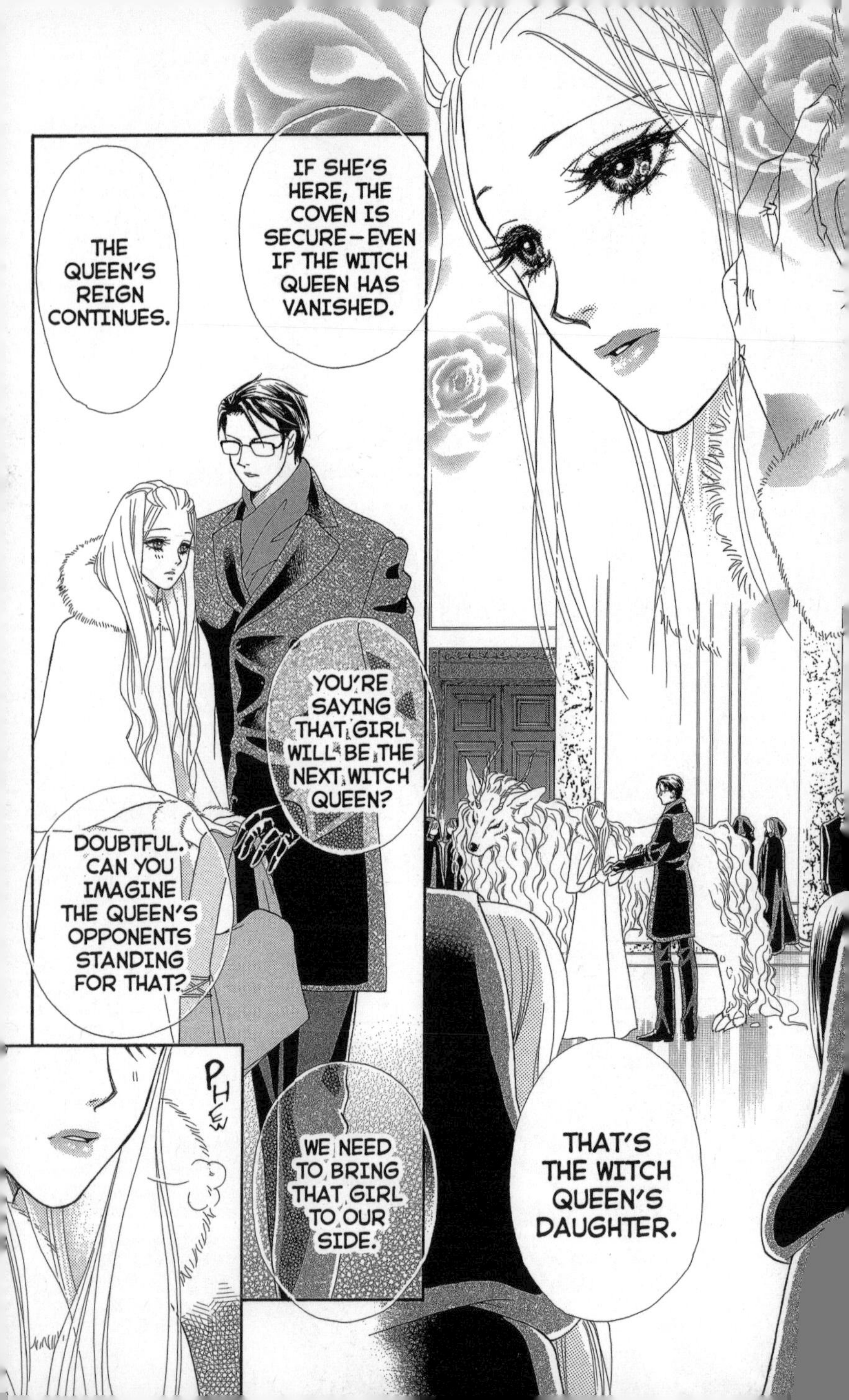
THAT'S THE WITCH QUEEN'S DAUGHTER.
IF SHE'S HERE, THE COVEN IS SECURE—EVEN IF THE WITCH QUEEN HAS VANISHED.
THE QUEEN'S REIGN CONTINUES.
YOU'RE SAYING THAT GIRL WILL BE THE NEXT WITCH QUEEN?
DOUBTFUL. CAN YOU IMAGINE THE QUEEN'S OPPONENTS STANDING FOR THAT?
WE NEED TO BRING THAT GIRL TO OUR SIDE.
PHEW

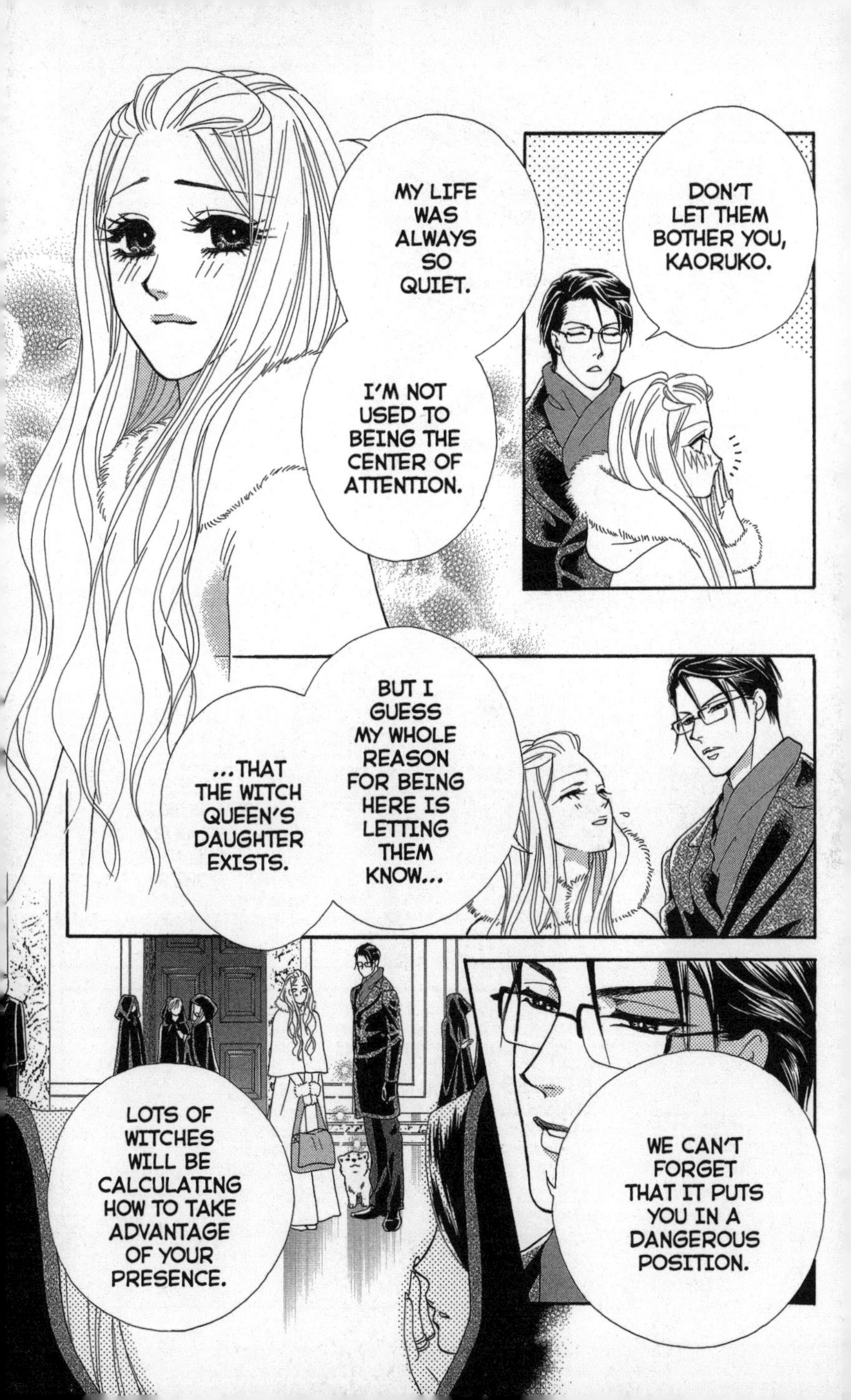
DON'T LET THEM BOTHER YOU, KAORUKO.
MY LIFE WAS ALWAYS SO QUIET.
I'M NOT USED TO BEING THE CENTER OF ATTENTION.
BUT I GUESS MY WHOLE REASON FOR BEING HERE IS LETTING THEM KNOW...
...THAT THE WITCH QUEEN'S DAUGHTER EXISTS.
WE CAN'T FORGET THAT IT PUTS YOU IN A DANGEROUS POSITION.
LOTS OF WITCHES WILL BE CALCULATING HOW TO TAKE ADVANTAGE OF YOUR PRESENCE.

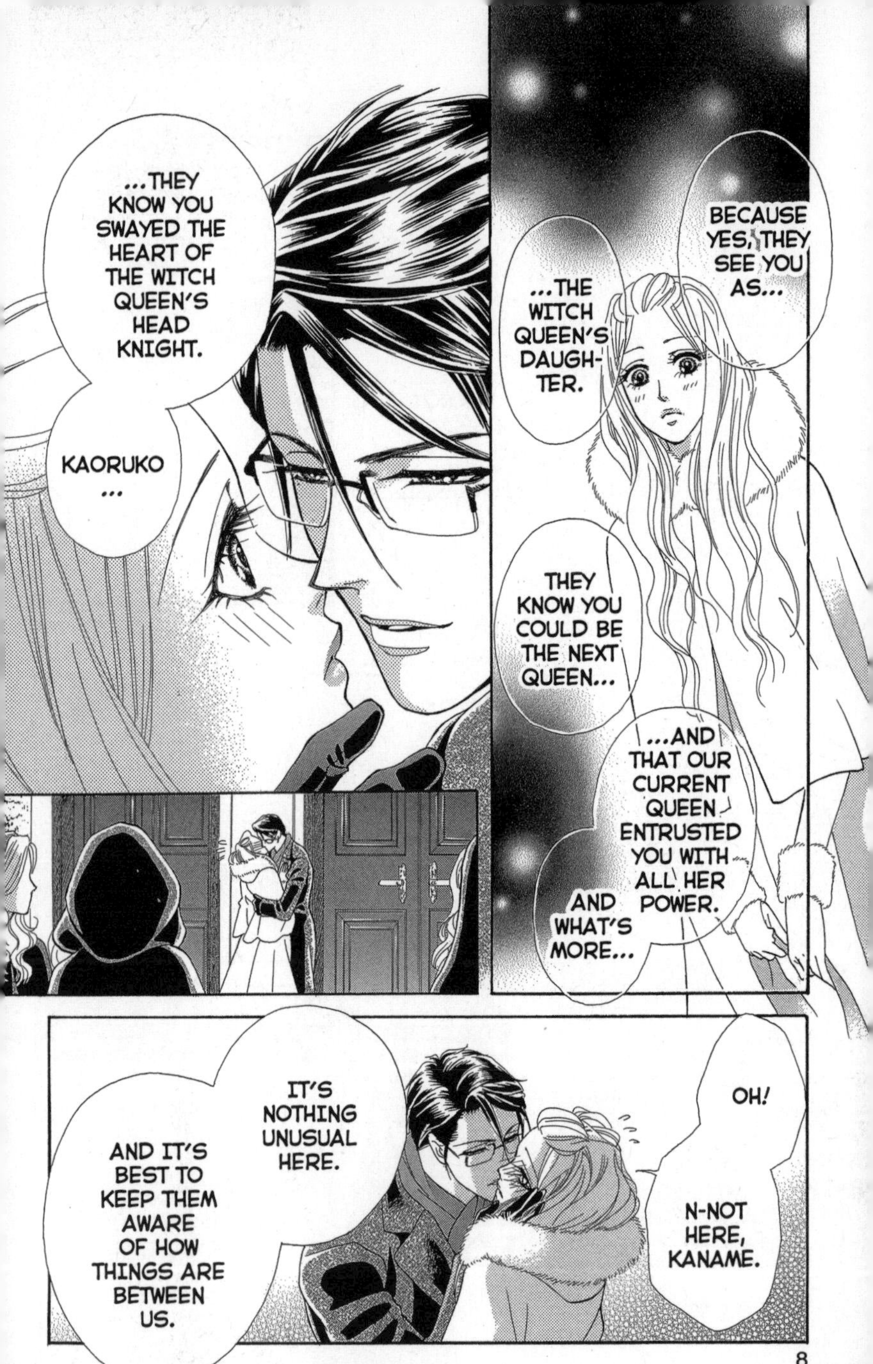
BECAUSE YES, THEY SEE YOU AS...
...THE WITCH QUEEN'S DAUGHTER.
THEY KNOW YOU COULD BE THE NEXT QUEEN...
...AND THAT OUR CURRENT QUEEN ENTRUSTED YOU WITH ALL HER POWER.
AND WHAT'S MORE...
...THEY KNOW YOU SWAYED THE HEART OF THE WITCH QUEEN'S HEAD KNIGHT.
KAORUKO...
OH!
N-NOT HERE, KANAME.
IT'S NOTHING UNUSUAL HERE.
AND IT'S BEST TO KEEP THEM AWARE OF HOW THINGS ARE BETWEEN US.

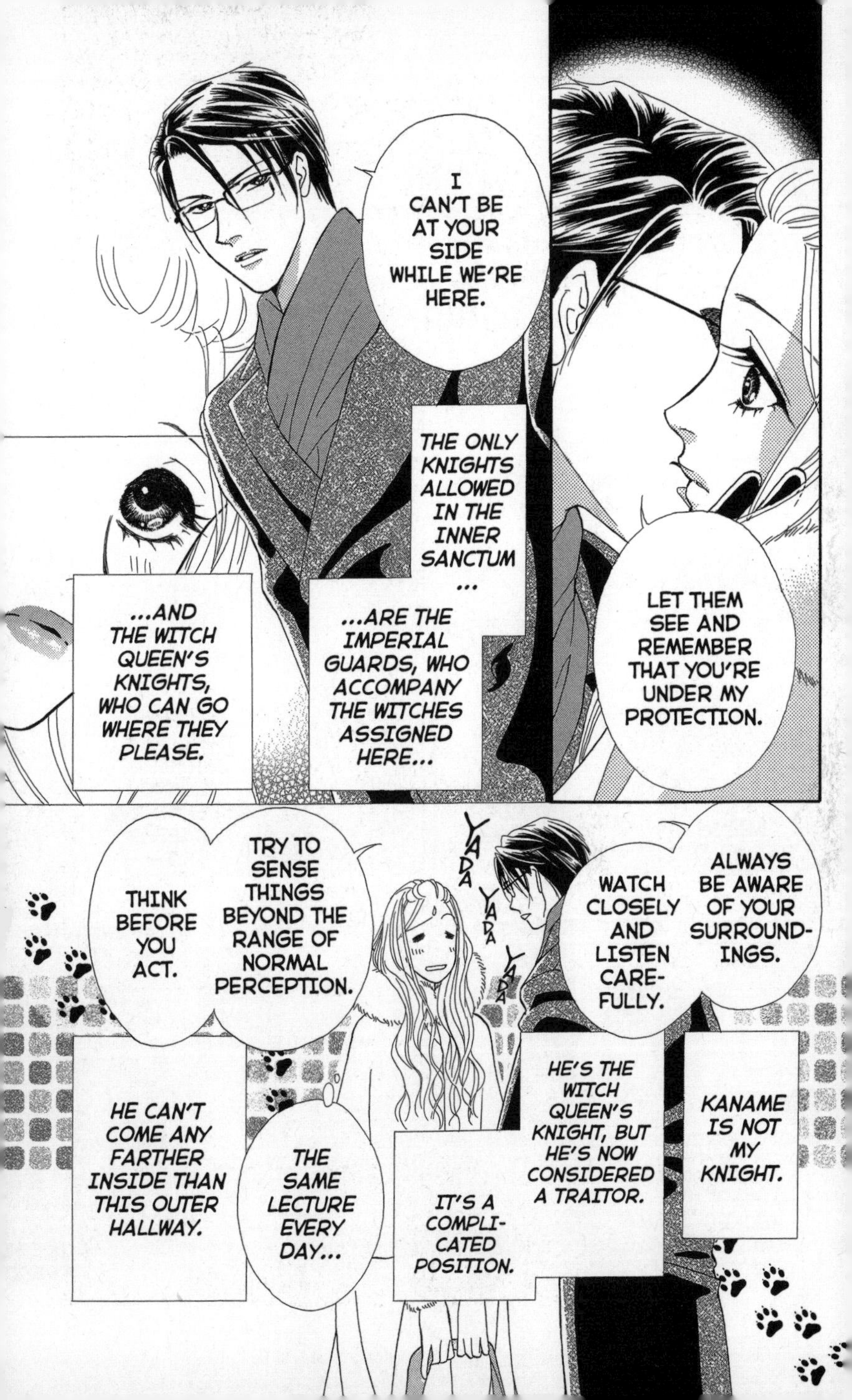
LET THEM SEE AND REMEMBER THAT YOU'RE UNDER MY PROTECTION.
I CAN'T BE AT YOUR SIDE WHILE WE'RE HERE.
THE ONLY KNIGHTS ALLOWED IN THE INNER SANCTUM ...
...ARE THE IMPERIAL GUARDS, WHO ACCOMPANY THE WITCHES ASSIGNED HERE...
...AND THE WITCH QUEEN'S KNIGHTS, WHO CAN GO WHERE THEY PLEASE.
ALWAYS BE AWARE OF YOUR SURROUND-INGS.
WATCH CLOSELY AND LISTEN CARE-FULLY.
YADA YADA YADA
TRY TO SENSE THINGS BEYOND THE RANGE OF NORMAL PERCEPTION.
THINK BEFORE YOU ACT.
KANAME IS NOT MY KNIGHT.
HE'S THE WITCH QUEEN'S KNIGHT, BUT HE'S NOW CONSIDERED A TRAITOR.
IT'S A COMPLI-CATED POSITION.
THE SAME LECTURE EVERY DAY...
HE CAN'T COME ANY FARTHER INSIDE THAN THIS OUTER HALLWAY.

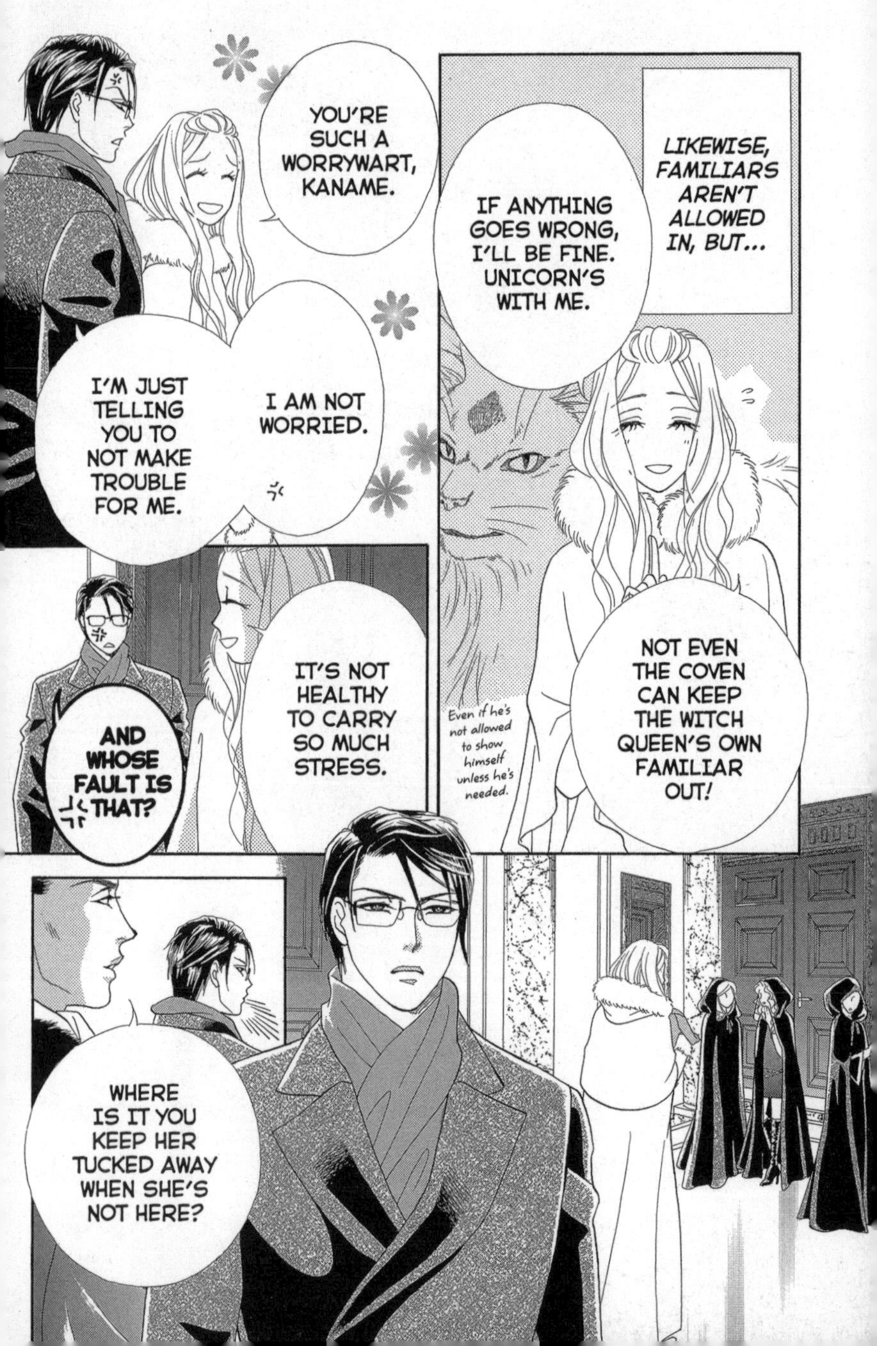
LIKEWISE, FAMILIARS AREN'T ALLOWED IN, BUT...
IF ANYTHING GOES WRONG, I'LL BE FINE. UNICORN'S WITH ME.
NOT EVEN THE COVEN CAN KEEP THE WITCH QUEEN'S OWN FAMILIAR OUT!
Even if he's not allowed to show himself unless he's needed.
YOU'RE SUCH A WORRYWART, KANAME.
I AM NOT WORRIED.
I'M JUST TELLING YOU TO NOT MAKE TROUBLE FOR ME.
IT'S NOT HEALTHY TO CARRY SO MUCH STRESS.
AND WHOSE FAULT IS THAT?
WHERE IS IT YOU KEEP HER TUCKED AWAY WHEN SHE'S NOT HERE?

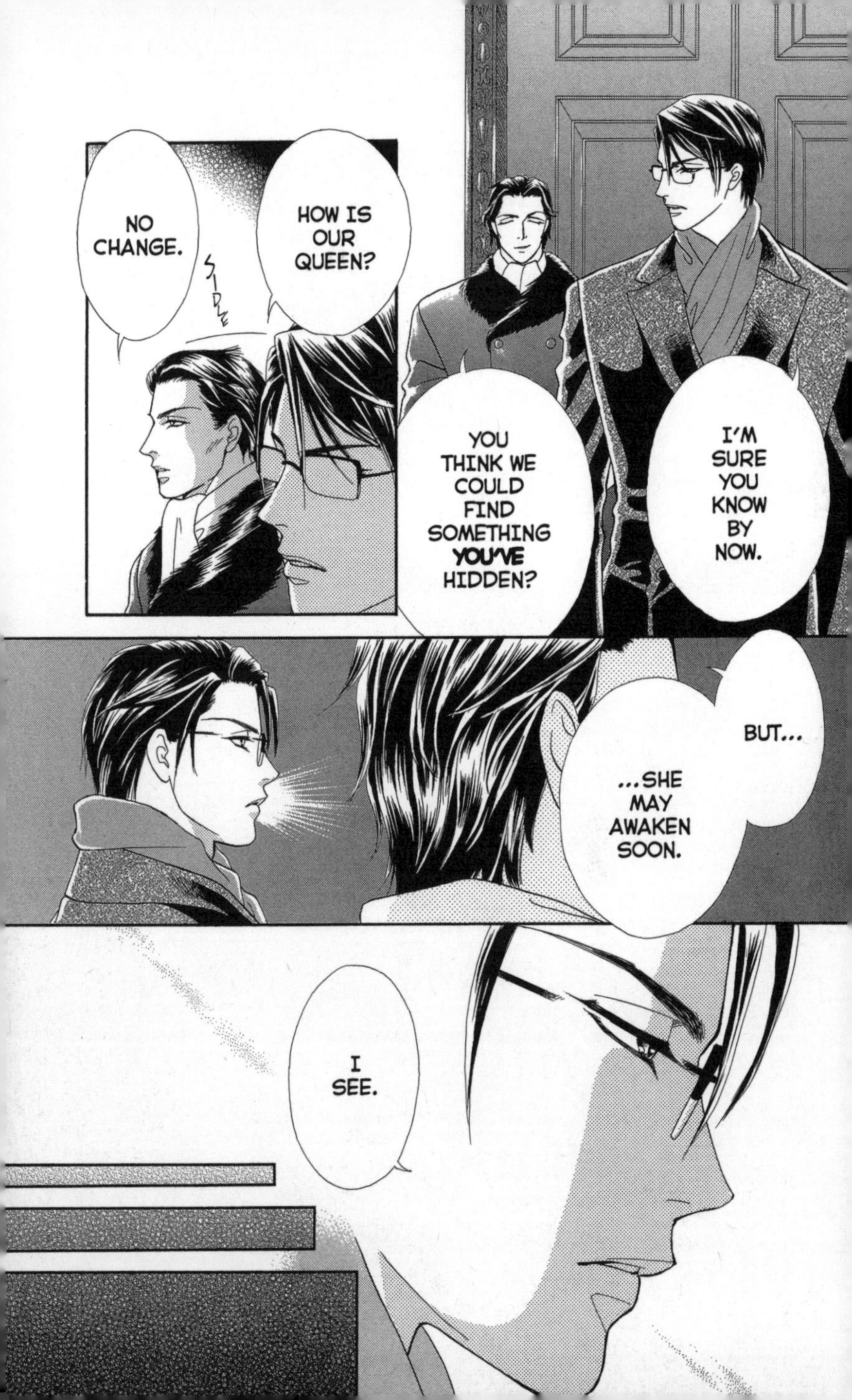
I'M SURE YOU KNOW BY NOW.
YOU THINK WE COULD FIND SOMETHING YOU'VE HIDDEN?
HOW IS OUR QUEEN?
SIDLE
NO CHANGE.
BUT...
...SHE MAY AWAKEN SOON.
I SEE.

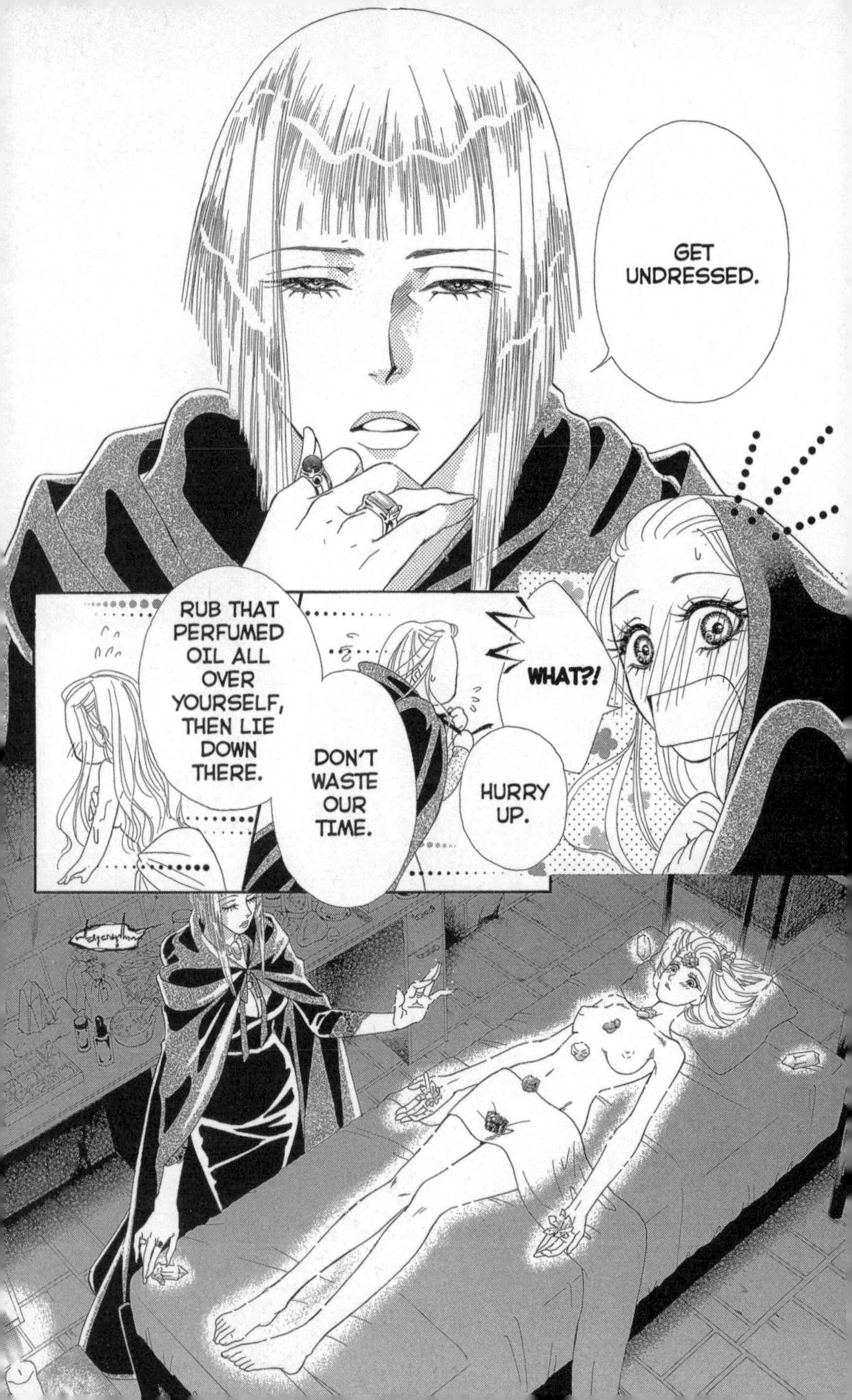
GET UNDRESSED.
WHAT?!
HURRY UP.
DON'T WASTE OUR TIME.
RUB THAT PERFUMED OIL ALL OVER YOURSELF, THEN LIE DOWN THERE.

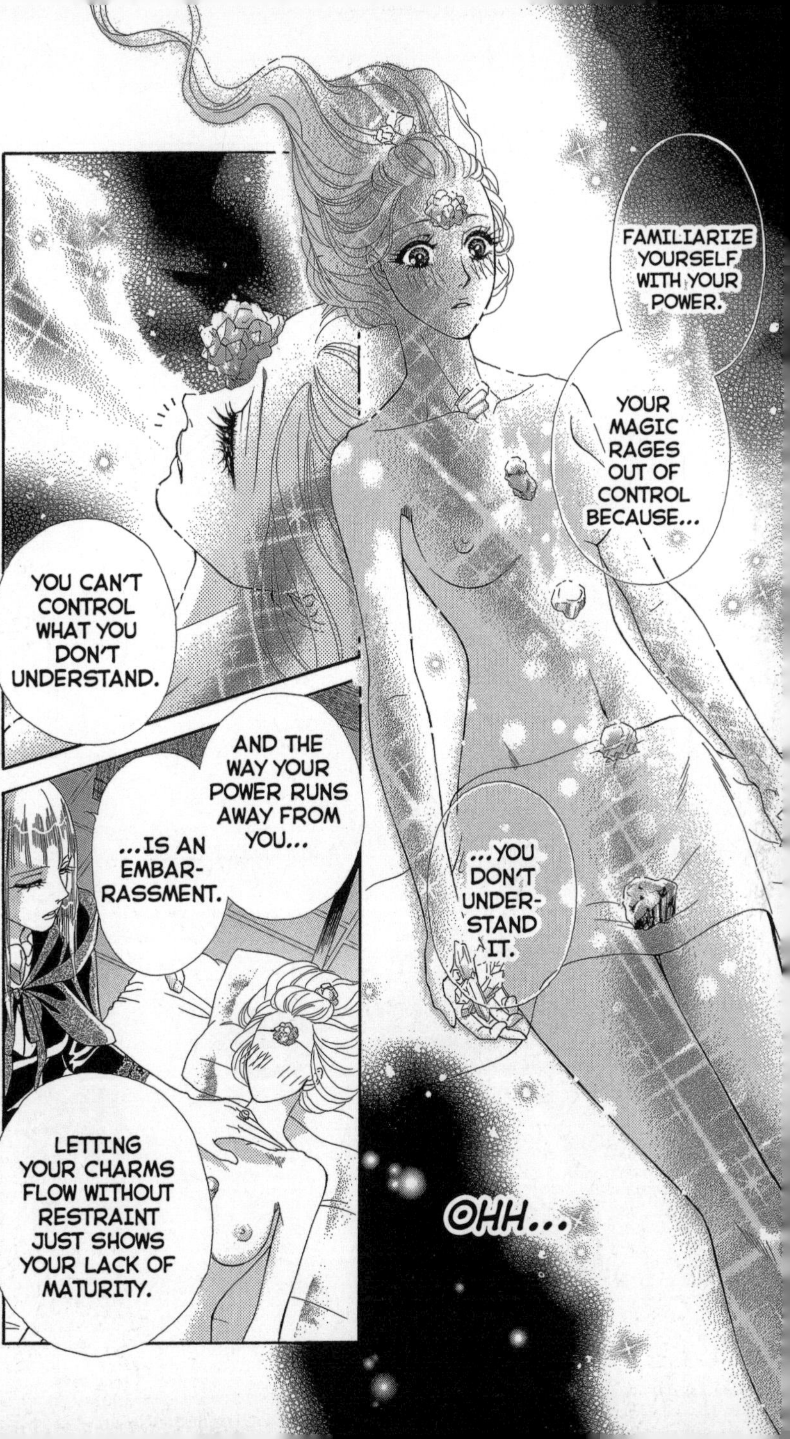
FAMILIARIZE YOURSELF WITH YOUR POWER.
YOUR MAGIC RAGES OUT OF CONTROL BECAUSE...
...YOU DON'T UNDER-STAND IT.
OHH...
YOU CAN'T CONTROL WHAT YOU DON'T UNDERSTAND.
AND THE WAY YOUR POWER RUNS AWAY FROM YOU...
...IS AN EMBAR-RASSMENT.
LETTING YOUR CHARMS FLOW WITHOUT RESTRAINT JUST SHOWS YOUR LACK OF MATURITY.

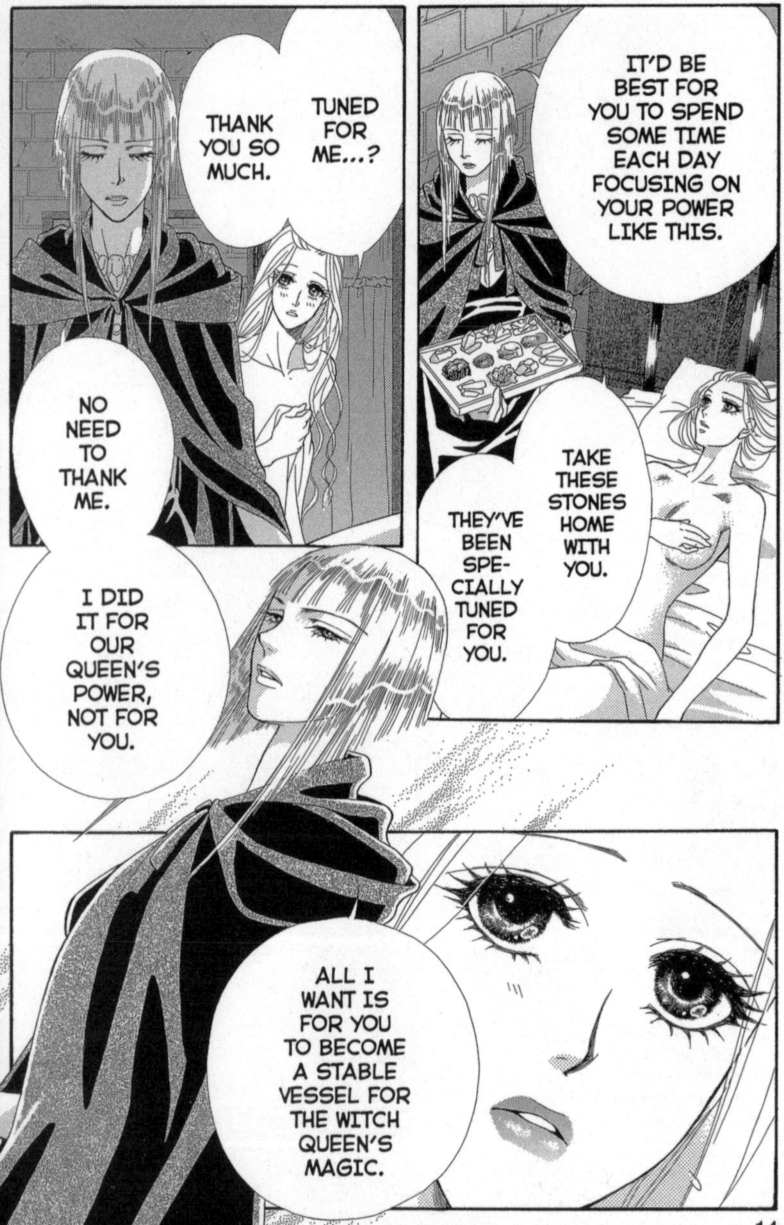
IT'D BE BEST FOR YOU TO SPEND SOME TIME EACH DAY FOCUSING ON YOUR POWER LIKE THIS.
TAKE THESE STONES HOME WITH YOU.
THEY'VE BEEN SPE-CIALLY TUNED FOR YOU.
TUNED FOR ME...?
THANK YOU SO MUCH.
NO NEED TO THANK ME.
I DID IT FOR OUR QUEEN'S POWER, NOT FOR YOU.
ALL I WANT IS FOR YOU TO BECOME A STABLE VESSEL FOR THE WITCH QUEEN'S MAGIC.

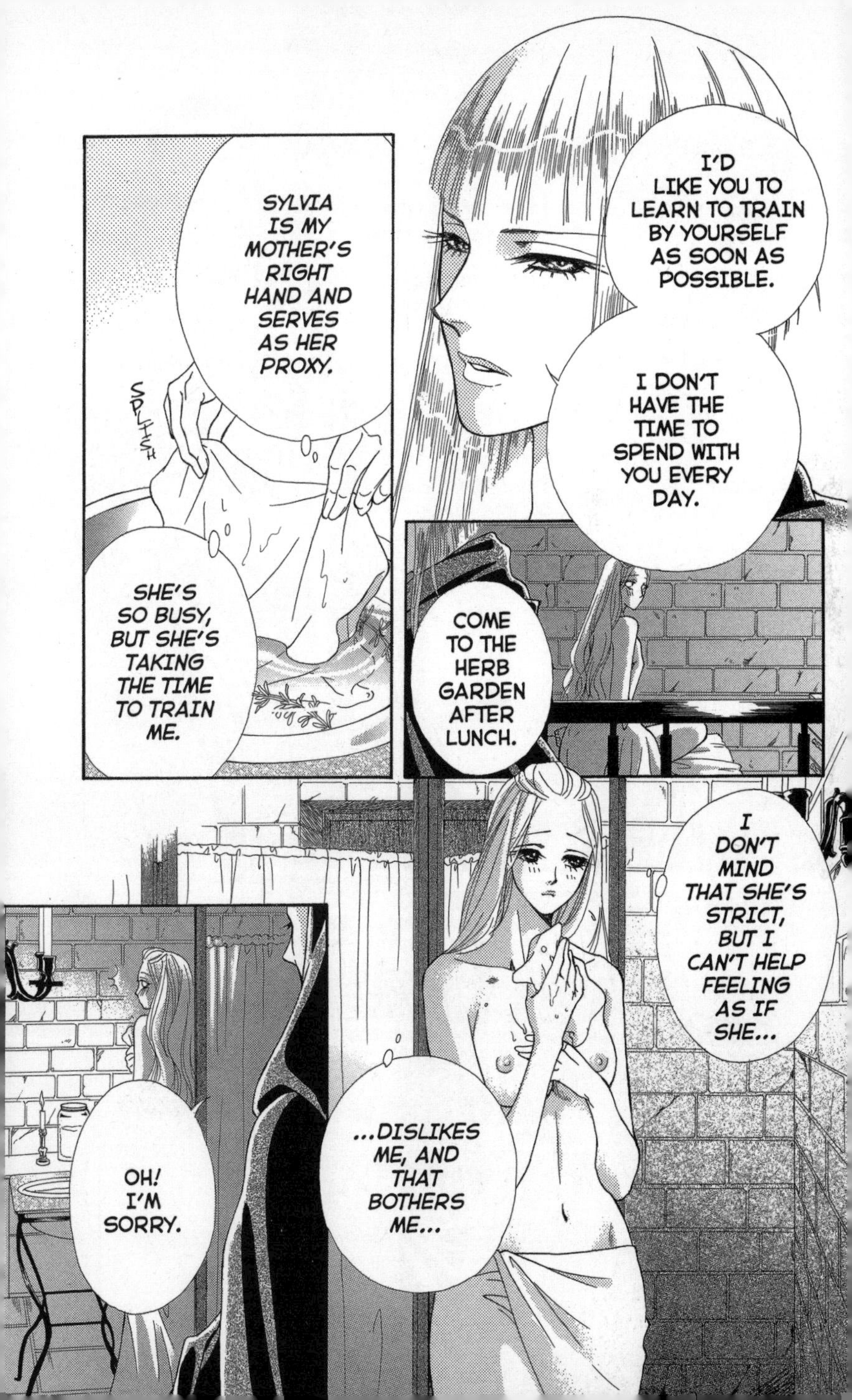
I'D LIKE YOU TO LEARN TO TRAIN BY YOURSELF AS SOON AS POSSIBLE.
I DON'T HAVE THE TIME TO SPEND WITH YOU EVERY DAY.
COME TO THE HERB GARDEN AFTER LUNCH.
SYLVIA IS MY MOTHER'S RIGHT HAND AND SERVES AS HER PROXY.
SPLISH
SHE'S SO BUSY, BUT SHE'S TAKING THE TIME TO TRAIN ME.
I DON'T MIND THAT SHE'S STRICT, BUT I CAN'T HELP FEELING AS IF SHE...
...DISLIKES ME, AND THAT BOTHERS ME...
OH! I'M SORRY.

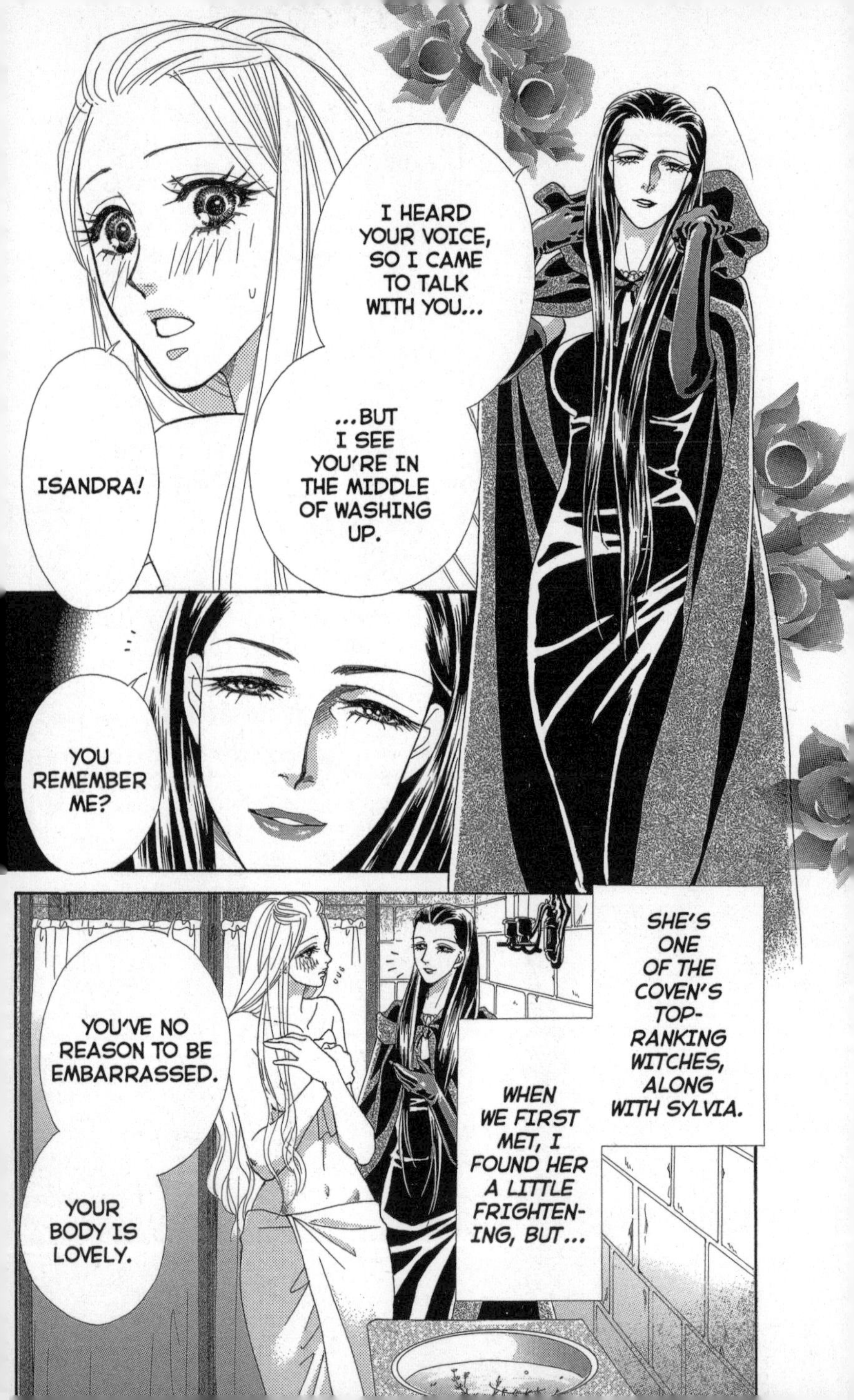
I HEARD YOUR VOICE, SO I CAME TO TALK WITH YOU...
...BUT I SEE YOU'RE IN THE MIDDLE OF WASHING UP.
ISANDRA!
YOU REMEMBER ME?
SHE'S ONE OF THE COVEN'S TOP-RANKING WITCHES, ALONG WITH SYLVIA.
WHEN WE FIRST MET, I FOUND HER A LITTLE FRIGHTEN-ING, BUT...
YOU'VE NO REASON TO BE EMBARRASSED.
YOUR BODY IS LOVELY.

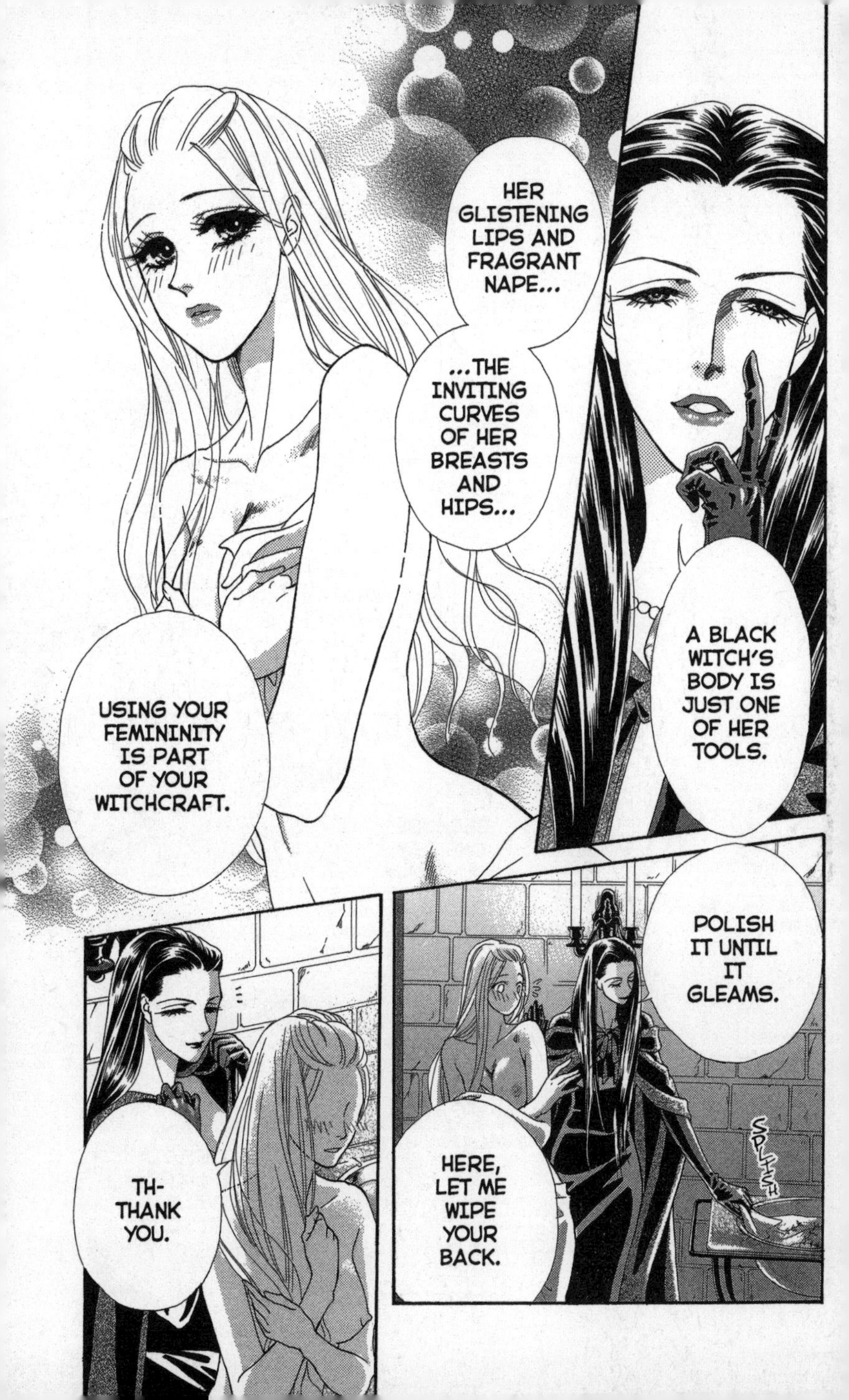
HER GLISTENING LIPS AND FRAGRANT NAPE...
...THE INVITING CURVES OF HER BREASTS AND HIPS...
A BLACK WITCH'S BODY IS JUST ONE OF HER TOOLS.
USING YOUR FEMININITY IS PART OF YOUR WITCHCRAFT.
POLISH IT UNTIL IT GLEAMS.
SPLISH
HERE, LET ME WIPE YOUR BACK.
TH- THANK YOU.

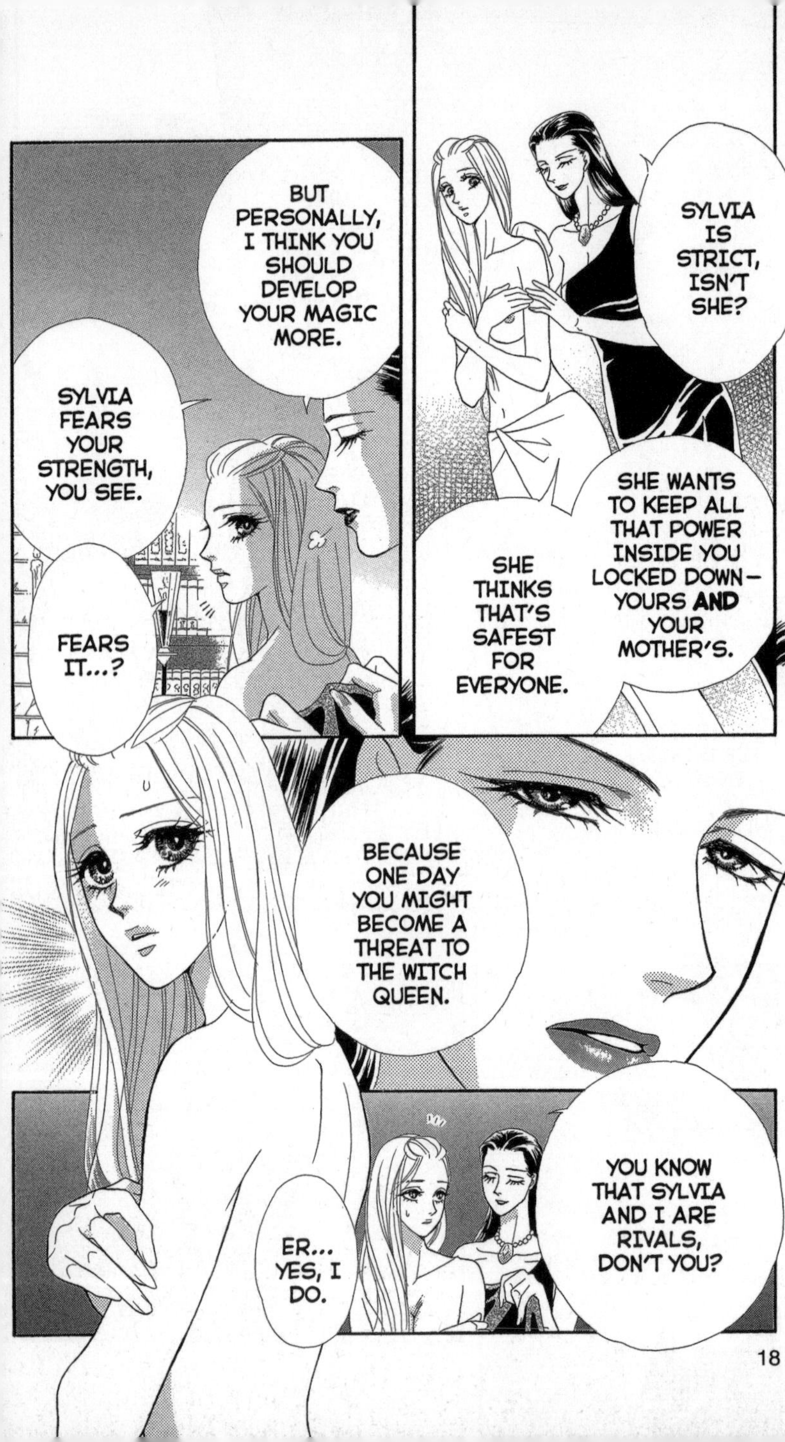

SYLVIA IS STRICT, ISN'T SHE?
SHE WANTS TO KEEP ALL THAT POWER INSIDE YOU LOCKED DOWN—YOURS **AND** YOUR MOTHER'S.
SHE THINKS THAT'S SAFEST FOR EVERYONE.
BUT PERSONALLY, I THINK YOU SHOULD DEVELOP YOUR MAGIC MORE.
SYLVIA FEARS YOUR STRENGTH, YOU SEE.
FEARS IT...?
BECAUSE ONE DAY YOU MIGHT BECOME A THREAT TO THE WITCH QUEEN.
YOU KNOW THAT SYLVIA AND I ARE RIVALS, DON'T YOU?
ER... YES, I DO.

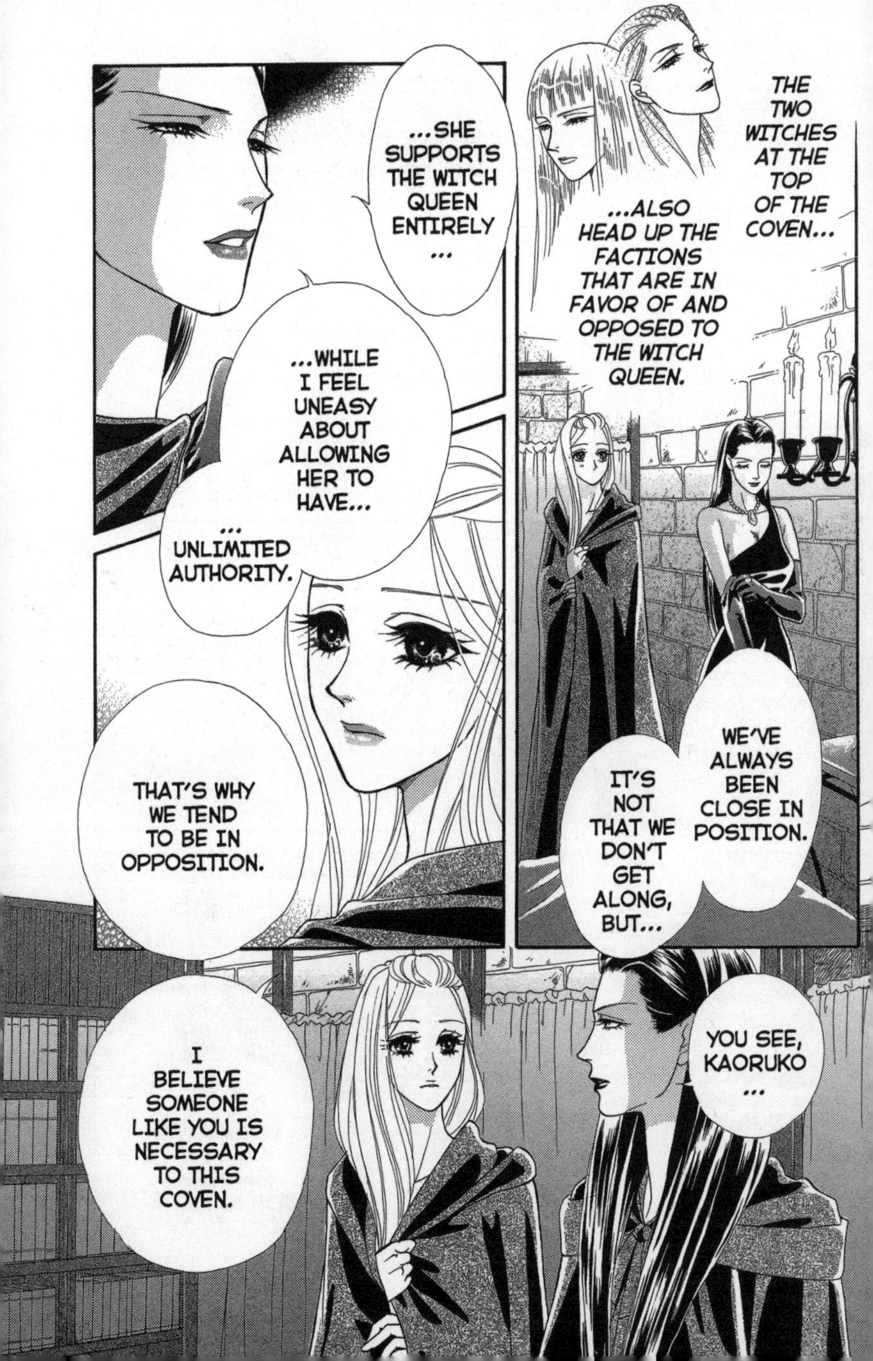
THE TWO WITCHES AT THE TOP OF THE COVEN...
...ALSO HEAD UP THE FACTIONS THAT ARE IN FAVOR OF AND OPPOSED TO THE WITCH QUEEN.
WE'VE ALWAYS BEEN CLOSE IN POSITION.
IT'S NOT THAT WE DON'T GET ALONG, BUT...
...SHE SUPPORTS THE WITCH QUEEN ENTIRELY...
...WHILE I FEEL UNEASY ABOUT ALLOWING HER TO HAVE...
...UNLIMITED AUTHORITY.
THAT'S WHY WE TEND TO BE IN OPPOSITION.
YOU SEE, KAORUKO...
I BELIEVE SOMEONE LIKE YOU IS NECESSARY TO THIS COVEN.

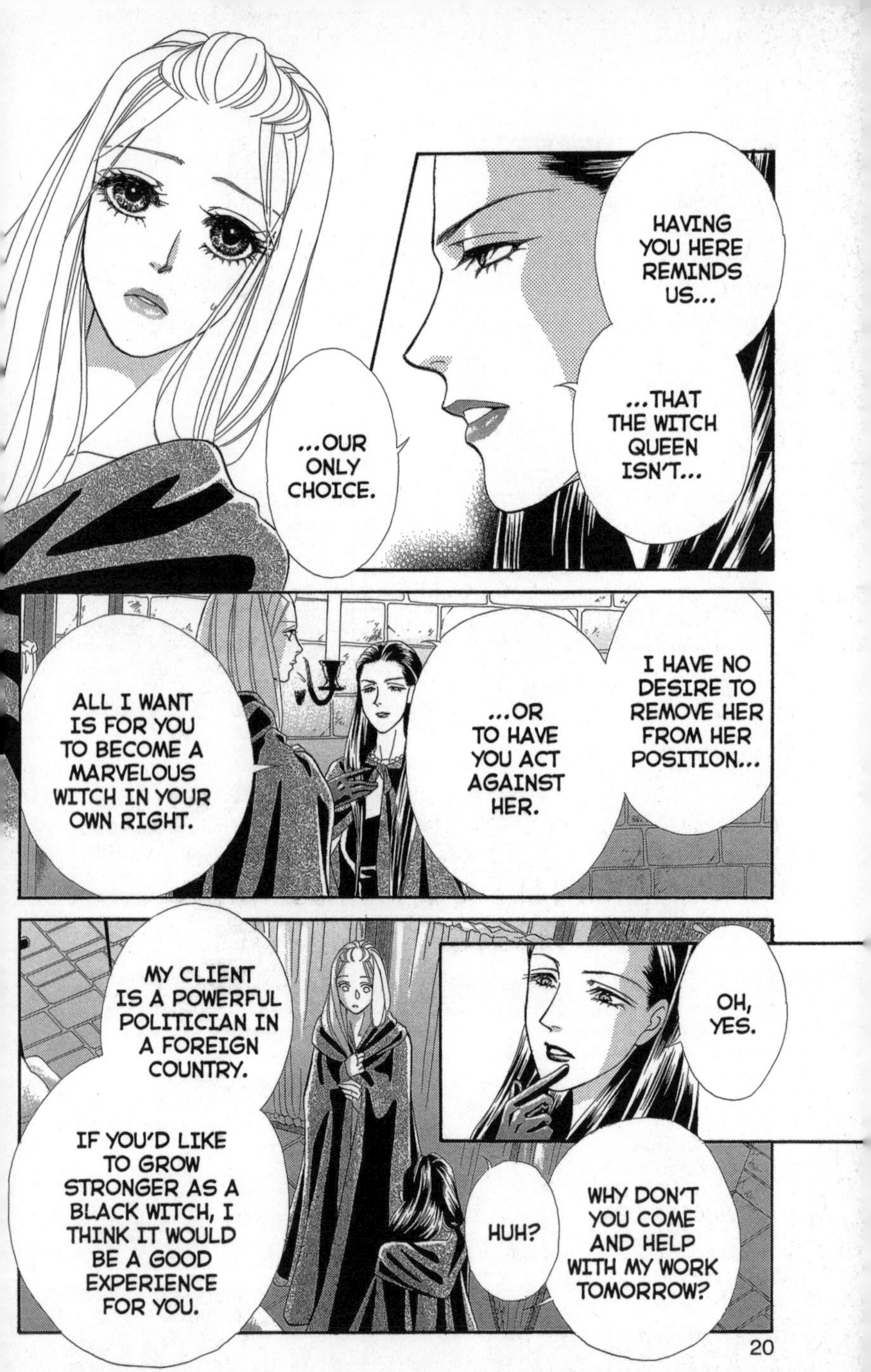
HAVING YOU HERE REMINDS US...
...THAT THE WITCH QUEEN ISN'T...
...OUR ONLY CHOICE.
I HAVE NO DESIRE TO REMOVE HER FROM HER POSITION...
...OR TO HAVE YOU ACT AGAINST HER.
ALL I WANT IS FOR YOU TO BECOME A MARVELOUS WITCH IN YOUR OWN RIGHT.
OH, YES.
WHY DON'T YOU COME AND HELP WITH MY WORK TOMORROW?
HUH?
MY CLIENT IS A POWERFUL POLITICIAN IN A FOREIGN COUNTRY.
IF YOU'D LIKE TO GROW STRONGER AS A BLACK WITCH, I THINK IT WOULD BE A GOOD EXPERIENCE FOR YOU.

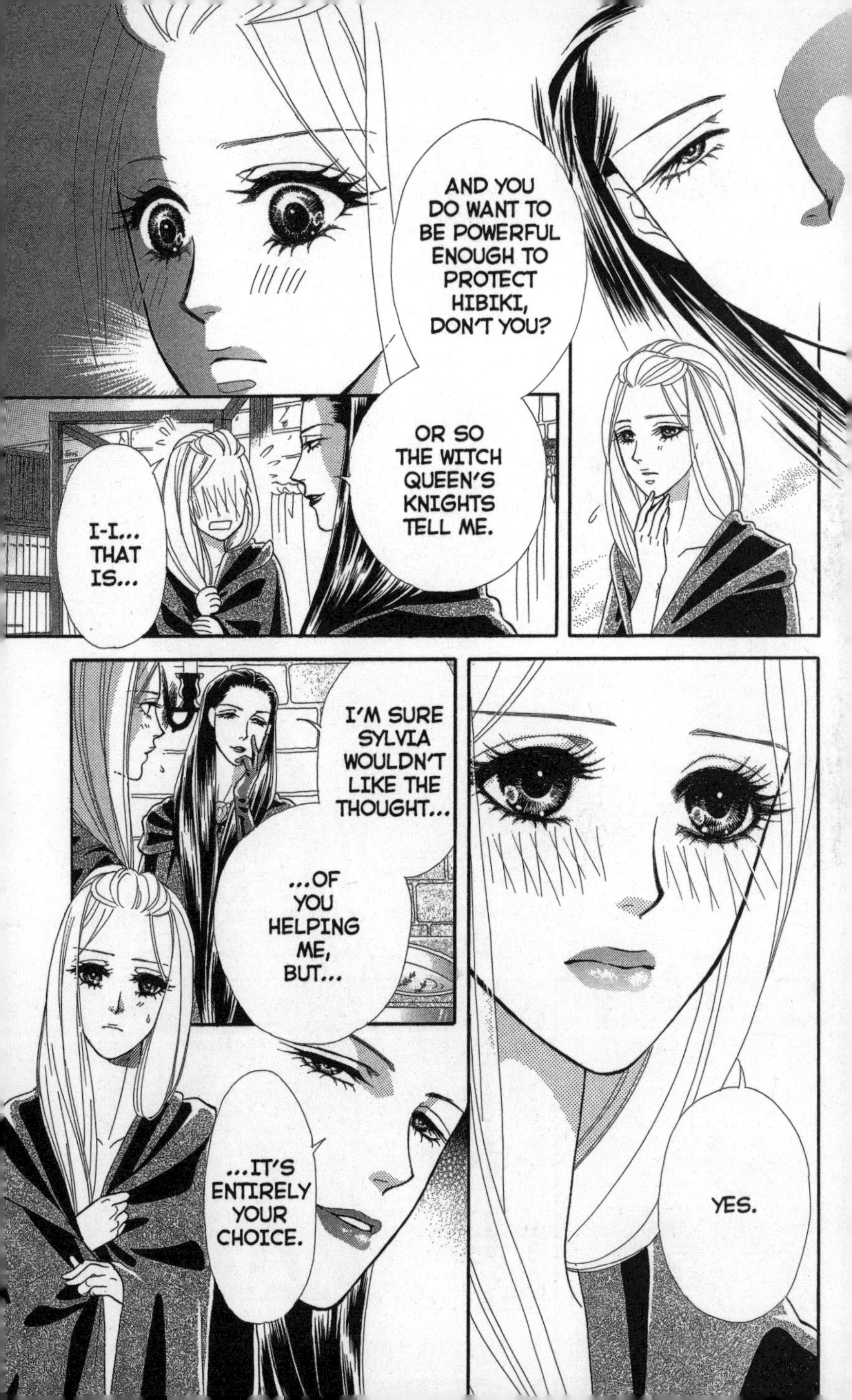
AND YOU DO WANT TO BE POWERFUL ENOUGH TO PROTECT HIBIKI, DON'T YOU?
OR SO THE WITCH QUEEN'S KNIGHTS TELL ME.
I-I... THAT IS...
YES.
I'M SURE SYLVIA WOULDN'T LIKE THE THOUGHT...
...OF YOU HELPING ME, BUT...
...IT'S ENTIRELY YOUR CHOICE.

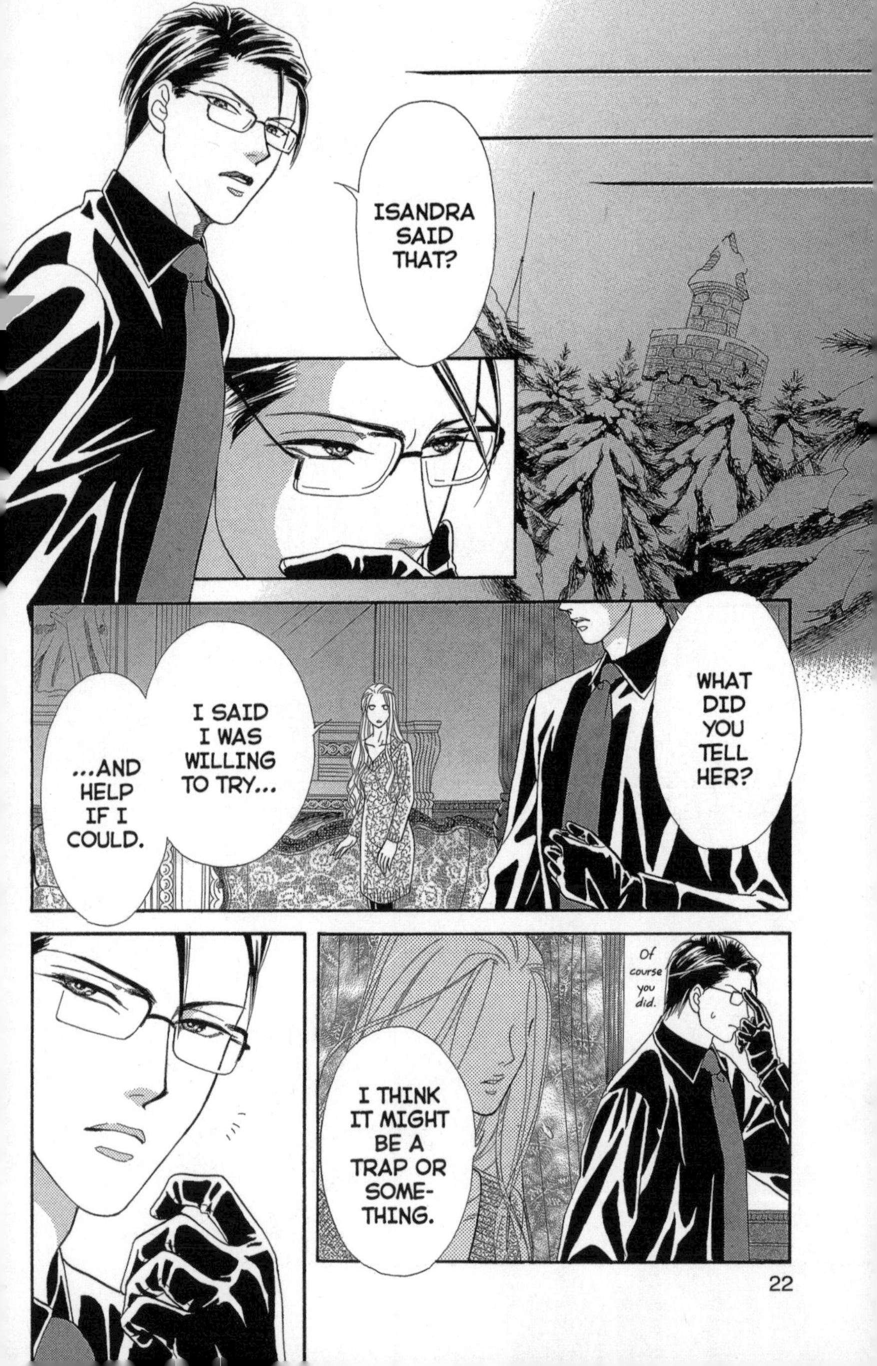
ISANDRA SAID THAT?
WHAT DID YOU TELL HER?
I SAID I WAS WILLING TO TRY...
...AND HELP IF I COULD.
Of course you did.
I THINK IT MIGHT BE A TRAP OR SOME-THING.

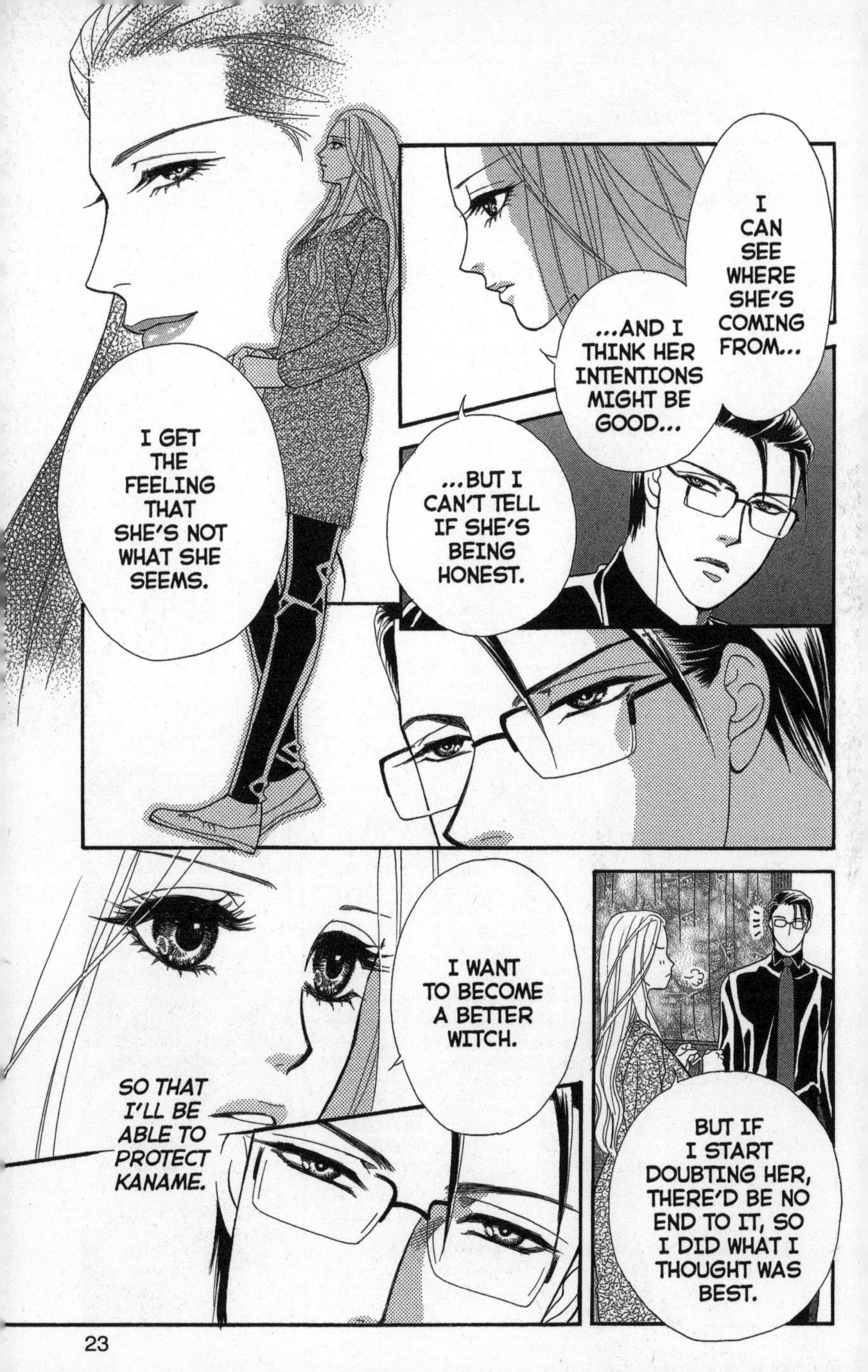
I CAN SEE WHERE SHE'S COMING FROM...
...AND I THINK HER INTENTIONS MIGHT BE GOOD...
...BUT I CAN'T TELL IF SHE'S BEING HONEST.
I GET THE FEELING THAT SHE'S NOT WHAT SHE SEEMS.
BUT IF I START DOUBTING HER, THERE'D BE NO END TO IT, SO I DID WHAT I THOUGHT WAS BEST.
I WANT TO BECOME A BETTER WITCH.
SO THAT I'LL BE ABLE TO PROTECT KANAME.

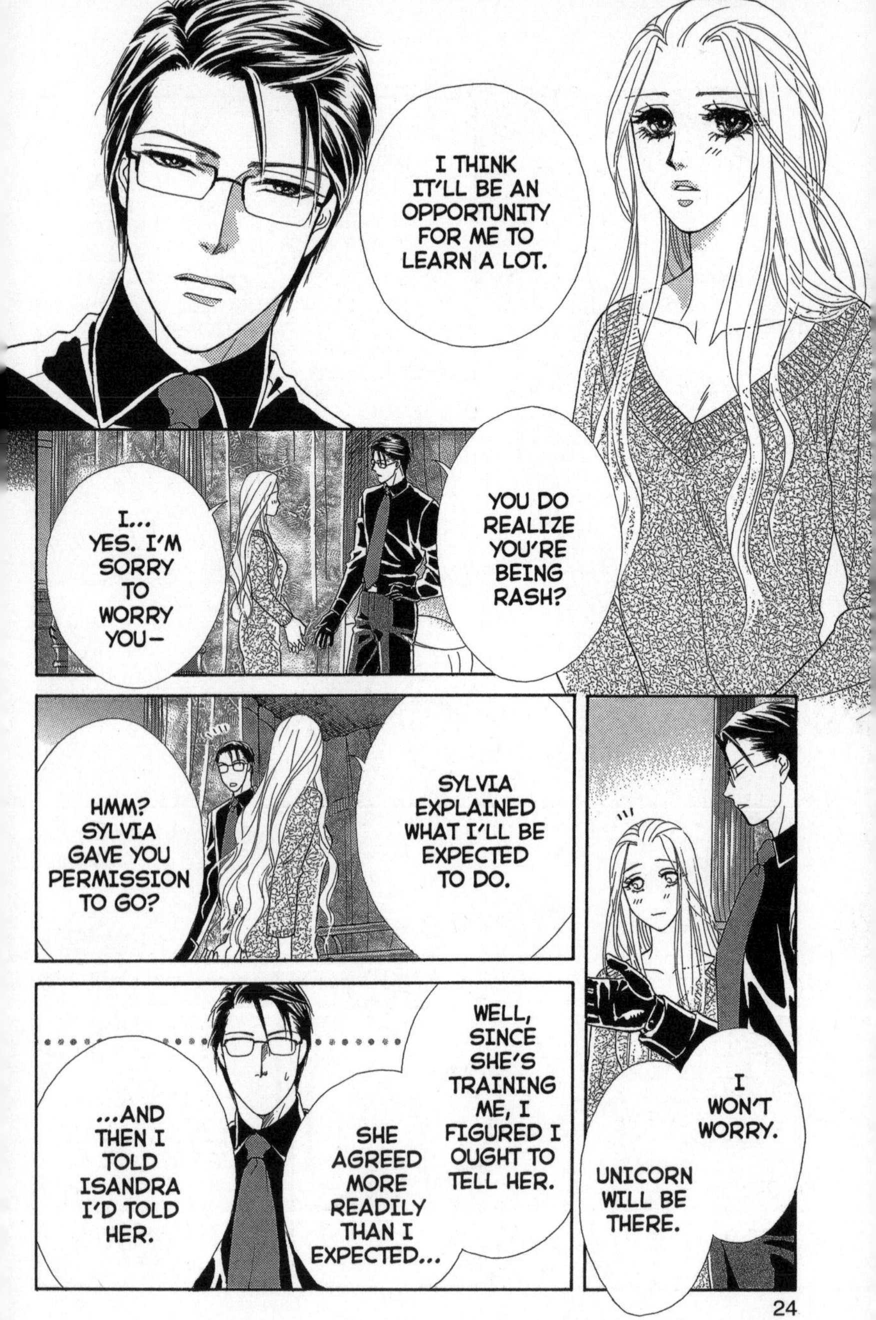

I THINK IT'LL BE AN OPPORTUNITY FOR ME TO LEARN A LOT.
YOU DO REALIZE YOU'RE BEING RASH?
I... YES. I'M SORRY TO WORRY YOU—
I WON'T WORRY.
UNICORN WILL BE THERE.
SYLVIA EXPLAINED WHAT I'LL BE EXPECTED TO DO.
HMM? SYLVIA GAVE YOU PERMISSION TO GO?
WELL, SINCE SHE'S TRAINING ME, I FIGURED I OUGHT TO TELL HER.
SHE AGREED MORE READILY THAN I EXPECTED...
...AND THEN I TOLD ISANDRA I'D TOLD HER.

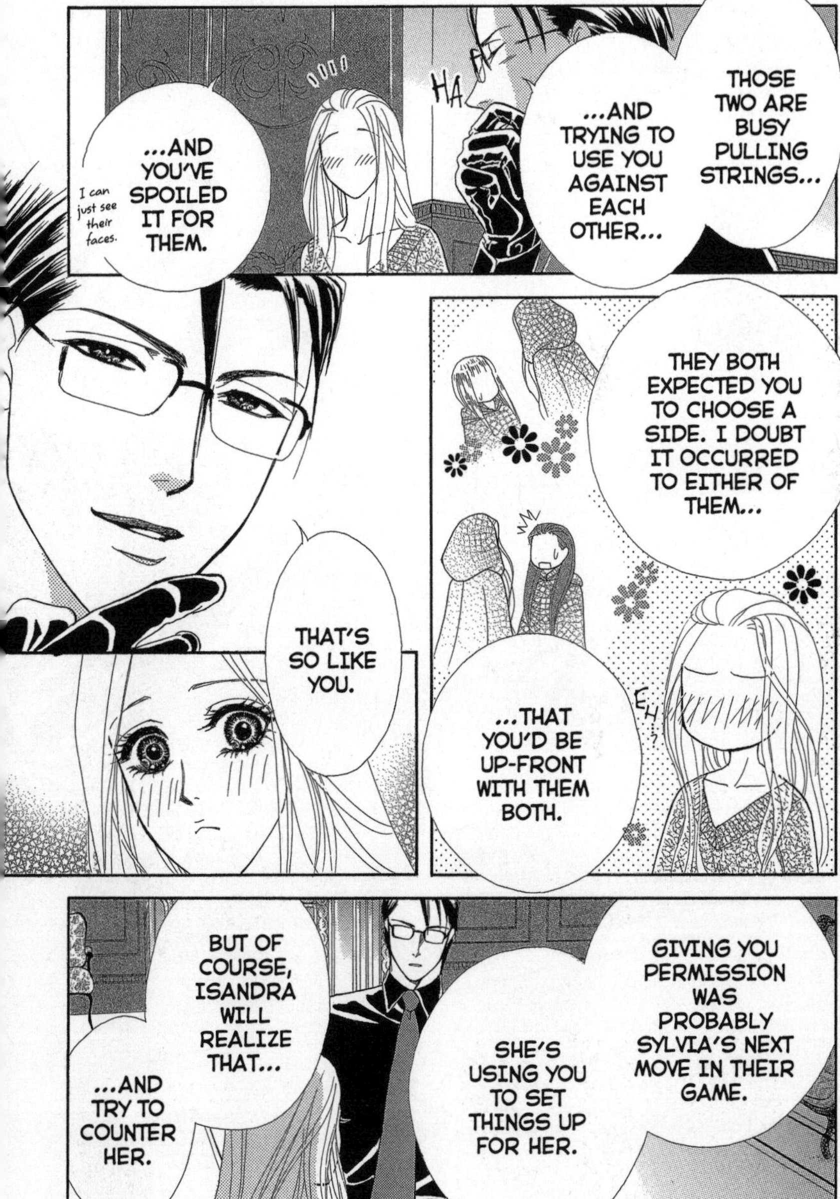
THOSE TWO ARE BUSY PULLING STRINGS...
...AND TRYING TO USE YOU AGAINST EACH OTHER...
HA
...AND YOU'VE SPOILED IT FOR THEM.
I can just see their faces.
THEY BOTH EXPECTED YOU TO CHOOSE A SIDE. I DOUBT IT OCCURRED TO EITHER OF THEM...
EH?
...THAT YOU'D BE UP-FRONT WITH THEM BOTH.
THAT'S SO LIKE YOU.
GIVING YOU PERMISSION WAS PROBABLY SYLVIA'S NEXT MOVE IN THEIR GAME.
SHE'S USING YOU TO SET THINGS UP FOR HER.
BUT OF COURSE, ISANDRA WILL REALIZE THAT...
...AND TRY TO COUNTER HER.

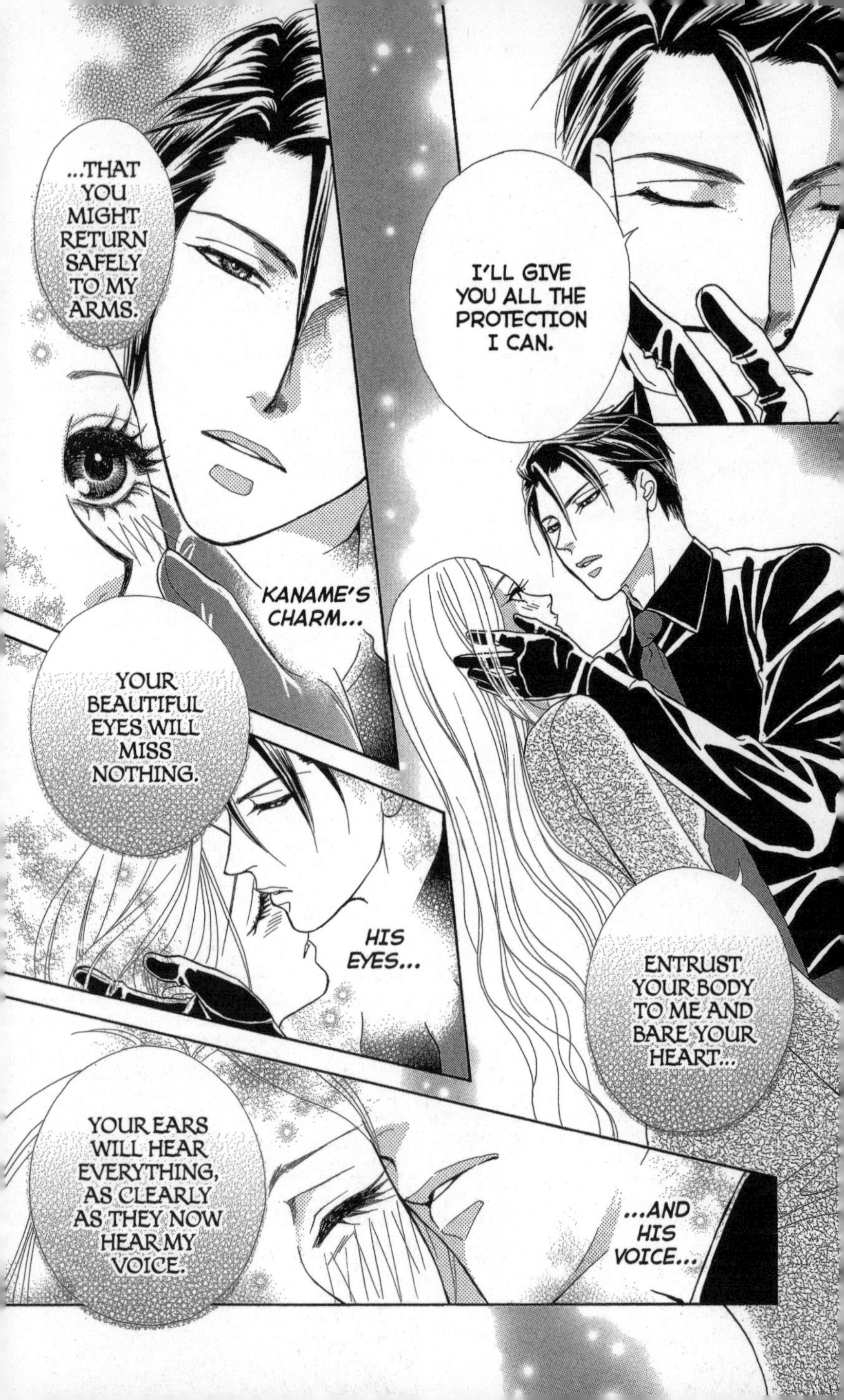
I'LL GIVE YOU ALL THE PROTECTION I CAN.
ENTRUST YOUR BODY TO ME AND BARE YOUR HEART...
...THAT YOU MIGHT RETURN SAFELY TO MY ARMS.
KANAME'S CHARM...
YOUR BEAUTIFUL EYES WILL MISS NOTHING.
HIS EYES...
YOUR EARS WILL HEAR EVERYTHING, AS CLEARLY AS THEY NOW HEAR MY VOICE.
...AND HIS VOICE...

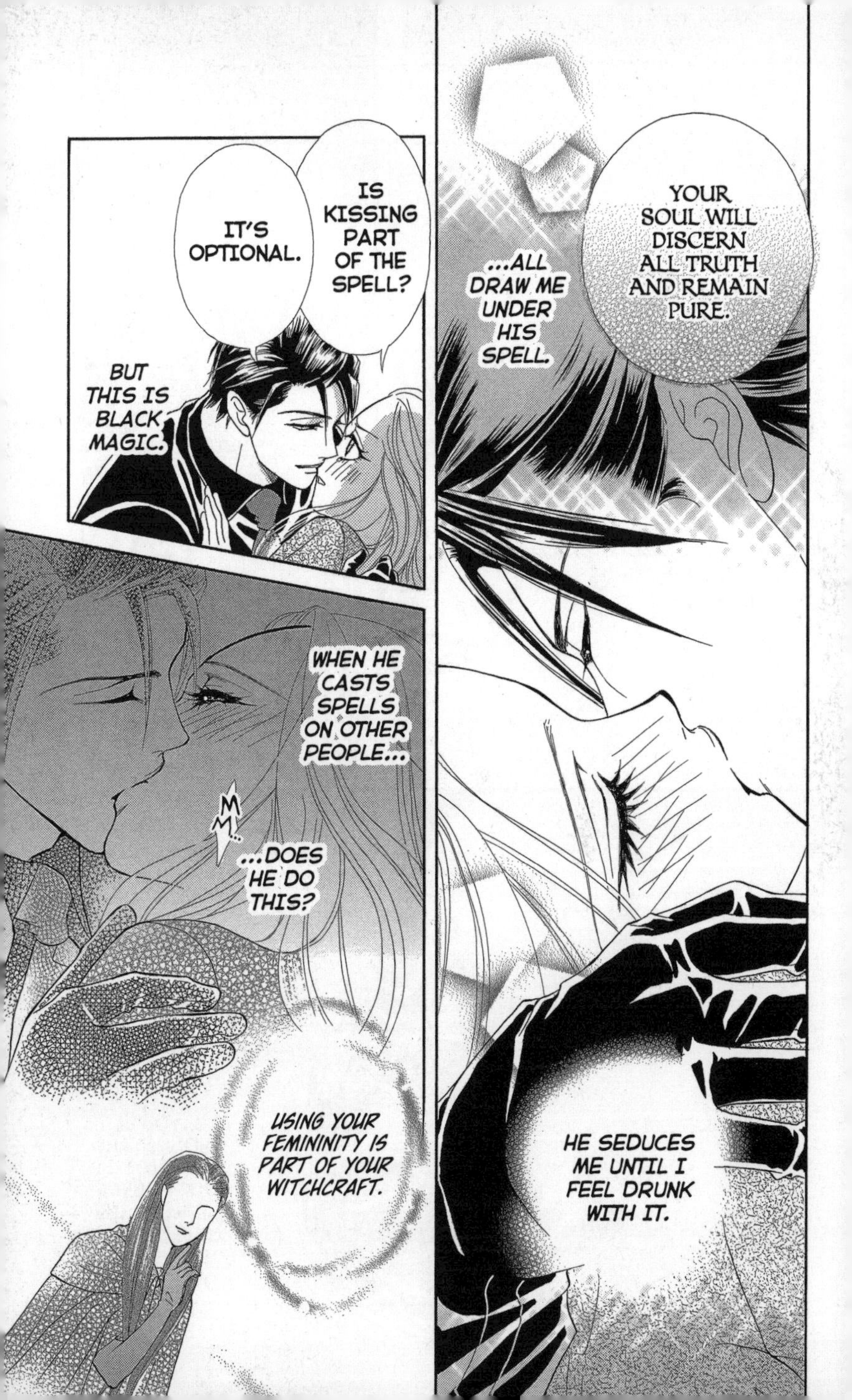
YOUR SOUL WILL DISCERN ALL TRUTH AND REMAIN PURE.
...ALL DRAW ME UNDER HIS SPELL.
HE SEDUCES ME UNTIL I FEEL DRUNK WITH IT.
IS KISSING PART OF THE SPELL?
IT'S OPTIONAL.
BUT THIS IS BLACK MAGIC.
WHEN HE CASTS SPELLS ON OTHER PEOPLE...
MM..
...DOES HE DO THIS?
USING YOUR FEMININITY IS PART OF YOUR WITCHCRAFT.

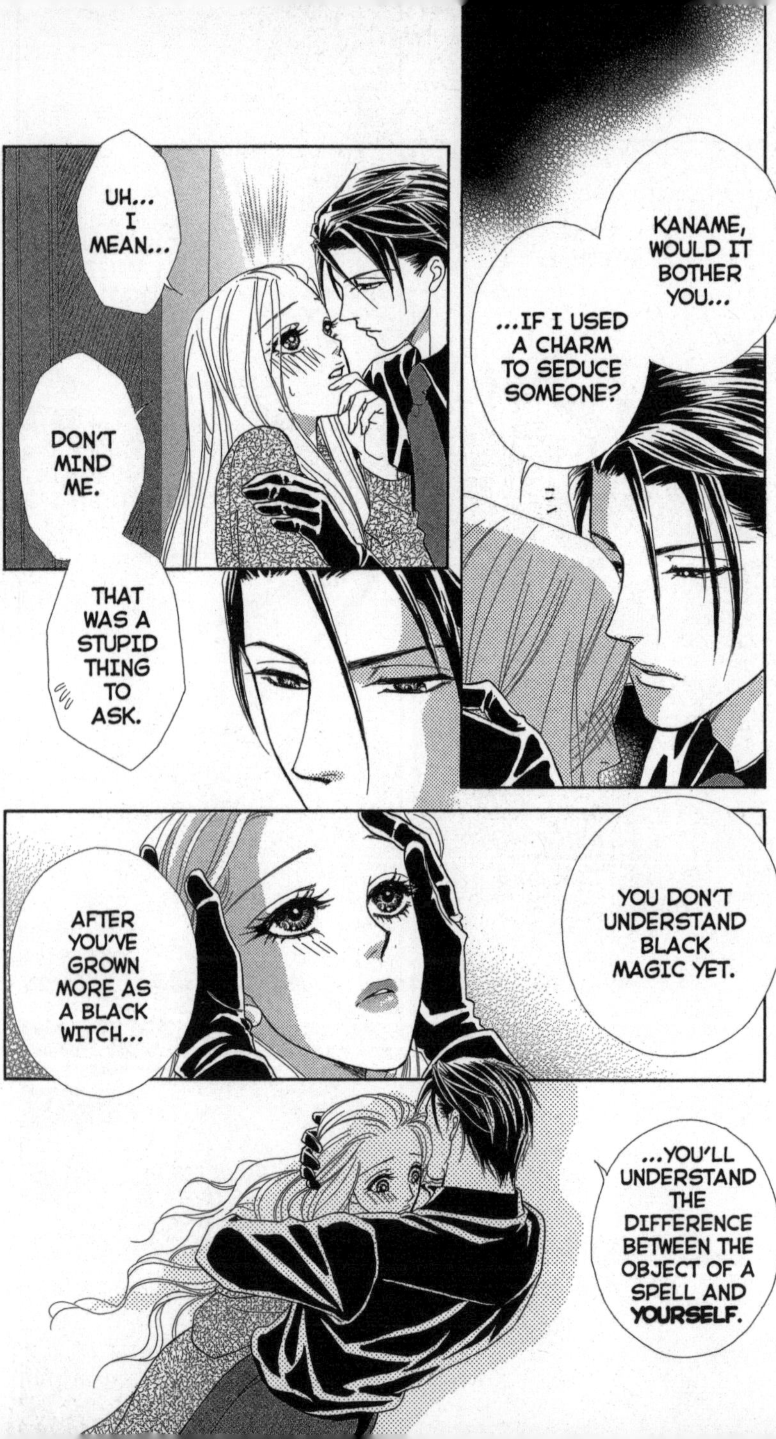
KANAME, WOULD IT BOTHER YOU...
...IF I USED A CHARM TO SEDUCE SOMEONE?
UH... I MEAN...
DON'T MIND ME.
THAT WAS A STUPID THING TO ASK.
YOU DON'T UNDERSTAND BLACK MAGIC YET.
AFTER YOU'VE GROWN MORE AS A BLACK WITCH...
...YOU'LL UNDERSTAND THE DIFFERENCE BETWEEN THE OBJECT OF A SPELL AND **YOURSELF**.

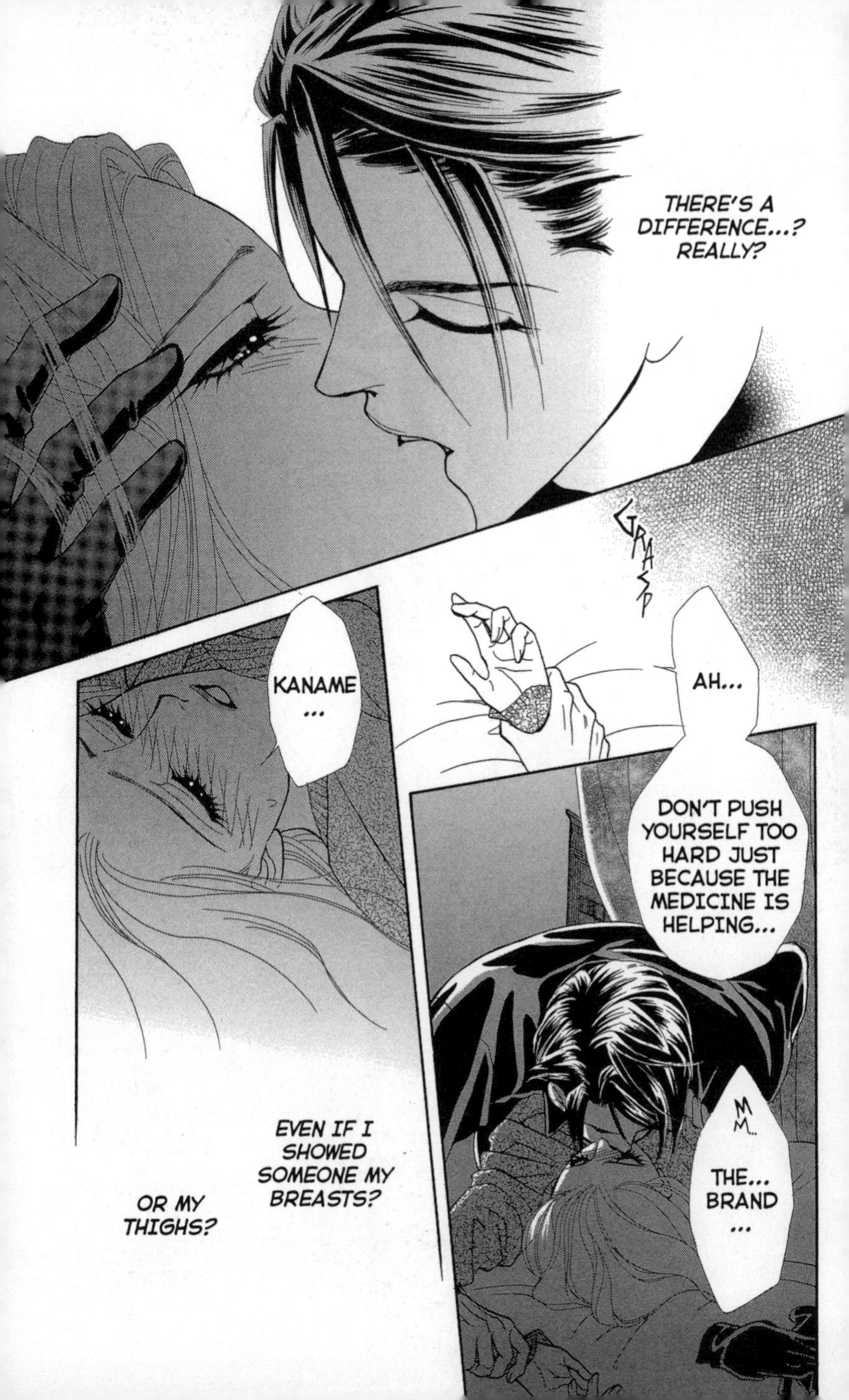
THERE'S A DIFFERENCE...? REALLY?
GRASP
AH...
DON'T PUSH YOURSELF TOO HARD JUST BECAUSE THE MEDICINE IS HELPING...
MM...
THE... BRAND ...
KANAME ...
EVEN IF I SHOWED SOMEONE MY BREASTS?
OR MY THIGHS?

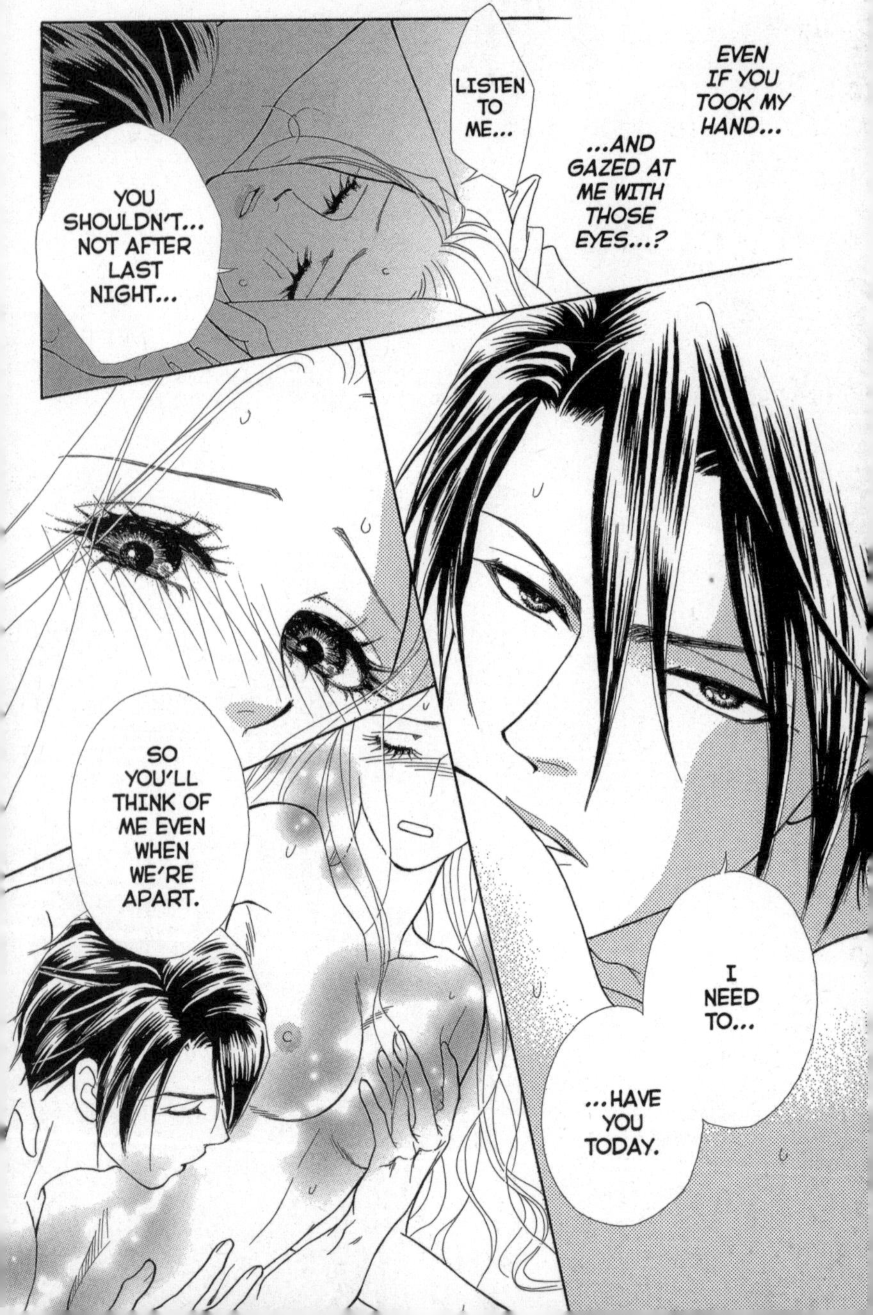
EVEN IF YOU TOOK MY HAND...
...AND GAZED AT ME WITH THOSE EYES...?
LISTEN TO ME...
YOU SHOULDN'T... NOT AFTER LAST NIGHT...
I NEED TO...
...HAVE YOU TODAY.
SO YOU'LL THINK OF ME EVEN WHEN WE'RE APART.

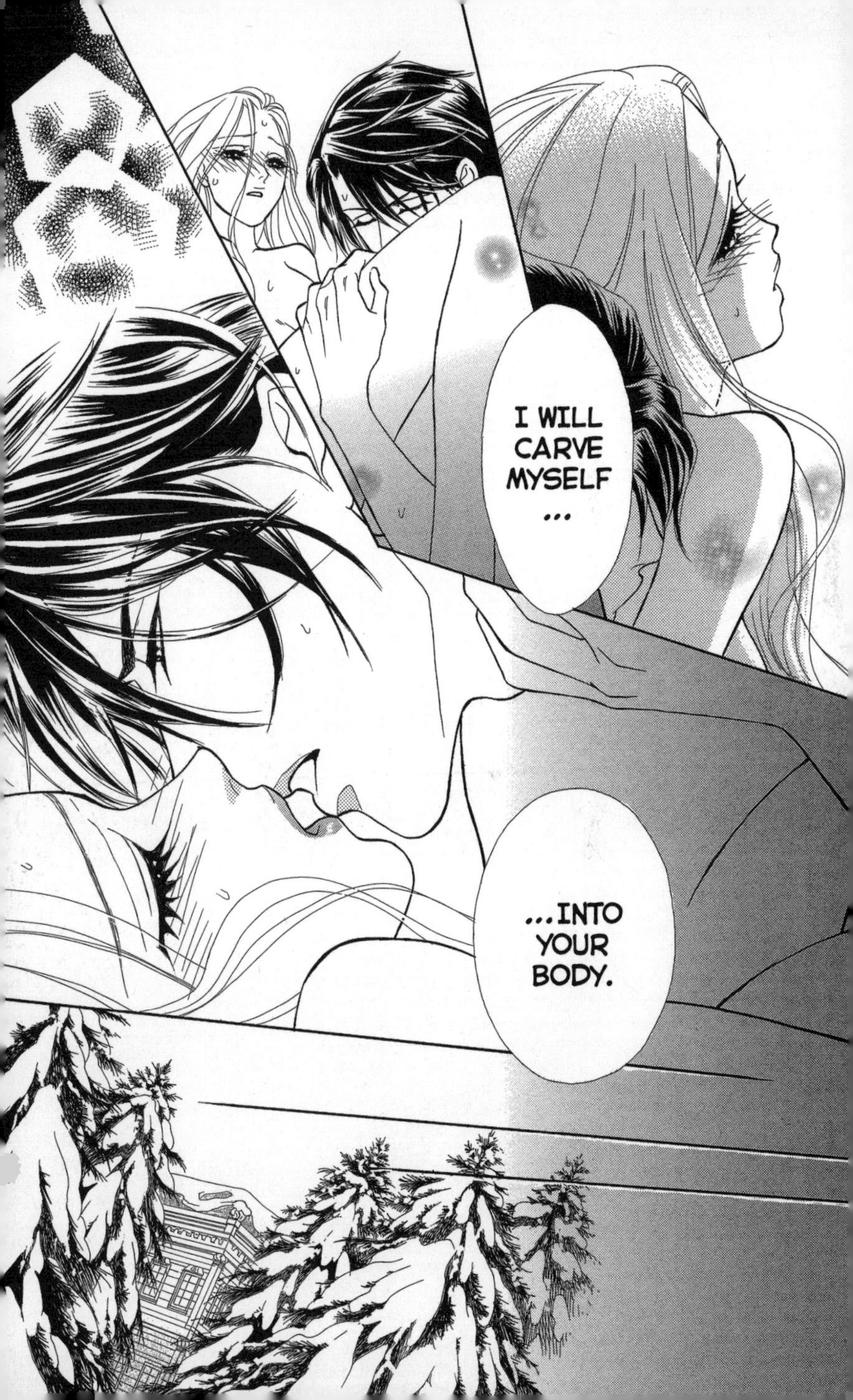
I WILL CARVE MYSELF ...
...INTO YOUR BODY.

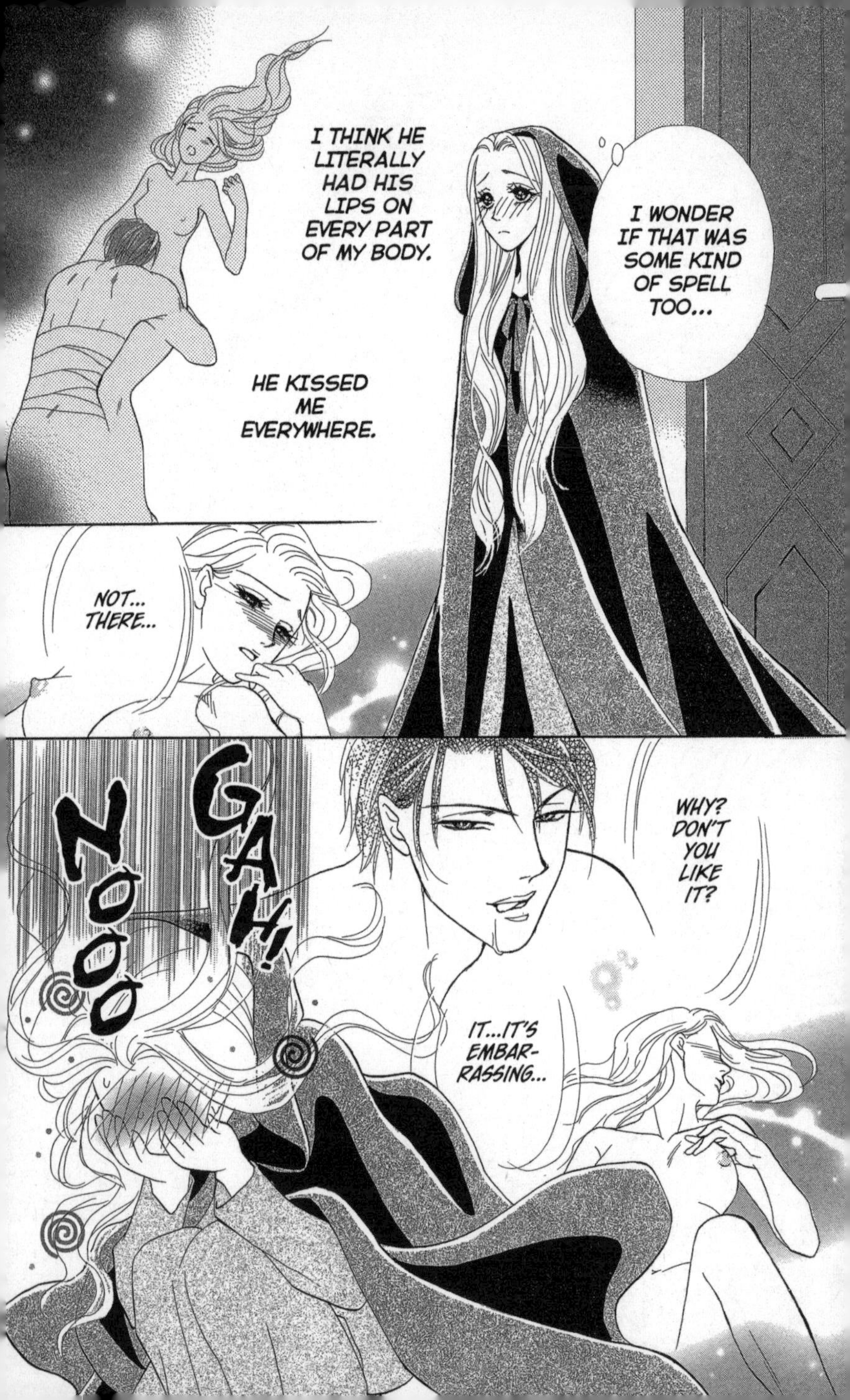
I WONDER IF THAT WAS SOME KIND OF SPELL TOO...
I THINK HE LITERALLY HAD HIS LIPS ON EVERY PART OF MY BODY.
HE KISSED ME EVERYWHERE.
NOT... THERE...
WHY? DON'T YOU LIKE IT?
IT...IT'S EMBAR-RASSING...
GAH! NOOO

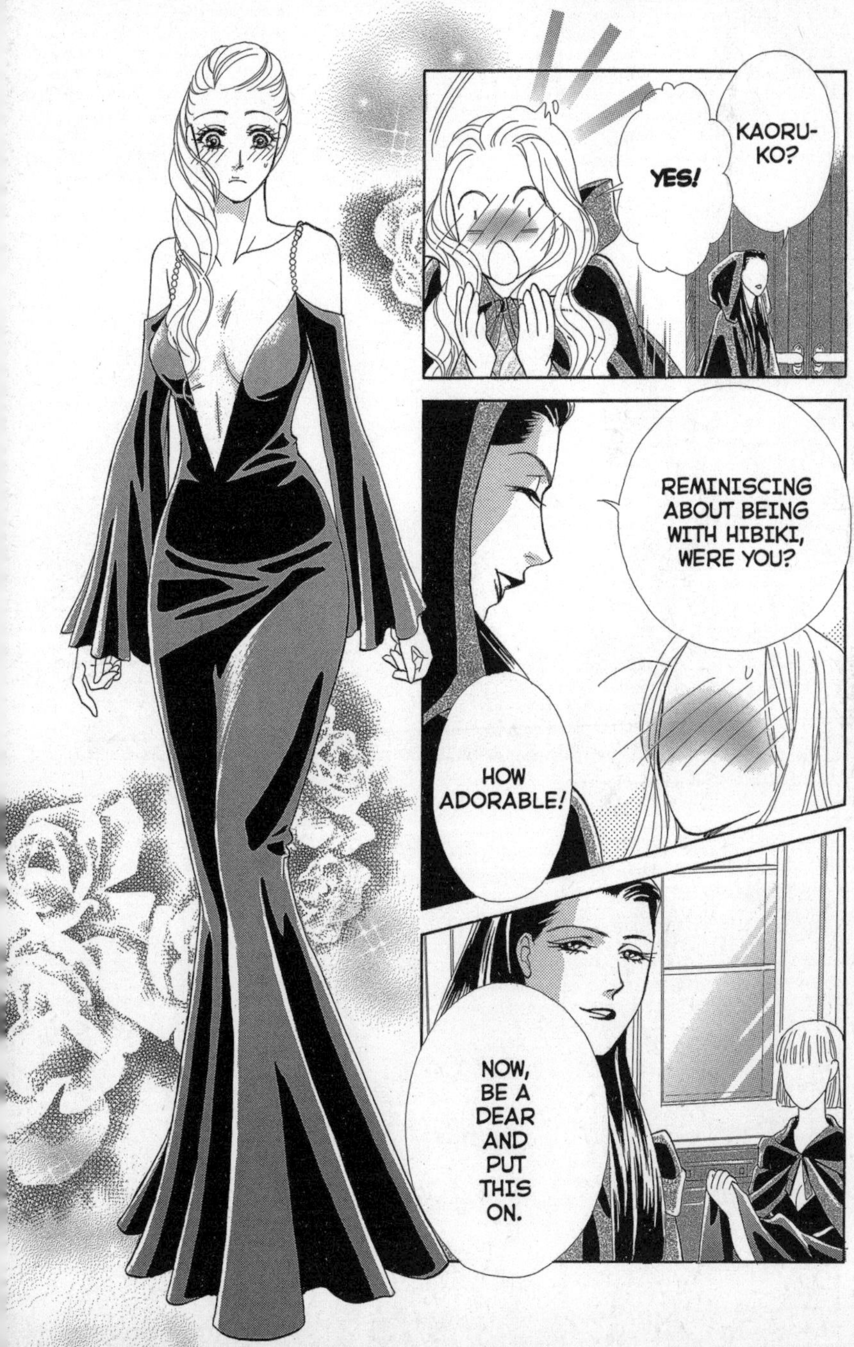
KAORU-KO?
YES!
REMINISCING ABOUT BEING WITH HIBIKI, WERE YOU?
HOW ADORABLE!
NOW, BE A DEAR AND PUT THIS ON.

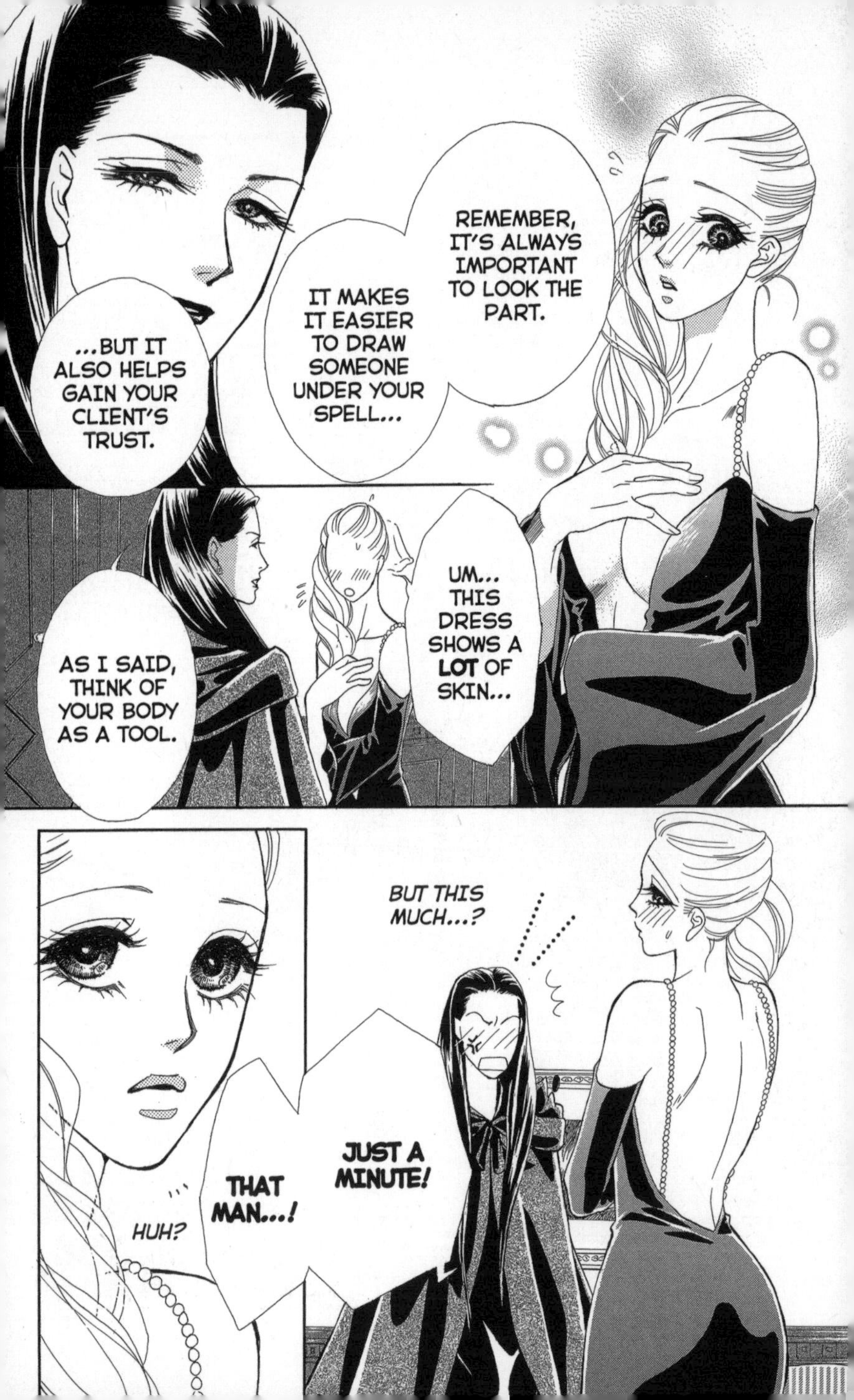
REMEMBER, IT'S ALWAYS IMPORTANT TO LOOK THE PART.
IT MAKES IT EASIER TO DRAW SOMEONE UNDER YOUR SPELL...
...BUT IT ALSO HELPS GAIN YOUR CLIENT'S TRUST.
UM... THIS DRESS SHOWS A LOT OF SKIN...
AS I SAID, THINK OF YOUR BODY AS A TOOL.
BUT THIS MUCH...?
JUST A MINUTE!
THAT MAN...!
HUH?

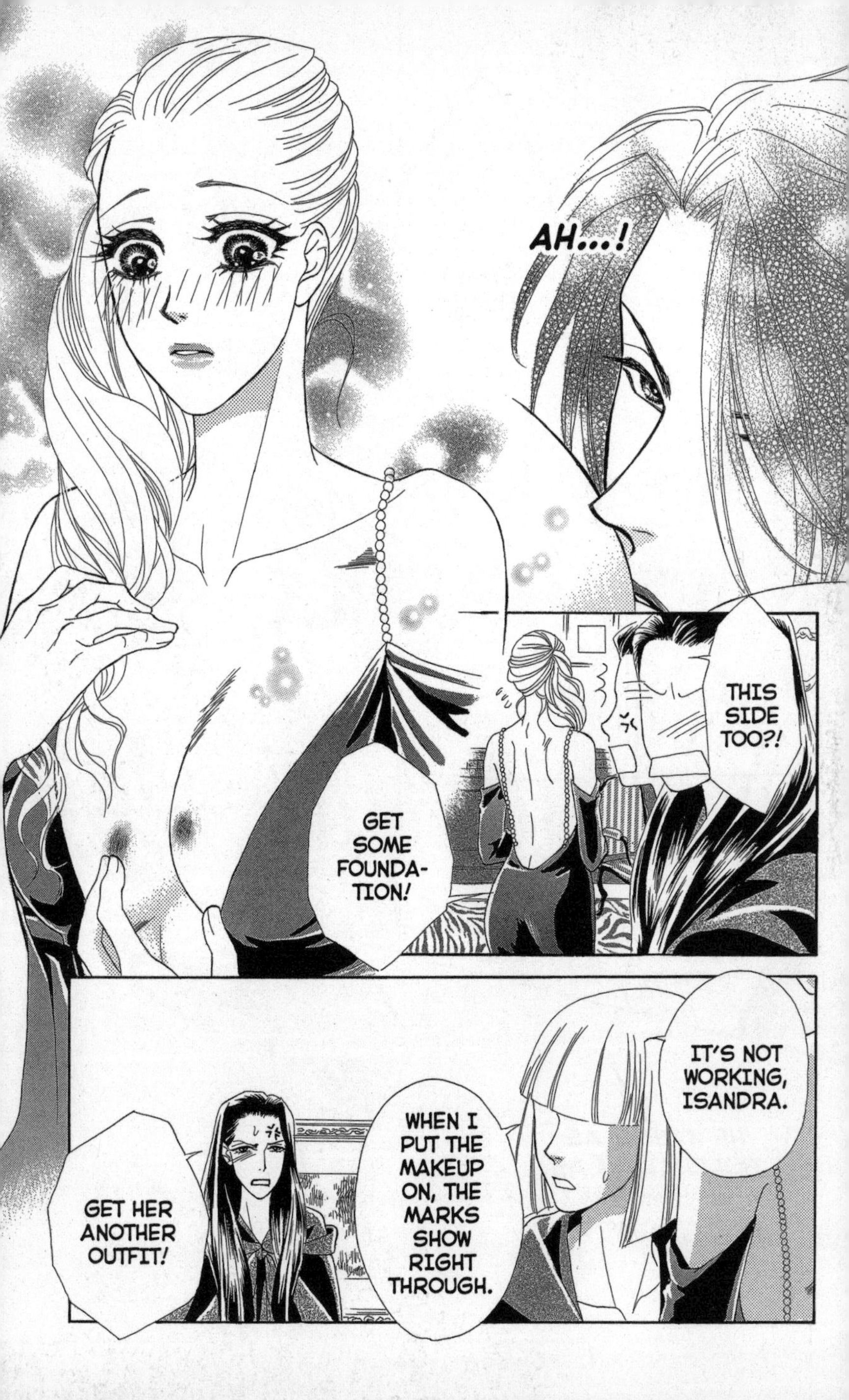
AH...!
THIS SIDE TOO?!
GET SOME FOUNDATION!
IT'S NOT WORKING, ISANDRA.
WHEN I PUT THE MAKEUP ON, THE MARKS SHOW RIGHT THROUGH.
GET HER ANOTHER OUTFIT!

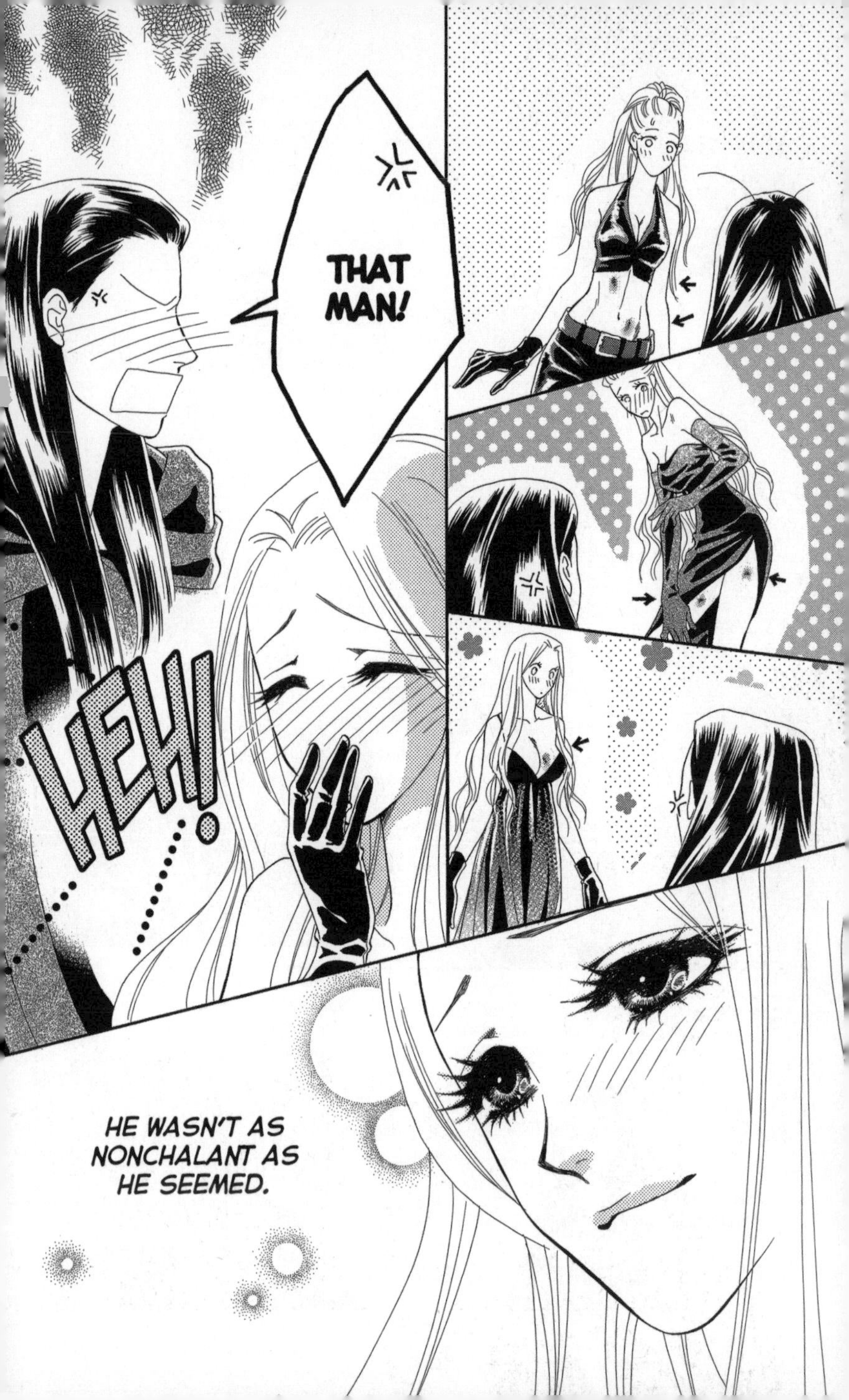
THAT MAN!
HEH!
HE WASN'T AS NONCHALANT AS HE SEEMED.

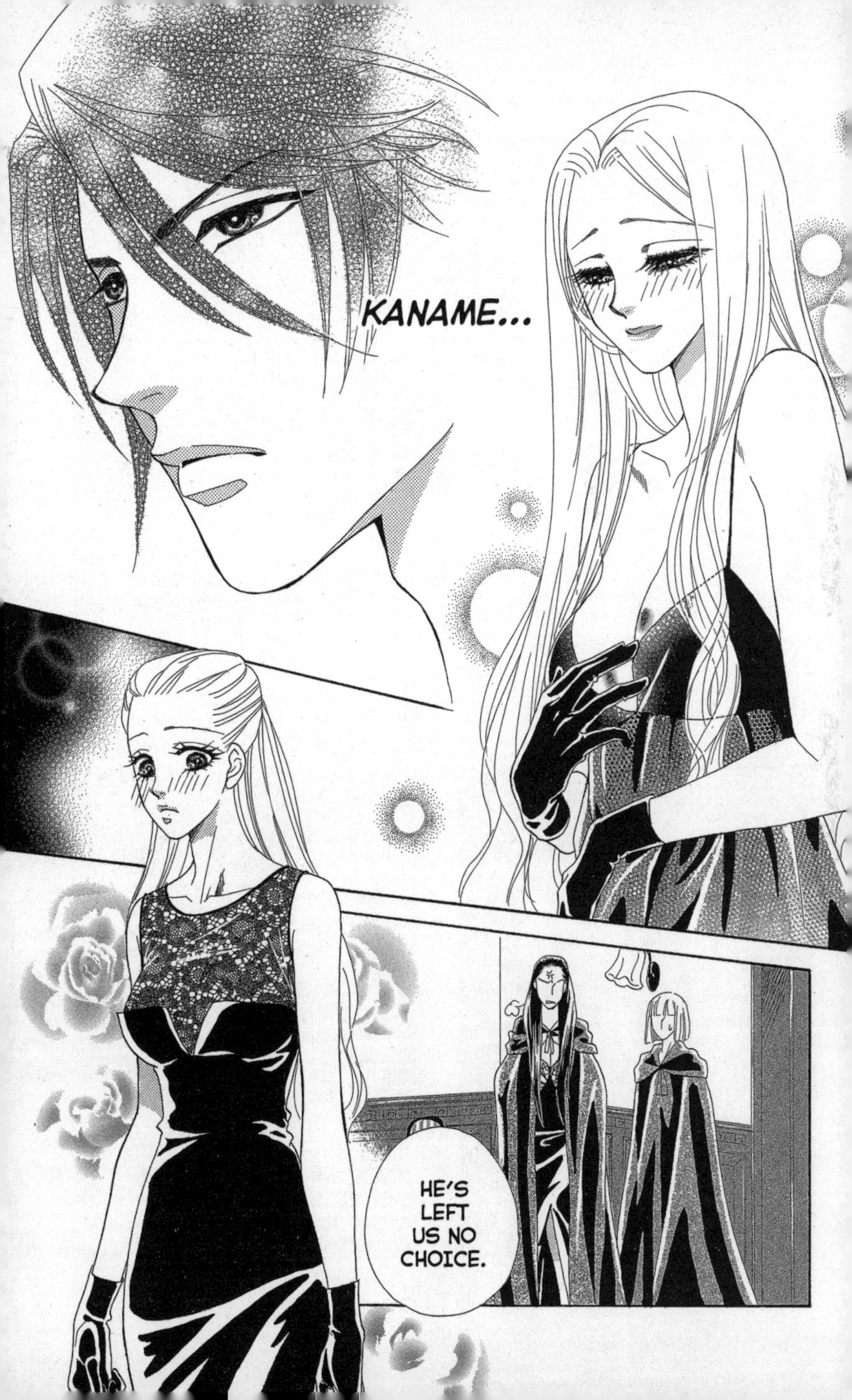
KANAME...
HE'S LEFT US NO CHOICE.

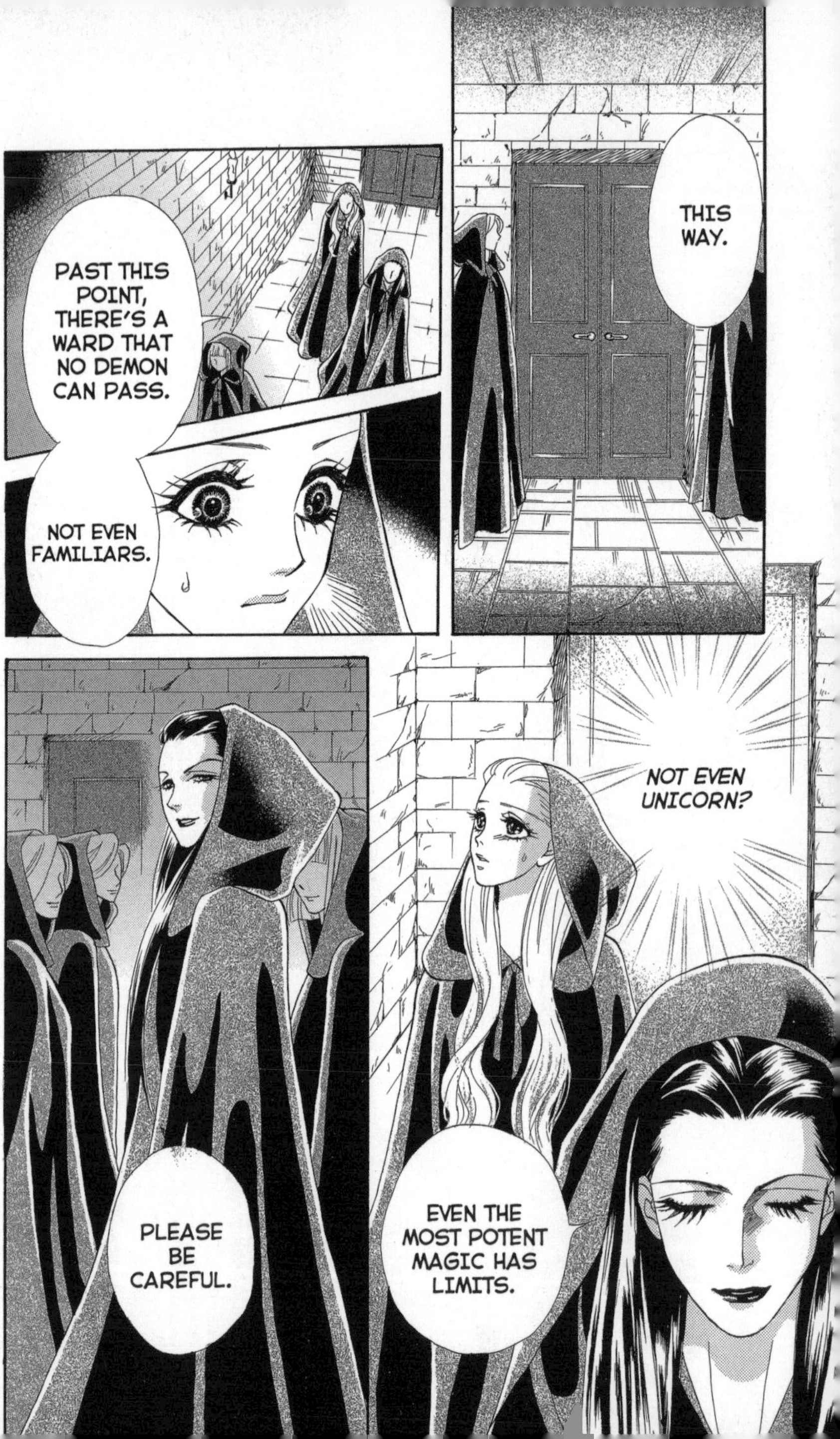
THIS WAY.
PAST THIS POINT, THERE'S A WARD THAT NO DEMON CAN PASS.
NOT EVEN FAMILIARS.
NOT EVEN UNICORN?
EVEN THE MOST POTENT MAGIC HAS LIMITS.
PLEASE BE CAREFUL.

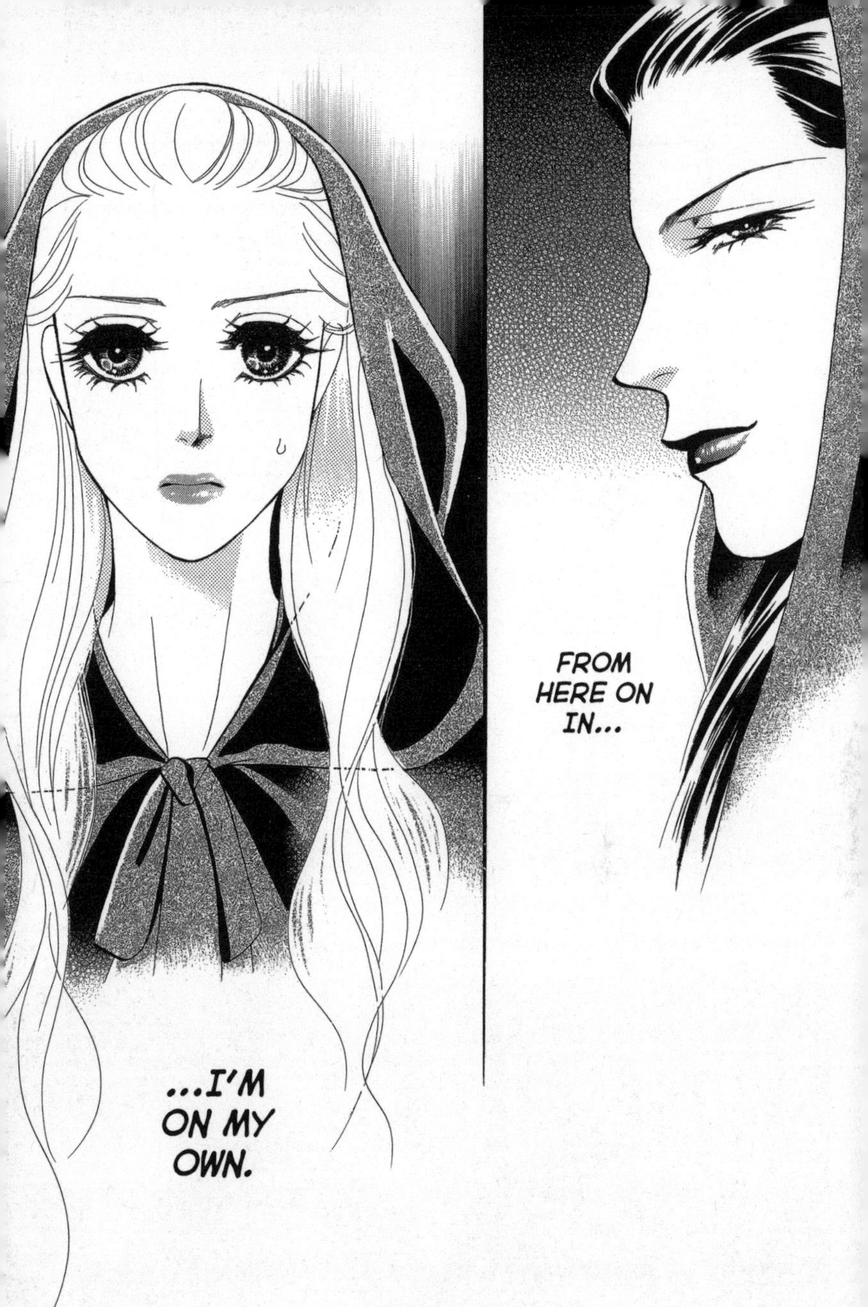
FROM HERE ON IN...
...I'M ON MY OWN.

SPELL 16: *TRAP*
–THE END–

– TRAP –

The stones Sylvia gave Koko were large chunks of things like garnet, tourmaline, topaz and emerald.

They're powerful tools in witchcraft, but they could be worth a fortune too.

It's scary carrying all these...

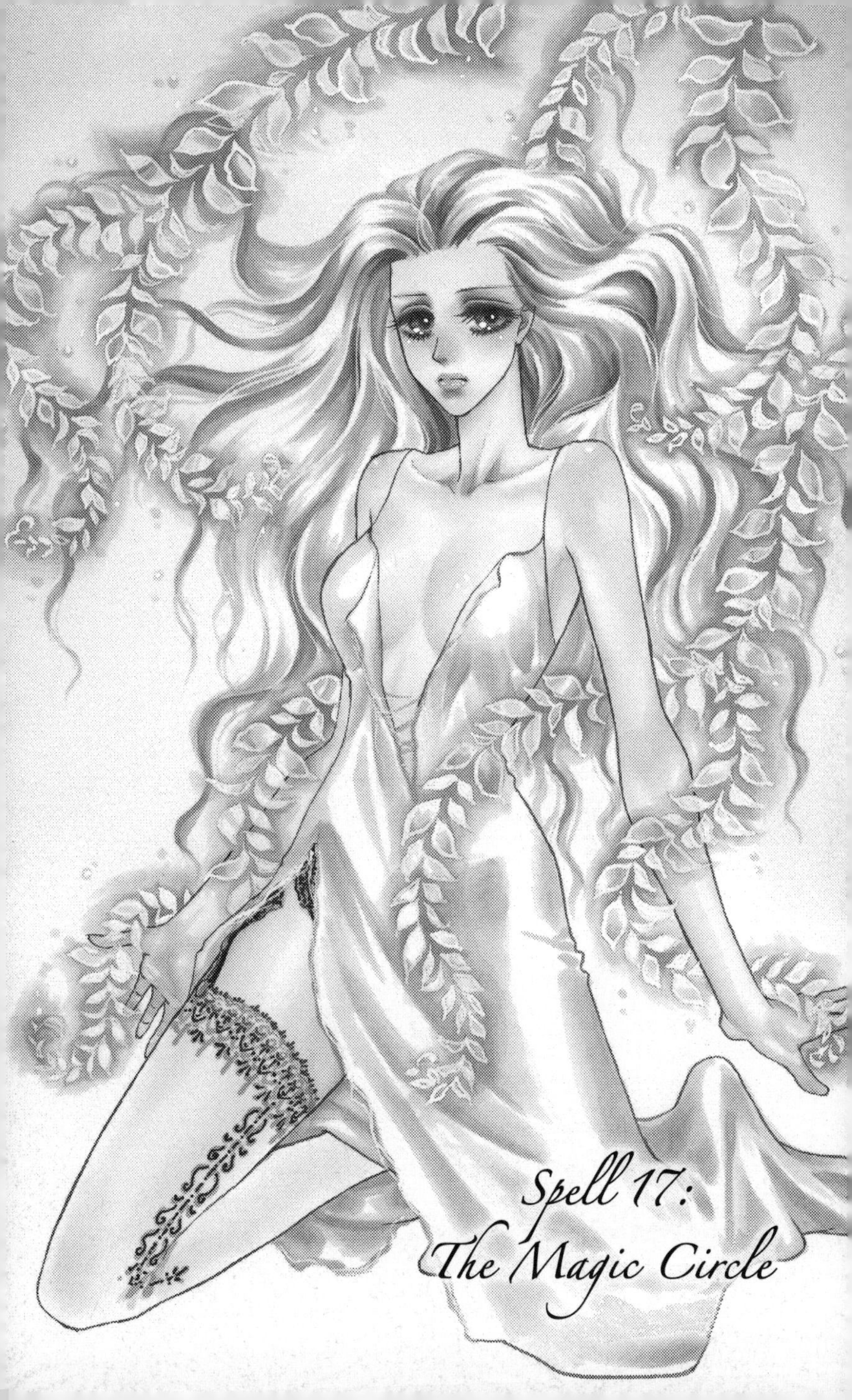
Spell 17:
The Magic Circle

It was so much fun drawing
the leaves twining around Koko
in the previous illustration!

If I had more time, I'd love
to paint more of them on a
bigger piece of paper...

She
always
does this
to me!

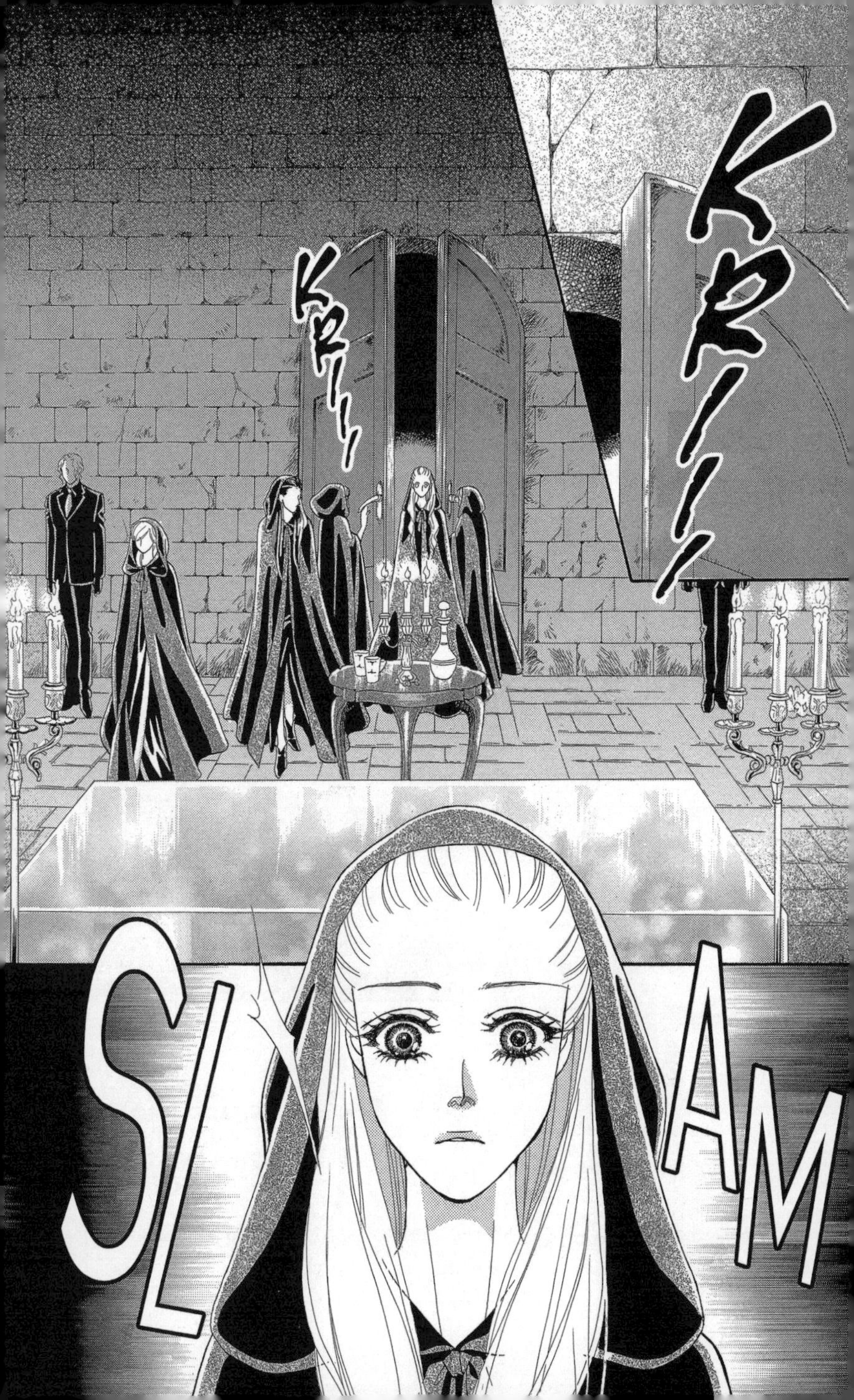
SLAM

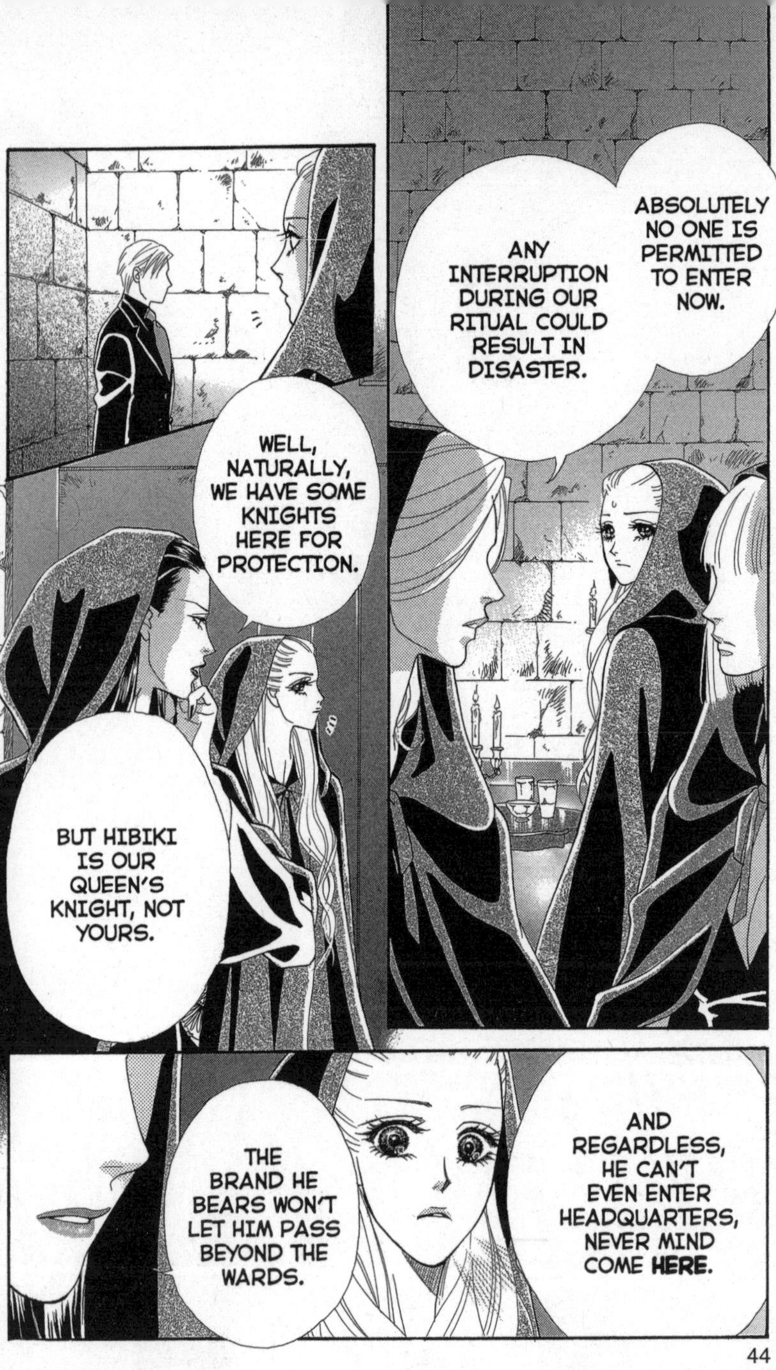
ABSOLUTELY NO ONE IS PERMITTED TO ENTER NOW.
ANY INTERRUPTION DURING OUR RITUAL COULD RESULT IN DISASTER.
WELL, NATURALLY, WE HAVE SOME KNIGHTS HERE FOR PROTECTION.
BUT HIBIKI IS OUR QUEEN'S KNIGHT, NOT YOURS.
AND REGARDLESS, HE CAN'T EVEN ENTER HEADQUARTERS, NEVER MIND COME **HERE**.
THE BRAND HE BEARS WON'T LET HIM PASS BEYOND THE WARDS.

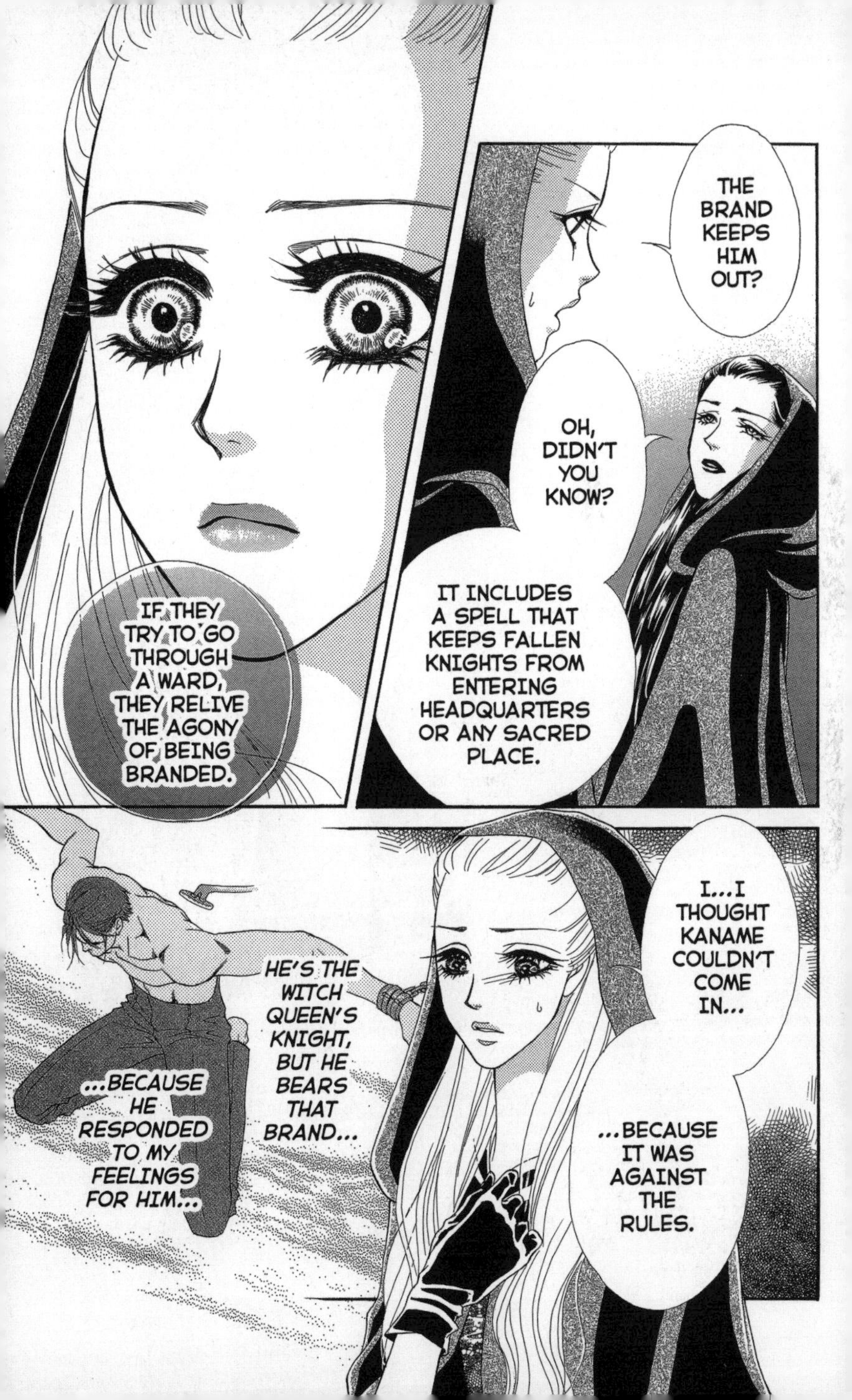
THE BRAND KEEPS HIM OUT?
OH, DIDN'T YOU KNOW?
IT INCLUDES A SPELL THAT KEEPS FALLEN KNIGHTS FROM ENTERING HEADQUARTERS OR ANY SACRED PLACE.
IF THEY TRY TO GO THROUGH A WARD, THEY RELIVE THE AGONY OF BEING BRANDED.
I...I THOUGHT KANAME COULDN'T COME IN...
...BECAUSE IT WAS AGAINST THE RULES.
HE'S THE WITCH QUEEN'S KNIGHT, BUT HE BEARS THAT BRAND...
...BECAUSE HE RESPONDED TO MY FEELINGS FOR HIM...

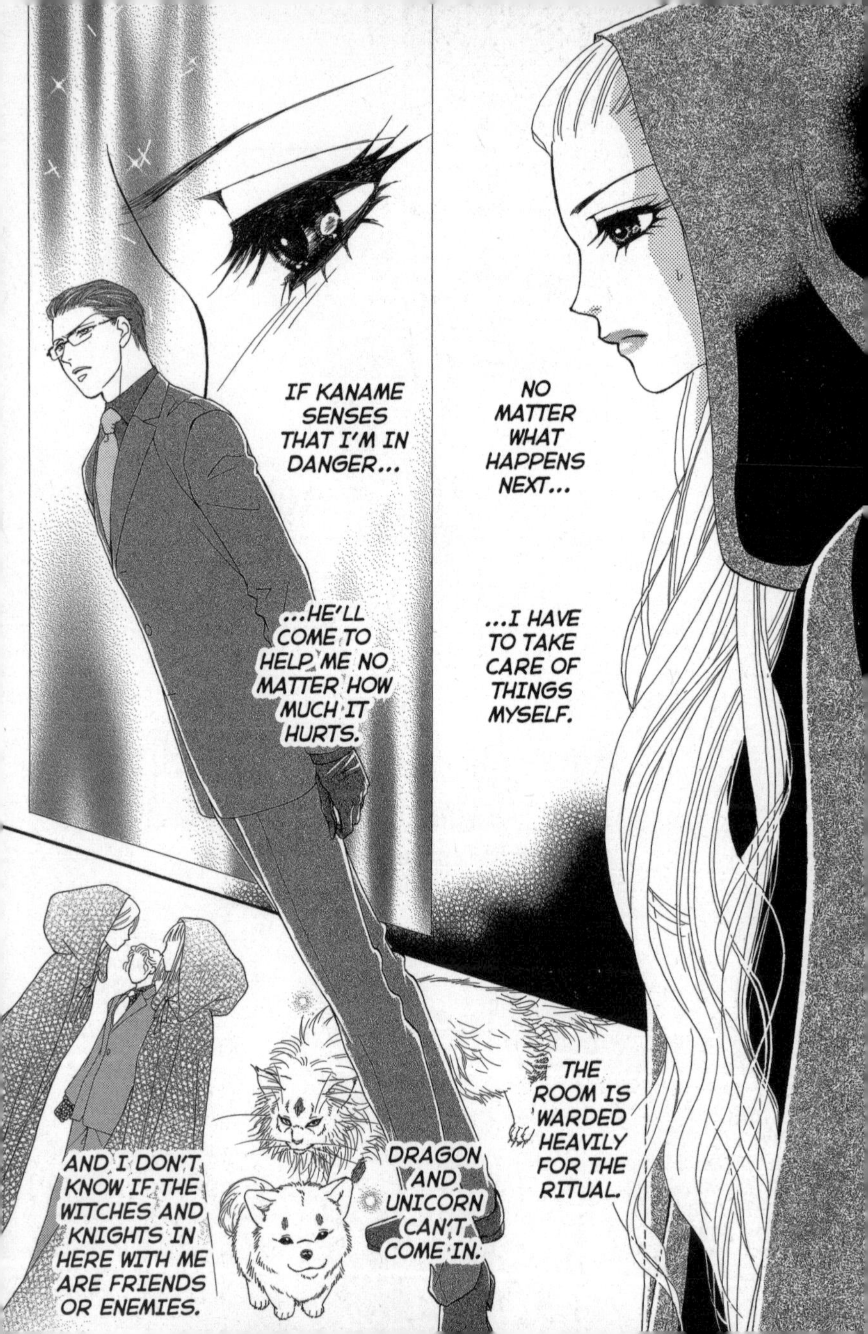
NO MATTER WHAT HAPPENS NEXT...
...I HAVE TO TAKE CARE OF THINGS MYSELF.
IF KANAME SENSES THAT I'M IN DANGER...
...HE'LL COME TO HELP ME NO MATTER HOW MUCH IT HURTS.
THE ROOM IS WARDED HEAVILY FOR THE RITUAL.
DRAGON AND UNICORN CAN'T COME IN.
AND I DON'T KNOW IF THE WITCHES AND KNIGHTS IN HERE WITH ME ARE FRIENDS OR ENEMIES.

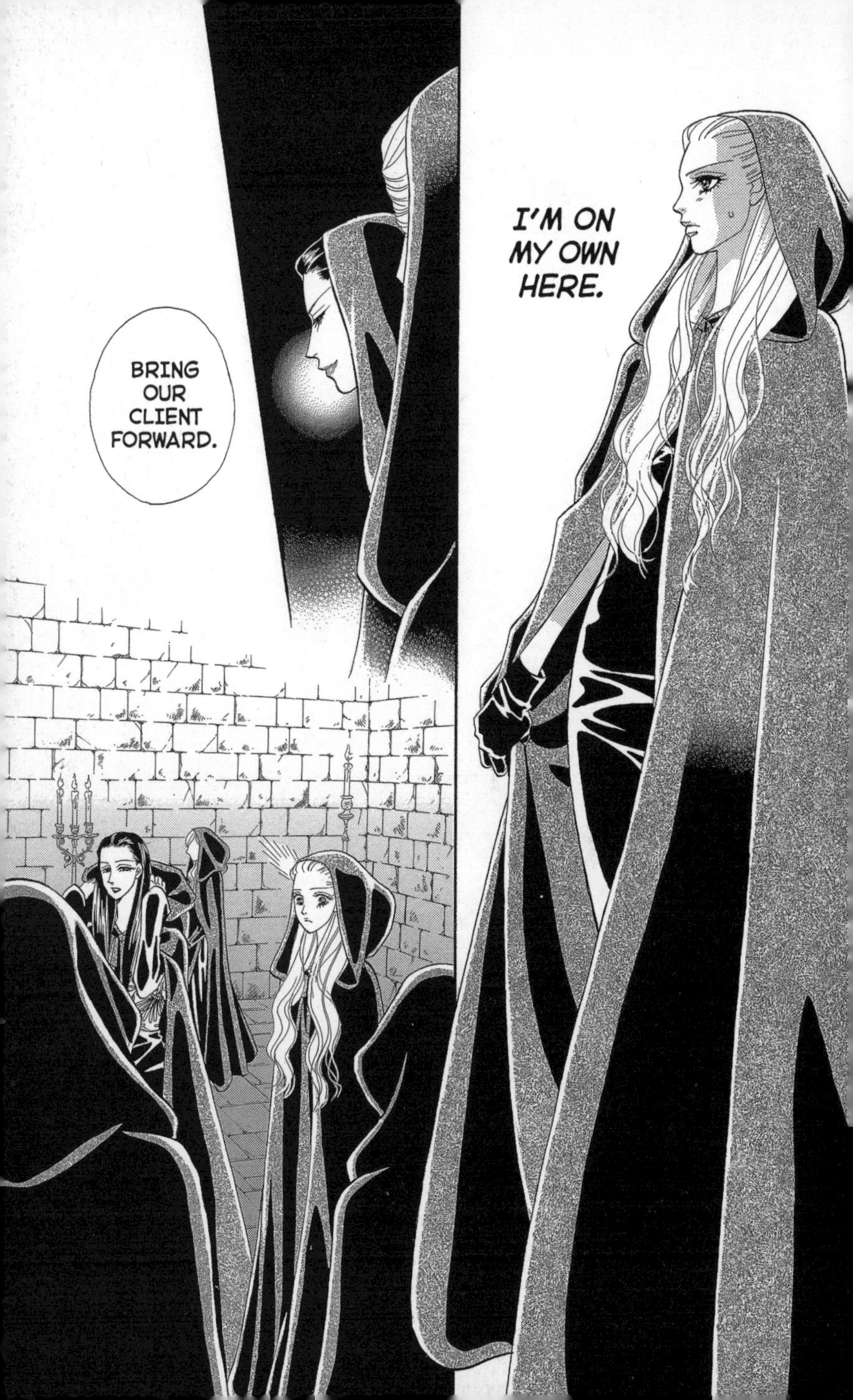
I'M ON MY OWN HERE.
BRING OUR CLIENT FORWARD.

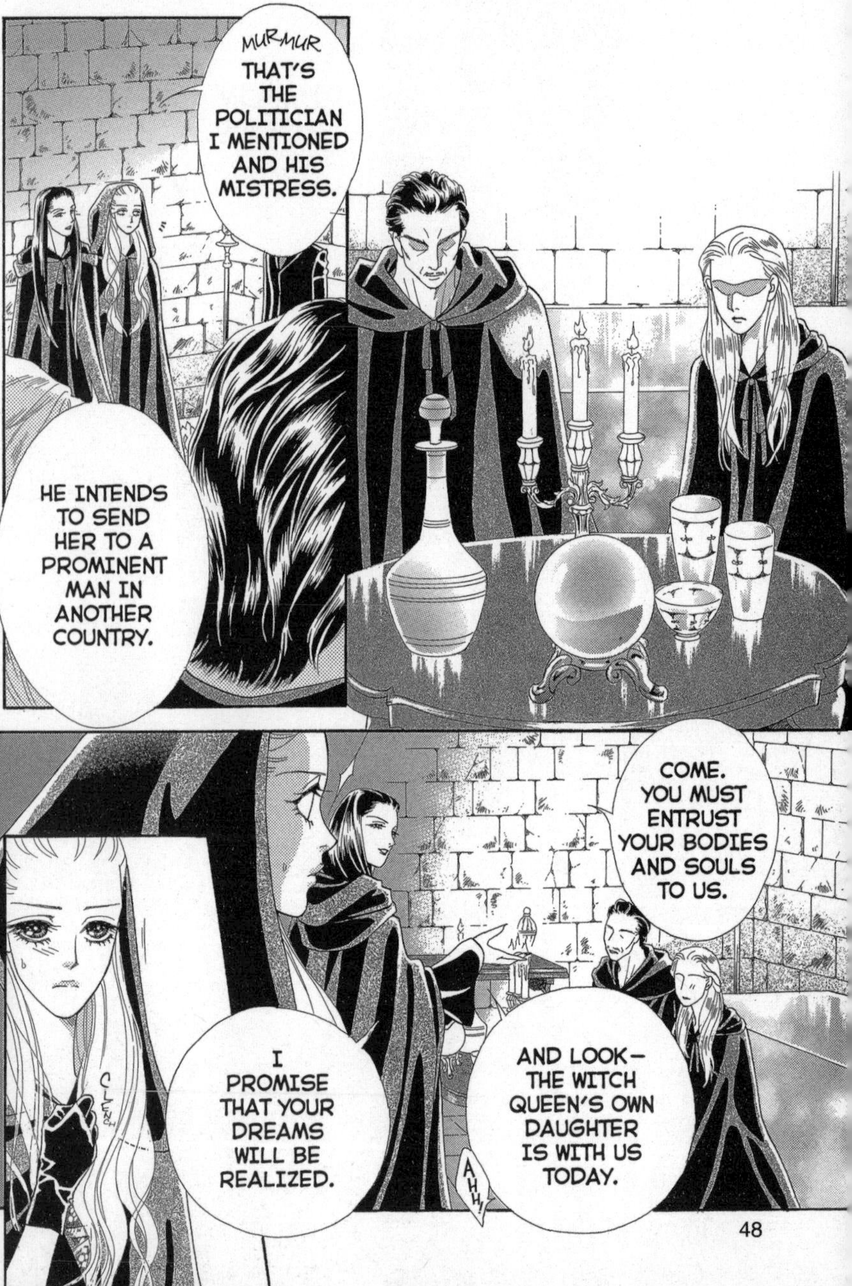
MURMUR
THAT'S THE POLITICIAN I MENTIONED AND HIS MISTRESS.
HE INTENDS TO SEND HER TO A PROMINENT MAN IN ANOTHER COUNTRY.
COME. YOU MUST ENTRUST YOUR BODIES AND SOULS TO US.
AND LOOK— THE WITCH QUEEN'S OWN DAUGHTER IS WITH US TODAY.
AHH!
I PROMISE THAT YOUR DREAMS WILL BE REALIZED.
CLENCH

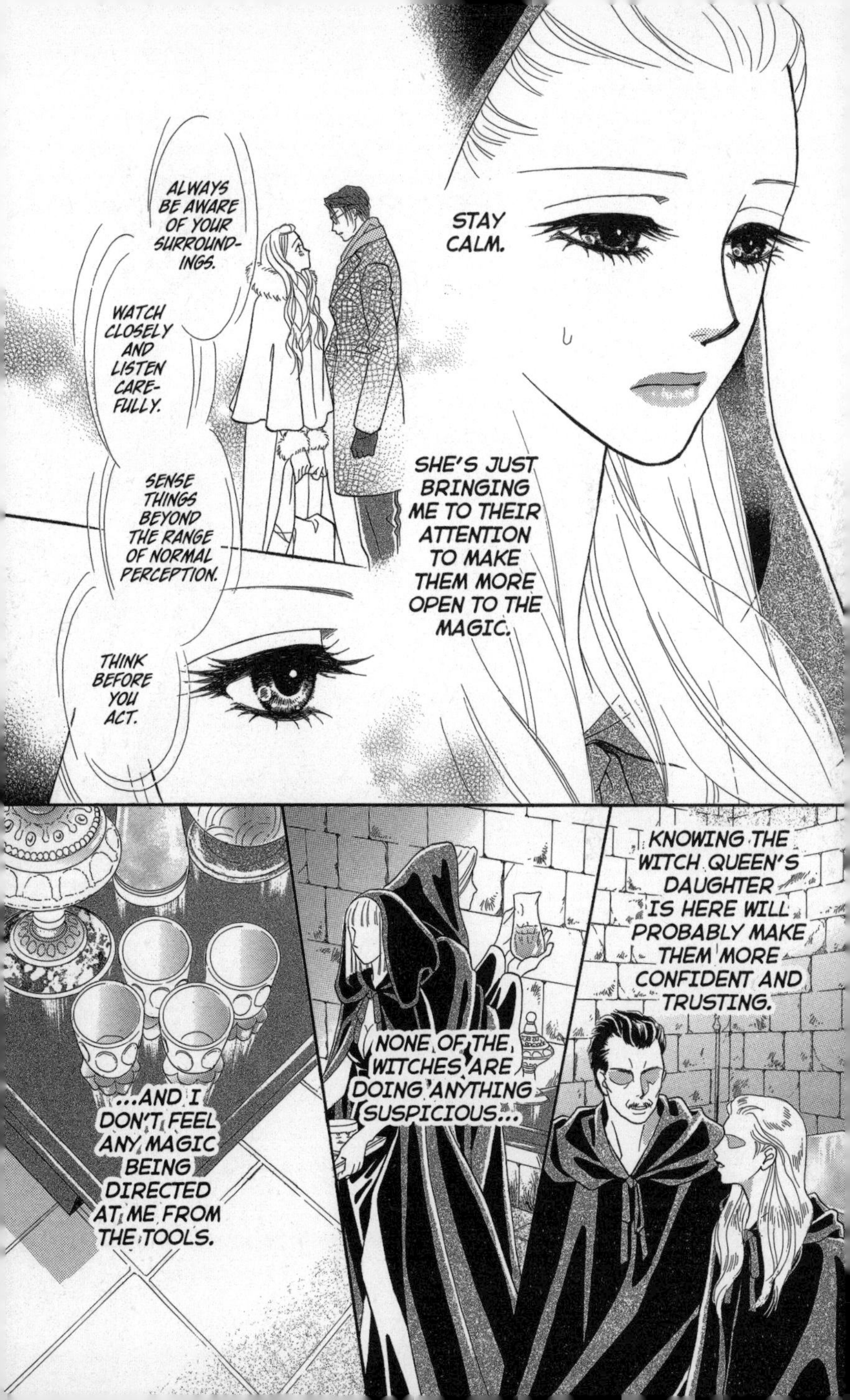
STAY CALM.
SHE'S JUST BRINGING ME TO THEIR ATTENTION TO MAKE THEM MORE OPEN TO THE MAGIC.
ALWAYS BE AWARE OF YOUR SURROUND-INGS.
WATCH CLOSELY AND LISTEN CARE-FULLY.
SENSE THINGS BEYOND THE RANGE OF NORMAL PERCEPTION.
THINK BEFORE YOU ACT.
KNOWING THE WITCH QUEEN'S DAUGHTER IS HERE WILL PROBABLY MAKE THEM MORE CONFIDENT AND TRUSTING.
NONE OF THE WITCHES ARE DOING ANYTHING SUSPICIOUS...
...AND I DON'T FEEL ANY MAGIC BEING DIRECTED AT ME FROM THE TOOLS.

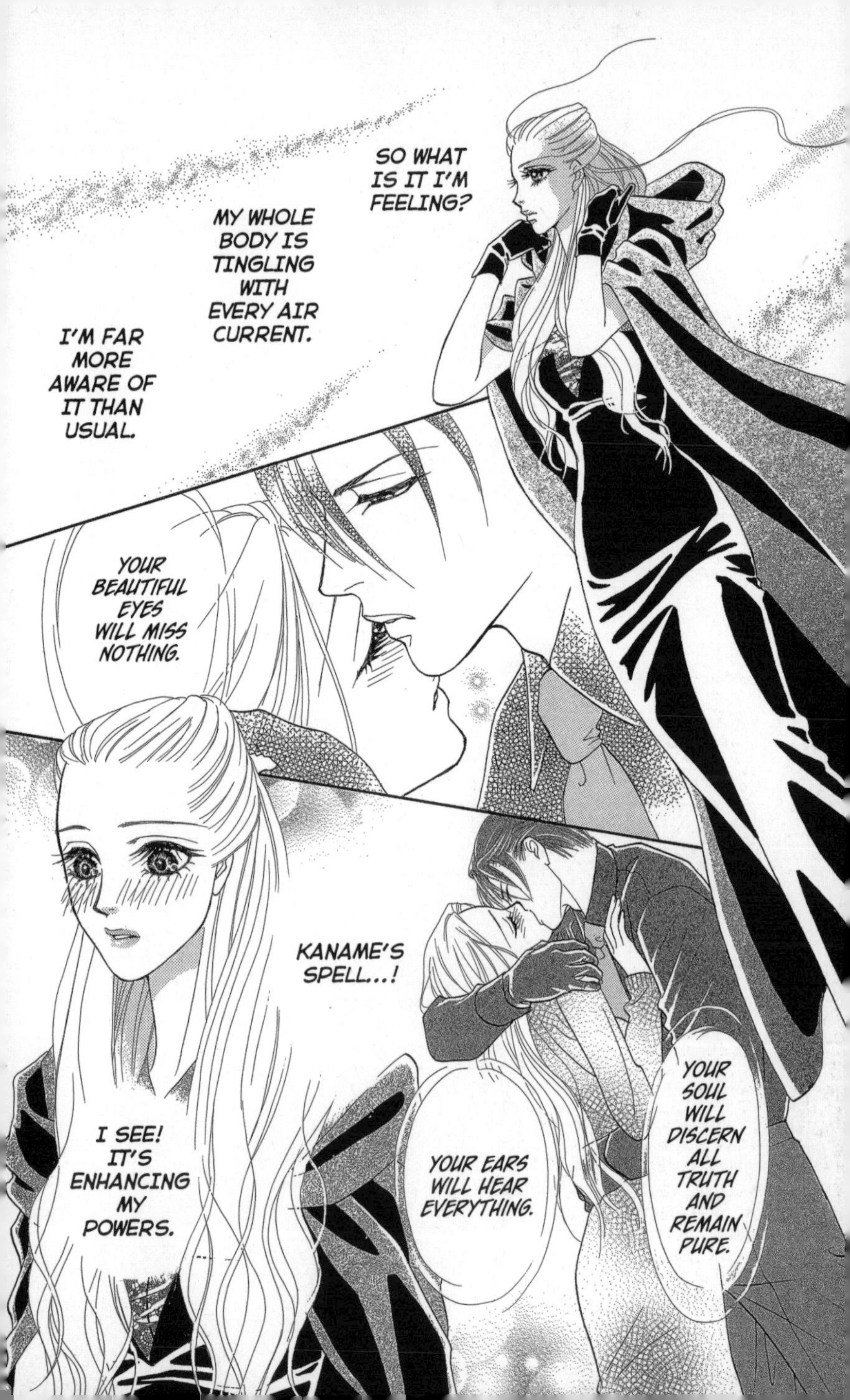
SO WHAT IS IT I'M FEELING?
MY WHOLE BODY IS TINGLING WITH EVERY AIR CURRENT.
I'M FAR MORE AWARE OF IT THAN USUAL.
YOUR BEAUTIFUL EYES WILL MISS NOTHING.
YOUR SOUL WILL DISCERN ALL TRUTH AND REMAIN PURE.
YOUR EARS WILL HEAR EVERYTHING.
KANAME'S SPELL...!
I SEE! IT'S ENHANCING MY POWERS.

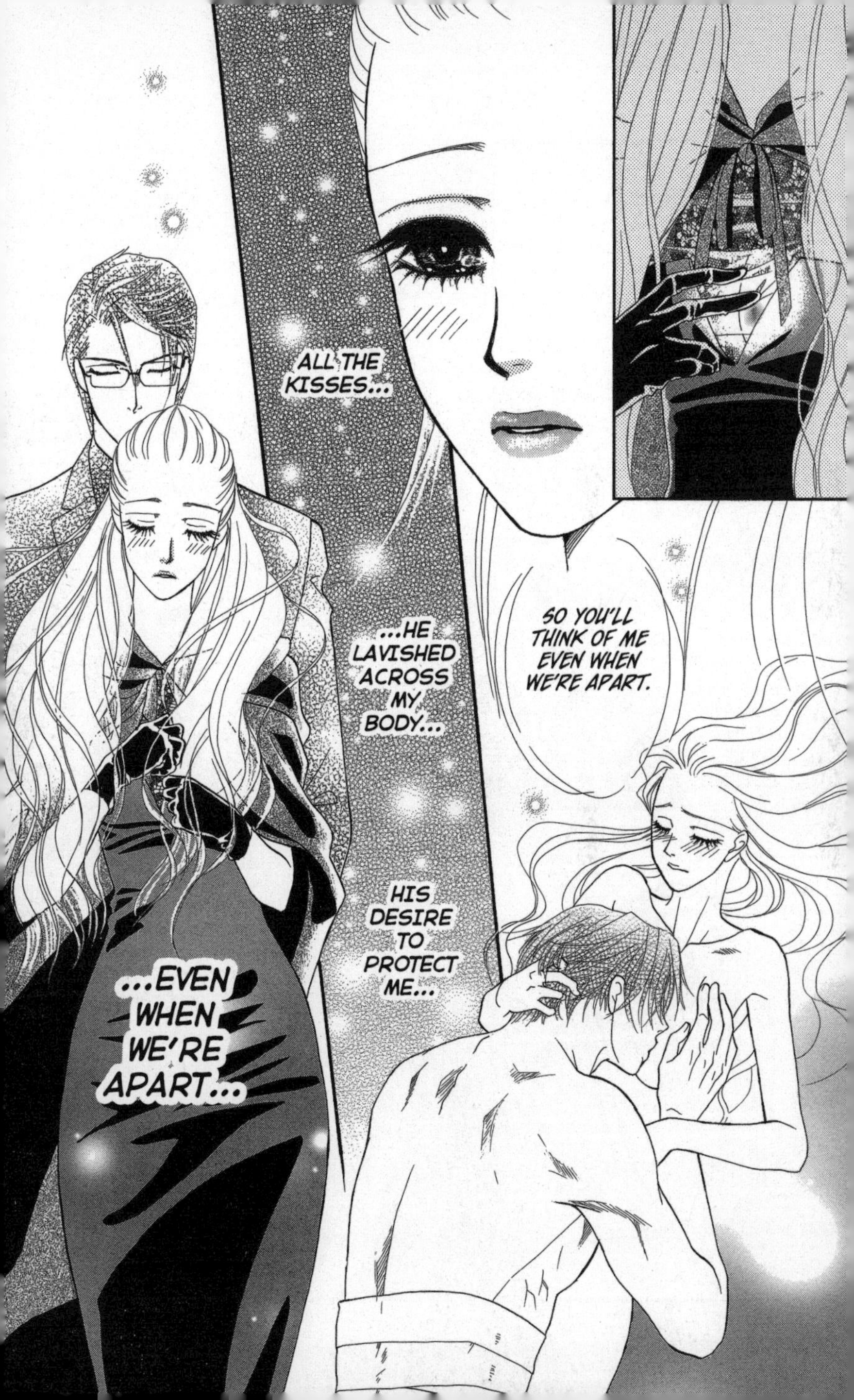
ALL THE KISSES...
SO YOU'LL THINK OF ME EVEN WHEN WE'RE APART.
...HE LAVISHED ACROSS MY BODY...
HIS DESIRE TO PROTECT ME...
...EVEN WHEN WE'RE APART...

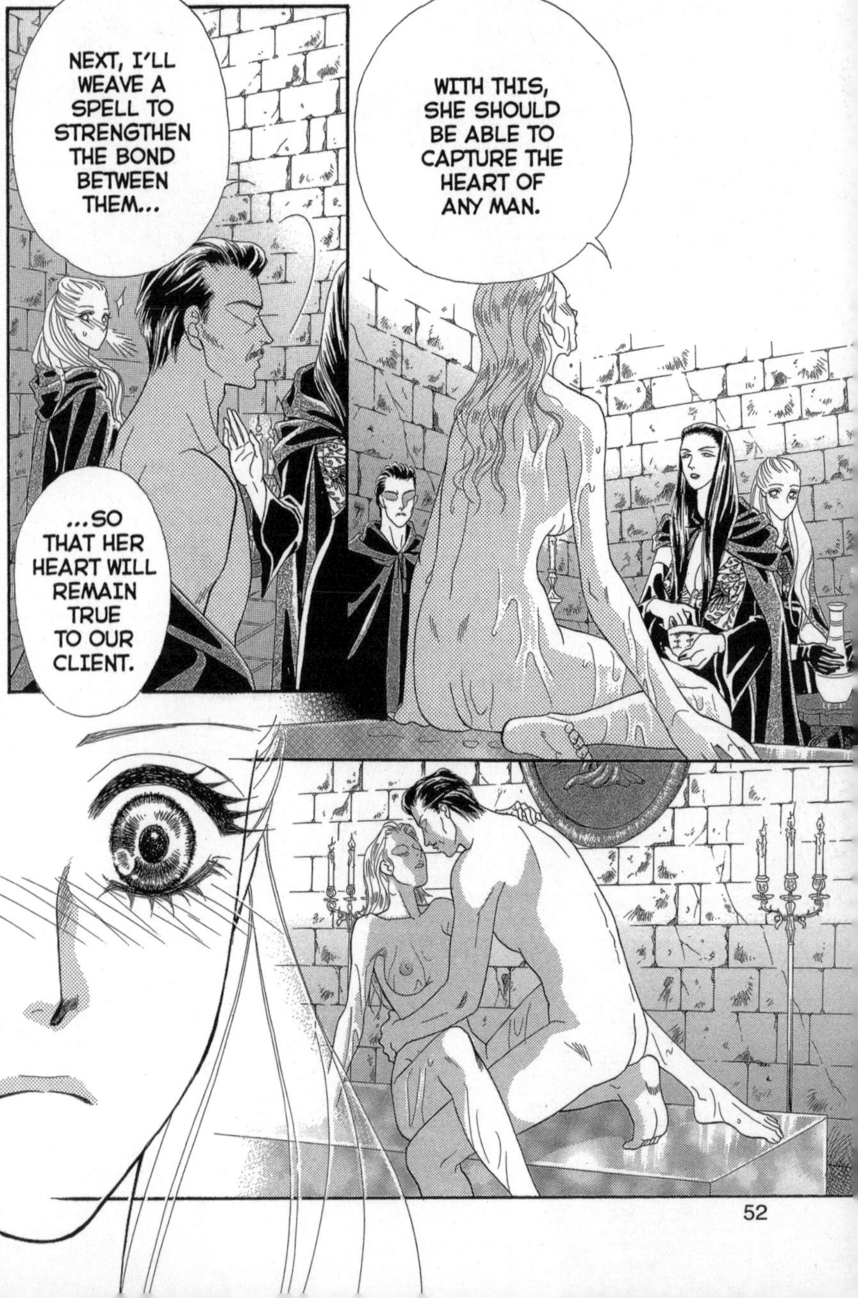
WITH THIS, SHE SHOULD BE ABLE TO CAPTURE THE HEART OF ANY MAN.
NEXT, I'LL WEAVE A SPELL TO STRENGTHEN THE BOND BETWEEN THEM...
...SO THAT HER HEART WILL REMAIN TRUE TO OUR CLIENT.

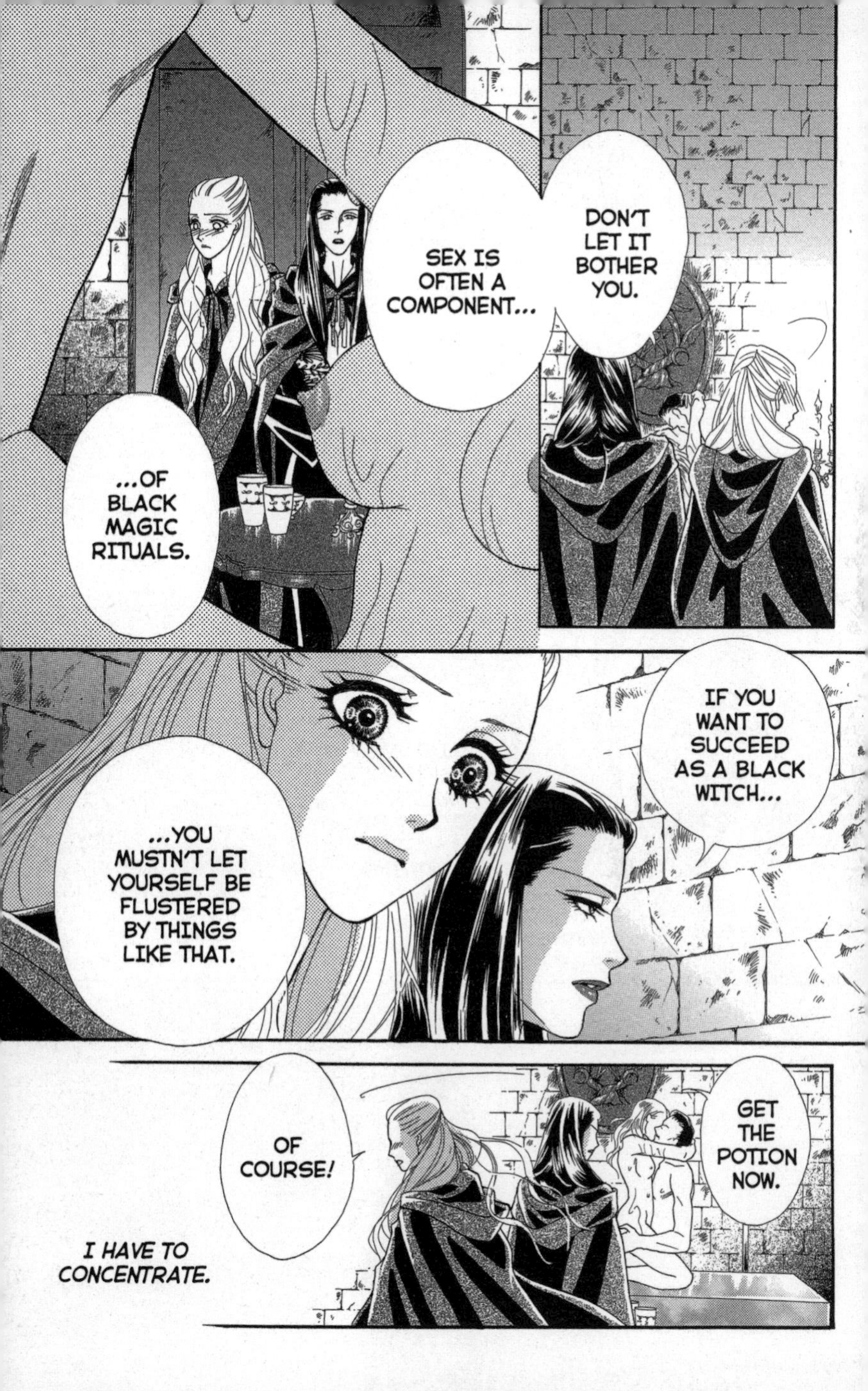
DON'T LET IT BOTHER YOU.
SEX IS OFTEN A COMPONENT...
...OF BLACK MAGIC RITUALS.
IF YOU WANT TO SUCCEED AS A BLACK WITCH...
...YOU MUSTN'T LET YOURSELF BE FLUSTERED BY THINGS LIKE THAT.
GET THE POTION NOW.
OF COURSE!
I HAVE TO CONCENTRATE.

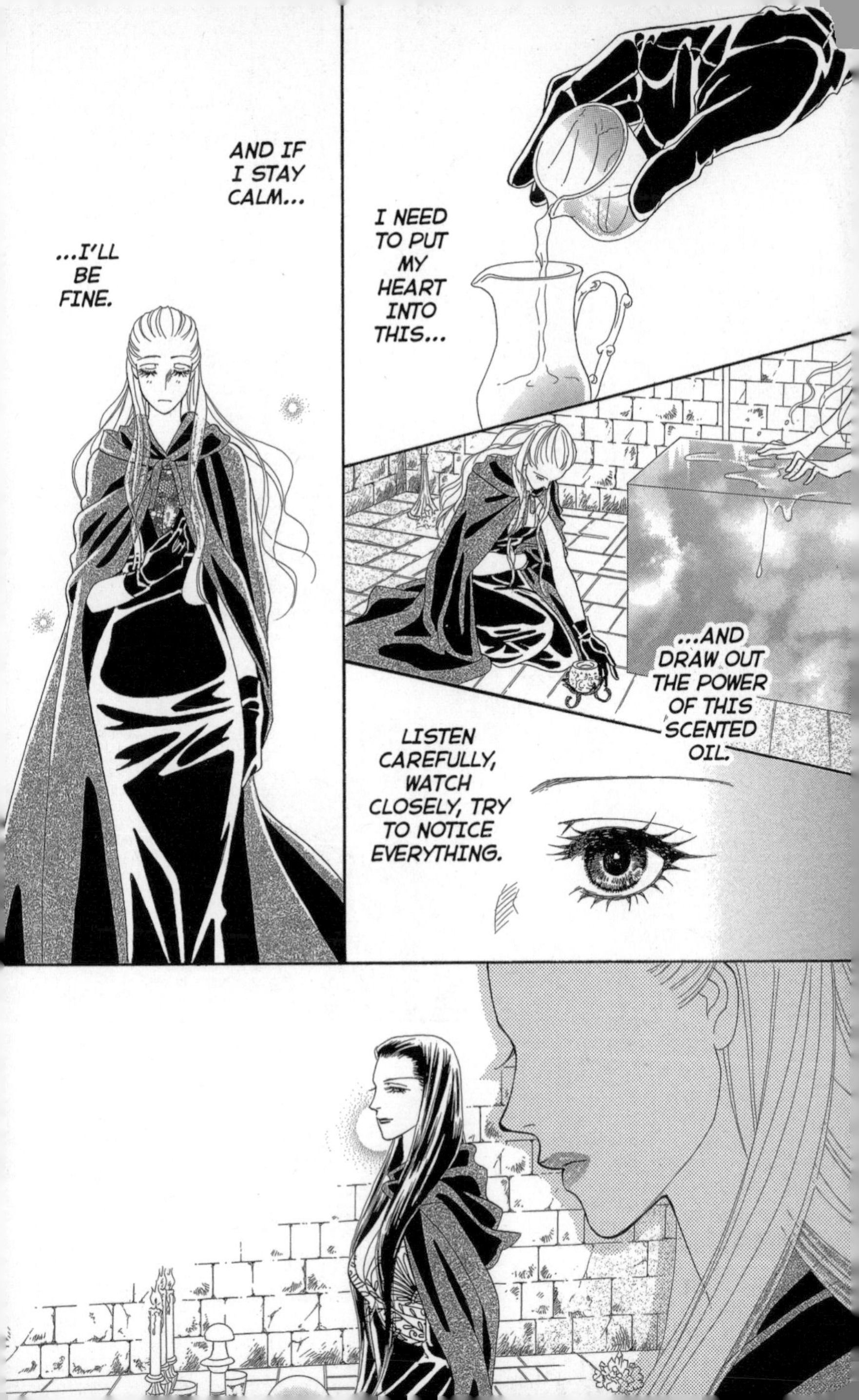
I NEED TO PUT MY HEART INTO THIS...
...AND DRAW OUT THE POWER OF THIS SCENTED OIL.
LISTEN CAREFULLY, WATCH CLOSELY, TRY TO NOTICE EVERYTHING.
AND IF I STAY CALM...
...I'LL BE FINE.

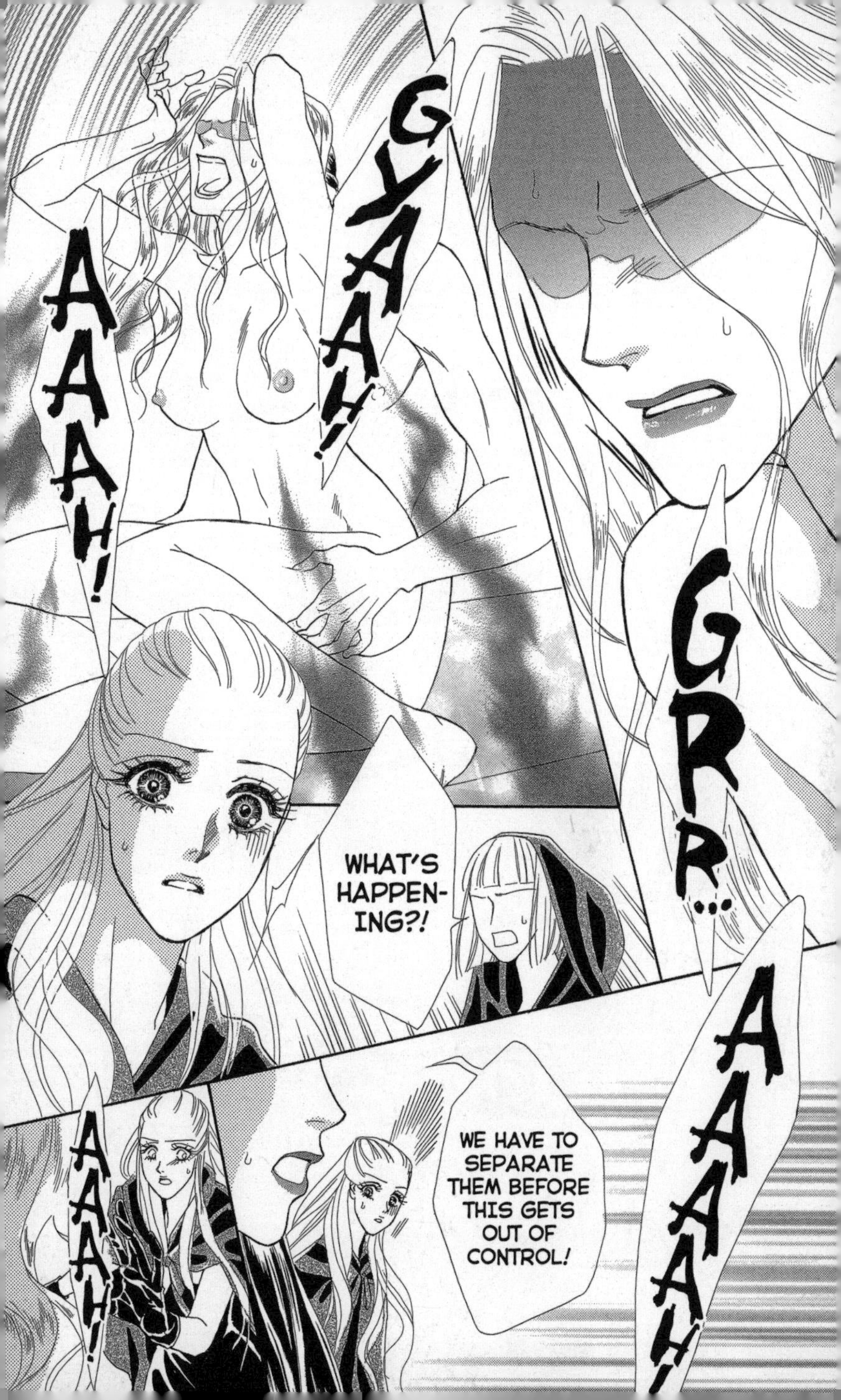
GRR...
GYAAH!
AAAH!
WHAT'S HAPPEN-ING?!
AAAAH!
WE HAVE TO SEPARATE THEM BEFORE THIS GETS OUT OF CONTROL!
AAAH!

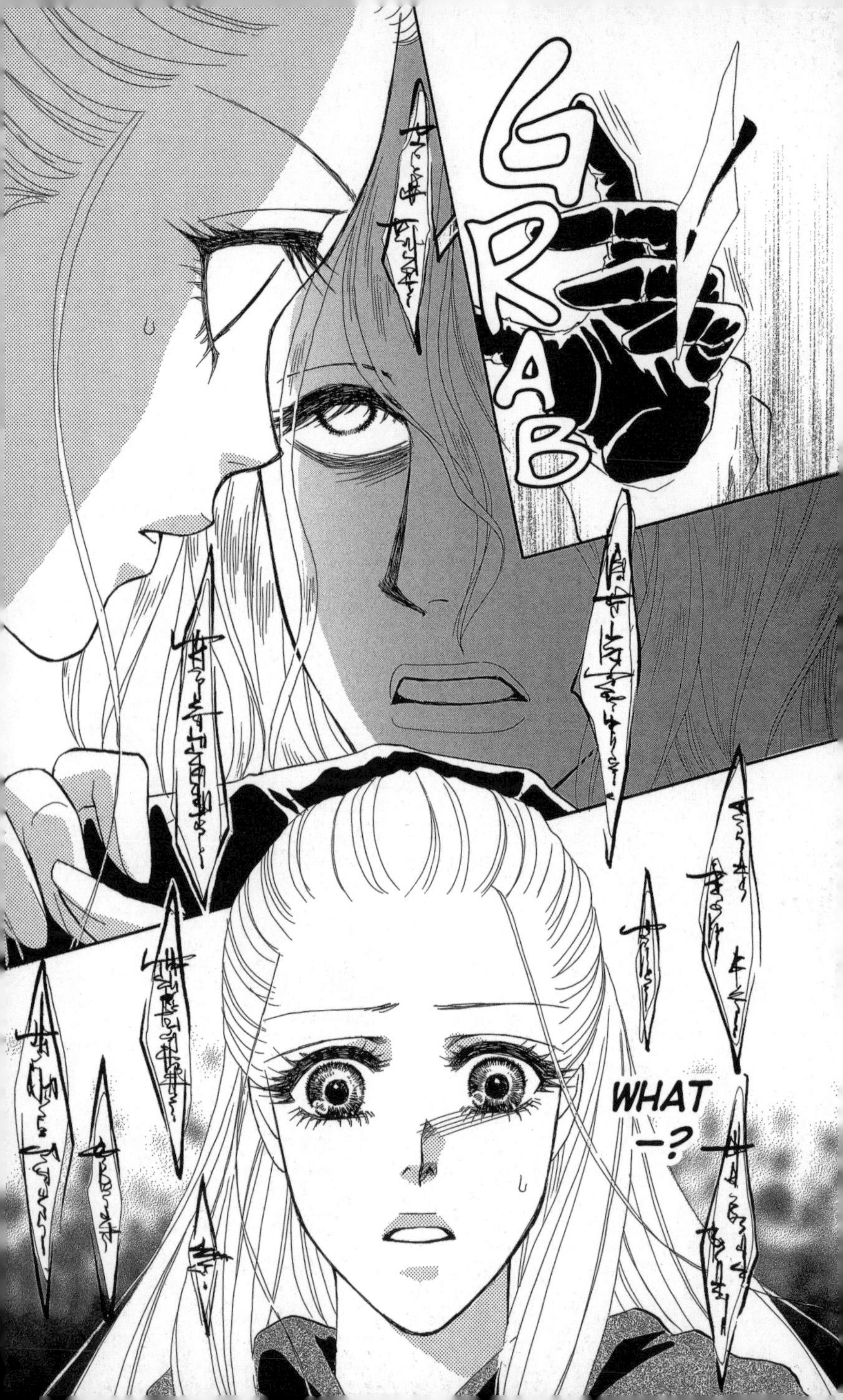
GRAB!
WHAT —?

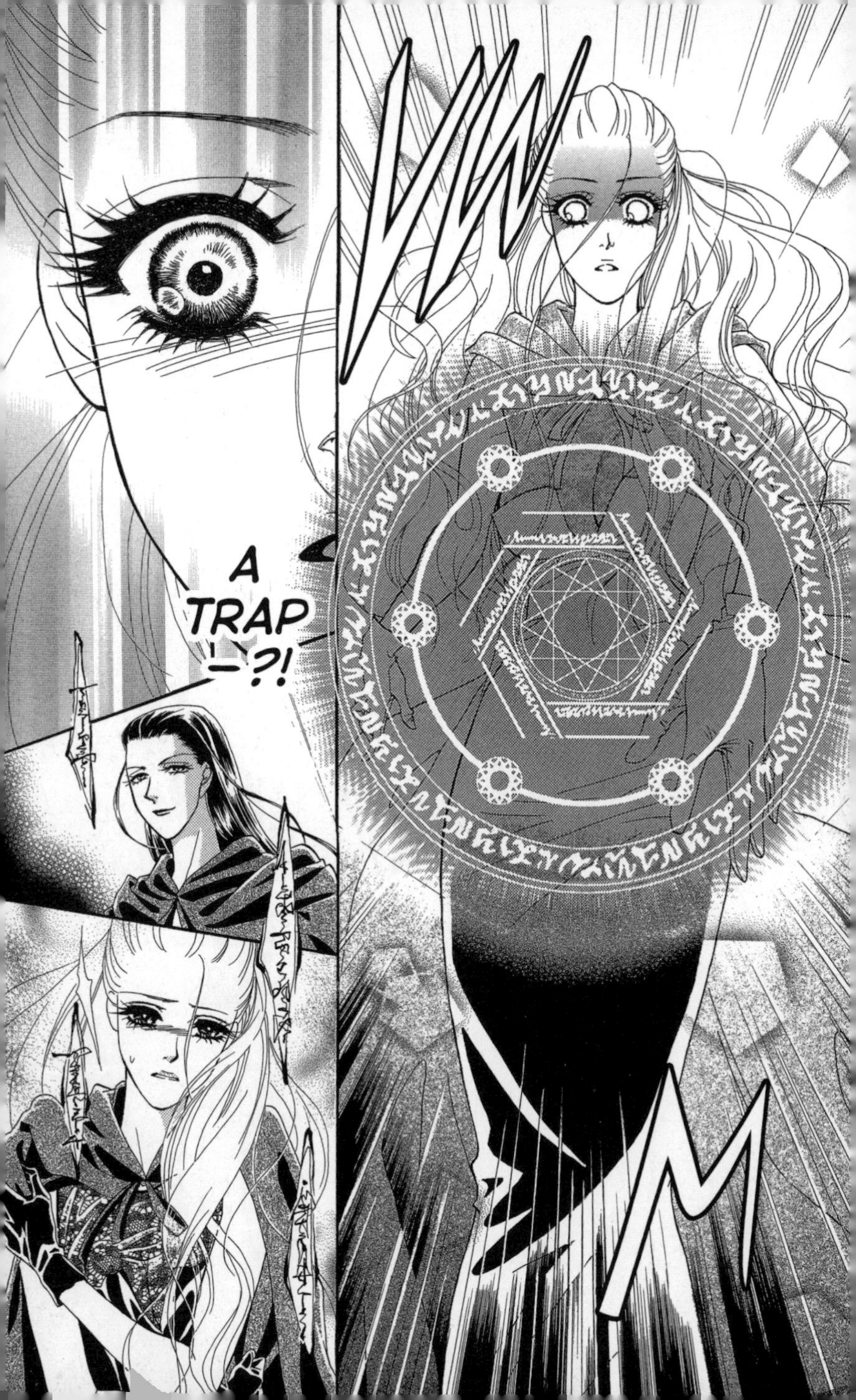
A TRAP—?!

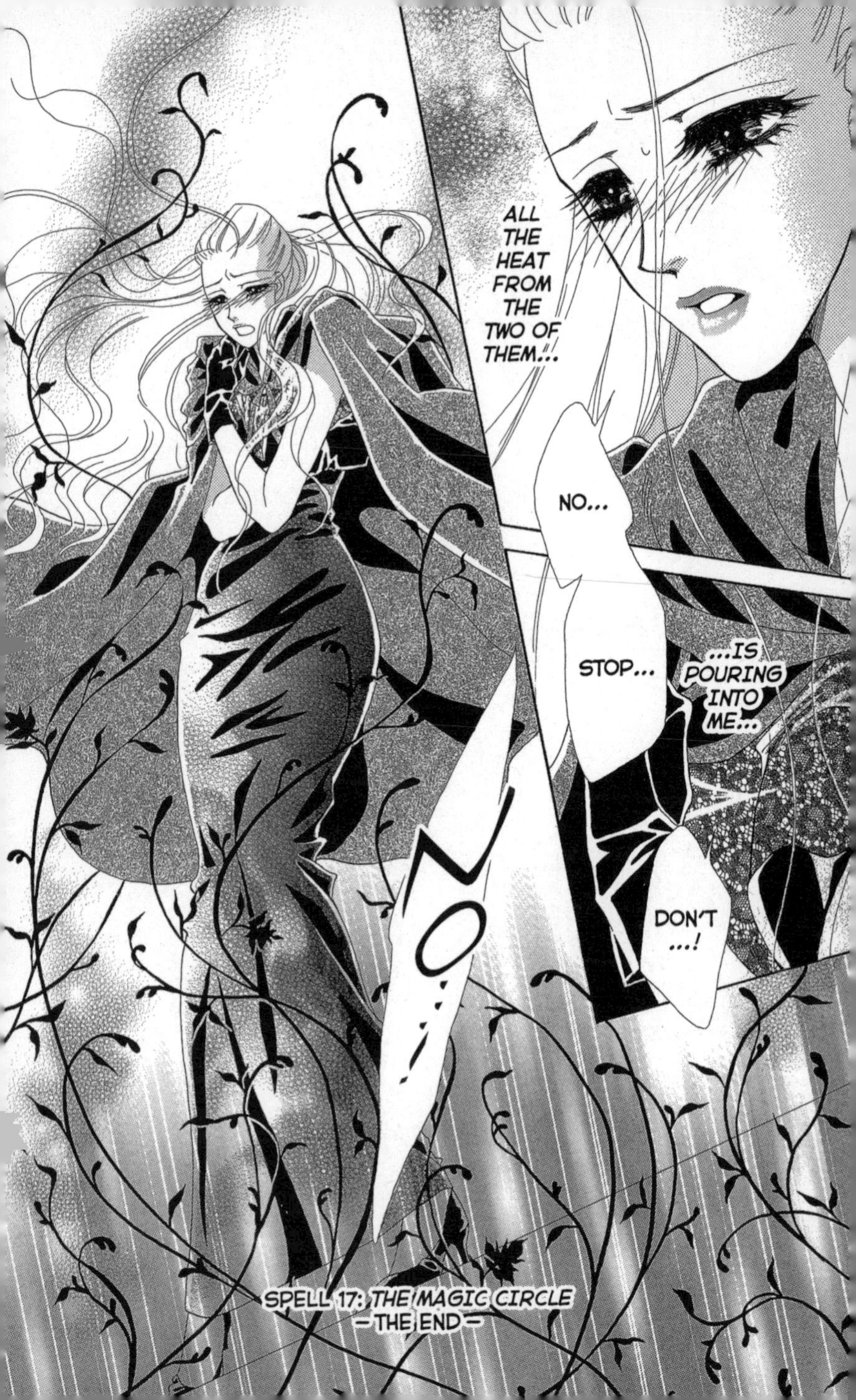
ALL THE HEAT FROM THE TWO OF THEM...
...IS POURING INTO ME...
NO...
STOP...
DON'T ...!
NO...!
SPELL 17: THE MAGIC CIRCLE
– THE END –

Spell 18: The Shield

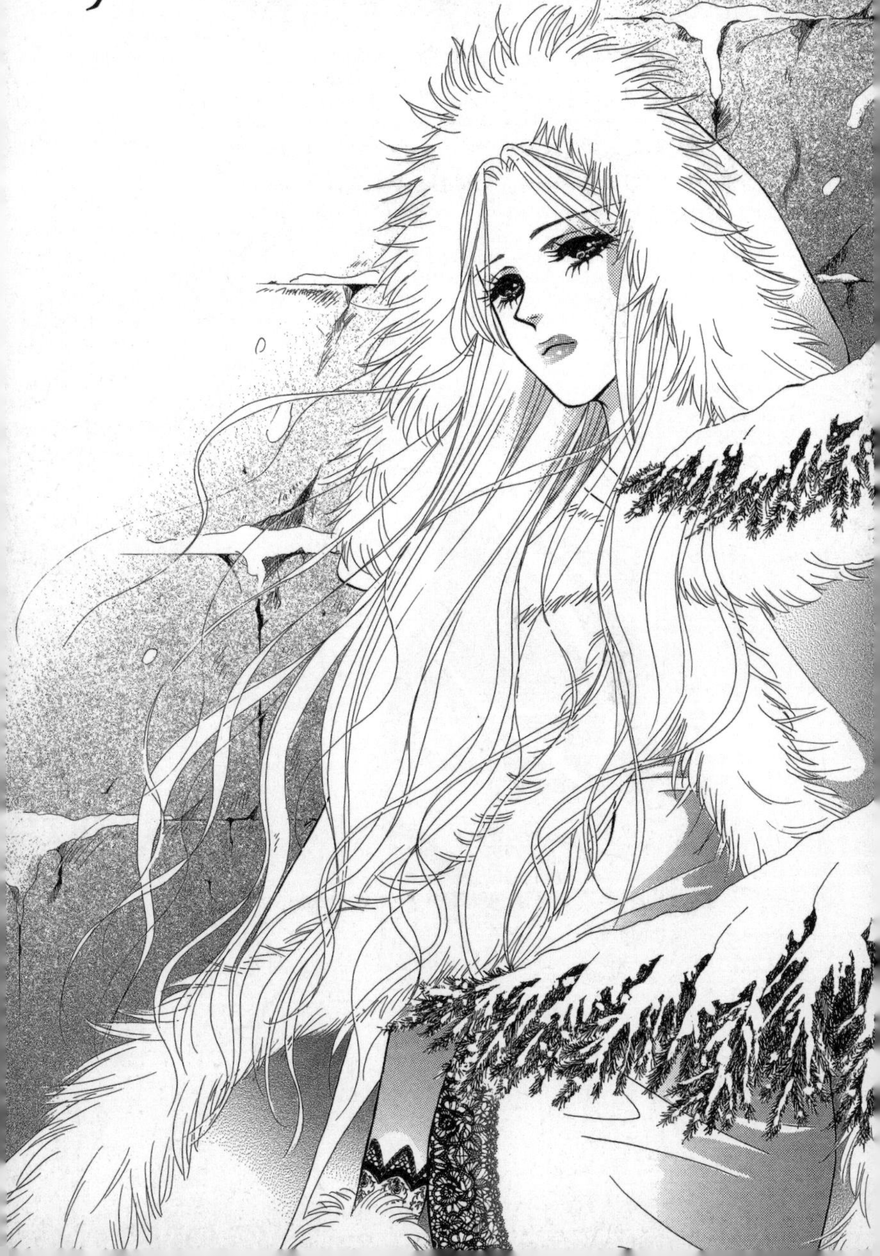

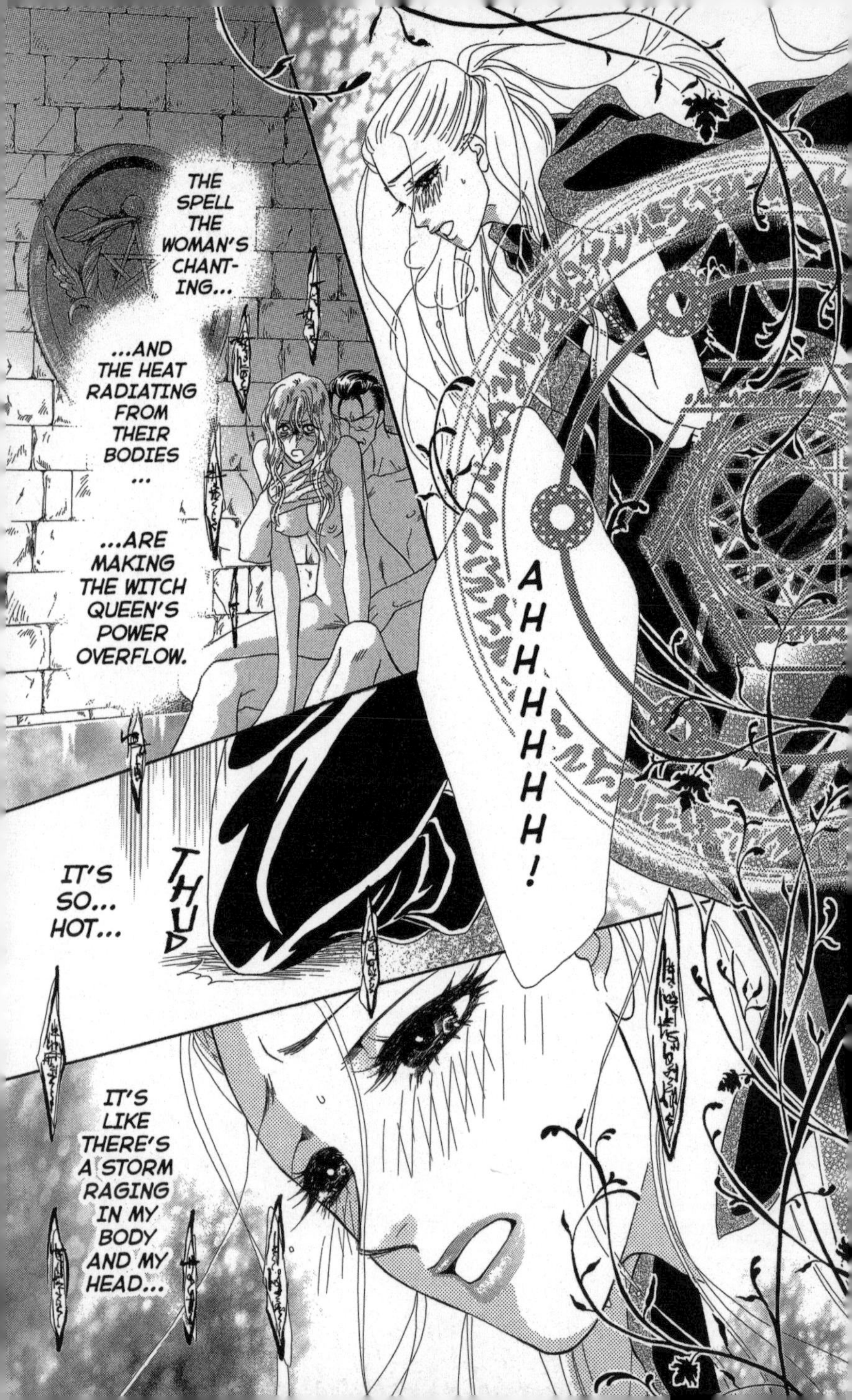
AHHHHHHHH!
THE SPELL THE WOMAN'S CHANT-ING...
...AND THE HEAT RADIATING FROM THEIR BODIES...
...ARE MAKING THE WITCH QUEEN'S POWER OVERFLOW.
THUD
IT'S SO... HOT...
IT'S LIKE THERE'S A STORM RAGING IN MY BODY AND MY HEAD...

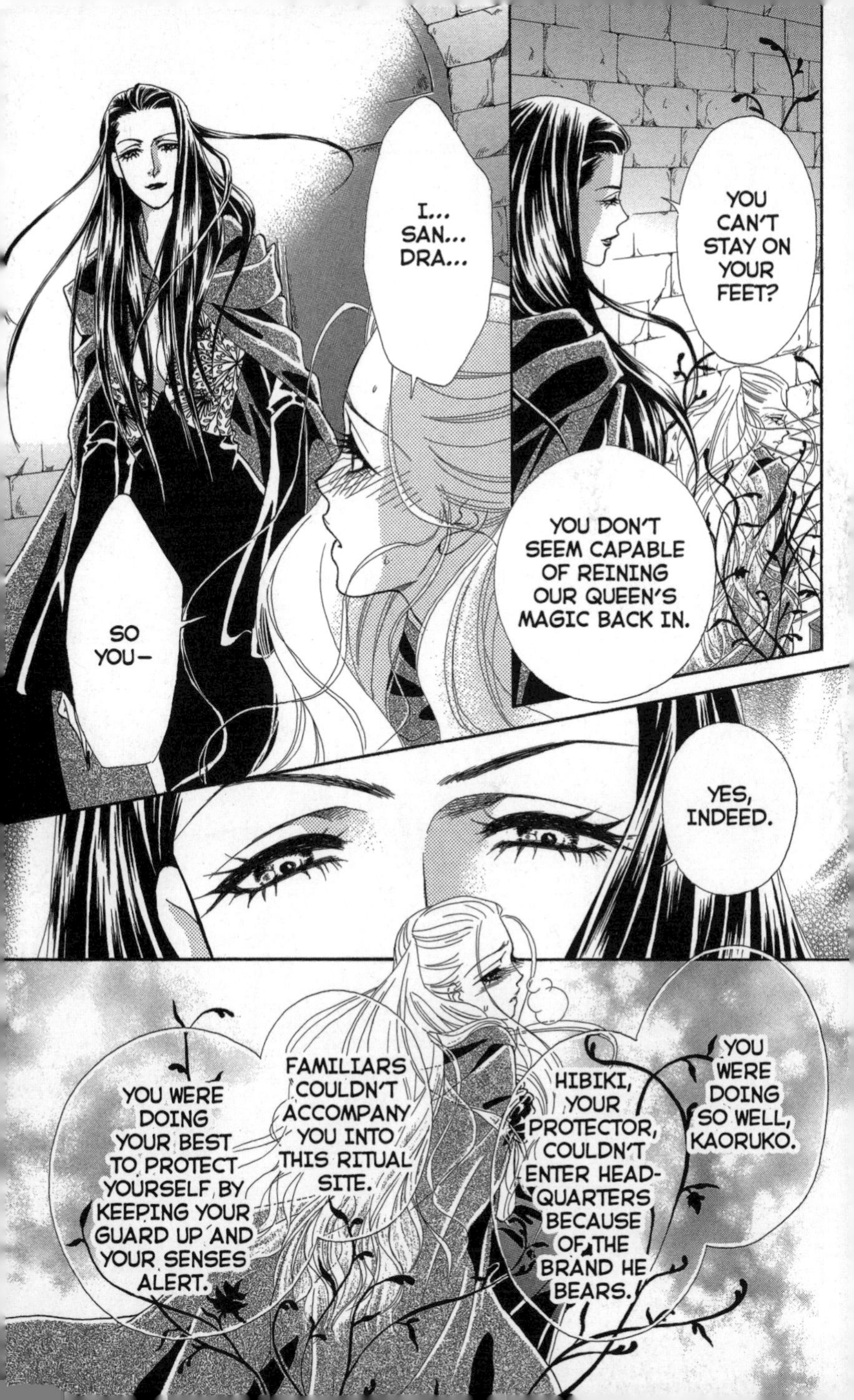
YOU CAN'T STAY ON YOUR FEET?
YOU DON'T SEEM CAPABLE OF REINING OUR QUEEN'S MAGIC BACK IN.
I... SAN... DRA...
SO YOU–
YES, INDEED.
YOU WERE DOING SO WELL, KAORUKO.
HIBIKI, YOUR PROTECTOR, COULDN'T ENTER HEAD-QUARTERS BECAUSE OF THE BRAND HE BEARS.
FAMILIARS COULDN'T ACCOMPANY YOU INTO THIS RITUAL SITE.
YOU WERE DOING YOUR BEST TO PROTECT YOURSELF BY KEEPING YOUR GUARD UP AND YOUR SENSES ALERT.

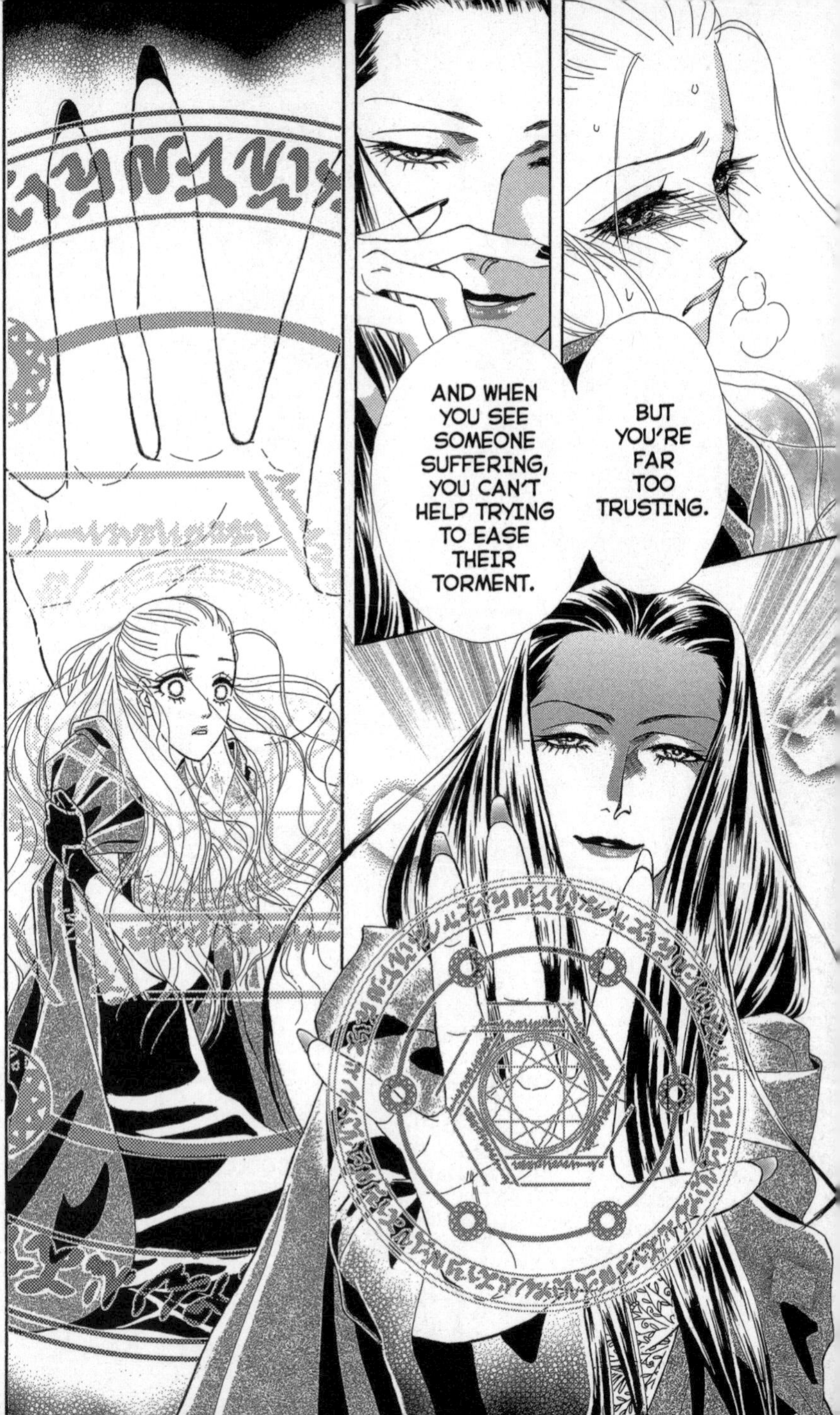
BUT YOU'RE FAR TOO TRUSTING.
AND WHEN YOU SEE SOMEONE SUFFERING, YOU CAN'T HELP TRYING TO EASE THEIR TORMENT.

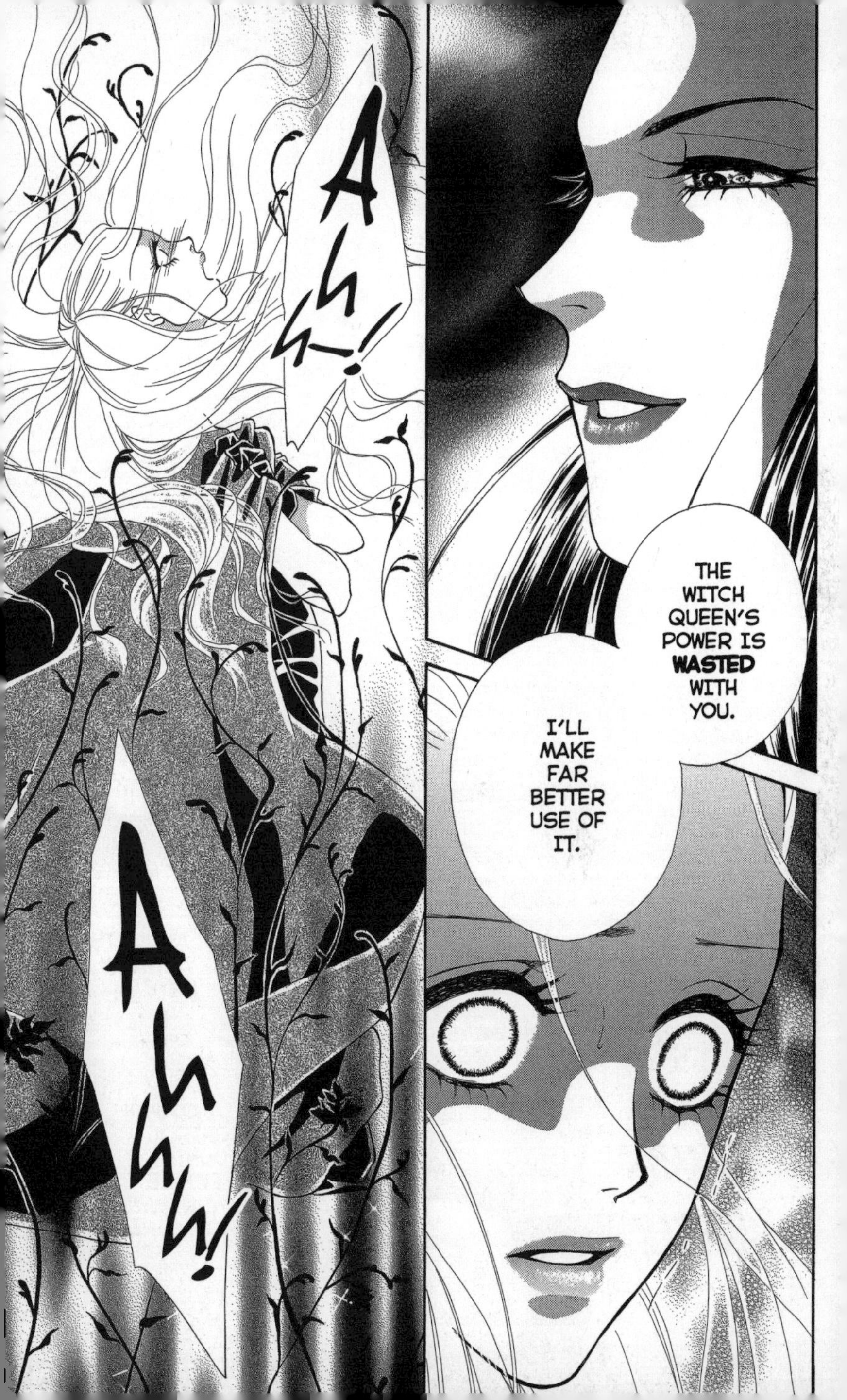
THE WITCH QUEEN'S POWER IS **WASTED** WITH YOU.
I'LL MAKE FAR BETTER USE OF IT.
Ahhh—!
Ahhhh!

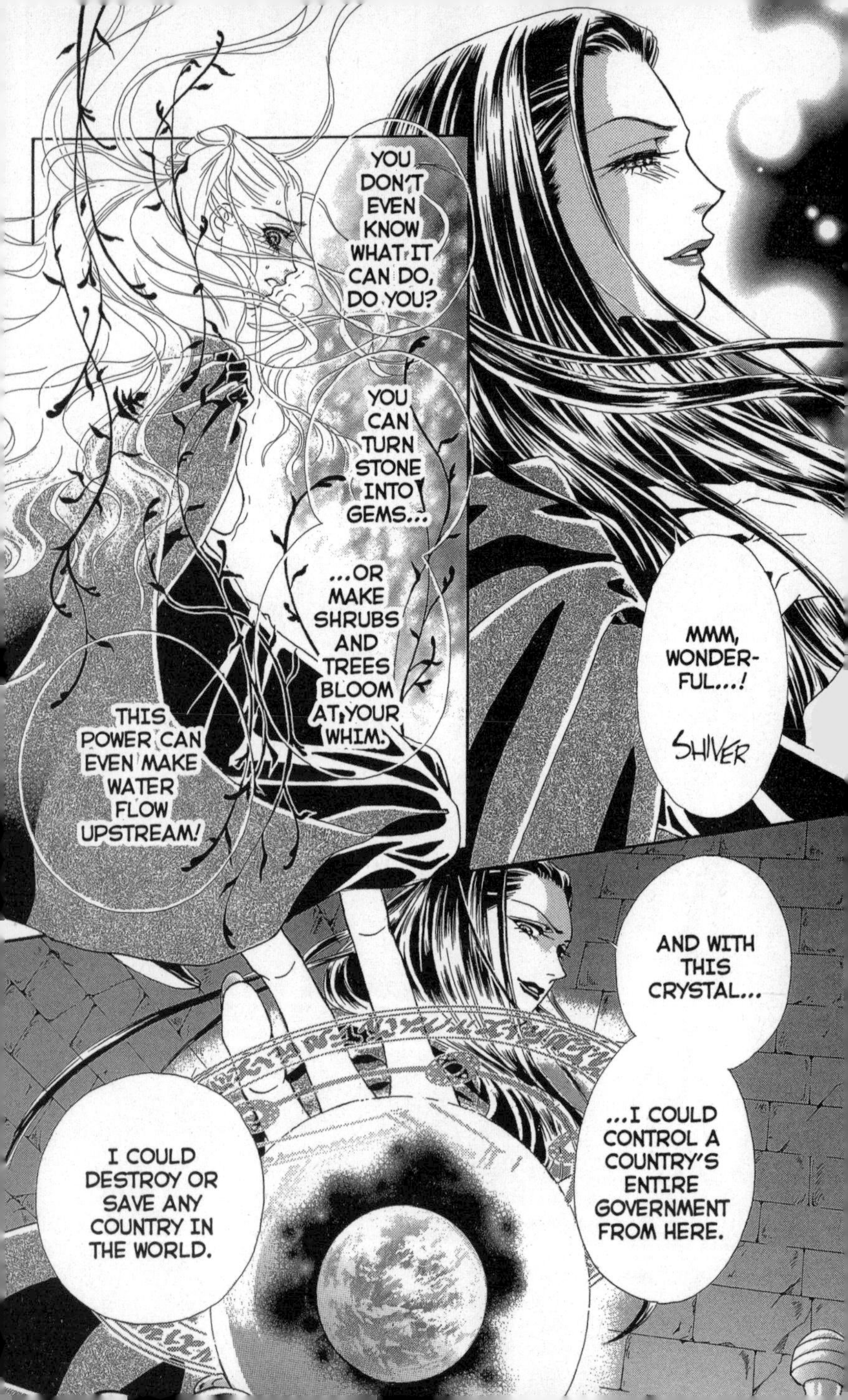

YOU DON'T EVEN KNOW WHAT IT CAN DO, DO YOU?
YOU CAN TURN STONE INTO GEMS...
...OR MAKE SHRUBS AND TREES BLOOM AT YOUR WHIM.
THIS POWER CAN EVEN MAKE WATER FLOW UPSTREAM!
MMM, WONDER-FUL...!
SHIVER
AND WITH THIS CRYSTAL...
...I COULD CONTROL A COUNTRY'S ENTIRE GOVERNMENT FROM HERE.
I COULD DESTROY OR SAVE ANY COUNTRY IN THE WORLD.

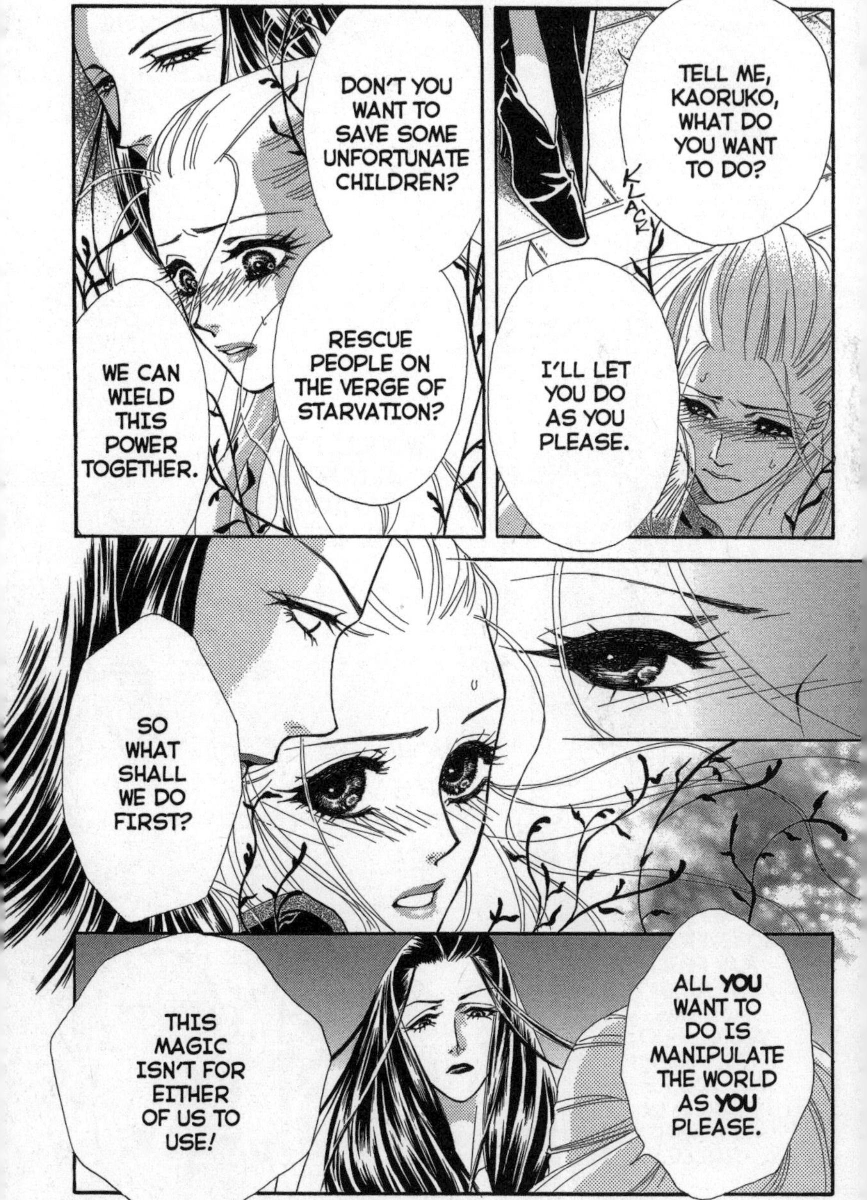
TELL ME, KAORUKO, WHAT DO YOU WANT TO DO?
KLACK
I'LL LET YOU DO AS YOU PLEASE.
DON'T YOU WANT TO SAVE SOME UNFORTUNATE CHILDREN?
RESCUE PEOPLE ON THE VERGE OF STARVATION?
WE CAN WIELD THIS POWER TOGETHER.
SO WHAT SHALL WE DO FIRST?
ALL **YOU** WANT TO DO IS MANIPULATE THE WORLD AS **YOU** PLEASE.
THIS MAGIC ISN'T FOR EITHER OF US TO USE!

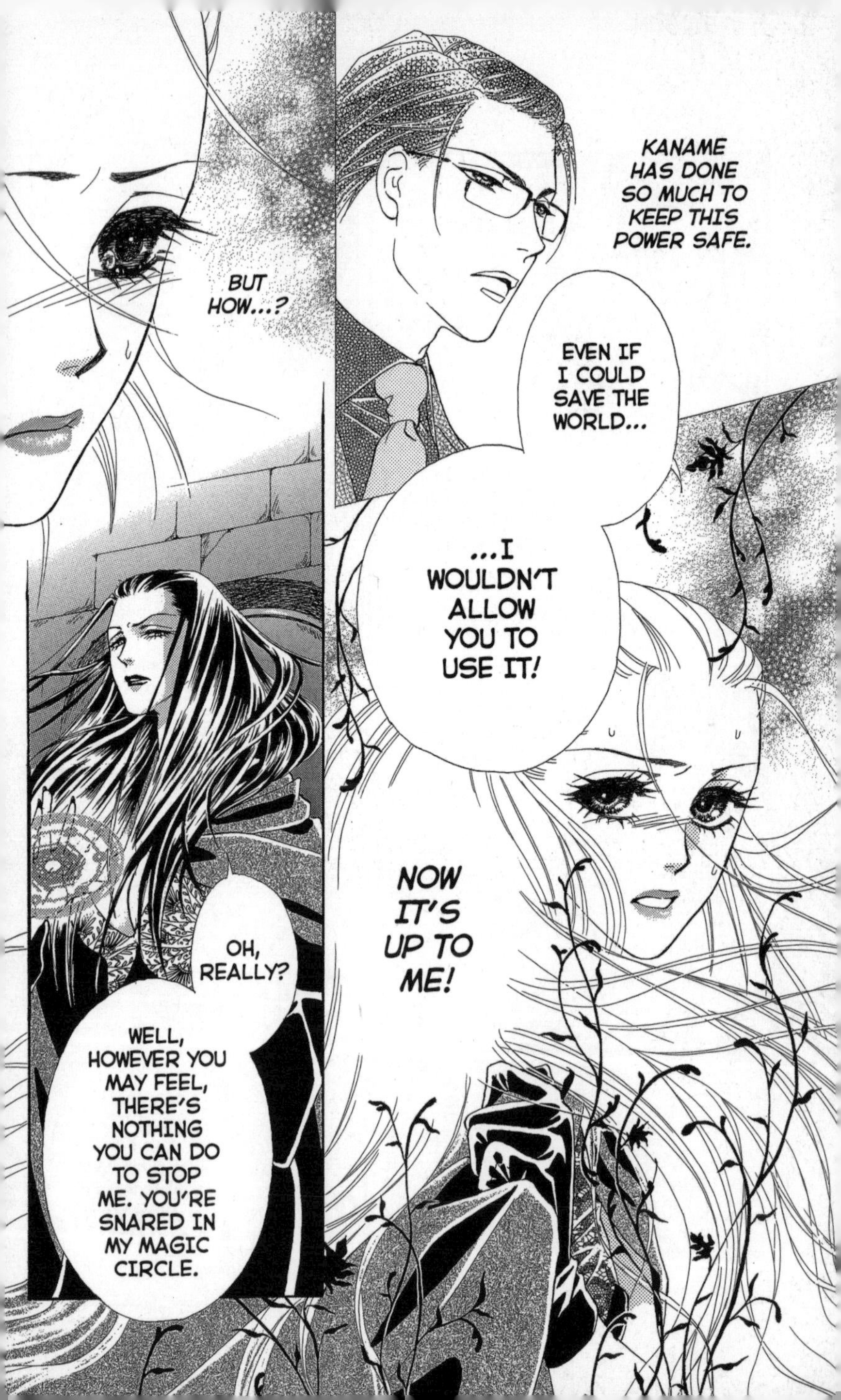
KANAME HAS DONE SO MUCH TO KEEP THIS POWER SAFE.
EVEN IF I COULD SAVE THE WORLD...
...I WOULDN'T ALLOW YOU TO USE IT!
BUT HOW...?
NOW IT'S UP TO ME!
OH, REALLY?
WELL, HOWEVER YOU MAY FEEL, THERE'S NOTHING YOU CAN DO TO STOP ME. YOU'RE SNARED IN MY MAGIC CIRCLE.

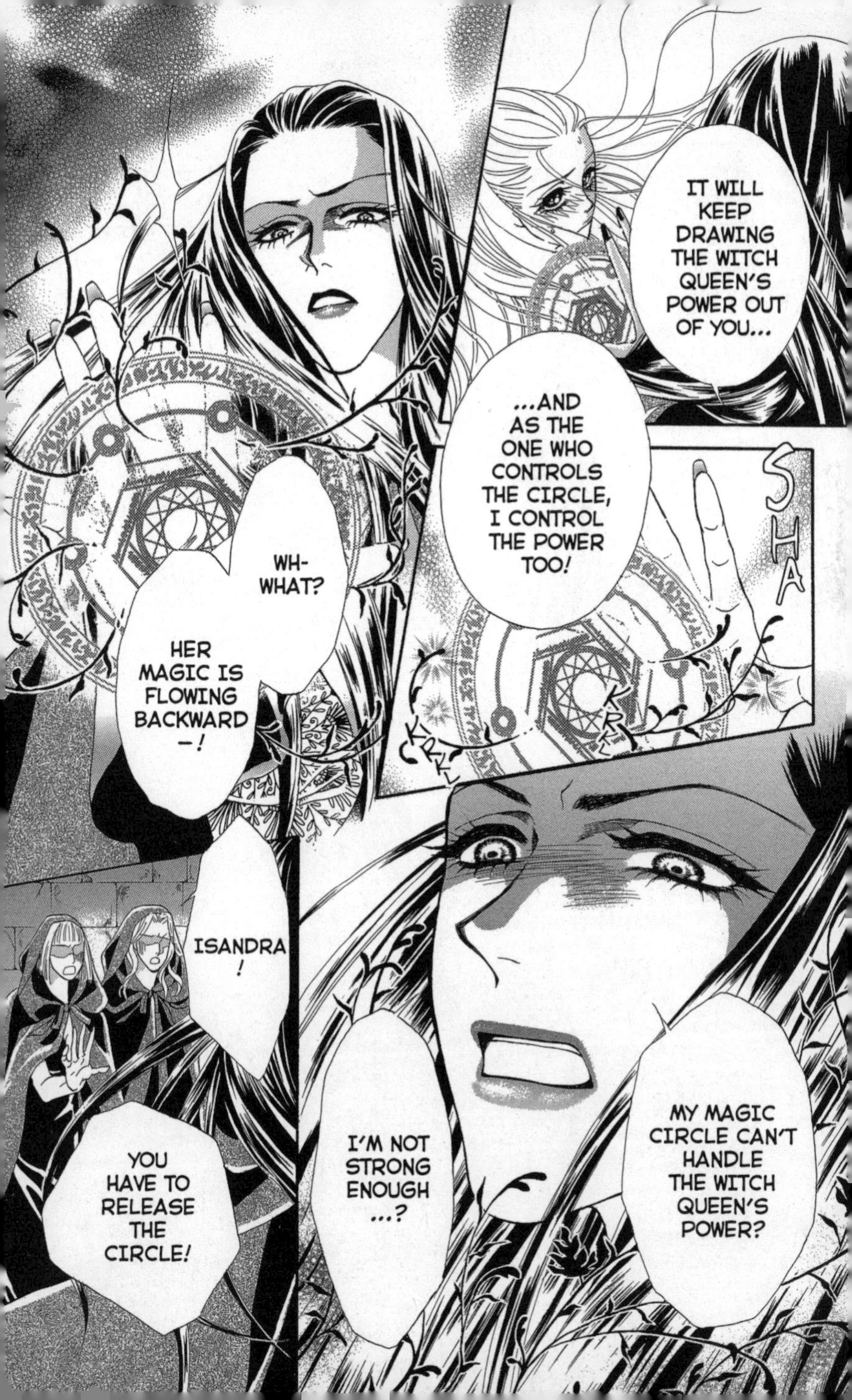
IT WILL KEEP DRAWING THE WITCH QUEEN'S POWER OUT OF YOU...
...AND AS THE ONE WHO CONTROLS THE CIRCLE, I CONTROL THE POWER TOO!
SHA
KRRKL
KRRKL
WH-WHAT?
HER MAGIC IS FLOWING BACKWARD—!
MY MAGIC CIRCLE CAN'T HANDLE THE WITCH QUEEN'S POWER?
I'M NOT STRONG ENOUGH...?
ISANDRA!
YOU HAVE TO RELEASE THE CIRCLE!

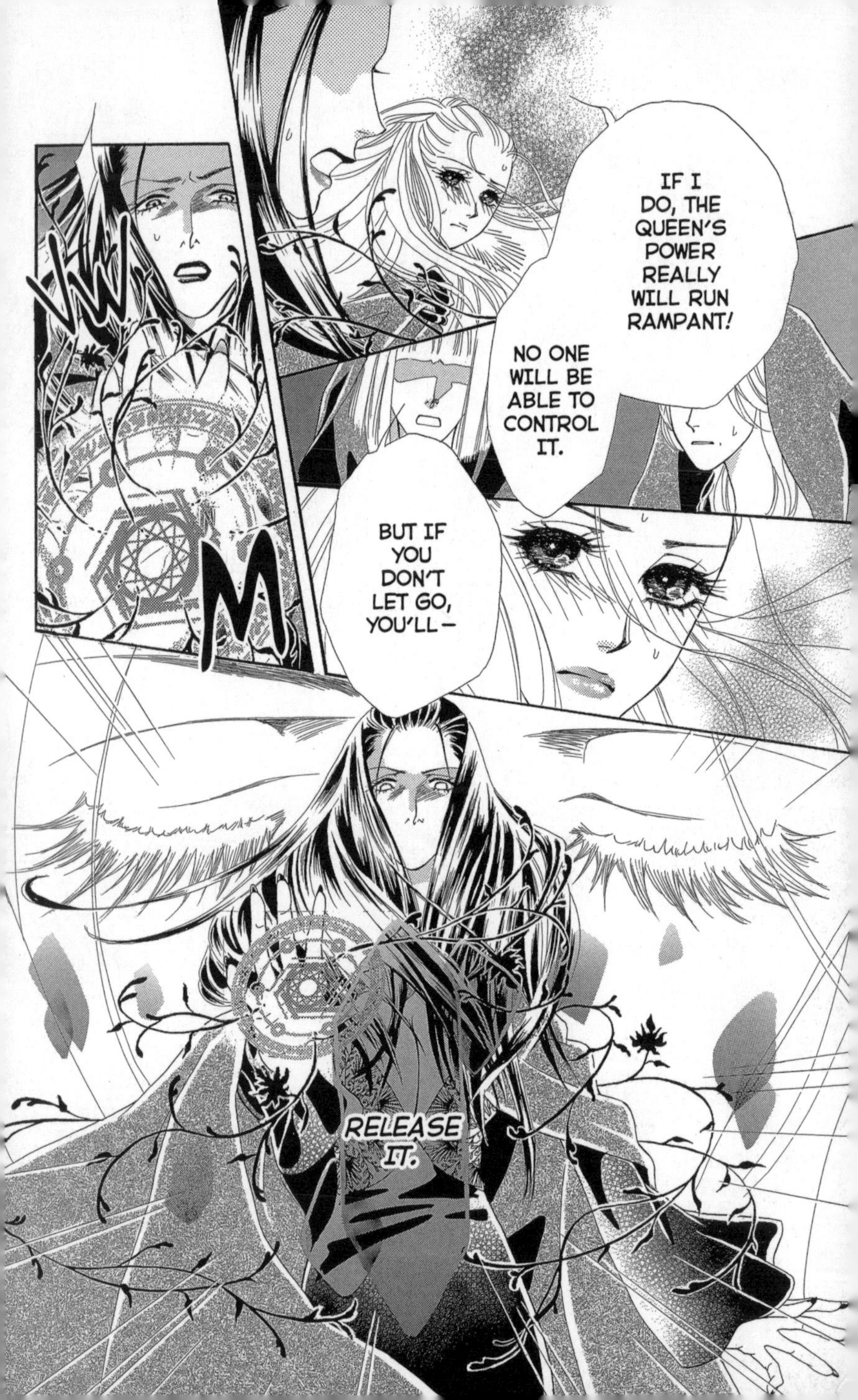
IF I DO, THE QUEEN'S POWER REALLY WILL RUN RAMPANT!
NO ONE WILL BE ABLE TO CONTROL IT.
BUT IF YOU DON'T LET GO, YOU'LL—
VW M
RELEASE IT.

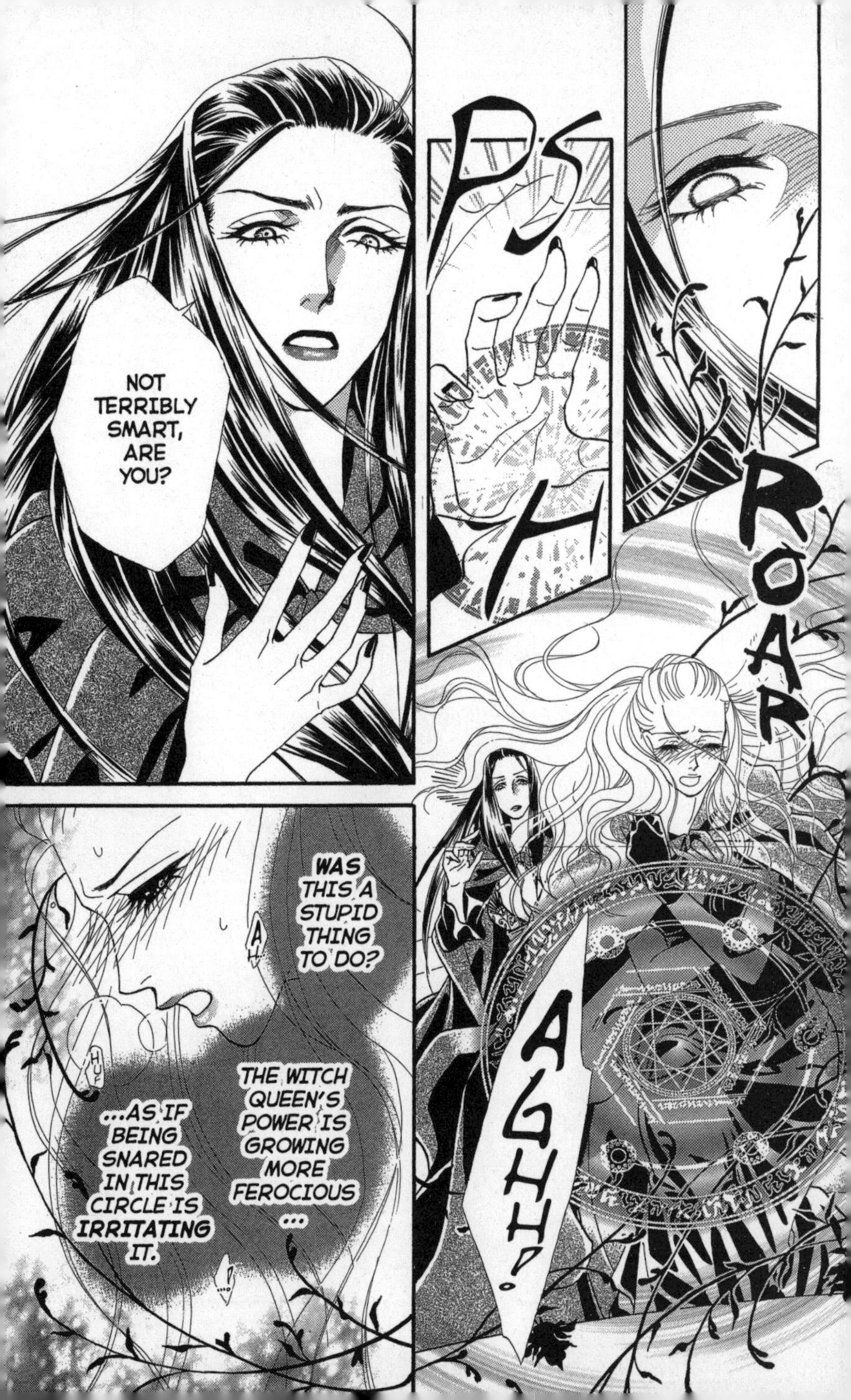
PSH
NOT TERRIBLY SMART, ARE YOU?
ROAR
AGHH!
WAS THIS A STUPID THING TO DO?
AH
THE WITCH QUEEN'S POWER IS GROWING MORE FEROCIOUS...
...AS IF BEING SNARED IN THIS CIRCLE IS IRRITATING IT.
HUF

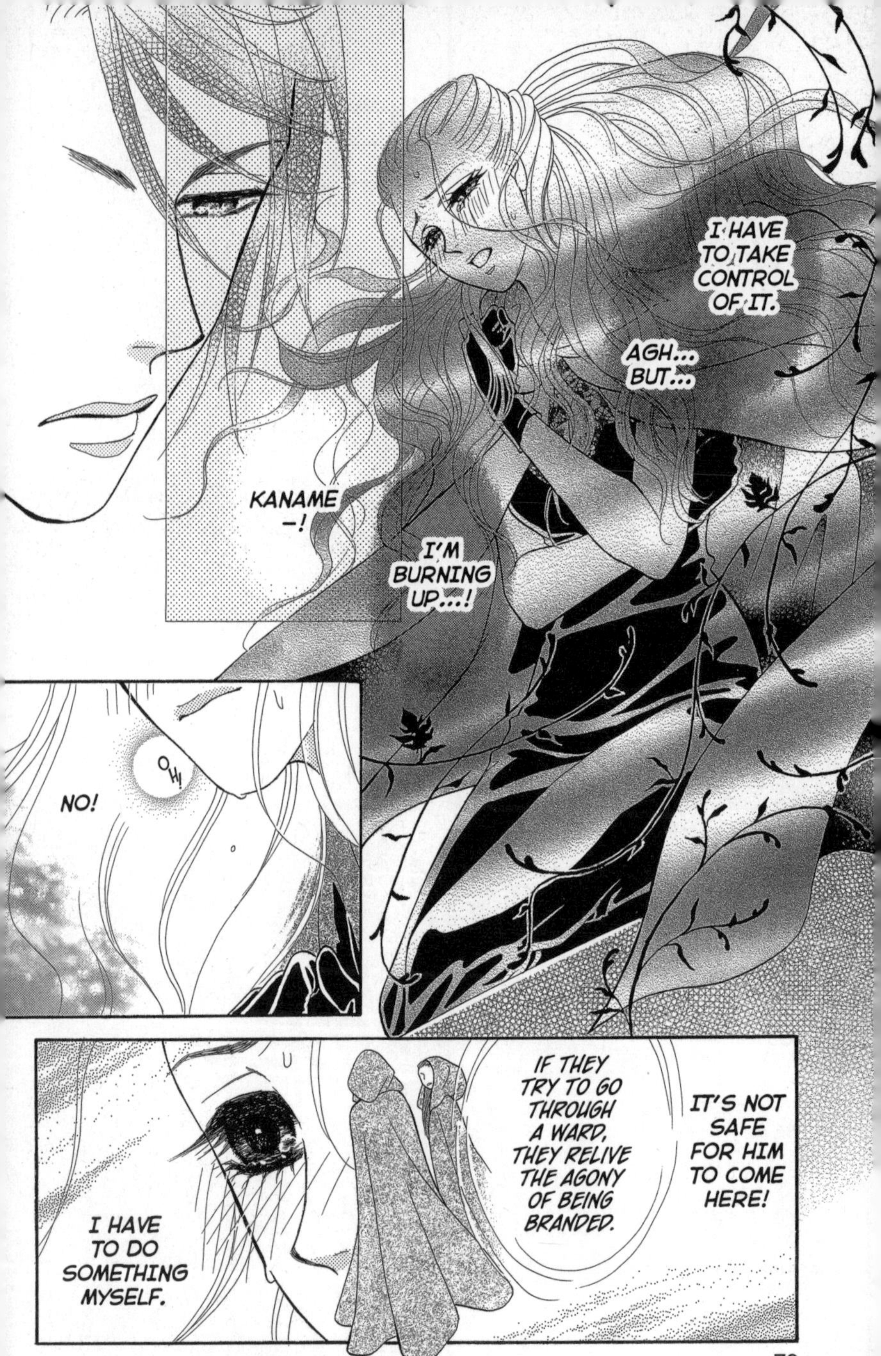
I HAVE TO TAKE CONTROL OF IT.
AGH... BUT...
I'M BURNING UP...!
KANAME —!
OH!
NO!
IT'S NOT SAFE FOR HIM TO COME HERE!
IF THEY TRY TO GO THROUGH A WARD, THEY RELIVE THE AGONY OF BEING BRANDED.
I HAVE TO DO SOMETHING MYSELF.

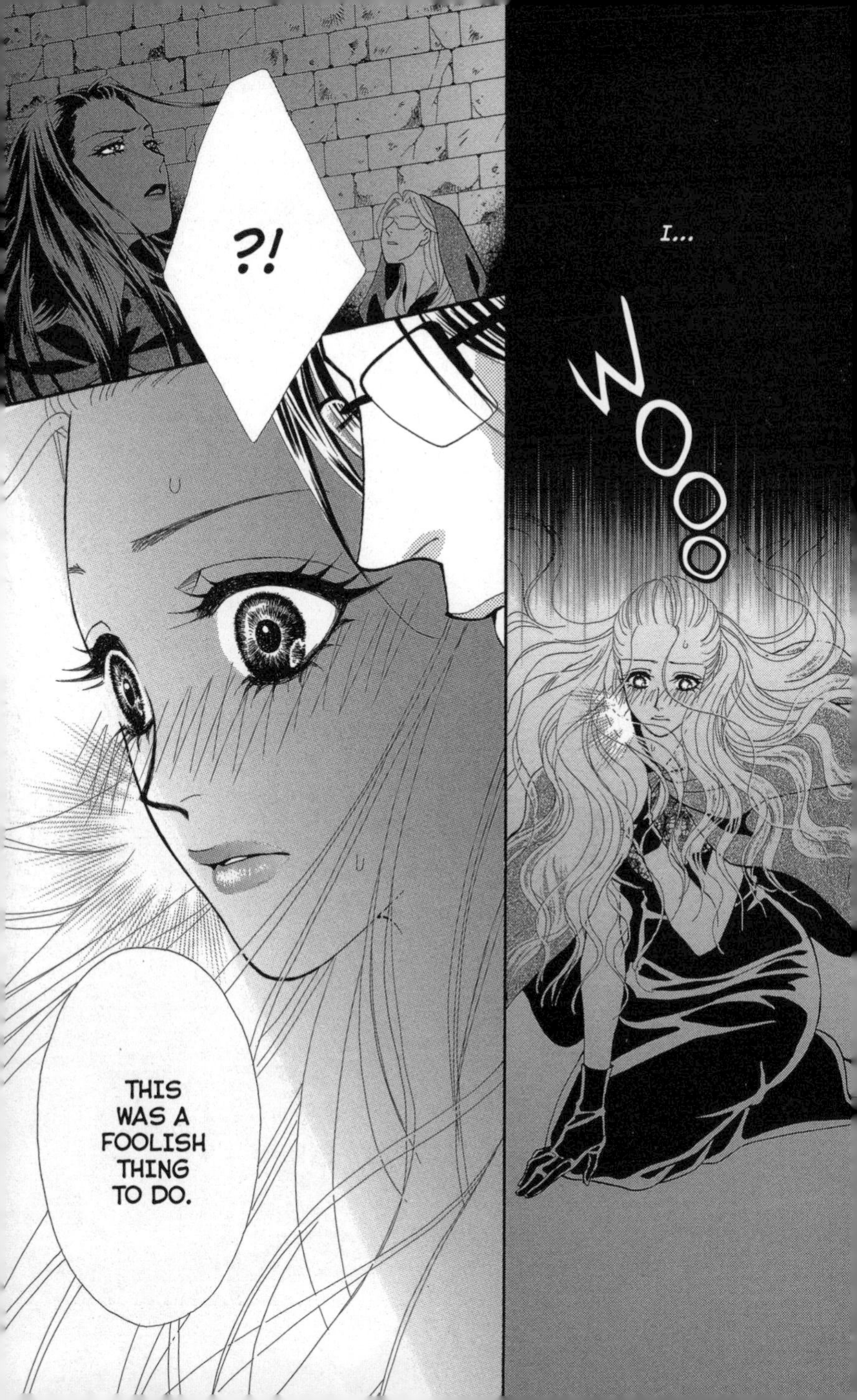
I...
WOOOO
?!
THIS WAS A FOOLISH THING TO DO.

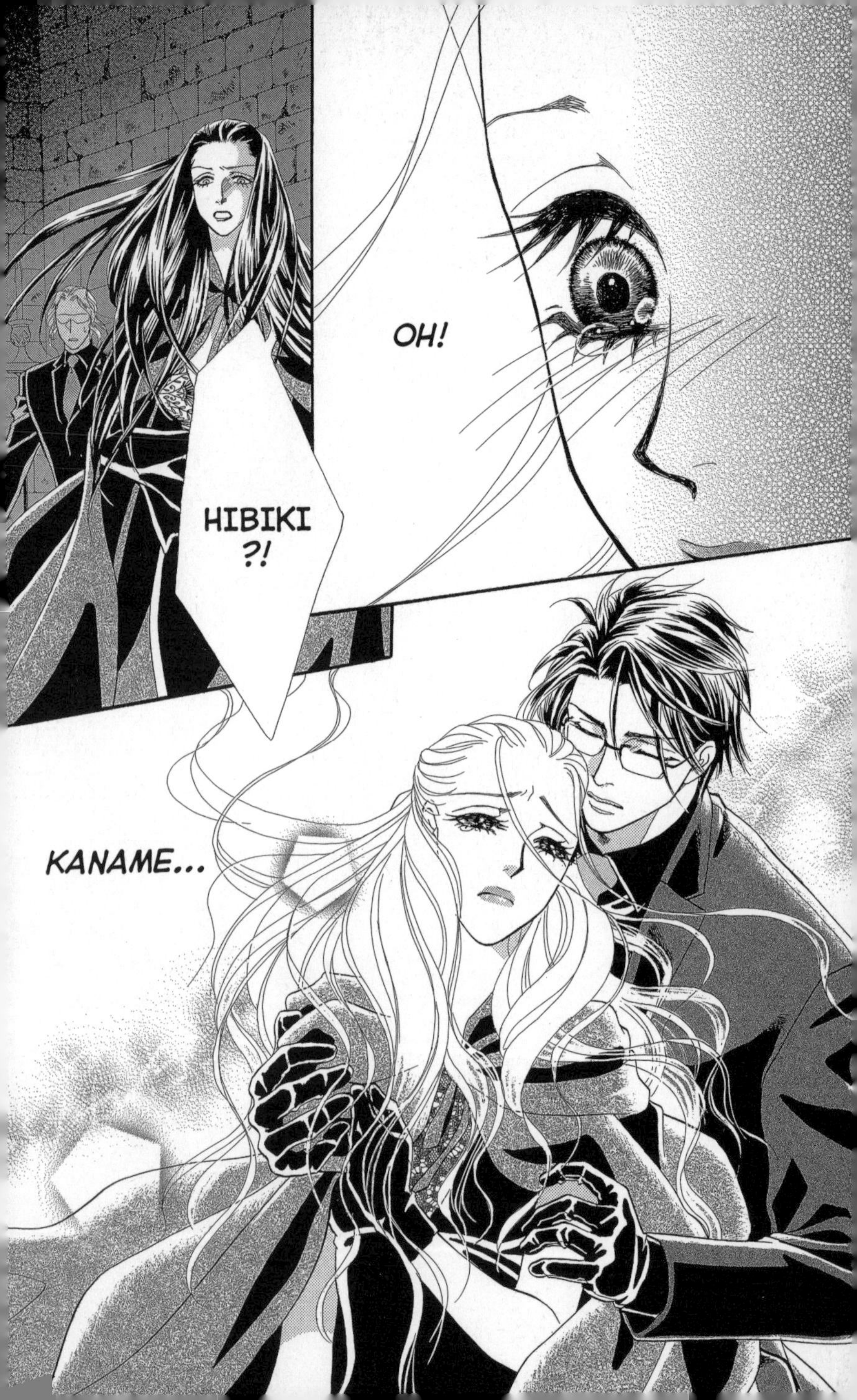
OH!
HIBIKI ?!
KANAME...

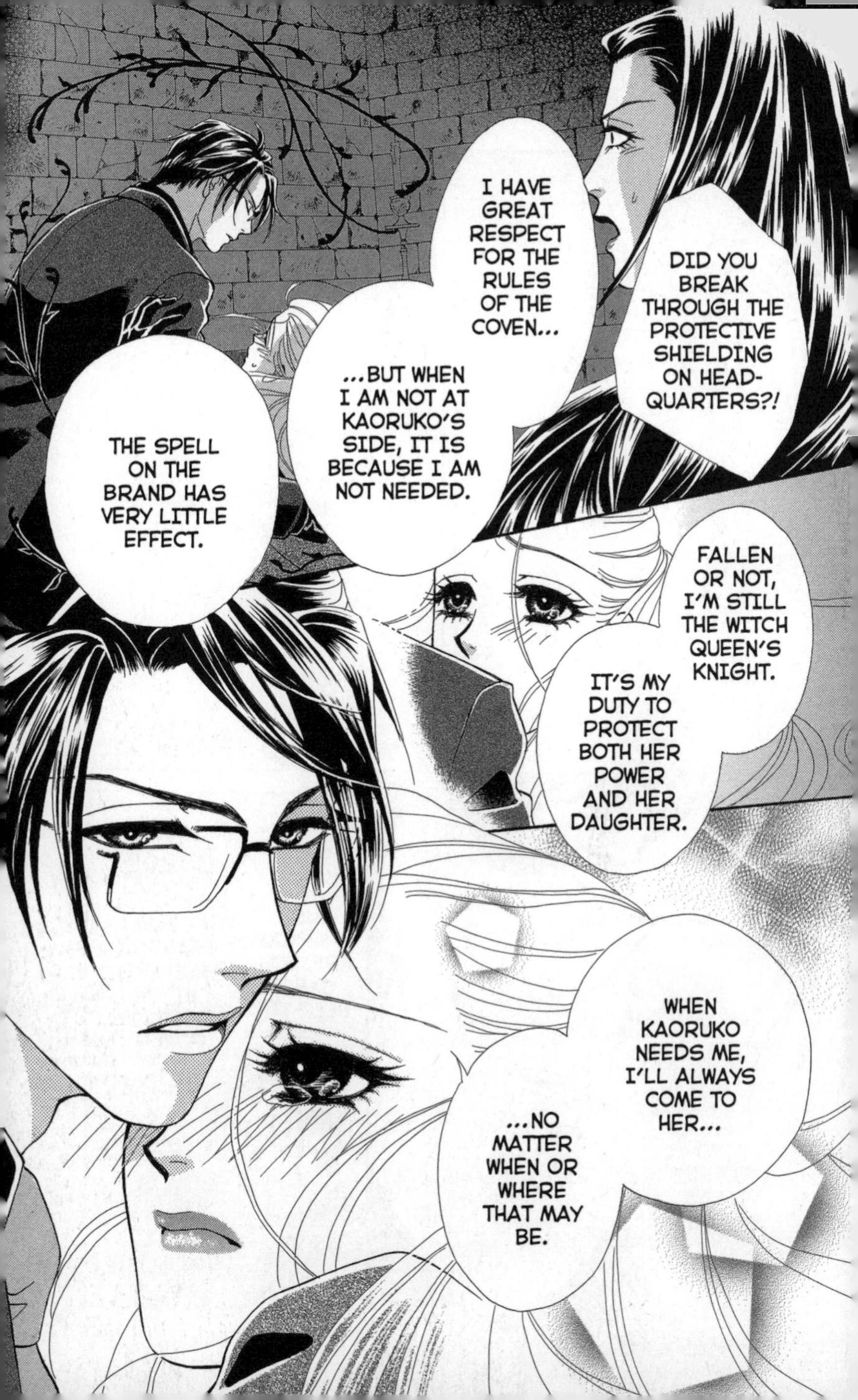
DID YOU BREAK THROUGH THE PROTECTIVE SHIELDING ON HEAD-QUARTERS?!
I HAVE GREAT RESPECT FOR THE RULES OF THE COVEN...
...BUT WHEN I AM NOT AT KAORUKO'S SIDE, IT IS BECAUSE I AM NOT NEEDED.
THE SPELL ON THE BRAND HAS VERY LITTLE EFFECT.
FALLEN OR NOT, I'M STILL THE WITCH QUEEN'S KNIGHT.
IT'S MY DUTY TO PROTECT BOTH HER POWER AND HER DAUGHTER.
WHEN KAORUKO NEEDS ME, I'LL ALWAYS COME TO HER...
...NO MATTER WHEN OR WHERE THAT MAY BE.

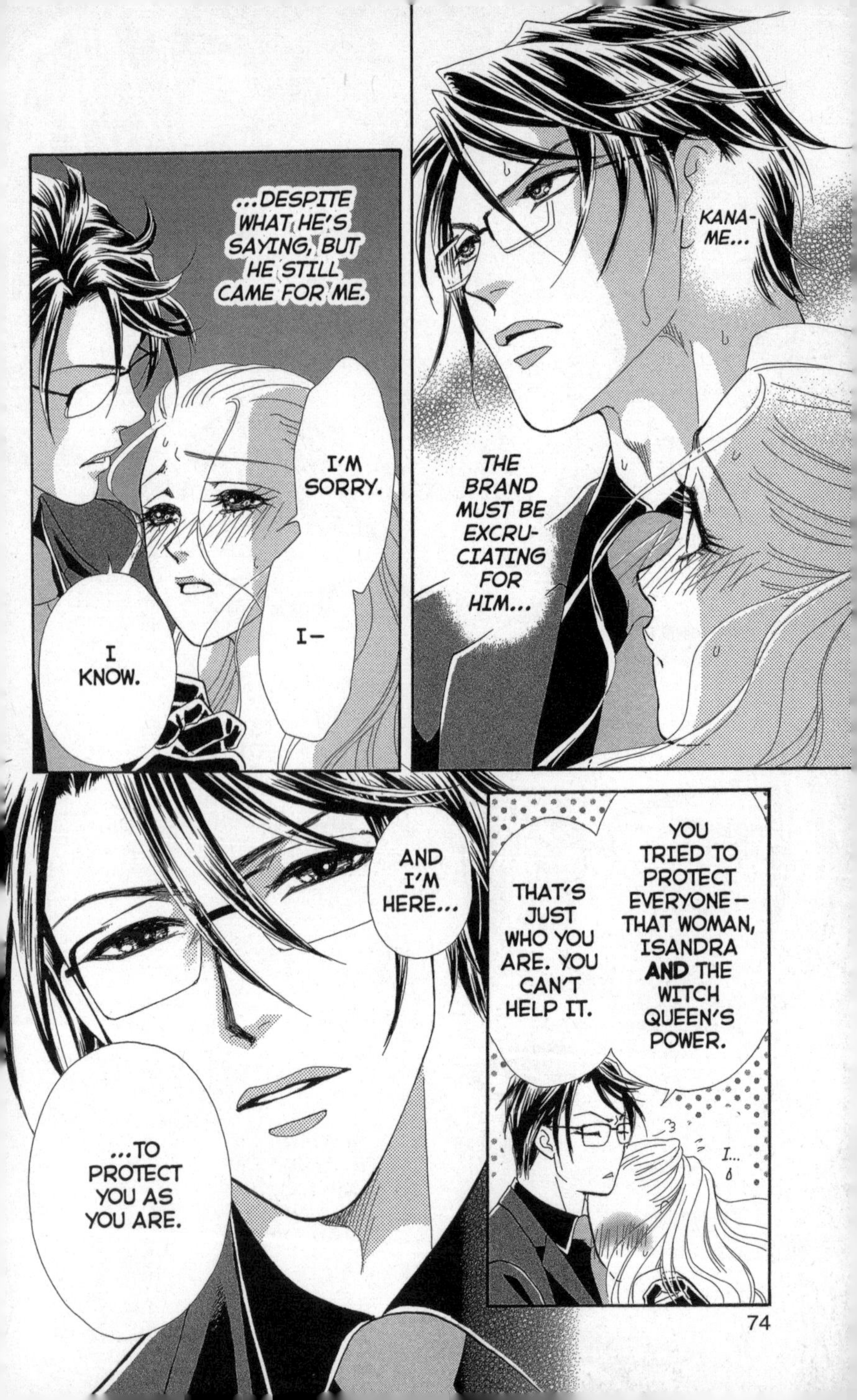
KANA-ME...
THE BRAND MUST BE EXCRUCIATING FOR HIM...
...DESPITE WHAT HE'S SAYING, BUT HE STILL CAME FOR ME.
I'M SORRY.
I—
I KNOW.
YOU TRIED TO PROTECT EVERYONE—THAT WOMAN, ISANDRA **AND** THE WITCH QUEEN'S POWER.
THAT'S JUST WHO YOU ARE. YOU CAN'T HELP IT.
I...
AND I'M HERE...
...TO PROTECT YOU AS YOU ARE.

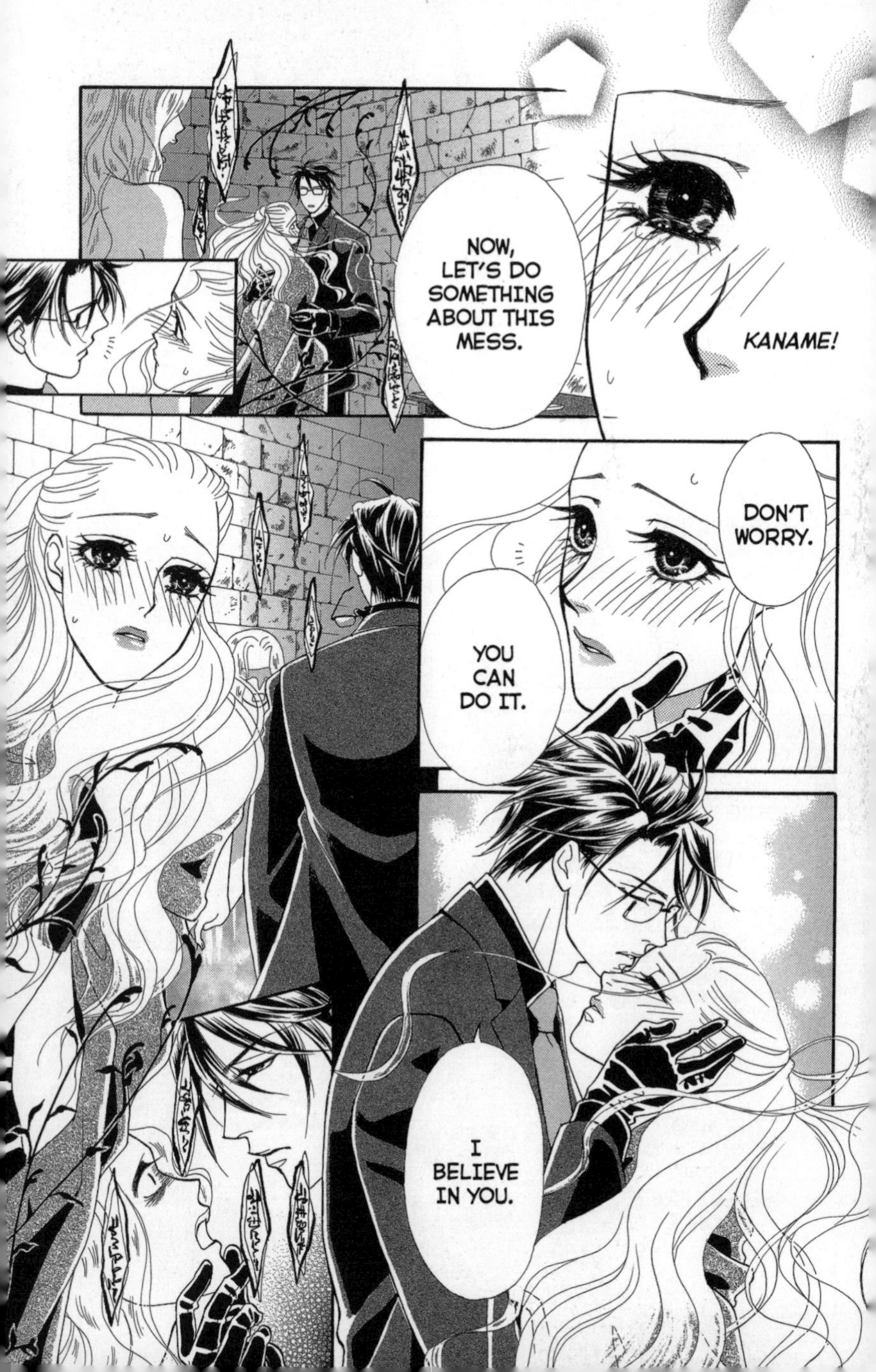
KANAME!
NOW, LET'S DO SOMETHING ABOUT THIS MESS.
DON'T WORRY.
YOU CAN DO IT.
I BELIEVE IN YOU.

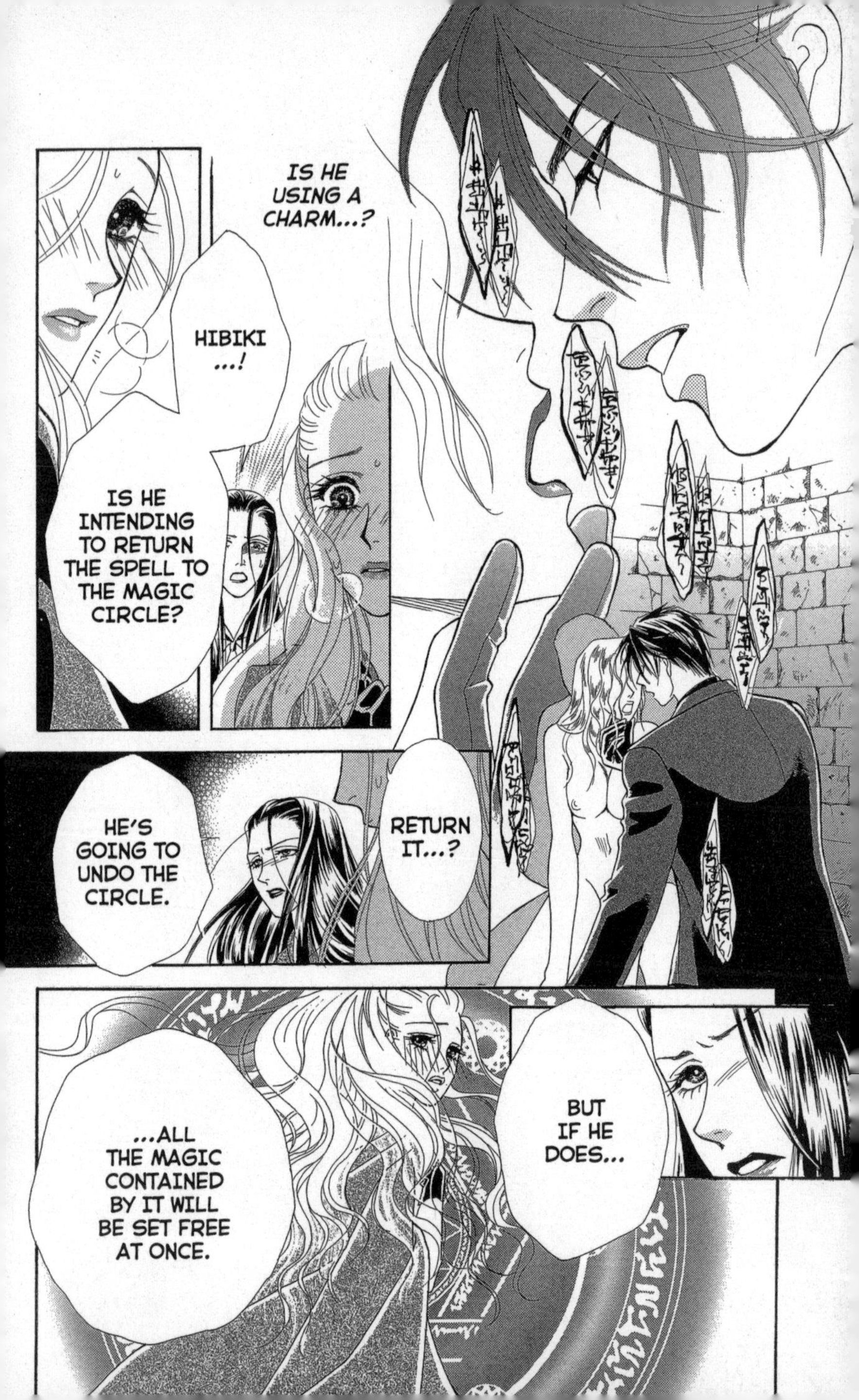
IS HE USING A CHARM...?
HIBIKI ...!
IS HE INTENDING TO RETURN THE SPELL TO THE MAGIC CIRCLE?
RETURN IT...?
HE'S GOING TO UNDO THE CIRCLE.
BUT IF HE DOES...
...ALL THE MAGIC CONTAINED BY IT WILL BE SET FREE AT ONCE.

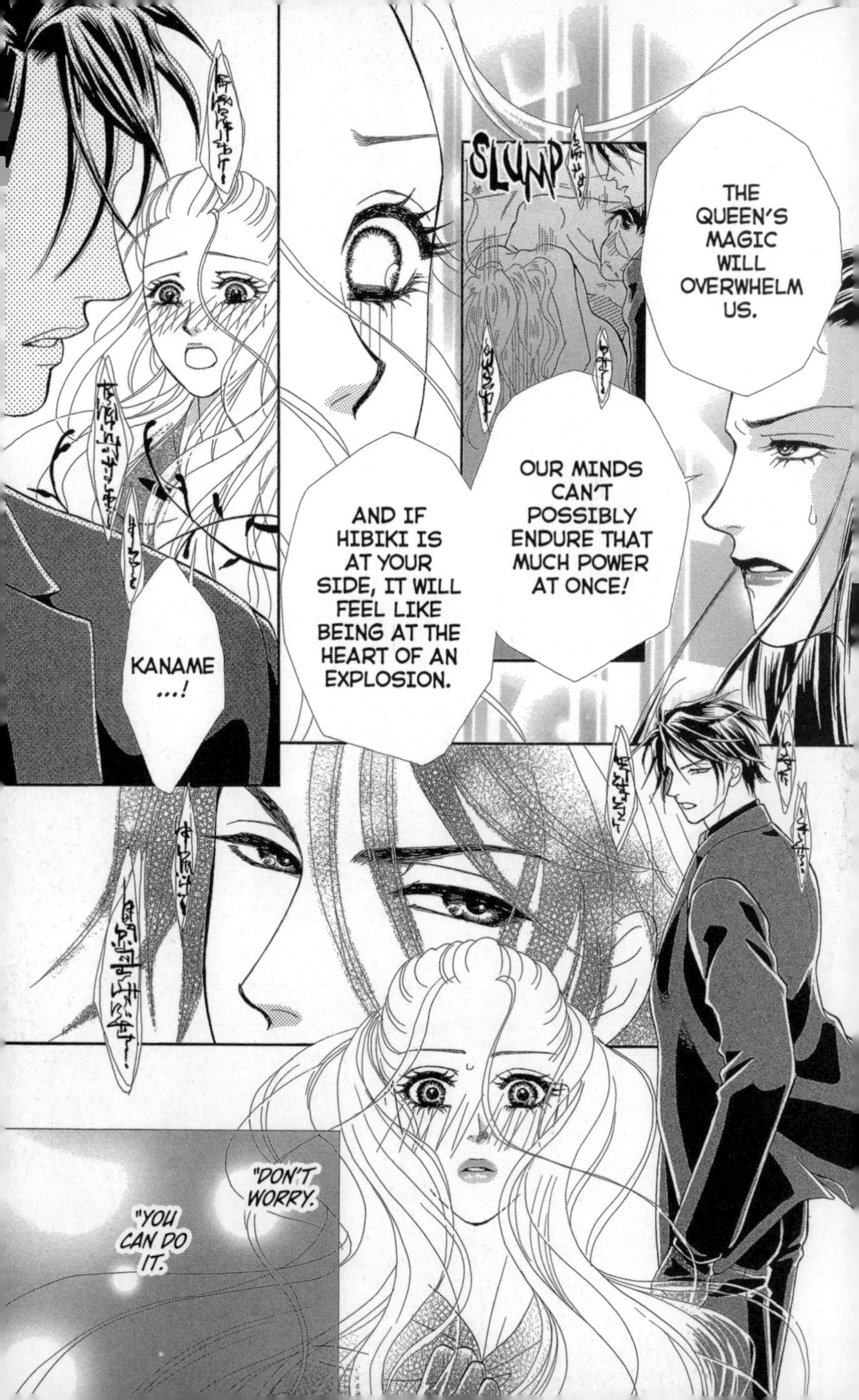

THE QUEEN'S MAGIC WILL OVERWHELM US.
SLUMP
OUR MINDS CAN'T POSSIBLY ENDURE THAT MUCH POWER AT ONCE!
AND IF HIBIKI IS AT YOUR SIDE, IT WILL FEEL LIKE BEING AT THE HEART OF AN EXPLOSION.
KANAME ...!
"DON'T WORRY.
"YOU CAN DO IT.

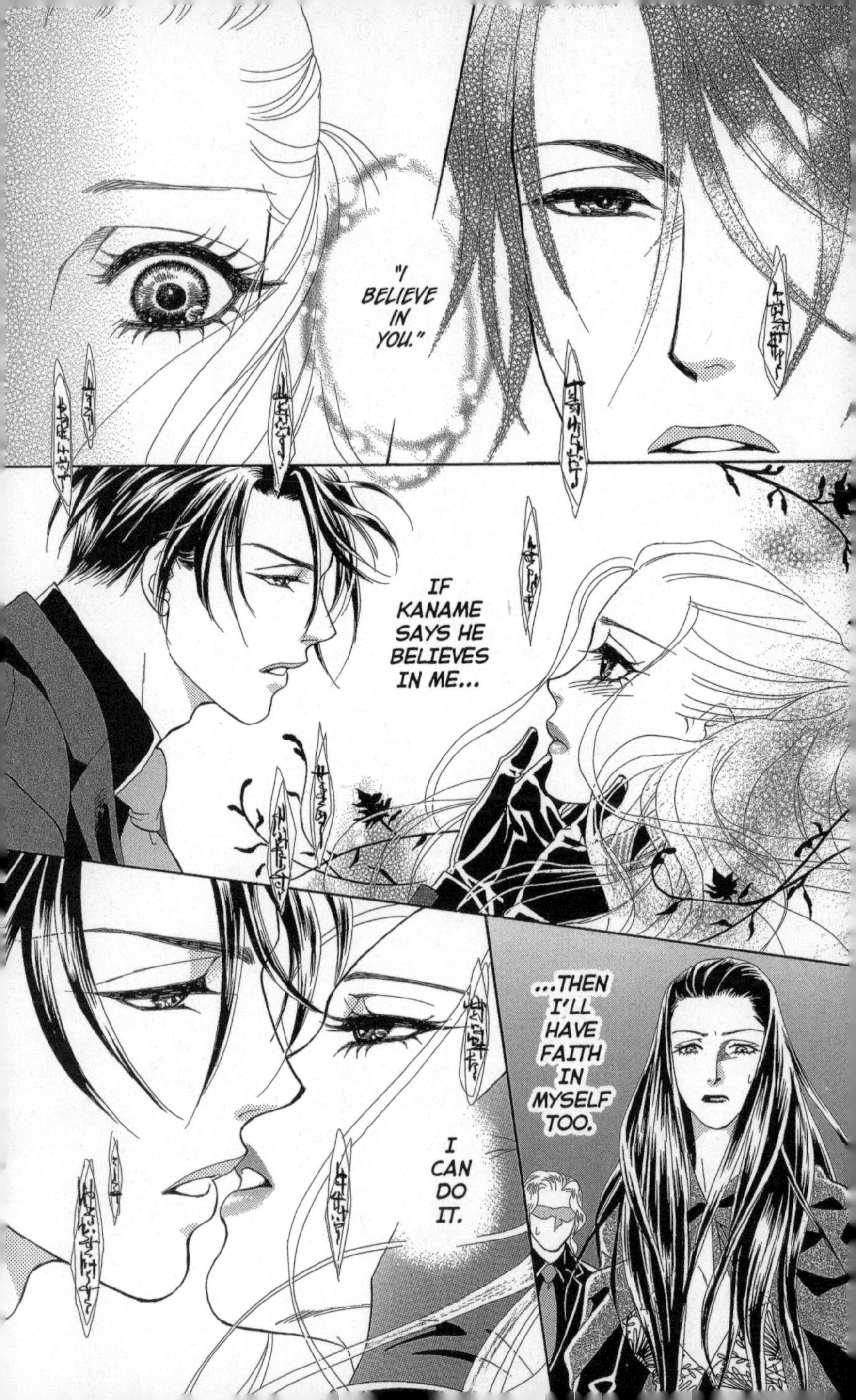
"I BELIEVE IN YOU."
IF KANAME SAYS HE BELIEVES IN ME...
...THEN I'LL HAVE FAITH IN MYSELF TOO.
I CAN DO IT.

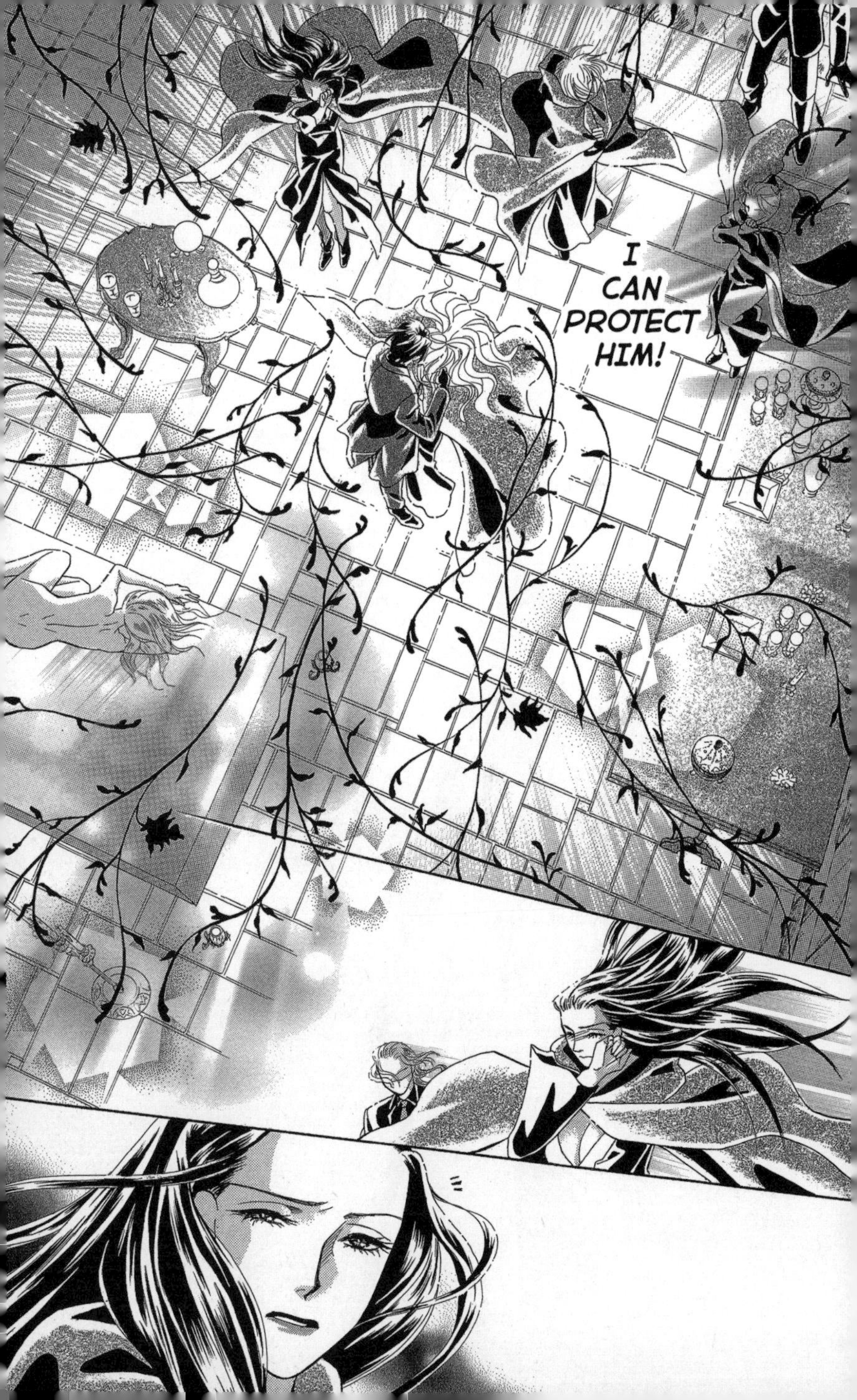
I CAN PROTECT HIM!

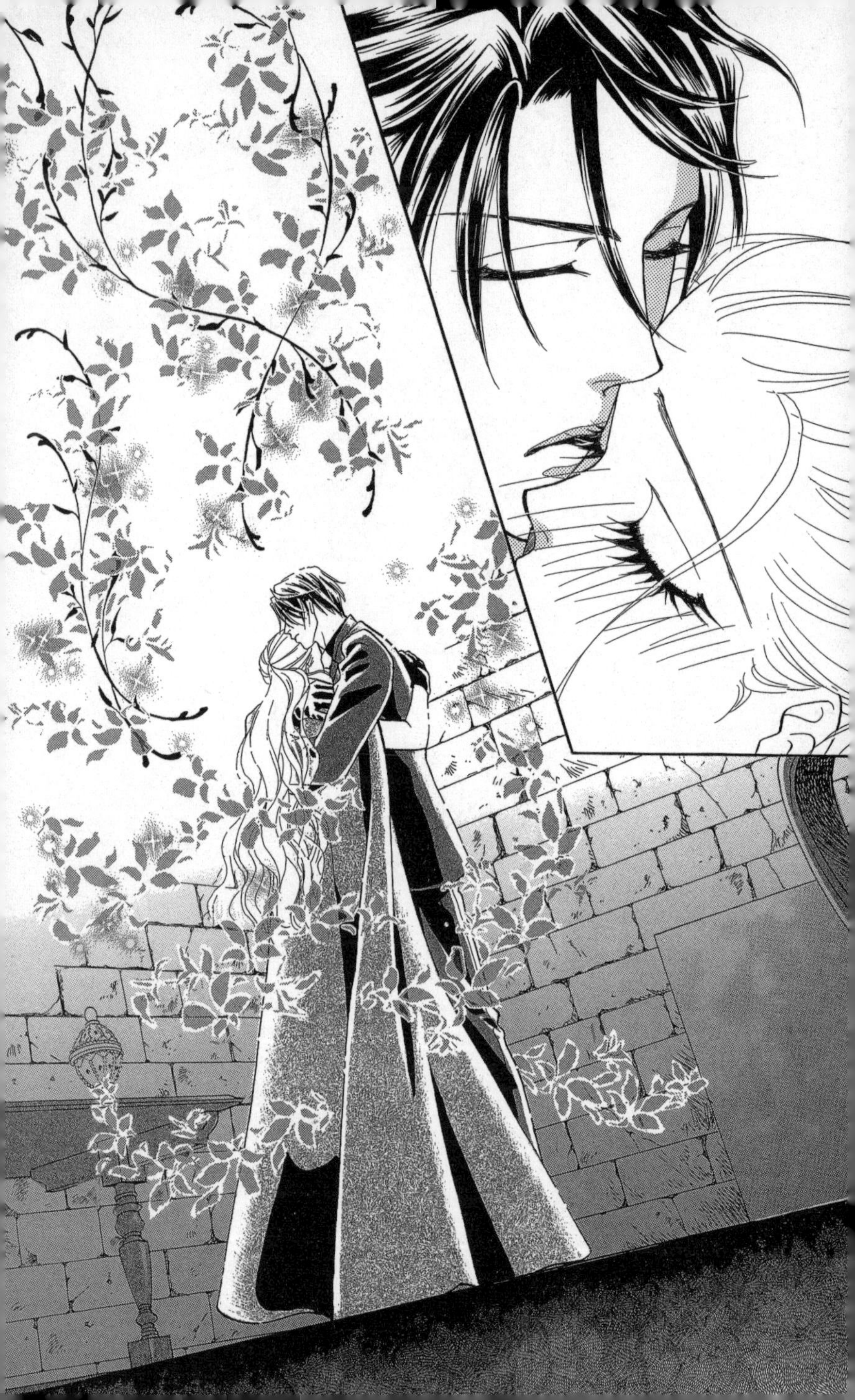

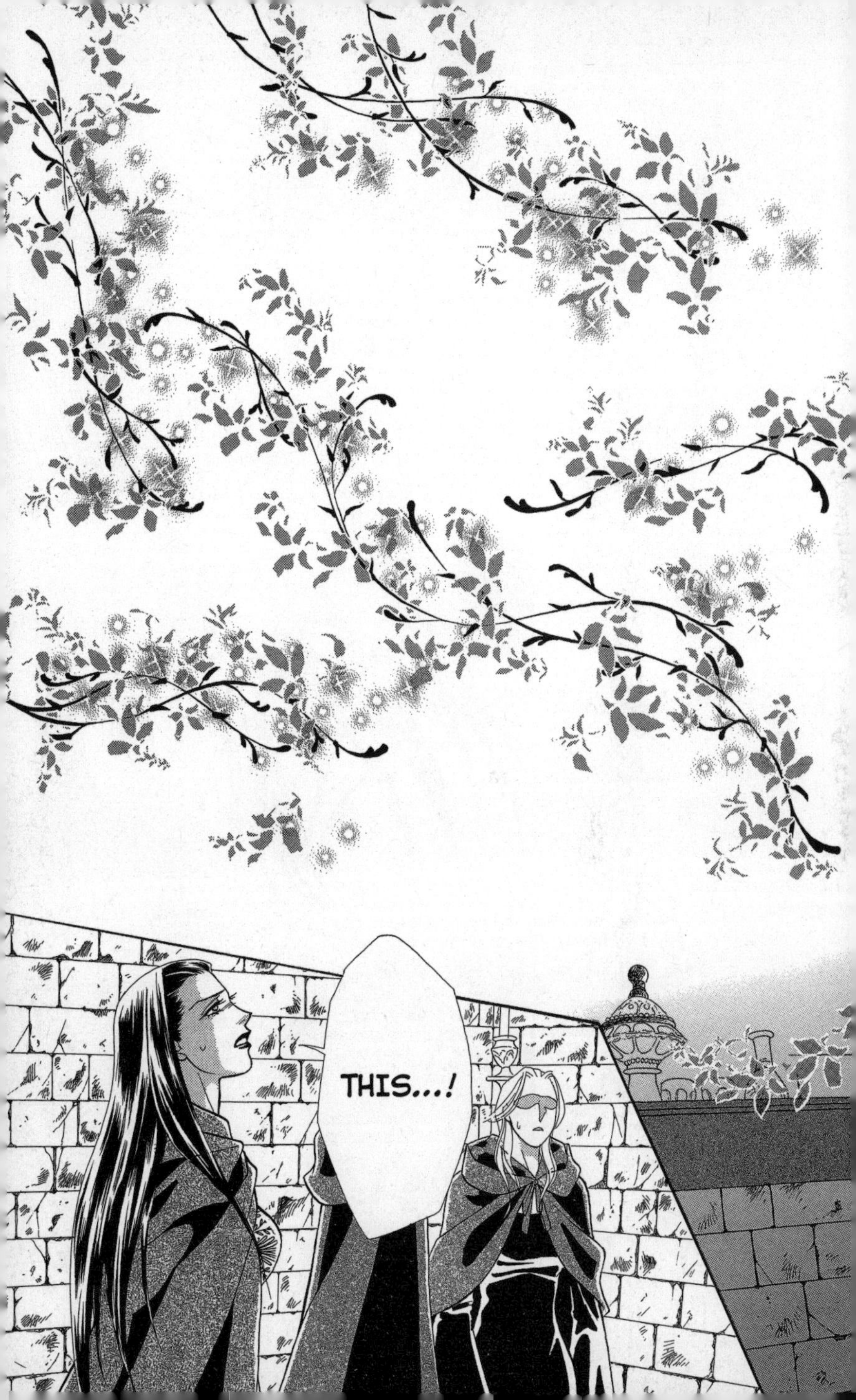
THIS...!

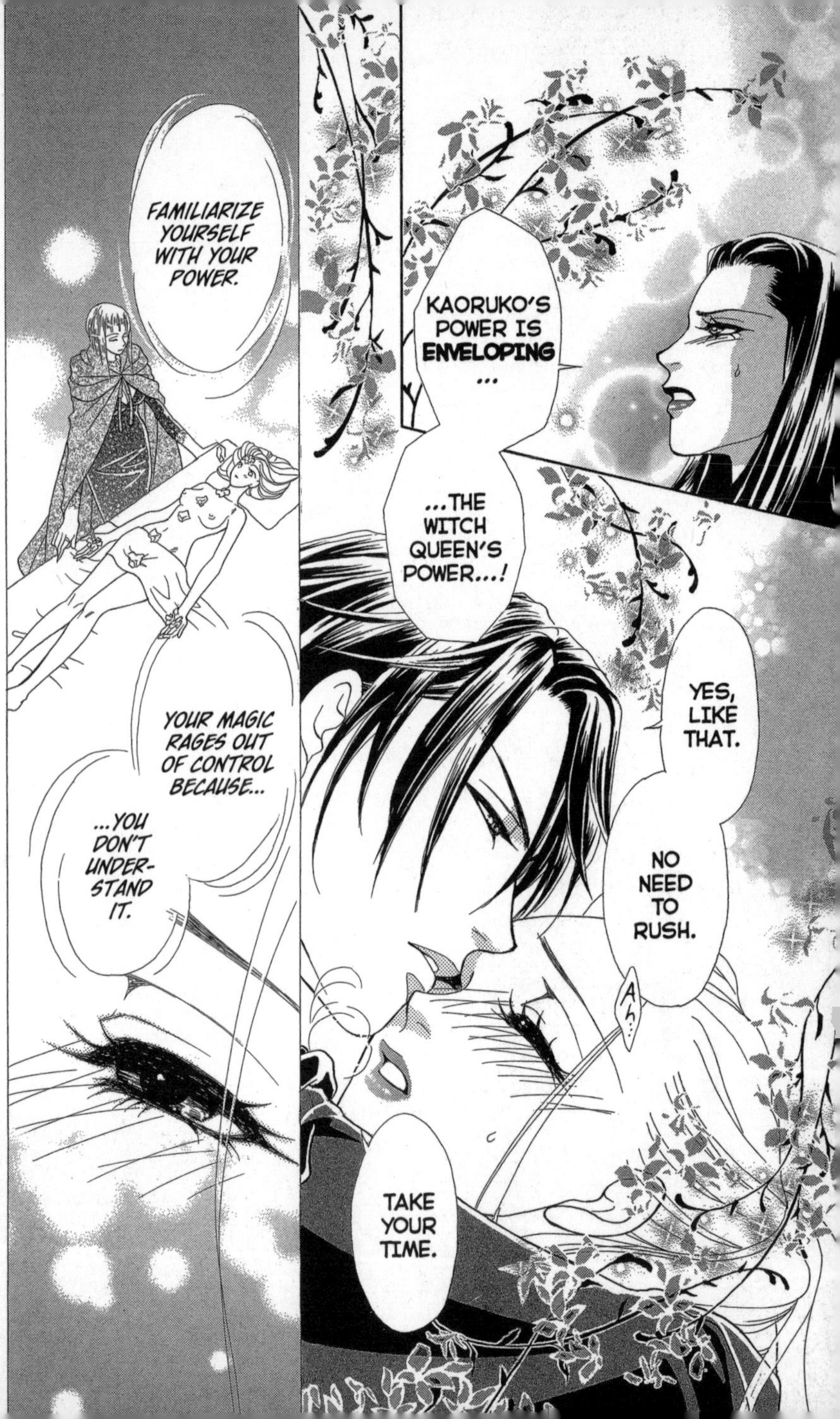
KAORUKO'S POWER IS **ENVELOPING** ...
...THE WITCH QUEEN'S POWER...!
YES, LIKE THAT.
NO NEED TO RUSH.
Ah...
TAKE YOUR TIME.
FAMILIARIZE YOURSELF WITH YOUR POWER.
YOUR MAGIC RAGES OUT OF CONTROL BECAUSE...
...YOU DON'T UNDER-STAND IT.

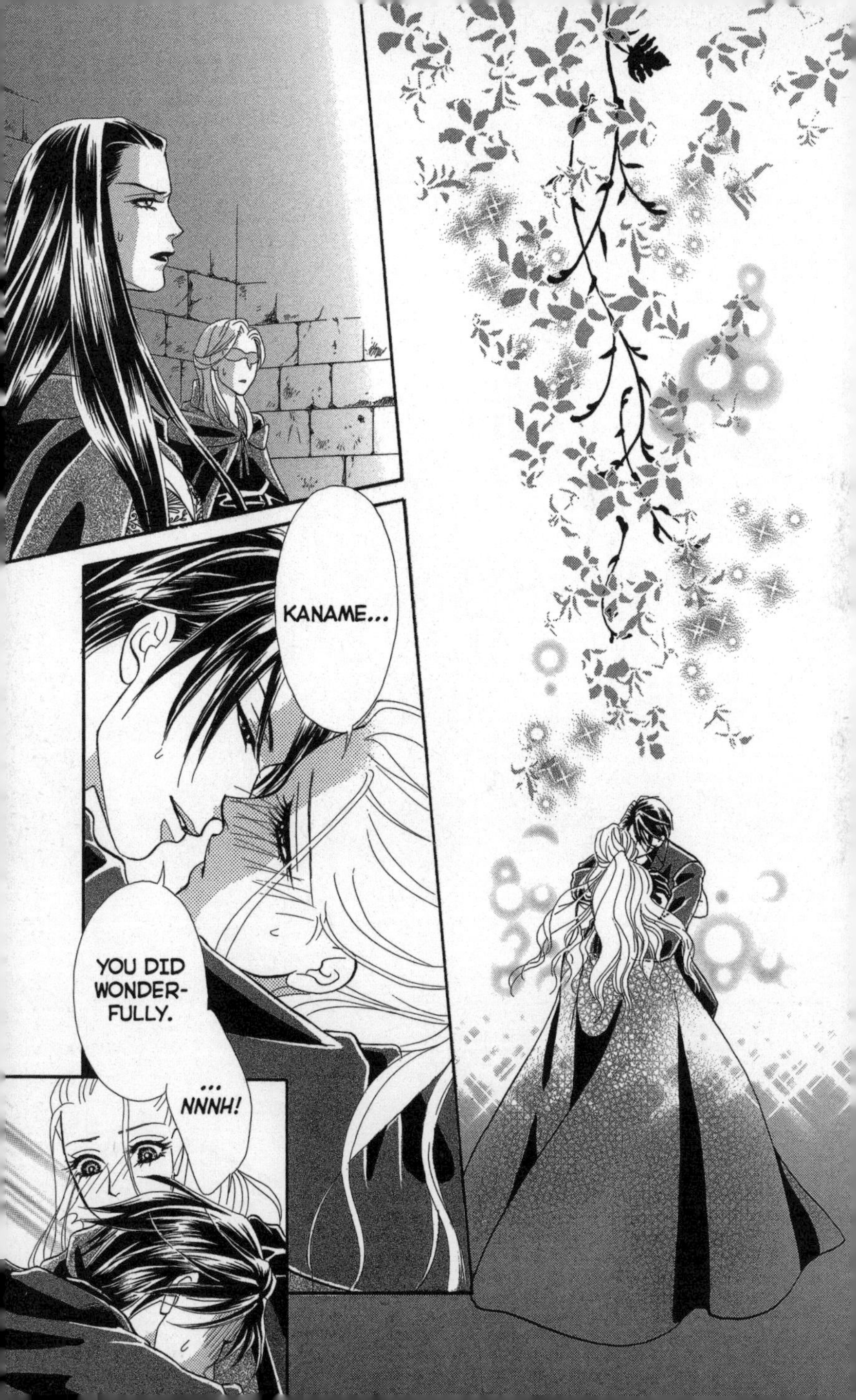
KANAME...
YOU DID WONDER-FULLY.
...NNNH!

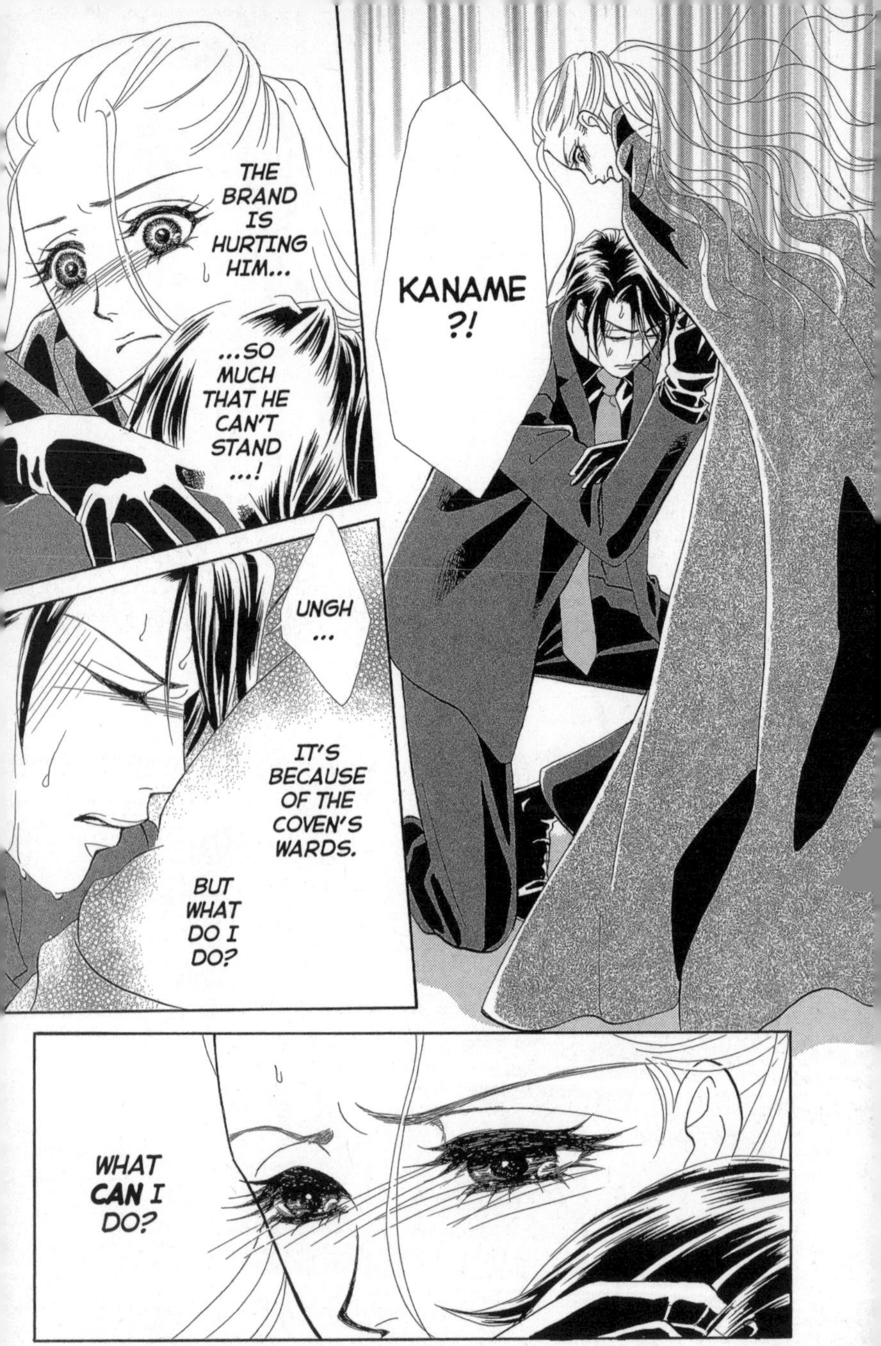
KANAME ?!
THE BRAND IS HURTING HIM...
...SO MUCH THAT HE CAN'T STAND ...!
UNGH ...
IT'S BECAUSE OF THE COVEN'S WARDS.
BUT WHAT DO I DO?
WHAT **CAN** I DO?

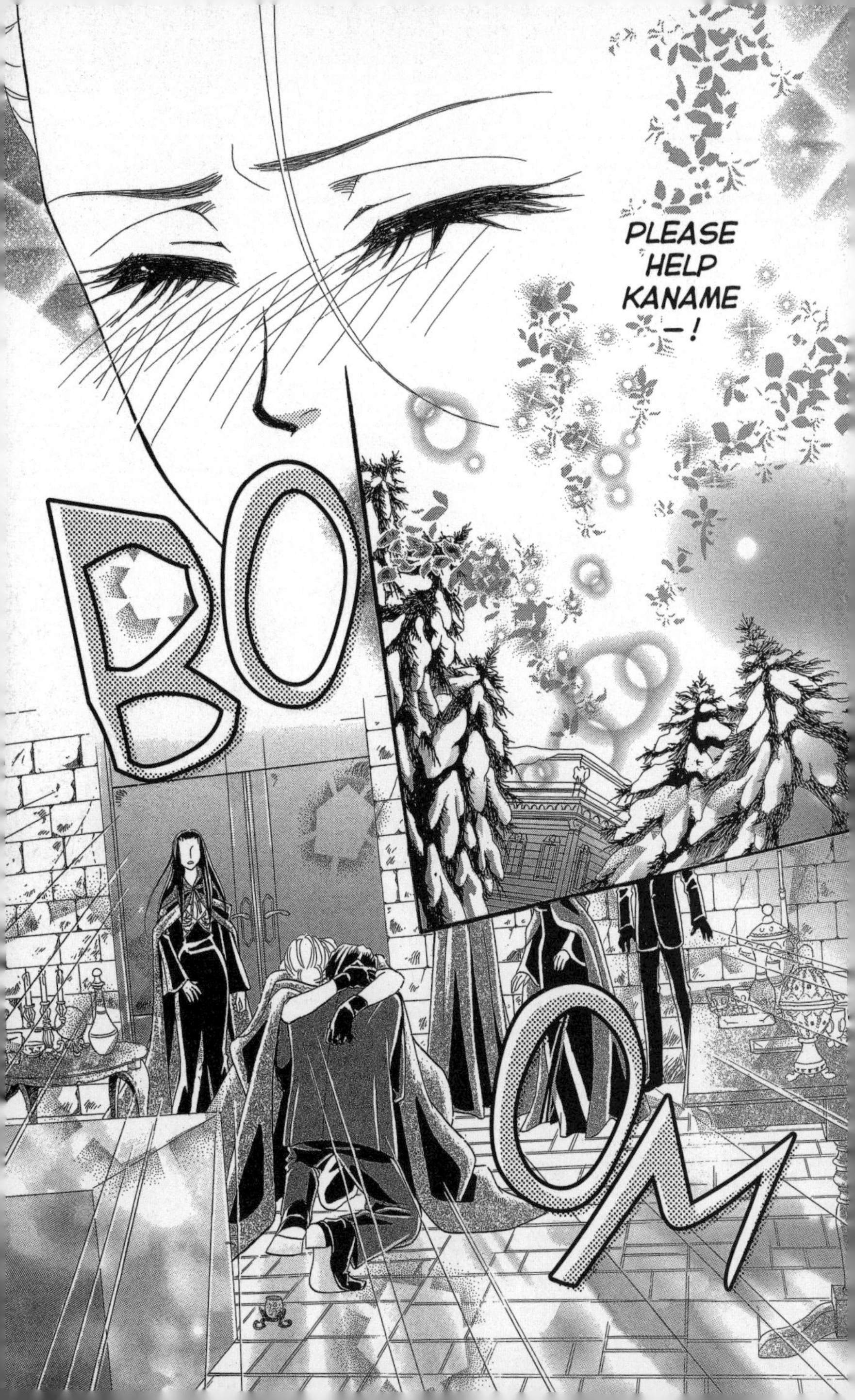
PLEASE HELP KANAME —!
BOOM

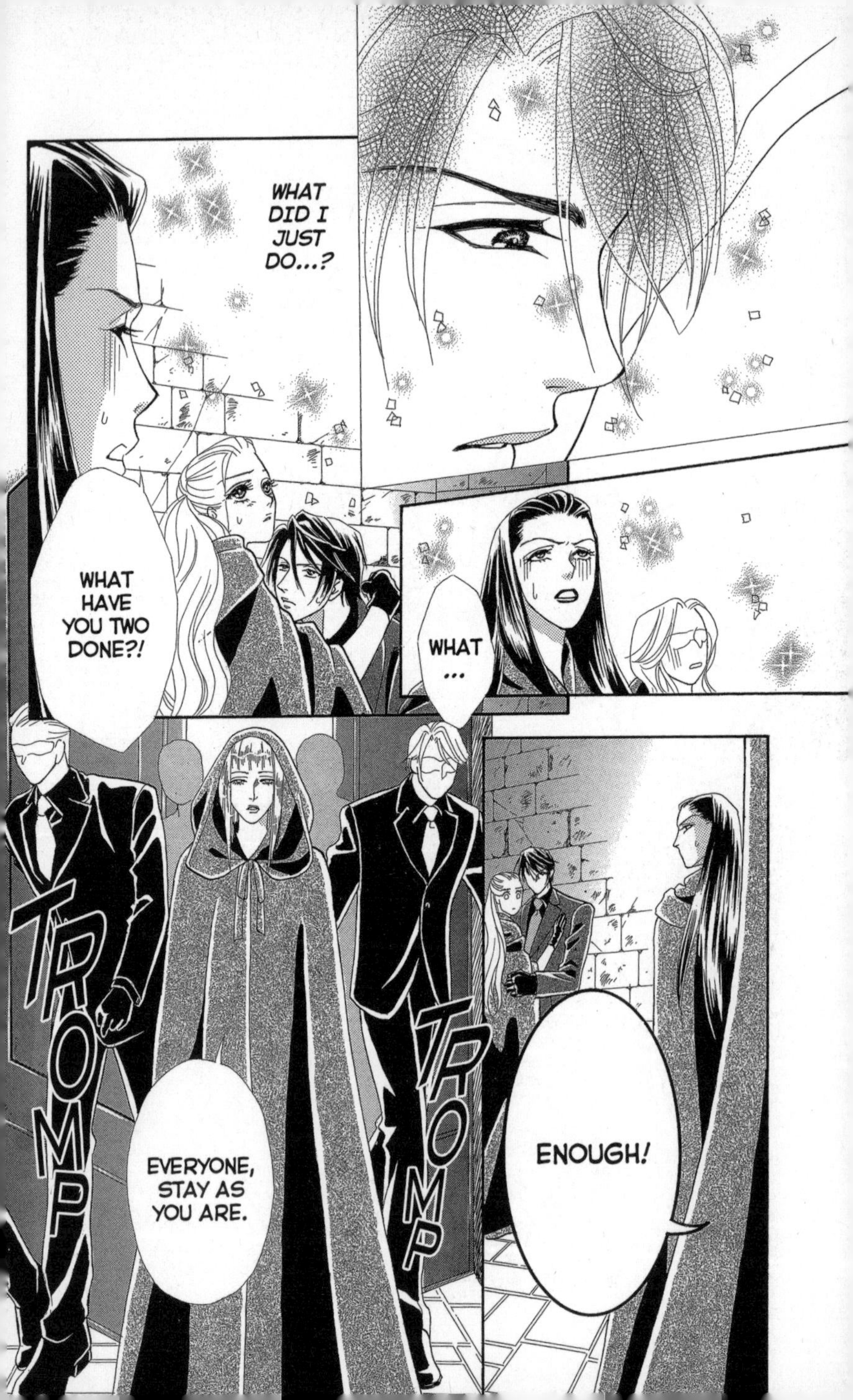
WHAT ...
WHAT DID I JUST DO...?
WHAT HAVE YOU TWO DONE?!
ENOUGH!
TROMP
TROMP
EVERYONE, STAY AS YOU ARE.

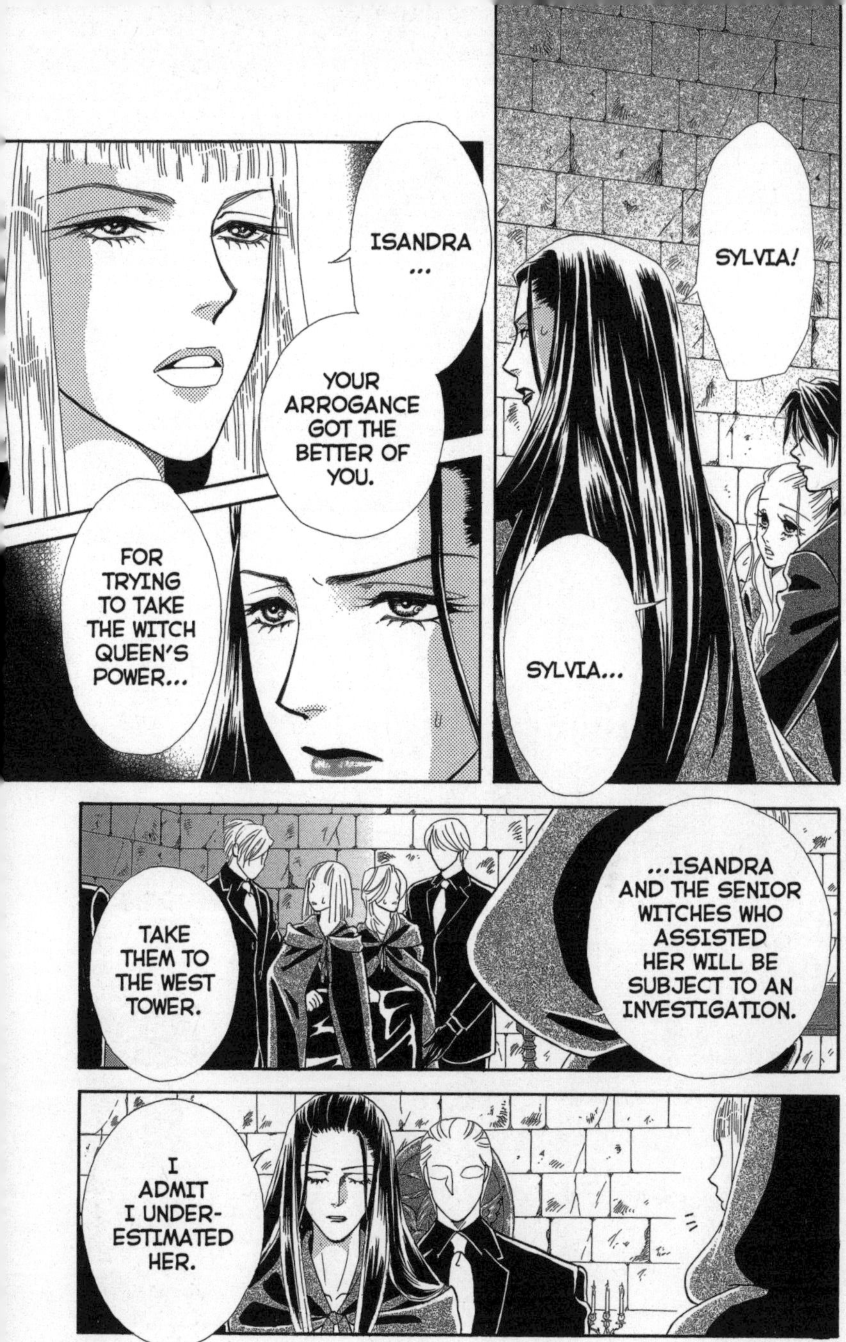
SYLVIA!
SYLVIA...
ISANDRA ...
YOUR ARROGANCE GOT THE BETTER OF YOU.
FOR TRYING TO TAKE THE WITCH QUEEN'S POWER...
...ISANDRA AND THE SENIOR WITCHES WHO ASSISTED HER WILL BE SUBJECT TO AN INVESTIGATION.
TAKE THEM TO THE WEST TOWER.
I ADMIT I UNDER-ESTIMATED HER.

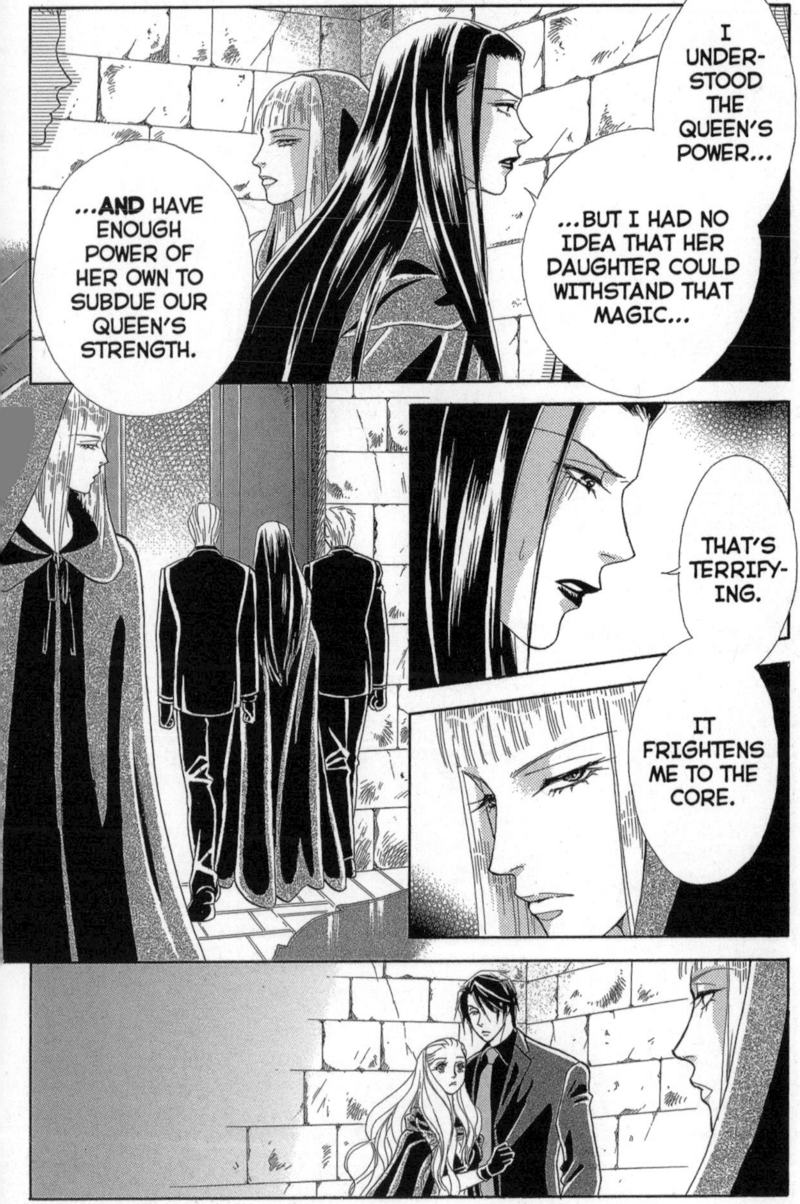
I UNDER-STOOD THE QUEEN'S POWER...
...BUT I HAD NO IDEA THAT HER DAUGHTER COULD WITHSTAND THAT MAGIC...
...**AND** HAVE ENOUGH POWER OF HER OWN TO SUBDUE OUR QUEEN'S STRENGTH.
THAT'S TERRIFY-ING.
IT FRIGHTENS ME TO THE CORE.

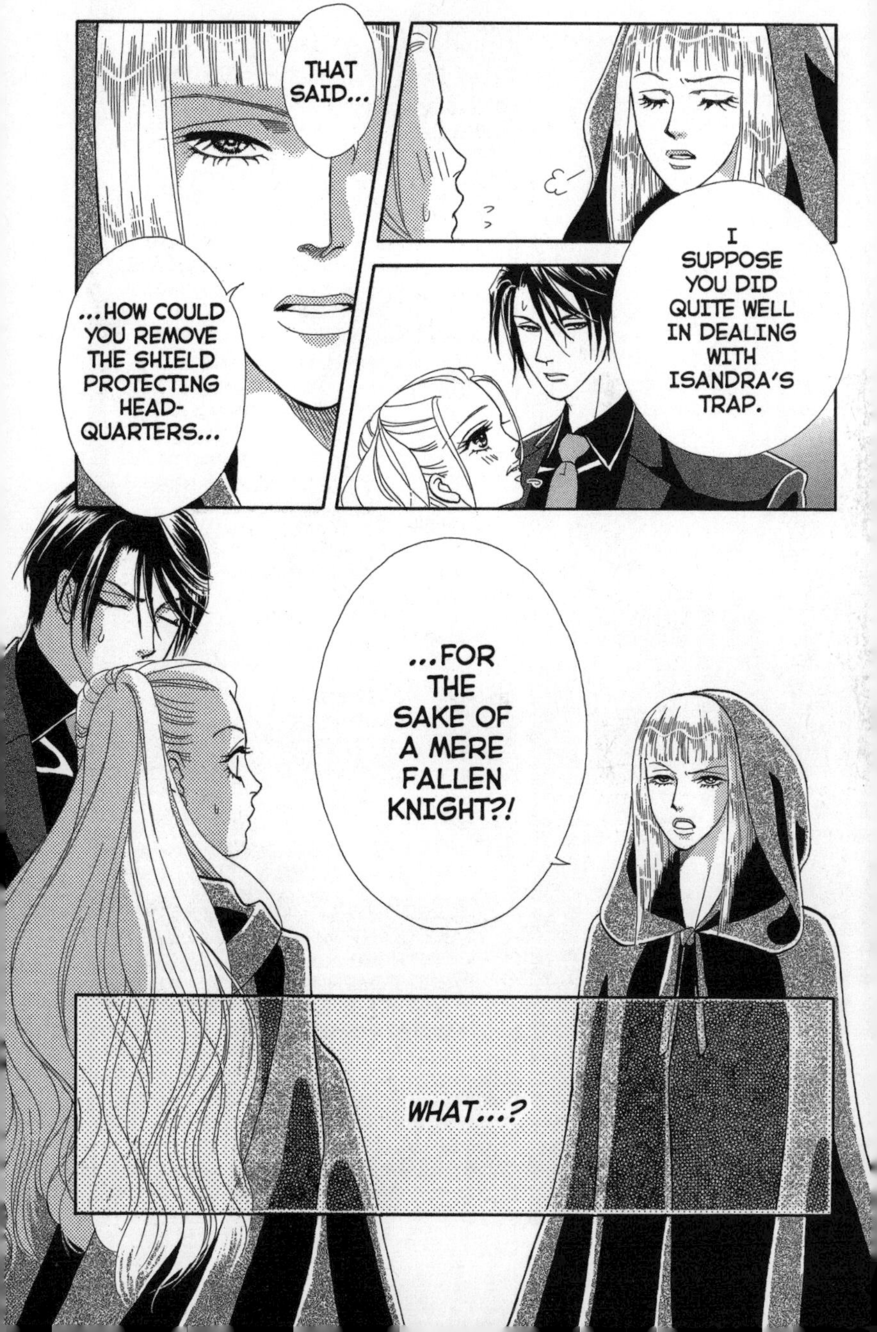
I SUPPOSE YOU DID QUITE WELL IN DEALING WITH ISANDRA'S TRAP.
THAT SAID...
...HOW COULD YOU REMOVE THE SHIELD PROTECTING HEAD-QUARTERS...
...FOR THE SAKE OF A MERE FALLEN KNIGHT?!
WHAT...?

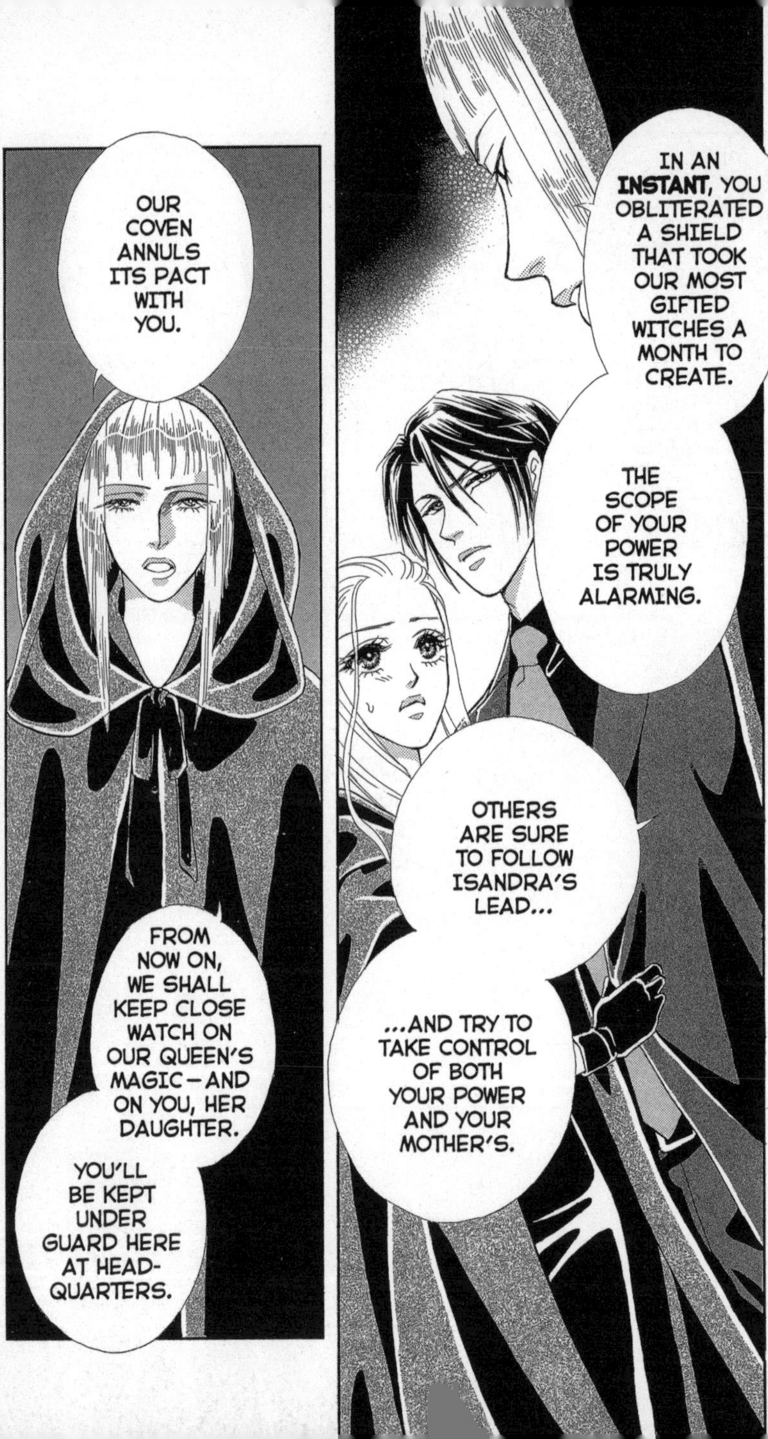
IN AN INSTANT, YOU OBLITERATED A SHIELD THAT TOOK OUR MOST GIFTED WITCHES A MONTH TO CREATE.
THE SCOPE OF YOUR POWER IS TRULY ALARMING.
OTHERS ARE SURE TO FOLLOW ISANDRA'S LEAD...
...AND TRY TO TAKE CONTROL OF BOTH YOUR POWER AND YOUR MOTHER'S.
OUR COVEN ANNULS ITS PACT WITH YOU.
FROM NOW ON, WE SHALL KEEP CLOSE WATCH ON OUR QUEEN'S MAGIC—AND ON YOU, HER DAUGHTER.
YOU'LL BE KEPT UNDER GUARD HERE AT HEAD-QUARTERS.

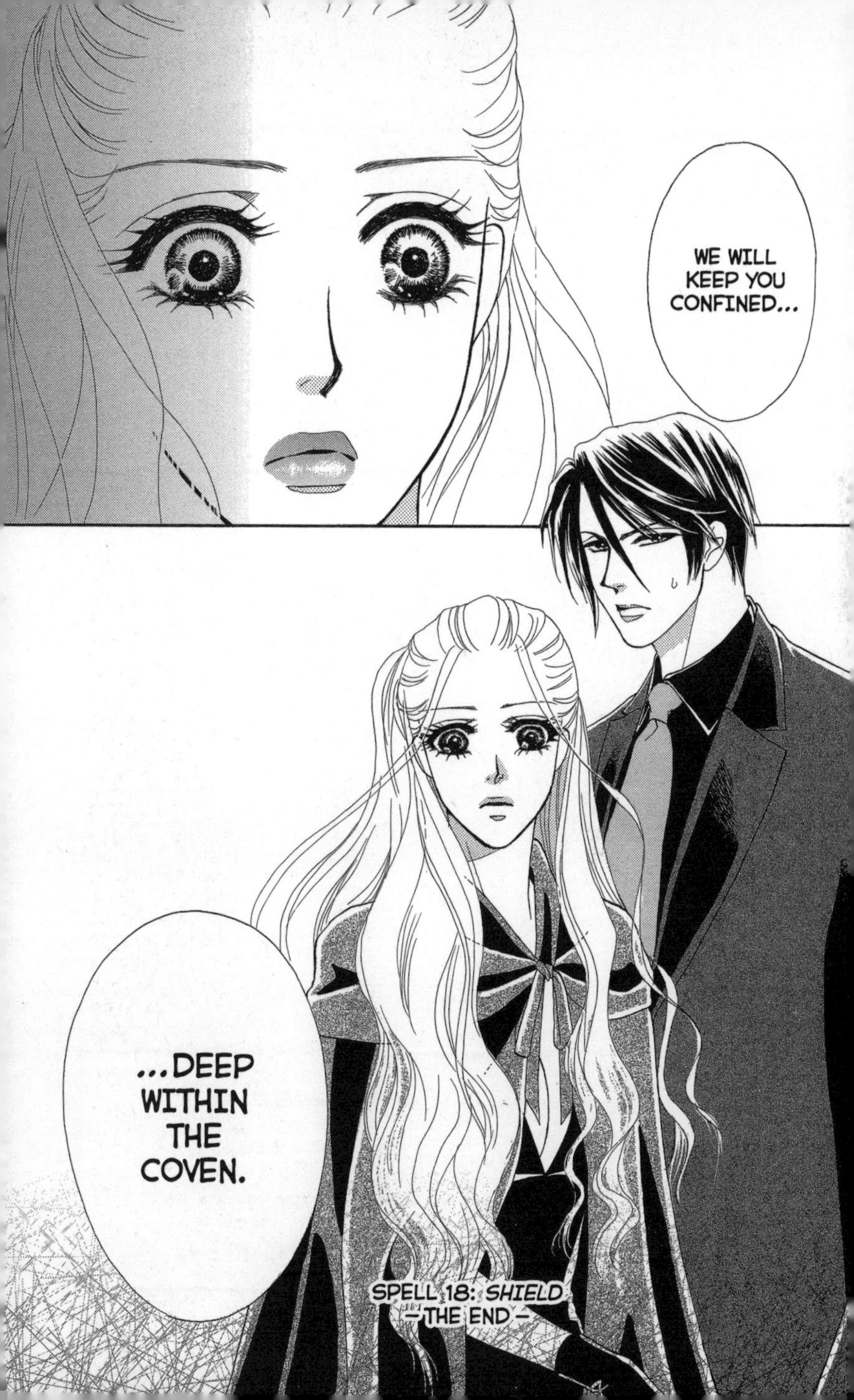
WE WILL KEEP YOU CONFINED...
...DEEP WITHIN THE COVEN.
SPELL 18: SHIELD
–THE END–

– THE MAGIC CIRCLE –

Some of you may have noticed that this chapter was shorter than usual. I was forced to shorten it because I was sick with the flu. I'd been working without much lead time, which caused problems for a lot of people—including you, my readers. I need to do some serious soul-searching.

– THE SHIELD –

I love drawing Isandra! ♪ I seem to have a thing for women who are mature and sexy. I actually like them a little riper. (Laugh)

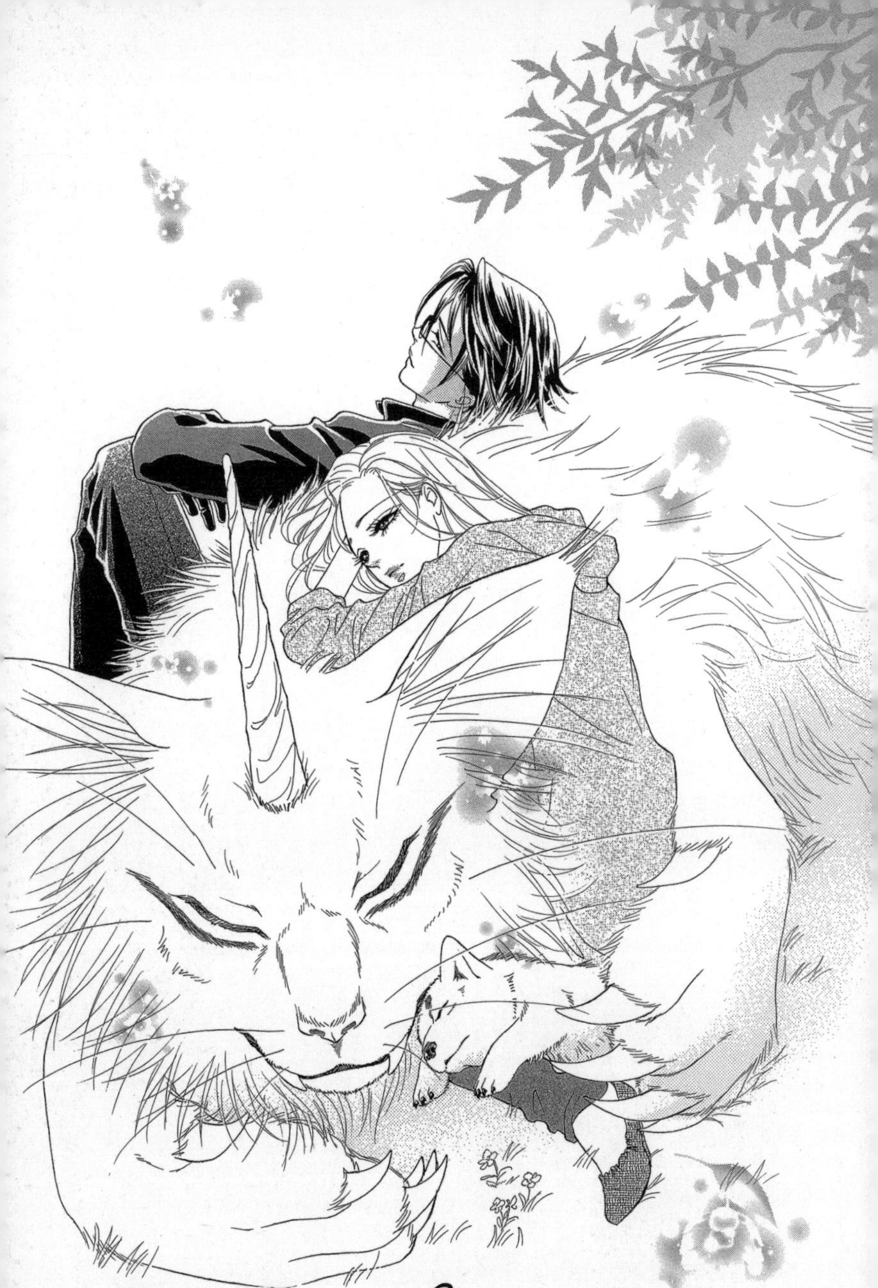

Spell 19: The Deep Forest

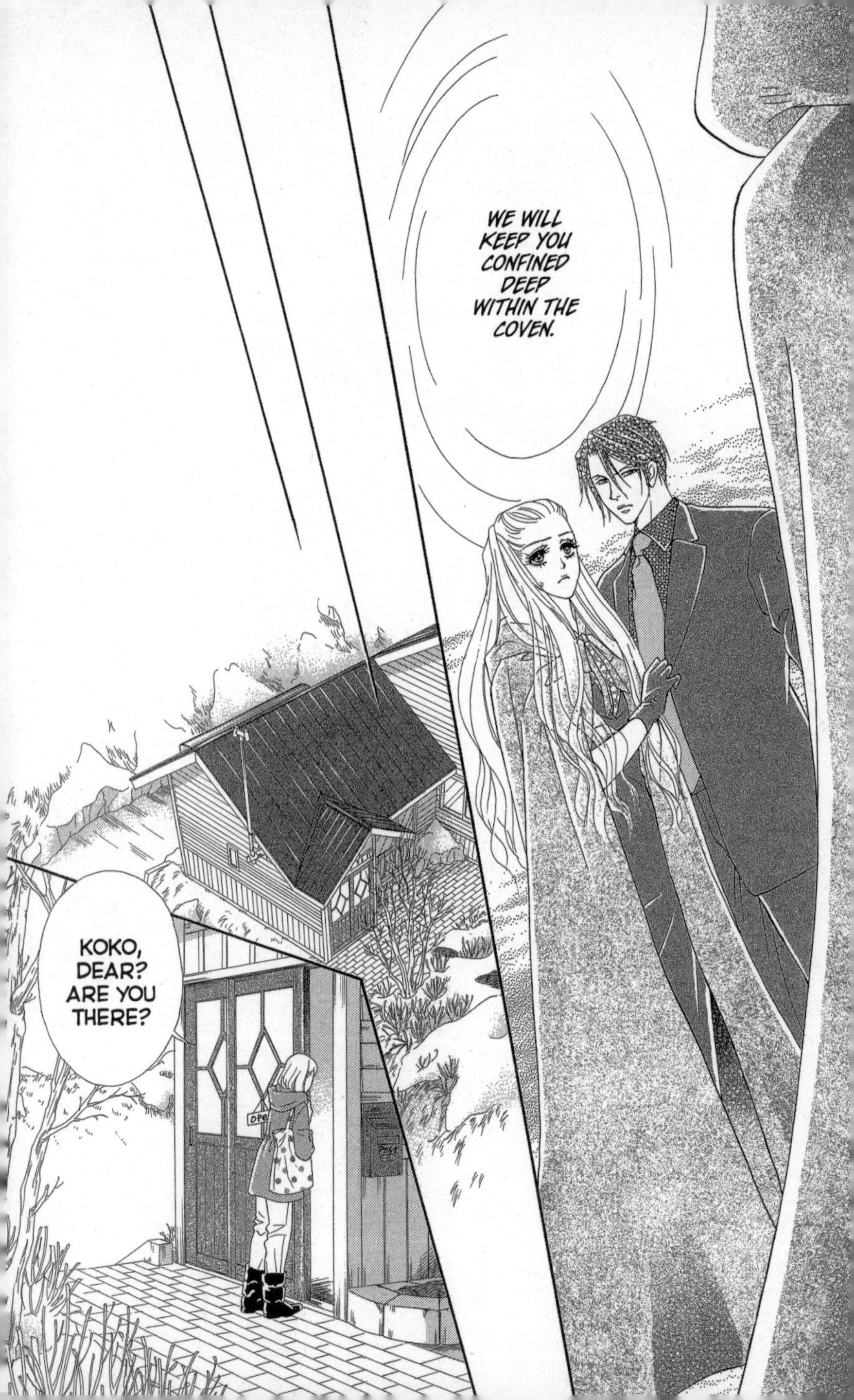
WE WILL KEEP YOU CONFINED DEEP WITHIN THE COVEN.
KOKO, DEAR? ARE YOU THERE?
Post

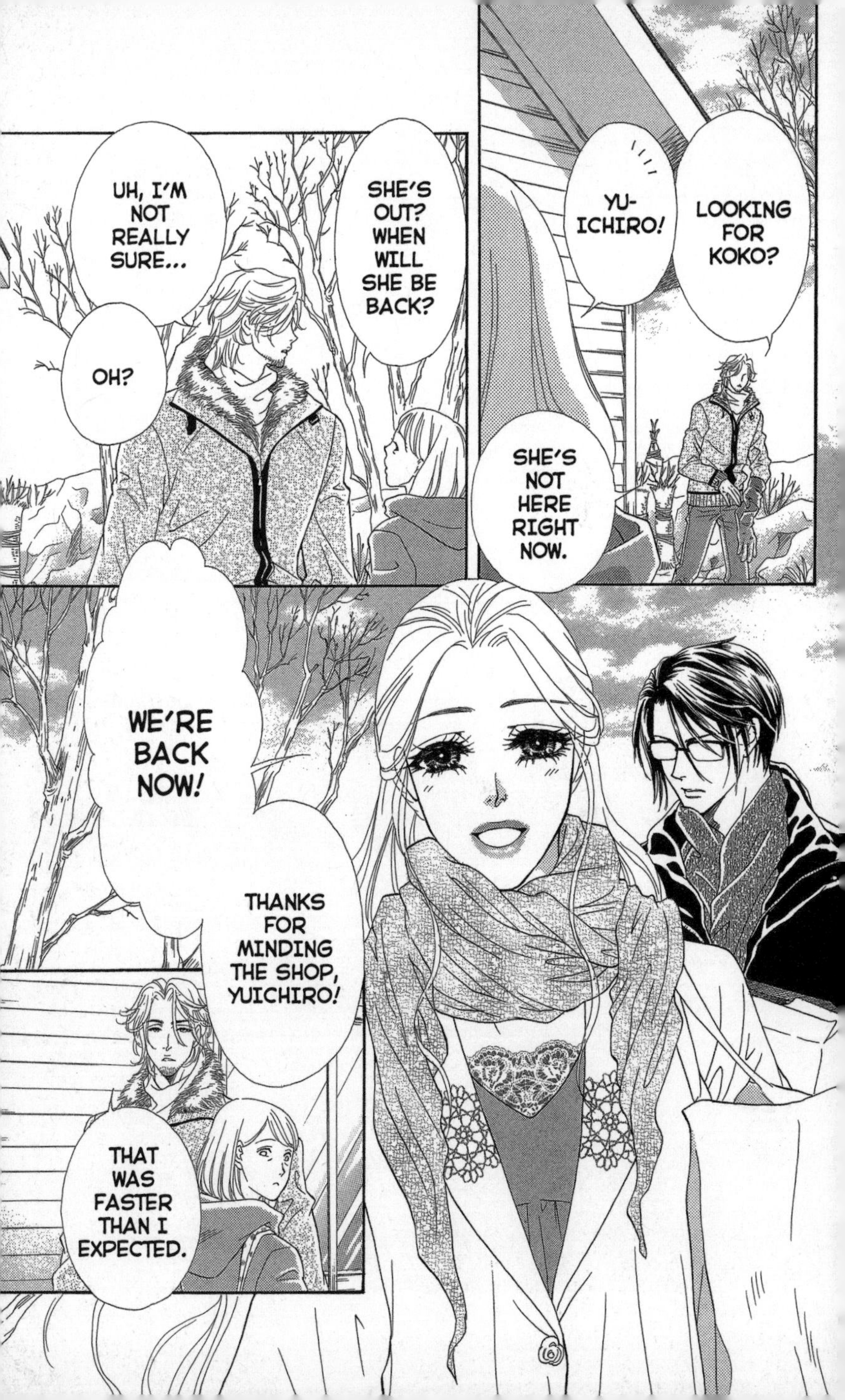
LOOKING FOR KOKO?
YU-ICHIRO!
SHE'S NOT HERE RIGHT NOW.
SHE'S OUT? WHEN WILL SHE BE BACK?
UH, I'M NOT REALLY SURE...
OH?
WE'RE BACK NOW!
THANKS FOR MINDING THE SHOP, YUICHIRO!
THAT WAS FASTER THAN I EXPECTED.

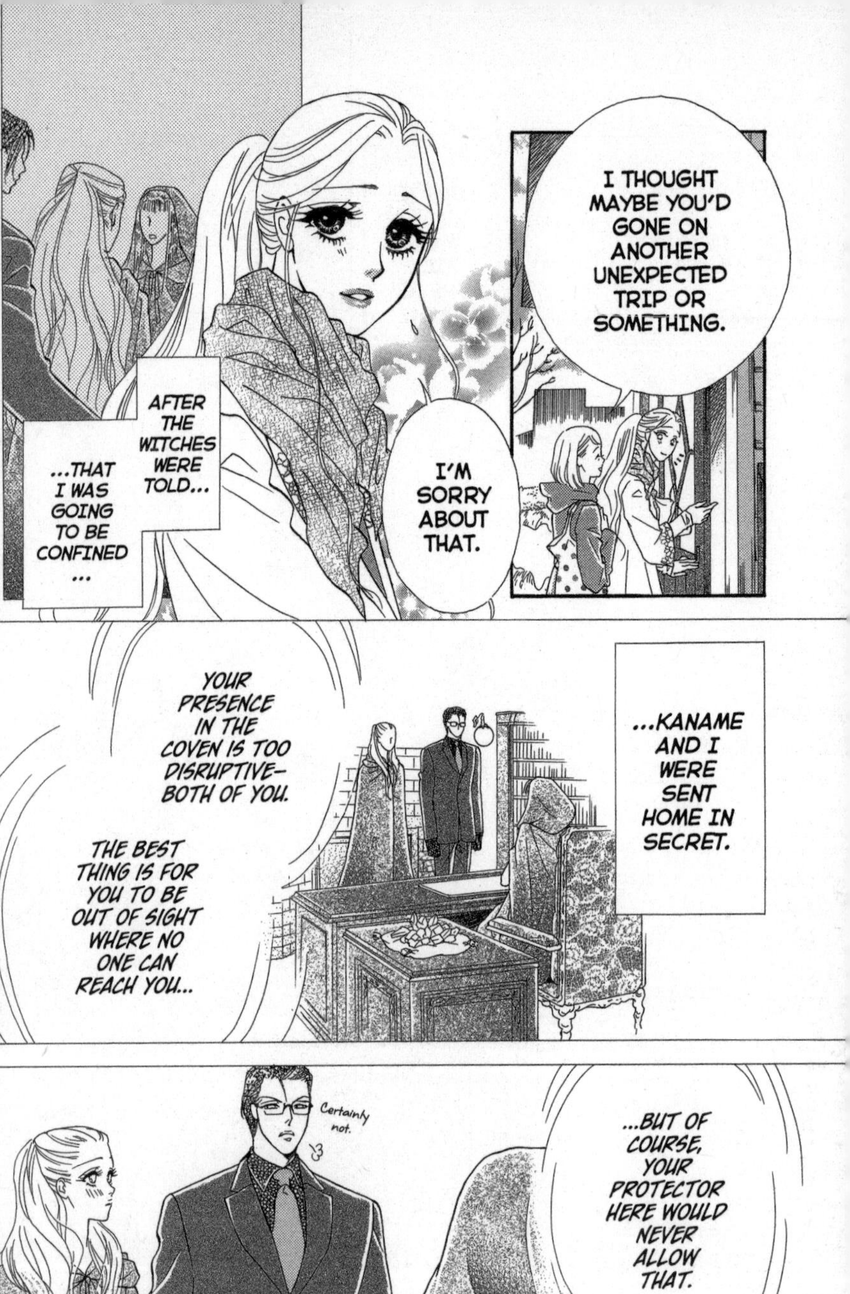
I THOUGHT MAYBE YOU'D GONE ON ANOTHER UNEXPECTED TRIP OR SOMETHING.
I'M SORRY ABOUT THAT.
AFTER THE WITCHES WERE TOLD...
...THAT I WAS GOING TO BE CONFINED...
...KANAME AND I WERE SENT HOME IN SECRET.
YOUR PRESENCE IN THE COVEN IS TOO DISRUPTIVE—BOTH OF YOU.
THE BEST THING IS FOR YOU TO BE OUT OF SIGHT WHERE NO ONE CAN REACH YOU...
...BUT OF COURSE, YOUR PROTECTOR HERE WOULD NEVER ALLOW THAT.
Certainly not.

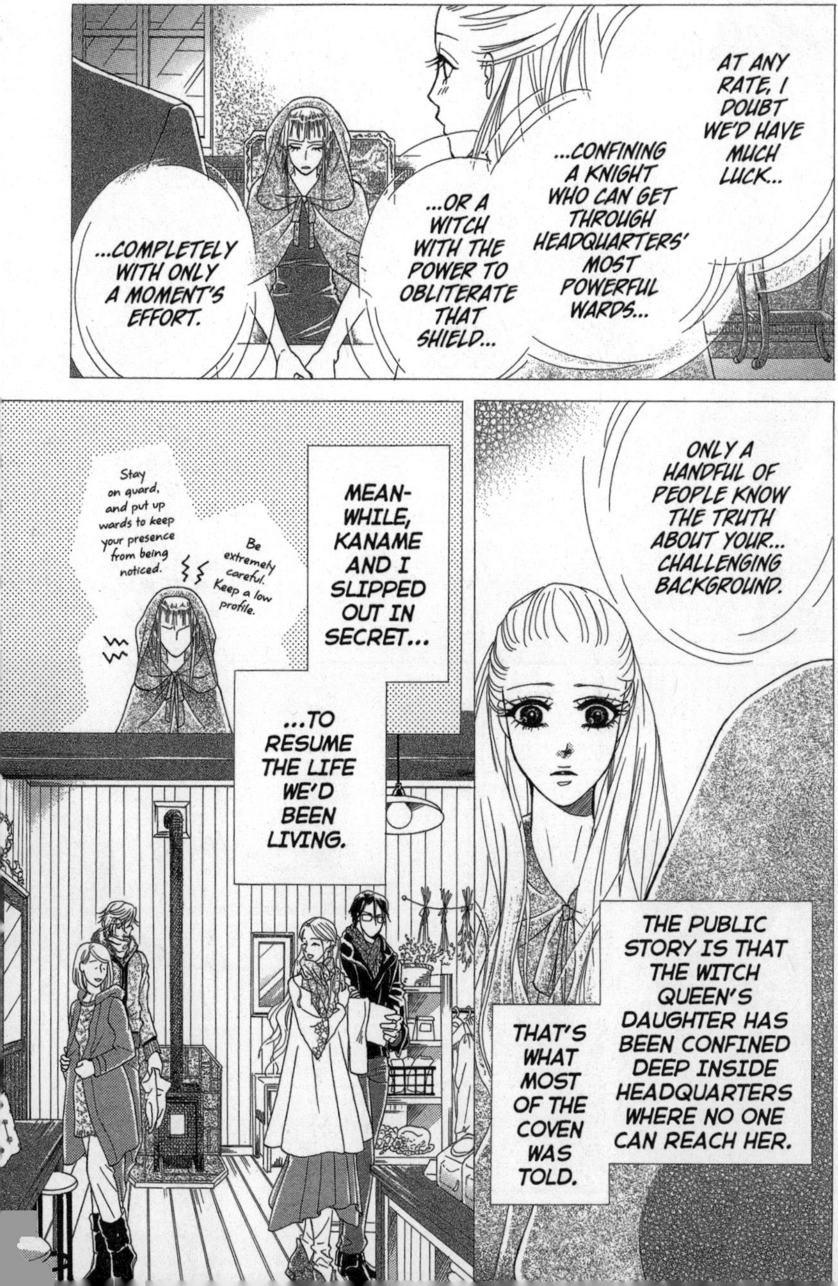
AT ANY RATE, I DOUBT WE'D HAVE MUCH LUCK...
...CONFINING A KNIGHT WHO CAN GET THROUGH HEADQUARTERS' MOST POWERFUL WARDS...
...OR A WITCH WITH THE POWER TO OBLITERATE THAT SHIELD...
...COMPLETELY WITH ONLY A MOMENT'S EFFORT.
ONLY A HANDFUL OF PEOPLE KNOW THE TRUTH ABOUT YOUR... CHALLENGING BACKGROUND.
THE PUBLIC STORY IS THAT THE WITCH QUEEN'S DAUGHTER HAS BEEN CONFINED DEEP INSIDE HEADQUARTERS WHERE NO ONE CAN REACH HER.
THAT'S WHAT MOST OF THE COVEN WAS TOLD.
MEAN-WHILE, KANAME AND I SLIPPED OUT IN SECRET...
Be extremely careful. Keep a low profile.
Stay on guard, and put up wards to keep your presence from being noticed.
...TO RESUME THE LIFE WE'D BEEN LIVING.

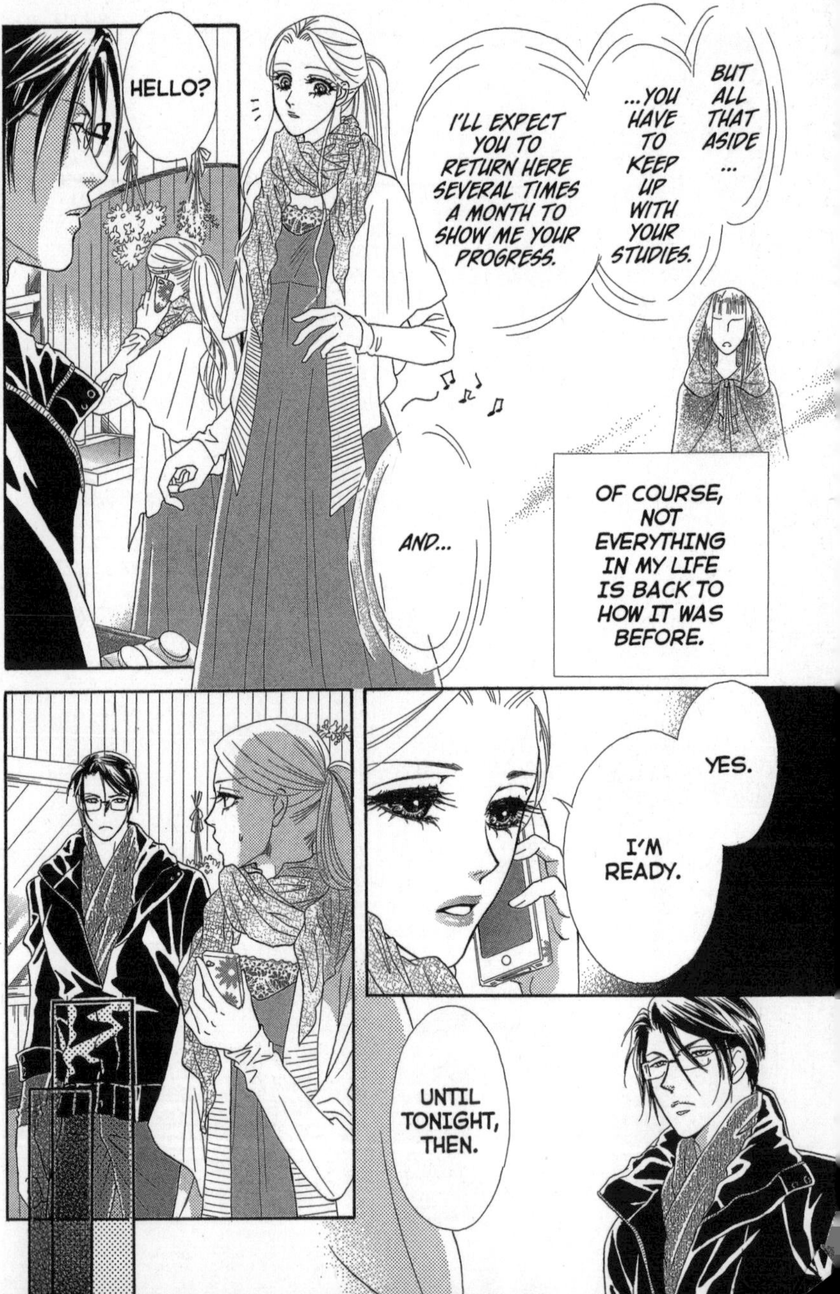
BUT ALL THAT ASIDE...
...YOU HAVE TO KEEP UP WITH YOUR STUDIES.
I'LL EXPECT YOU TO RETURN HERE SEVERAL TIMES A MONTH TO SHOW ME YOUR PROGRESS.
OF COURSE, NOT EVERYTHING IN MY LIFE IS BACK TO HOW IT WAS BEFORE.
AND...
HELLO?
YES.
I'M READY.
UNTIL TONIGHT, THEN.

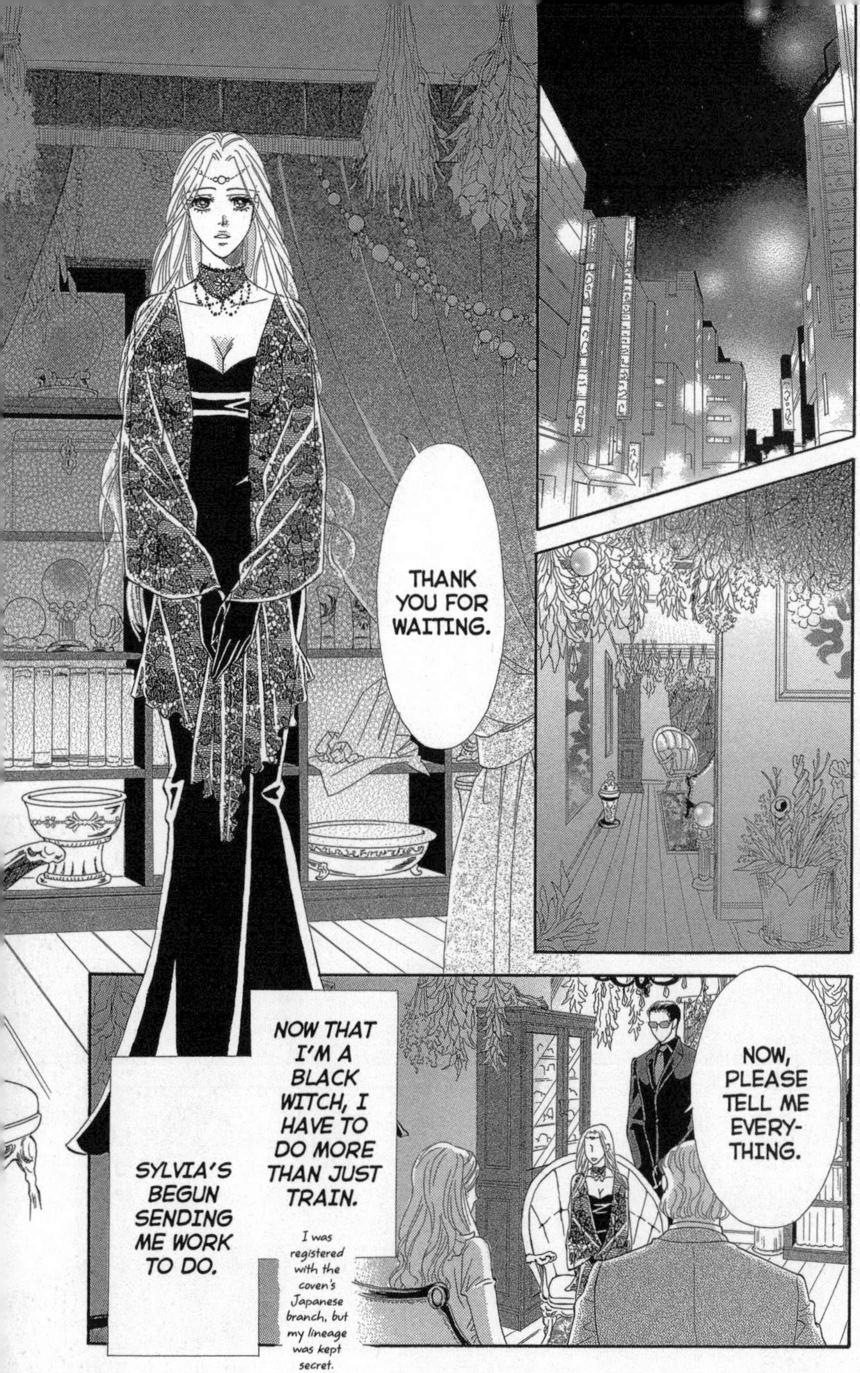
THANK YOU FOR WAITING.
NOW, PLEASE TELL ME EVERY-THING.
NOW THAT I'M A BLACK WITCH, I HAVE TO DO MORE THAN JUST TRAIN.
SYLVIA'S BEGUN SENDING ME WORK TO DO.
I was registered with the coven's Japanese branch, but my lineage was kept secret.

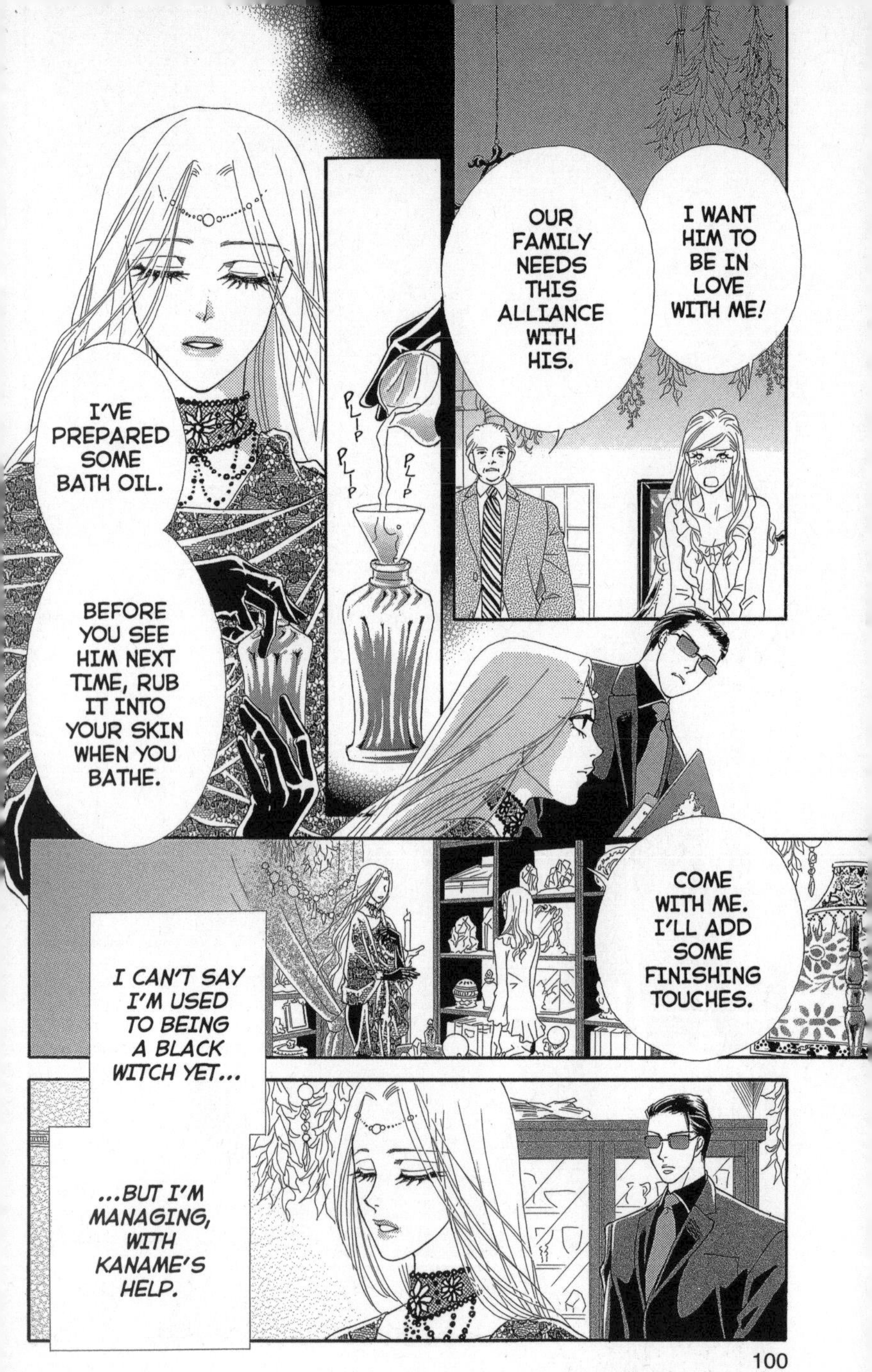
I WANT HIM TO BE IN LOVE WITH ME!
OUR FAMILY NEEDS THIS ALLIANCE WITH HIS.
PLIP PLIP PLIP
I'VE PREPARED SOME BATH OIL.
BEFORE YOU SEE HIM NEXT TIME, RUB IT INTO YOUR SKIN WHEN YOU BATHE.
COME WITH ME. I'LL ADD SOME FINISHING TOUCHES.
I CAN'T SAY I'M USED TO BEING A BLACK WITCH YET...
...BUT I'M MANAGING, WITH KANAME'S HELP.

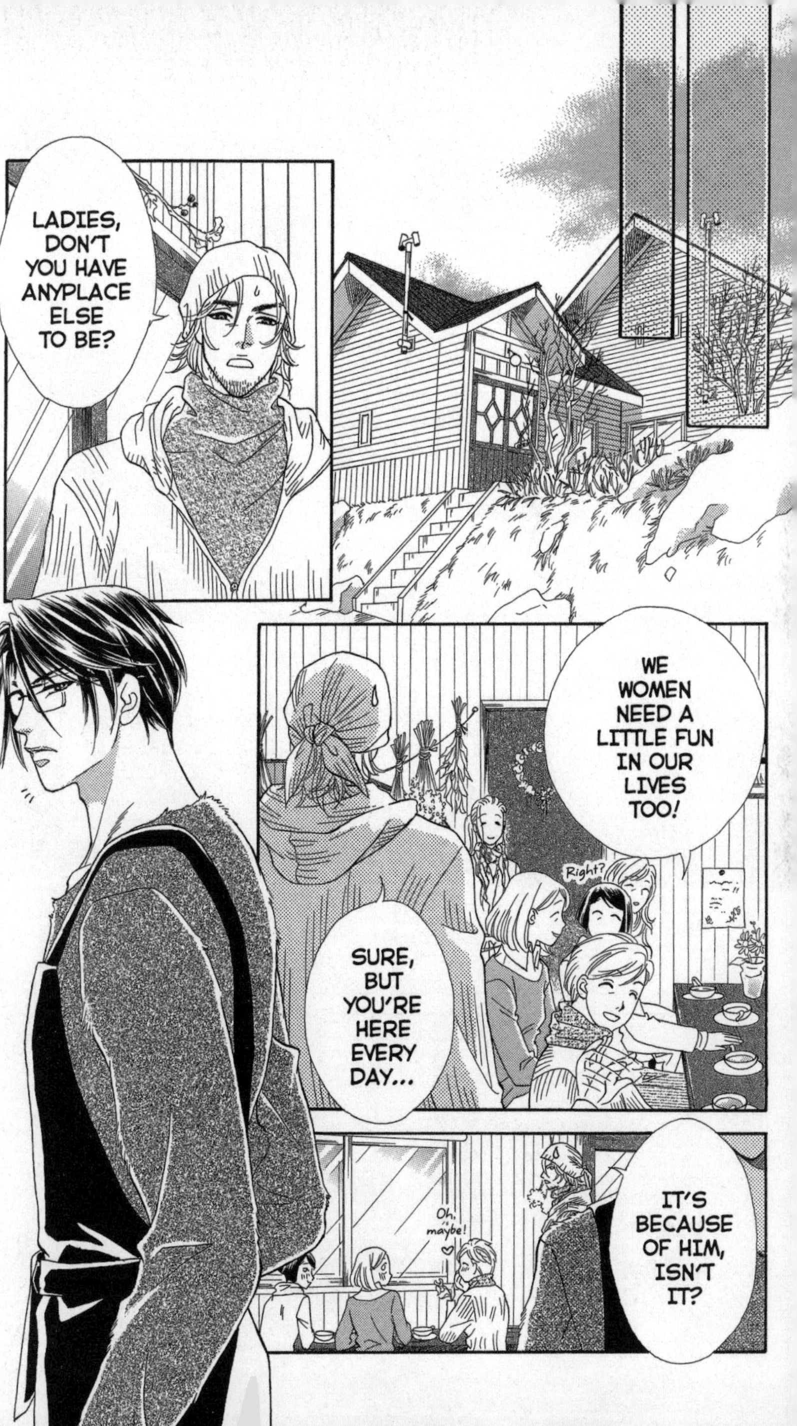
LADIES, DON'T YOU HAVE ANYPLACE ELSE TO BE?
WE WOMEN NEED A LITTLE FUN IN OUR LIVES TOO!
Right?
SURE, BUT YOU'RE HERE EVERY DAY...
IT'S BECAUSE OF HIM, ISN'T IT?
Oh, maybe!

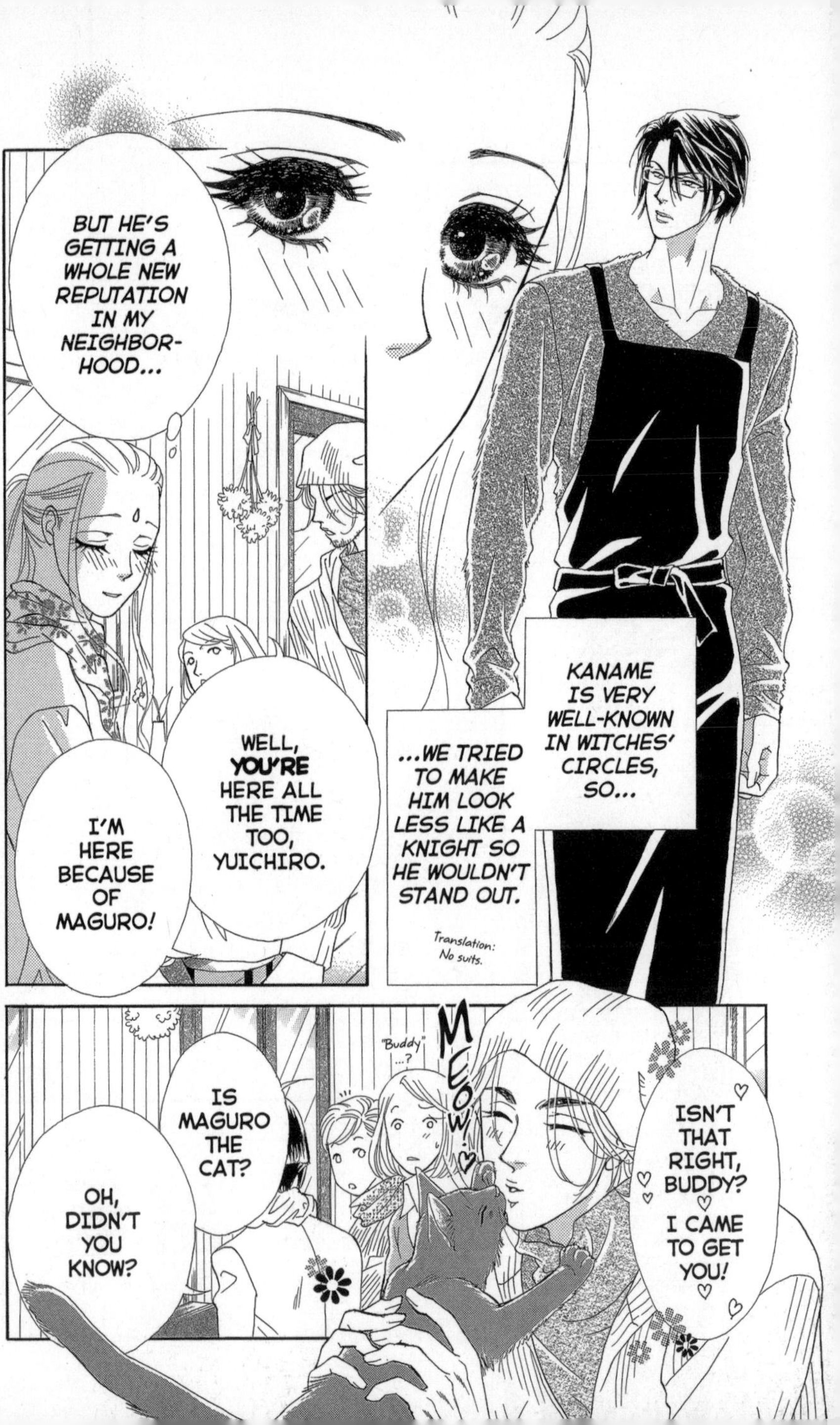
KANAME IS VERY WELL-KNOWN IN WITCHES' CIRCLES, SO...
...WE TRIED TO MAKE HIM LOOK LESS LIKE A KNIGHT SO HE WOULDN'T STAND OUT.
Translation: No suits.
BUT HE'S GETTING A WHOLE NEW REPUTATION IN MY NEIGHBORHOOD...
WELL, **YOU'RE** HERE ALL THE TIME TOO, YUICHIRO.
I'M HERE BECAUSE OF MAGURO!
MEOW!
ISN'T THAT RIGHT, BUDDY? I CAME TO GET YOU!
"Buddy" ...?
IS MAGURO THE CAT?
OH, DIDN'T YOU KNOW?

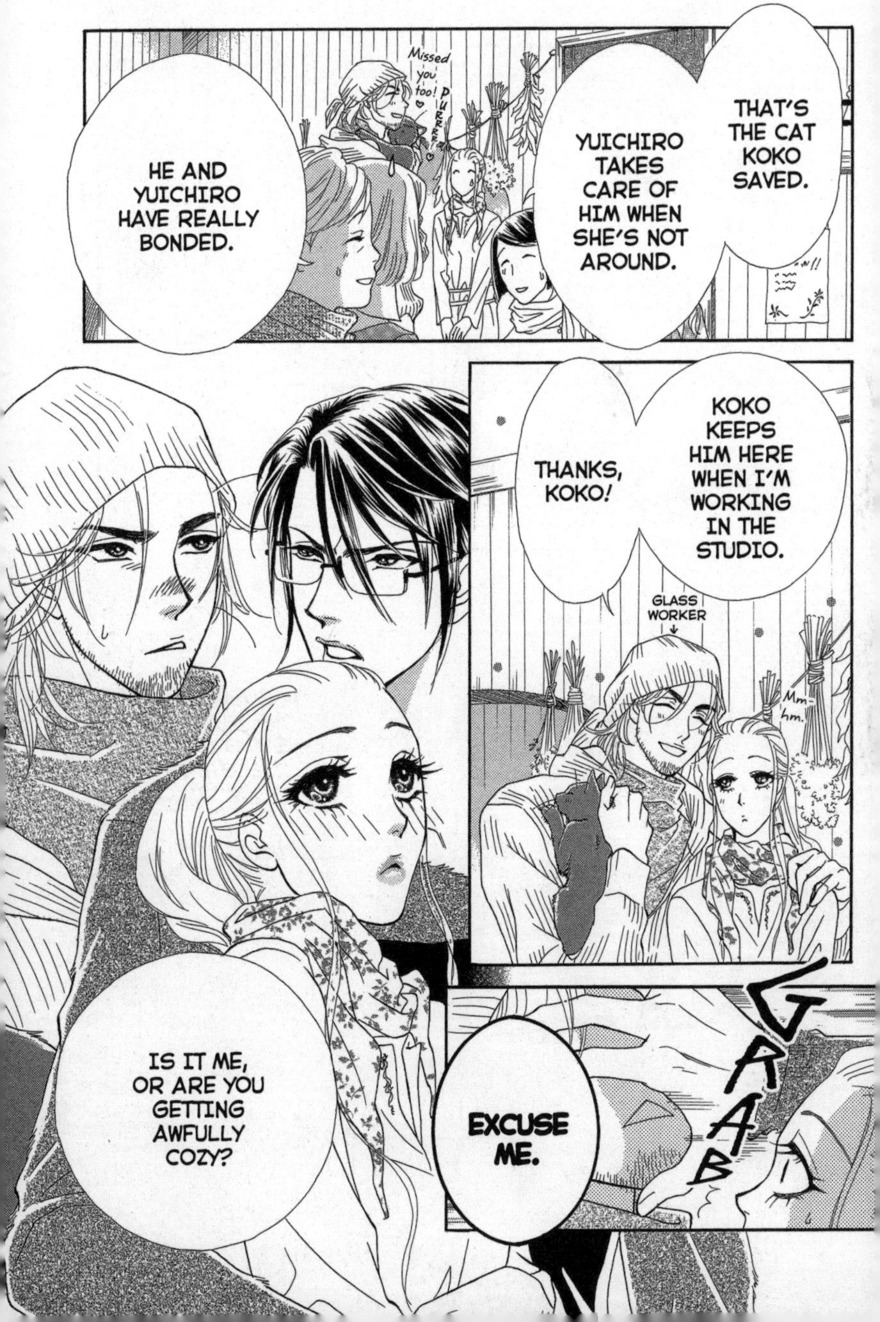
THAT'S THE CAT KOKO SAVED.
YUICHIRO TAKES CARE OF HIM WHEN SHE'S NOT AROUND.
Missed you too!
PURRR♡
HE AND YUICHIRO HAVE REALLY BONDED.
KOKO KEEPS HIM HERE WHEN I'M WORKING IN THE STUDIO.
THANKS, KOKO!
GLASS WORKER
Mm-hm.
GRAB
EXCUSE ME.
IS IT ME, OR ARE YOU GETTING AWFULLY COZY?

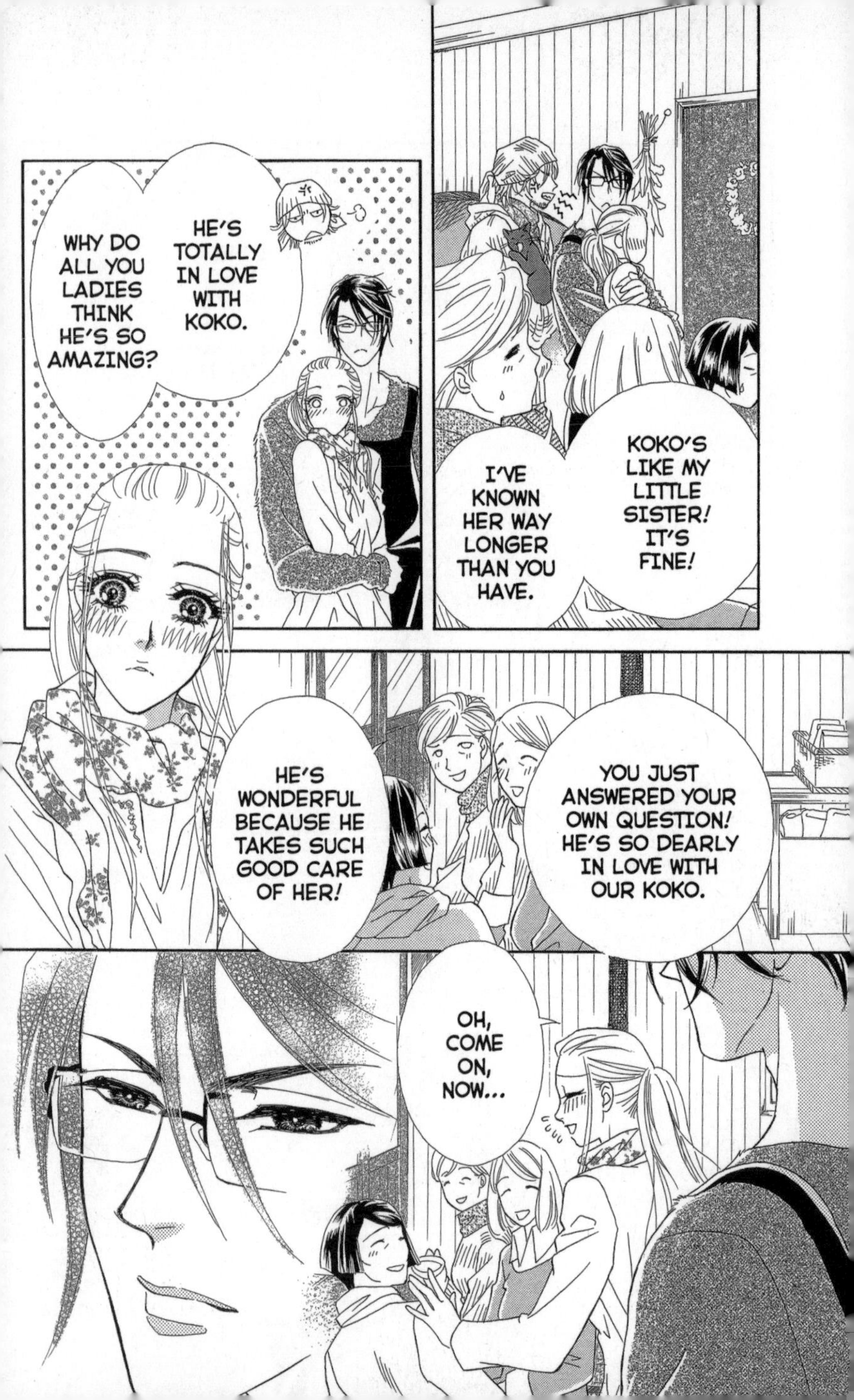
KOKO'S LIKE MY LITTLE SISTER! IT'S FINE!
I'VE KNOWN HER WAY LONGER THAN YOU HAVE.
HE'S TOTALLY IN LOVE WITH KOKO.
WHY DO ALL YOU LADIES THINK HE'S SO AMAZING?
YOU JUST ANSWERED YOUR OWN QUESTION! HE'S SO DEARLY IN LOVE WITH OUR KOKO.
HE'S WONDERFUL BECAUSE HE TAKES SUCH GOOD CARE OF HER!
OH, COME ON, NOW...

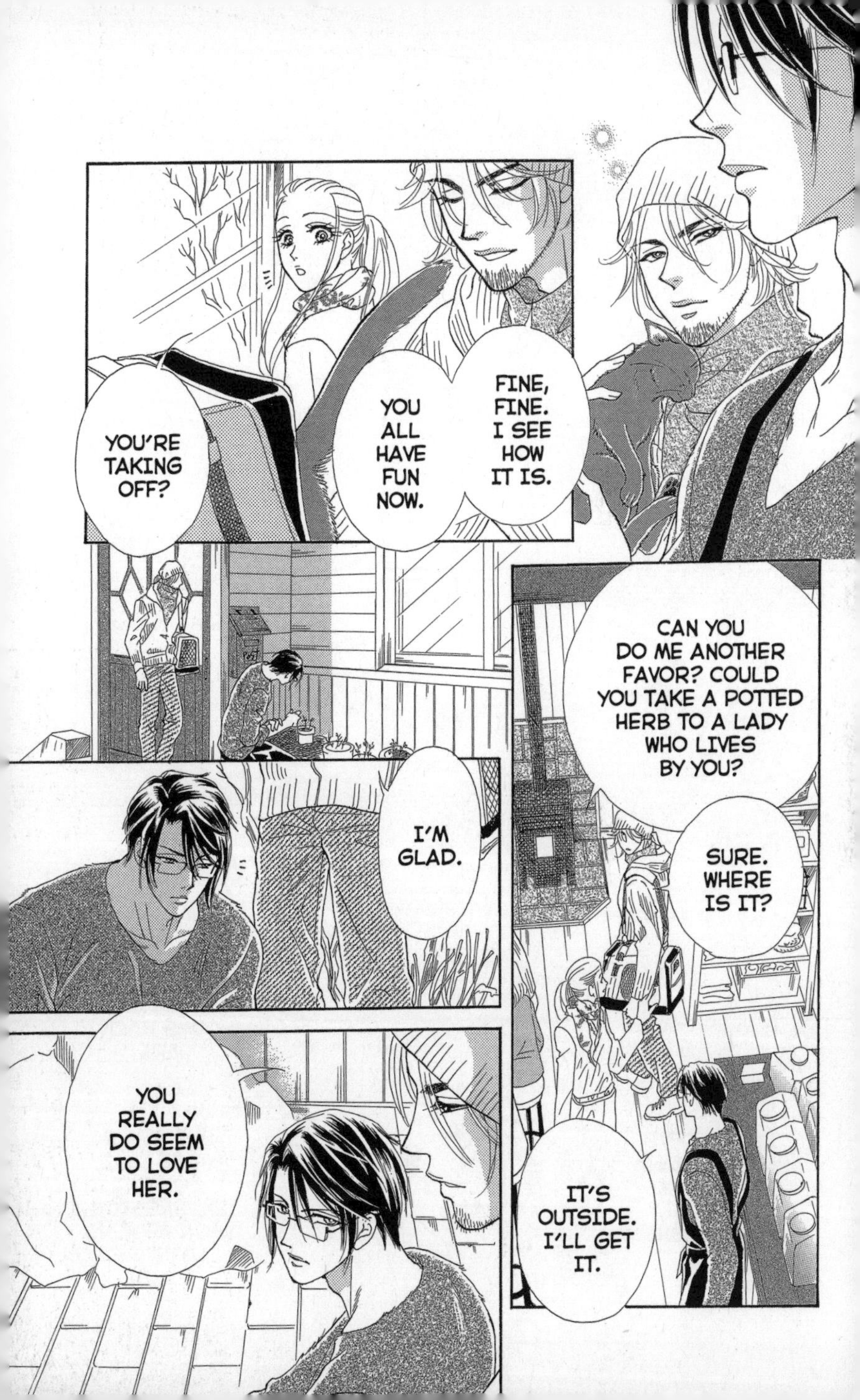
FINE, FINE. I SEE HOW IT IS.
YOU ALL HAVE FUN NOW.
YOU'RE TAKING OFF?
CAN YOU DO ME ANOTHER FAVOR? COULD YOU TAKE A POTTED HERB TO A LADY WHO LIVES BY YOU?
SURE. WHERE IS IT?
IT'S OUTSIDE. I'LL GET IT.
I'M GLAD.
YOU REALLY DO SEEM TO LOVE HER.

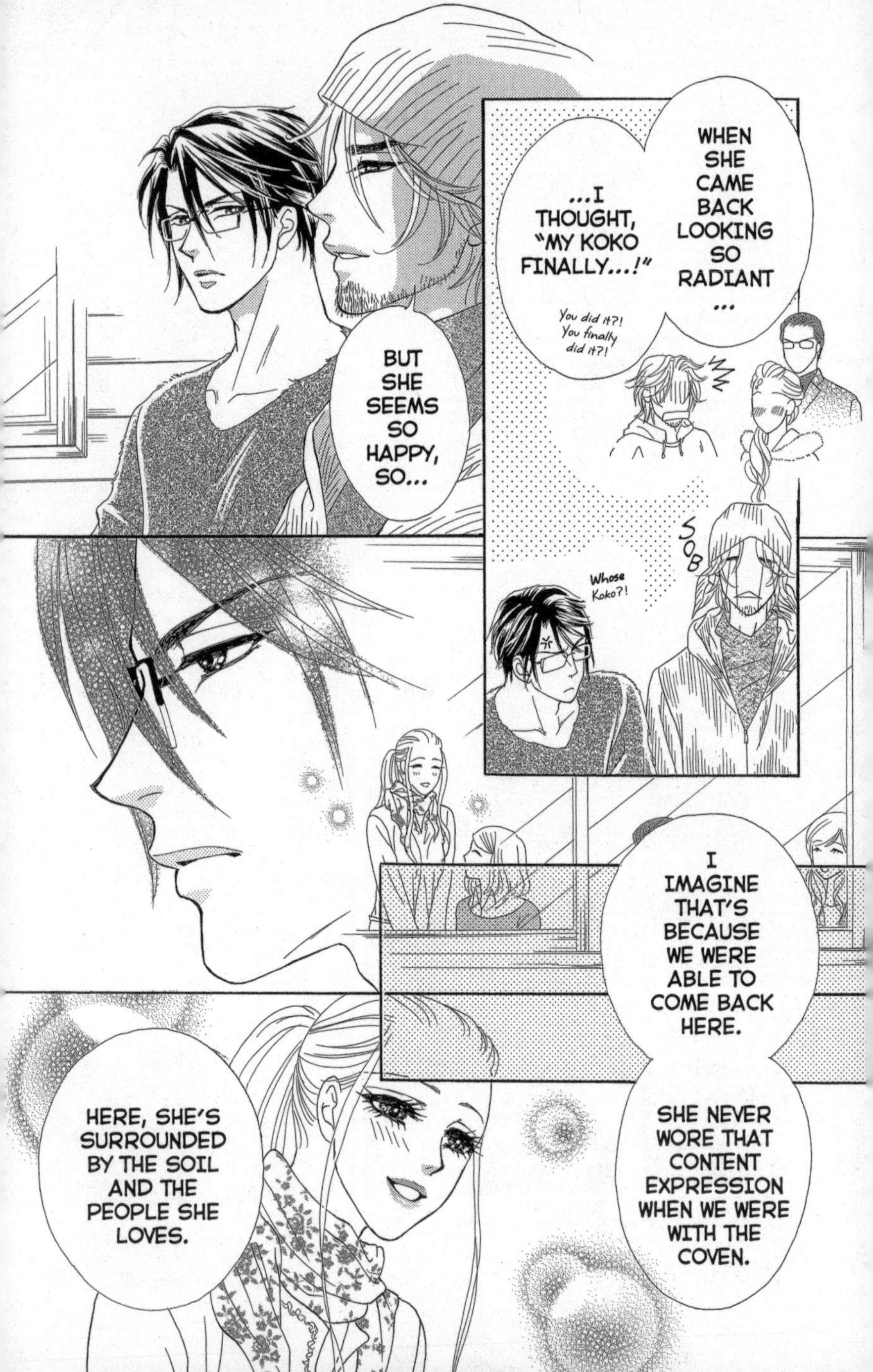
WHEN SHE CAME BACK LOOKING SO RADIANT...
...I THOUGHT, "MY KOKO FINALLY...!"
You did it?! You finally did it?!
SOB
Whose Koko?!
BUT SHE SEEMS SO HAPPY, SO...
I IMAGINE THAT'S BECAUSE WE WERE ABLE TO COME BACK HERE.
SHE NEVER WORE THAT CONTENT EXPRESSION WHEN WE WERE WITH THE COVEN.
HERE, SHE'S SURROUNDED BY THE SOIL AND THE PEOPLE SHE LOVES.

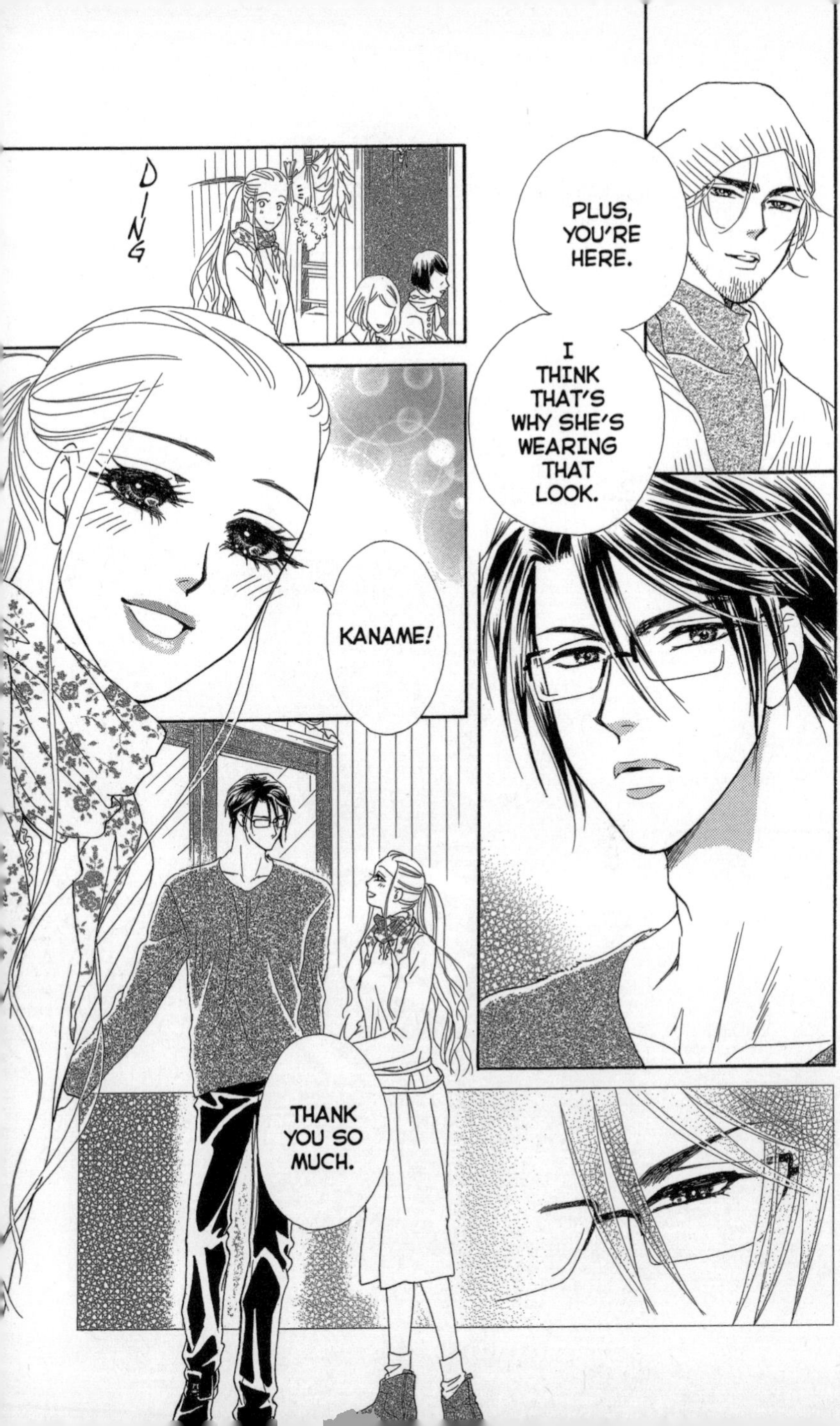
PLUS, YOU'RE HERE.
I THINK THAT'S WHY SHE'S WEARING THAT LOOK.
DING
KANAME!
THANK YOU SO MUCH.

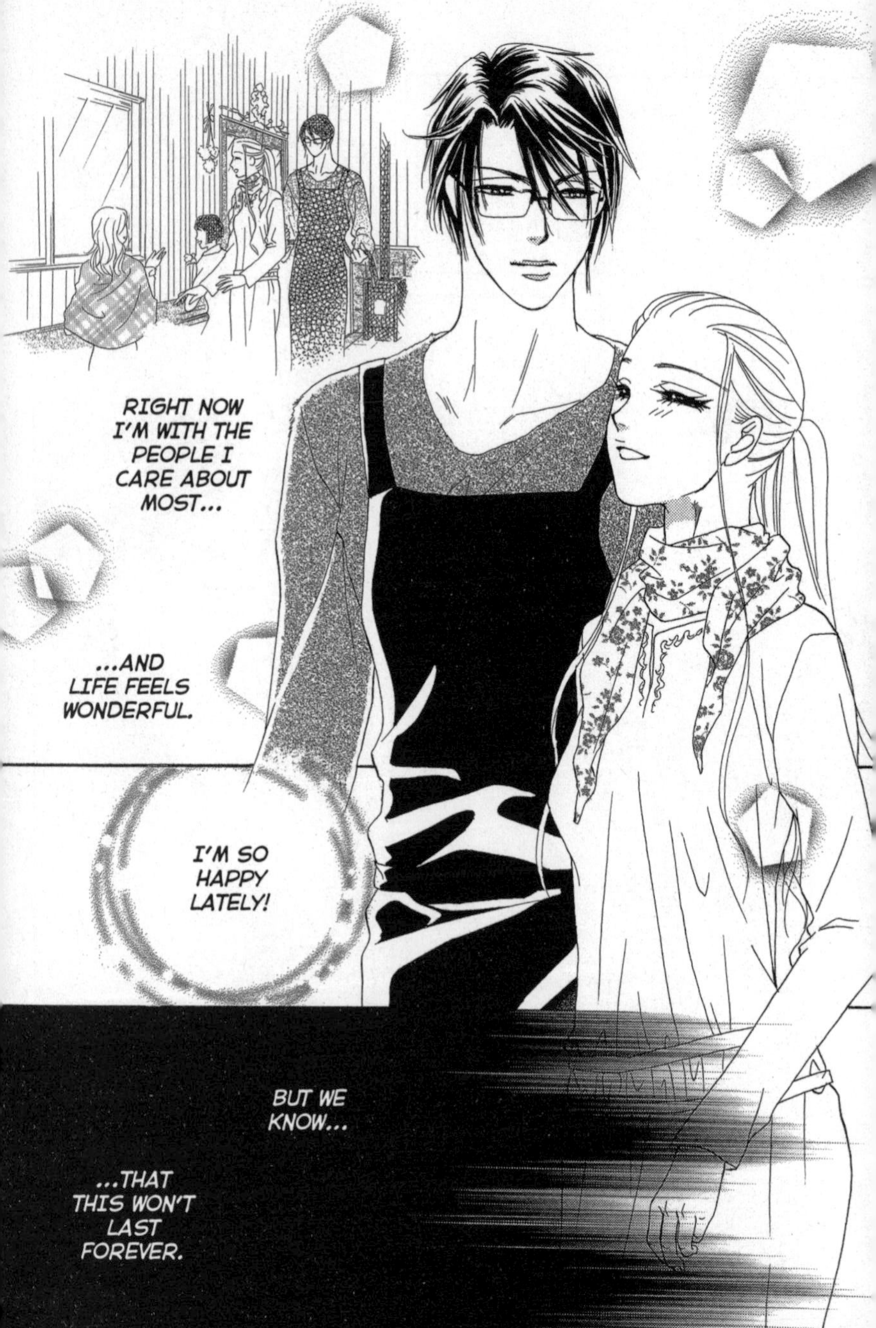
RIGHT NOW I'M WITH THE PEOPLE I CARE ABOUT MOST...
...AND LIFE FEELS WONDERFUL.
I'M SO HAPPY LATELY!
BUT WE KNOW...
...THAT THIS WON'T LAST FOREVER.

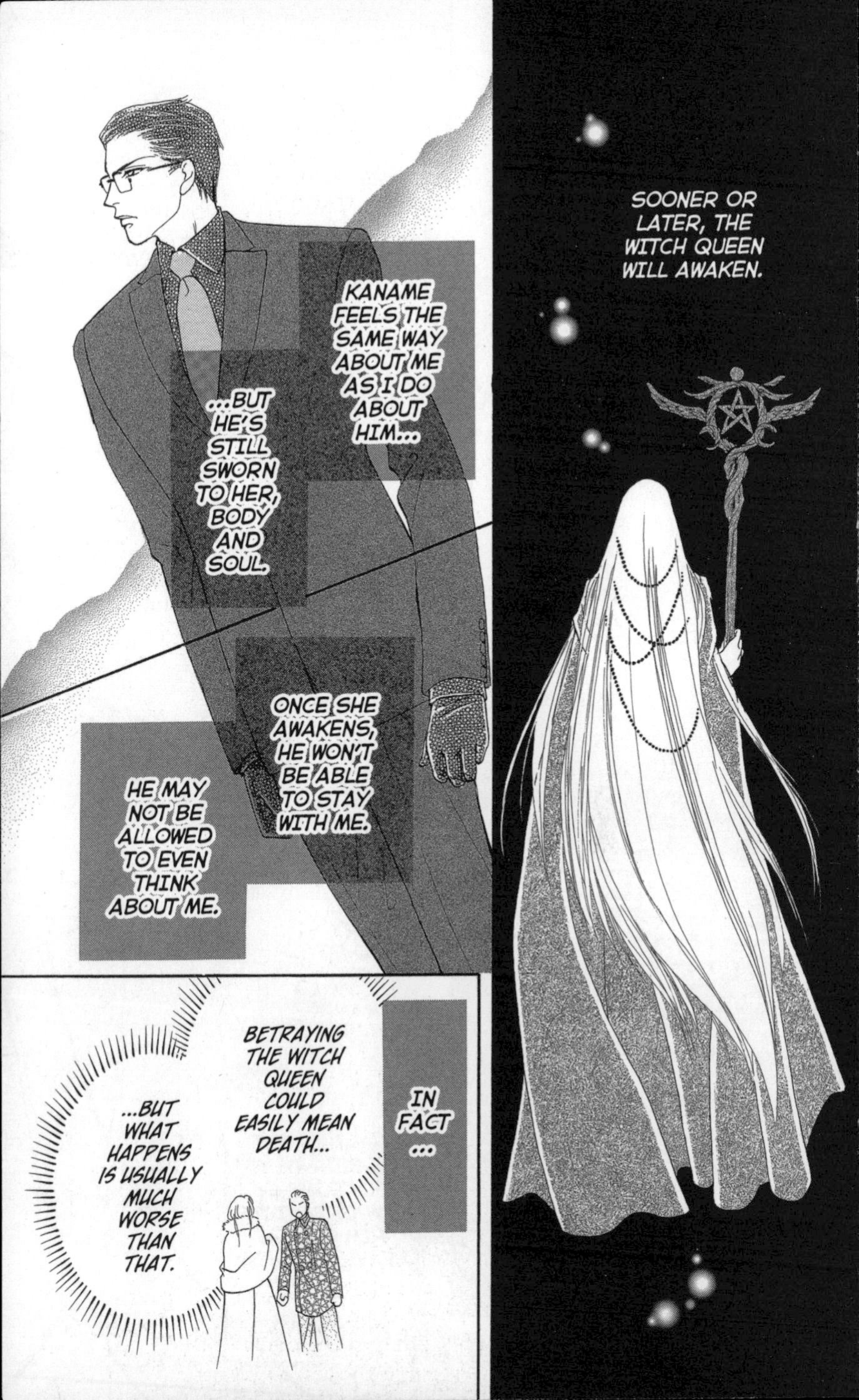
SOONER OR LATER, THE WITCH QUEEN WILL AWAKEN.
KANAME FEELS THE SAME WAY ABOUT ME AS I DO ABOUT HIM...
...BUT HE'S STILL SWORN TO HER, BODY AND SOUL.
ONCE SHE AWAKENS, HE WON'T BE ABLE TO STAY WITH ME.
HE MAY NOT BE ALLOWED TO EVEN THINK ABOUT ME.
IN FACT...
BETRAYING THE WITCH QUEEN COULD EASILY MEAN DEATH...
...BUT WHAT HAPPENS IS USUALLY MUCH WORSE THAN THAT.

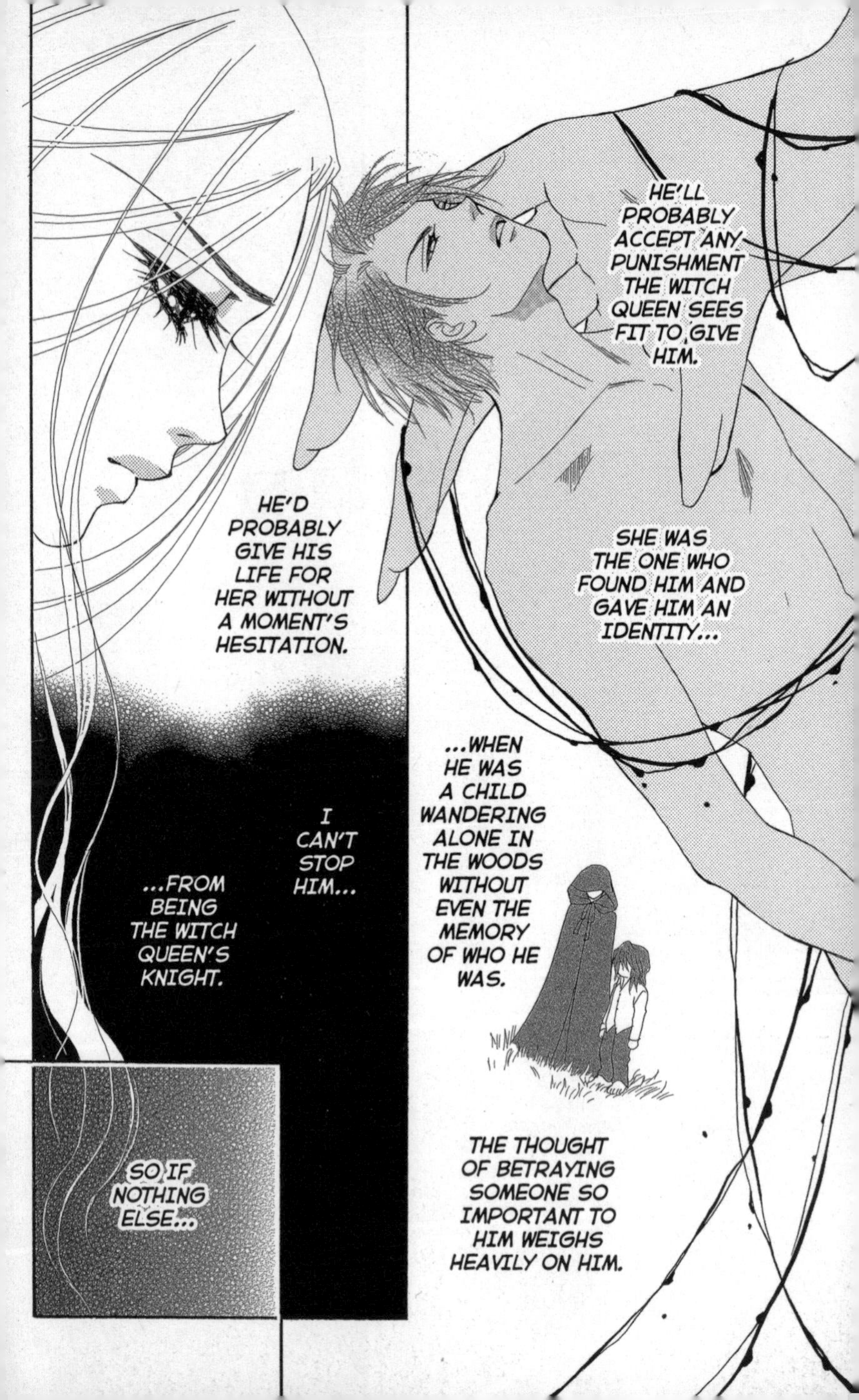
HE'LL PROBABLY ACCEPT ANY PUNISHMENT THE WITCH QUEEN SEES FIT TO GIVE HIM.
SHE WAS THE ONE WHO FOUND HIM AND GAVE HIM AN IDENTITY...
...WHEN HE WAS A CHILD WANDERING ALONE IN THE WOODS WITHOUT EVEN THE MEMORY OF WHO HE WAS.
THE THOUGHT OF BETRAYING SOMEONE SO IMPORTANT TO HIM WEIGHS HEAVILY ON HIM.
HE'D PROBABLY GIVE HIS LIFE FOR HER WITHOUT A MOMENT'S HESITATION.
I CAN'T STOP HIM...
...FROM BEING THE WITCH QUEEN'S KNIGHT.
SO IF NOTHING ELSE...

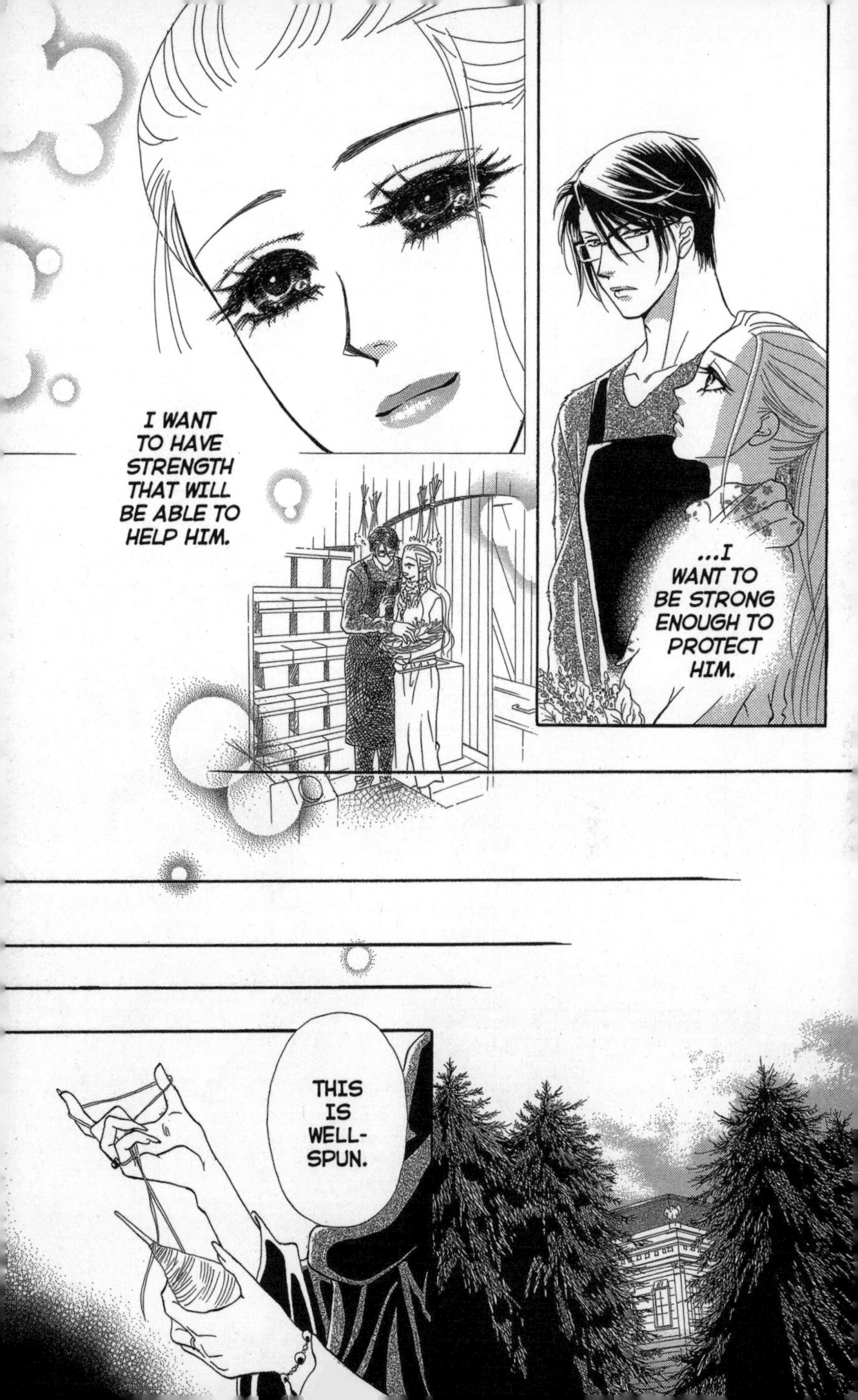
...I WANT TO BE STRONG ENOUGH TO PROTECT HIM.
I WANT TO HAVE STRENGTH THAT WILL BE ABLE TO HELP HIM.
THIS IS WELL-SPUN.

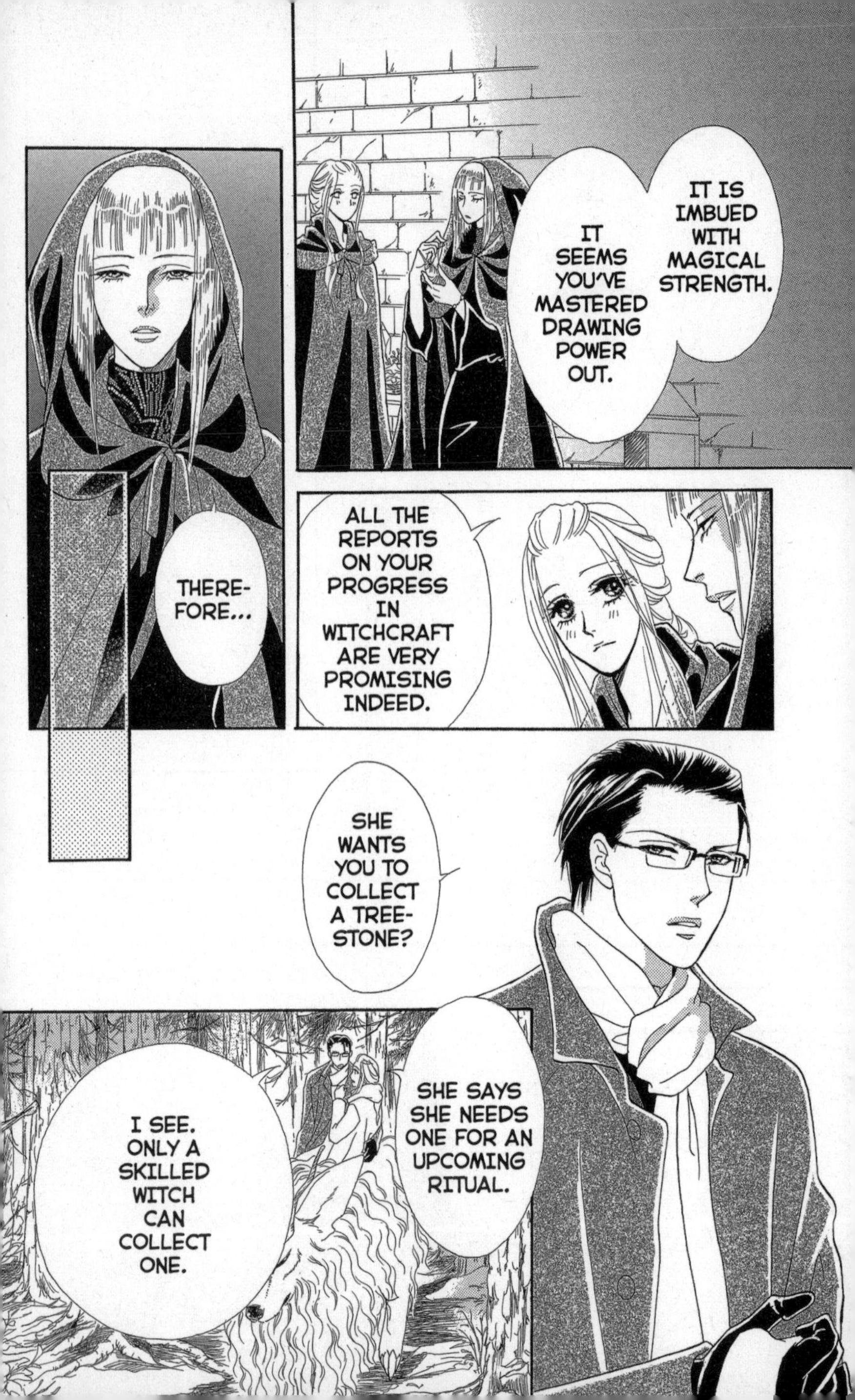
IT IS IMBUED WITH MAGICAL STRENGTH.
IT SEEMS YOU'VE MASTERED DRAWING POWER OUT.
ALL THE REPORTS ON YOUR PROGRESS IN WITCHCRAFT ARE VERY PROMISING INDEED.
THERE-FORE...
SHE WANTS YOU TO COLLECT A TREE-STONE?
SHE SAYS SHE NEEDS ONE FOR AN UPCOMING RITUAL.
I SEE. ONLY A SKILLED WITCH CAN COLLECT ONE.

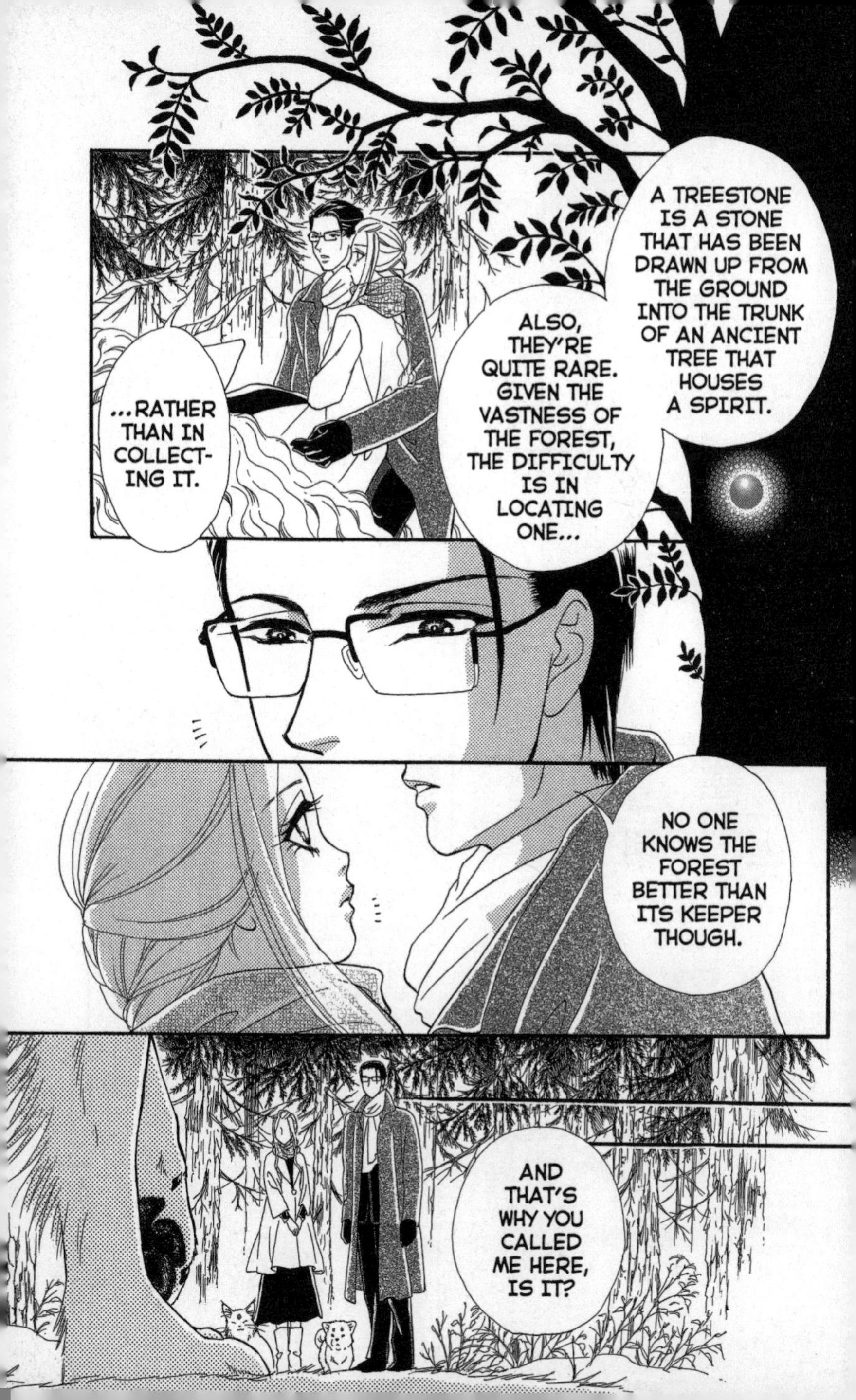
A TREESTONE IS A STONE THAT HAS BEEN DRAWN UP FROM THE GROUND INTO THE TRUNK OF AN ANCIENT TREE THAT HOUSES A SPIRIT.
ALSO, THEY'RE QUITE RARE. GIVEN THE VASTNESS OF THE FOREST, THE DIFFICULTY IS IN LOCATING ONE...
...RATHER THAN IN COLLECT-ING IT.
NO ONE KNOWS THE FOREST BETTER THAN ITS KEEPER THOUGH.
AND THAT'S WHY YOU CALLED ME HERE, IS IT?

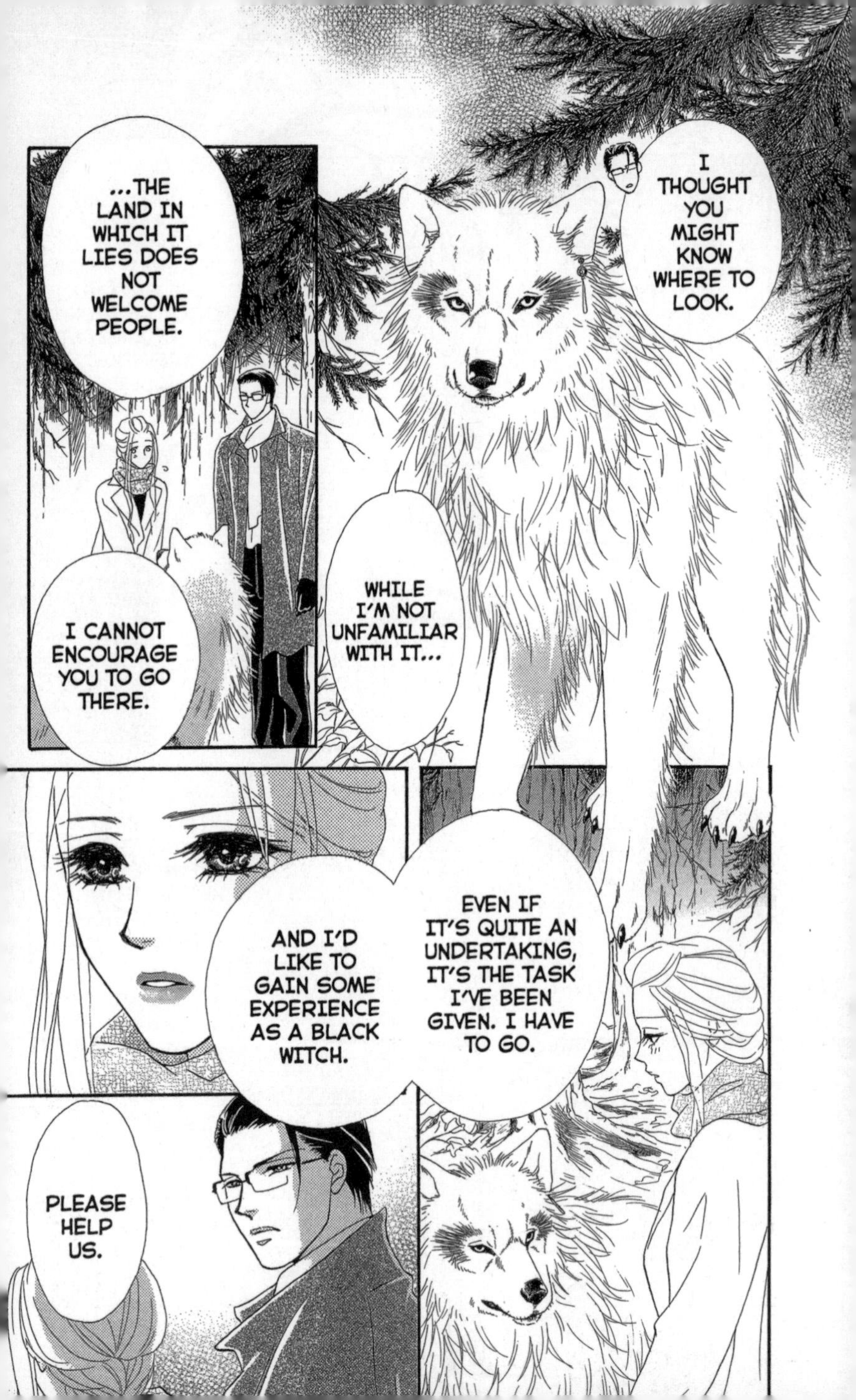
I THOUGHT YOU MIGHT KNOW WHERE TO LOOK.
WHILE I'M NOT UNFAMILIAR WITH IT...
...THE LAND IN WHICH IT LIES DOES NOT WELCOME PEOPLE.
I CANNOT ENCOURAGE YOU TO GO THERE.
EVEN IF IT'S QUITE AN UNDERTAKING, IT'S THE TASK I'VE BEEN GIVEN. I HAVE TO GO.
AND I'D LIKE TO GAIN SOME EXPERIENCE AS A BLACK WITCH.
PLEASE HELP US.

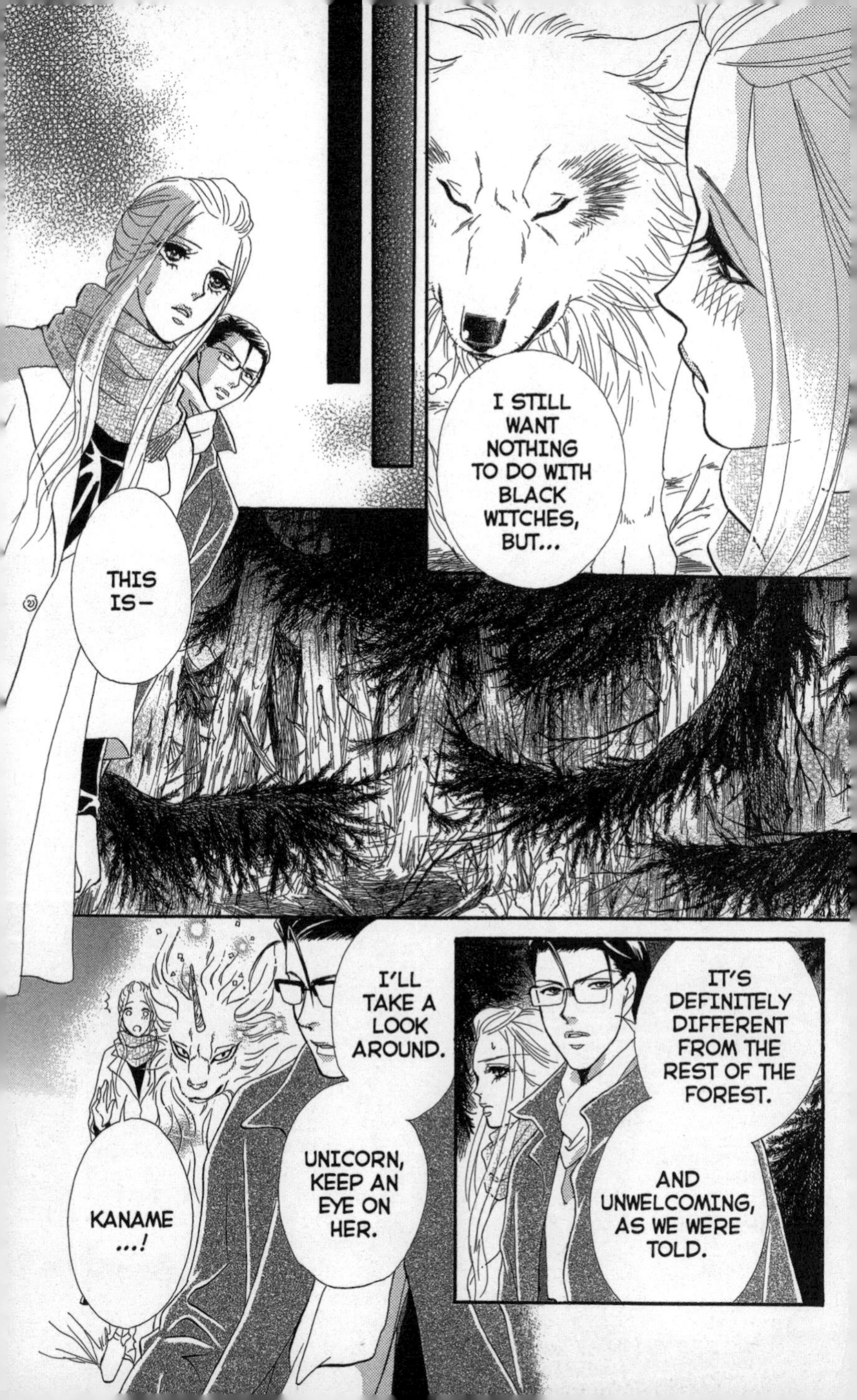
I STILL WANT NOTHING TO DO WITH BLACK WITCHES, BUT...
THIS IS—
IT'S DEFINITELY DIFFERENT FROM THE REST OF THE FOREST.
AND UNWELCOMING, AS WE WERE TOLD.
I'LL TAKE A LOOK AROUND.
UNICORN, KEEP AN EYE ON HER.
KANAME ...!

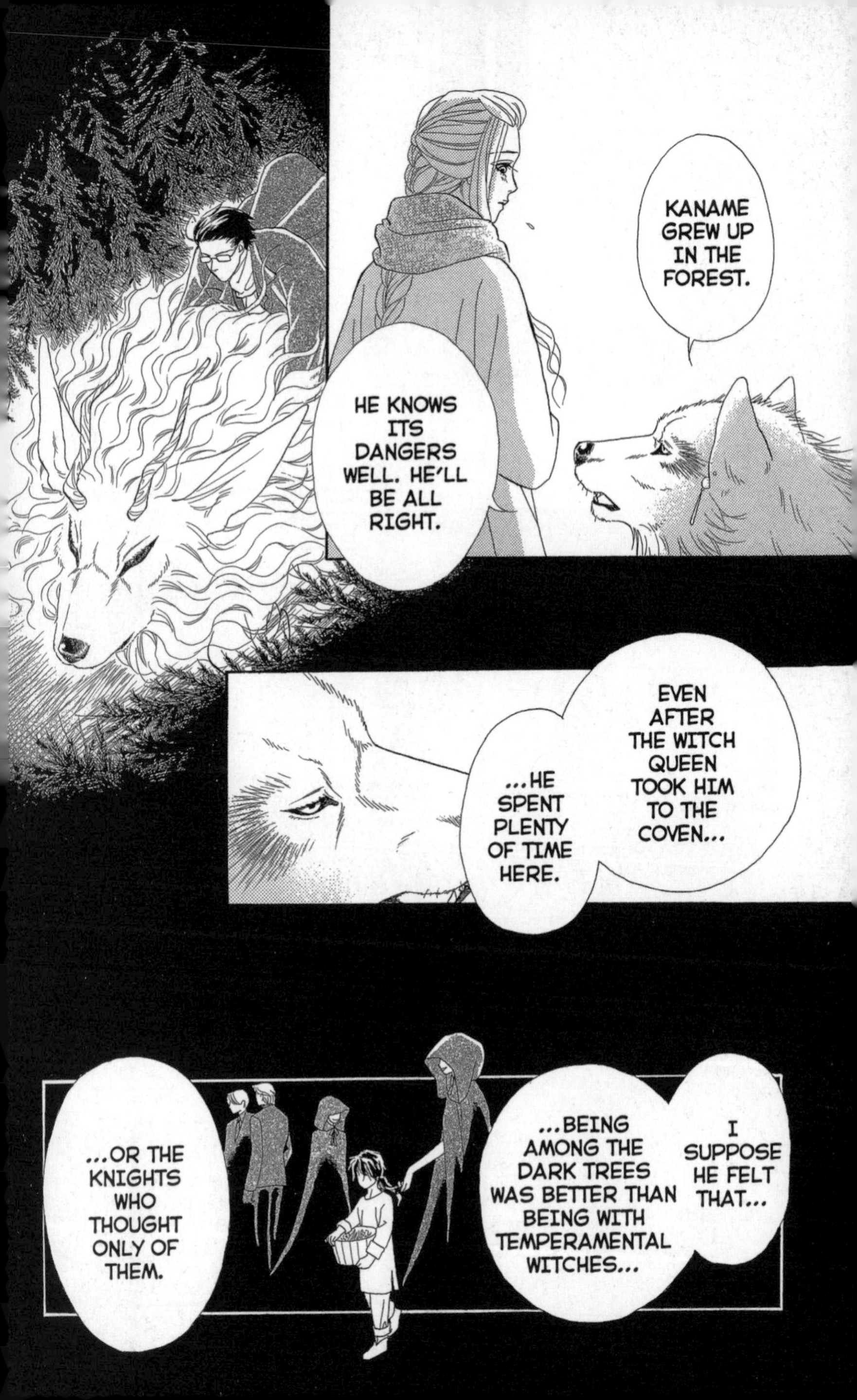
KANAME GREW UP IN THE FOREST.
HE KNOWS ITS DANGERS WELL. HE'LL BE ALL RIGHT.
EVEN AFTER THE WITCH QUEEN TOOK HIM TO THE COVEN...
...HE SPENT PLENTY OF TIME HERE.
I SUPPOSE HE FELT THAT...
...BEING AMONG THE DARK TREES WAS BETTER THAN BEING WITH TEMPERAMENTAL WITCHES...
...OR THE KNIGHTS WHO THOUGHT ONLY OF THEM.

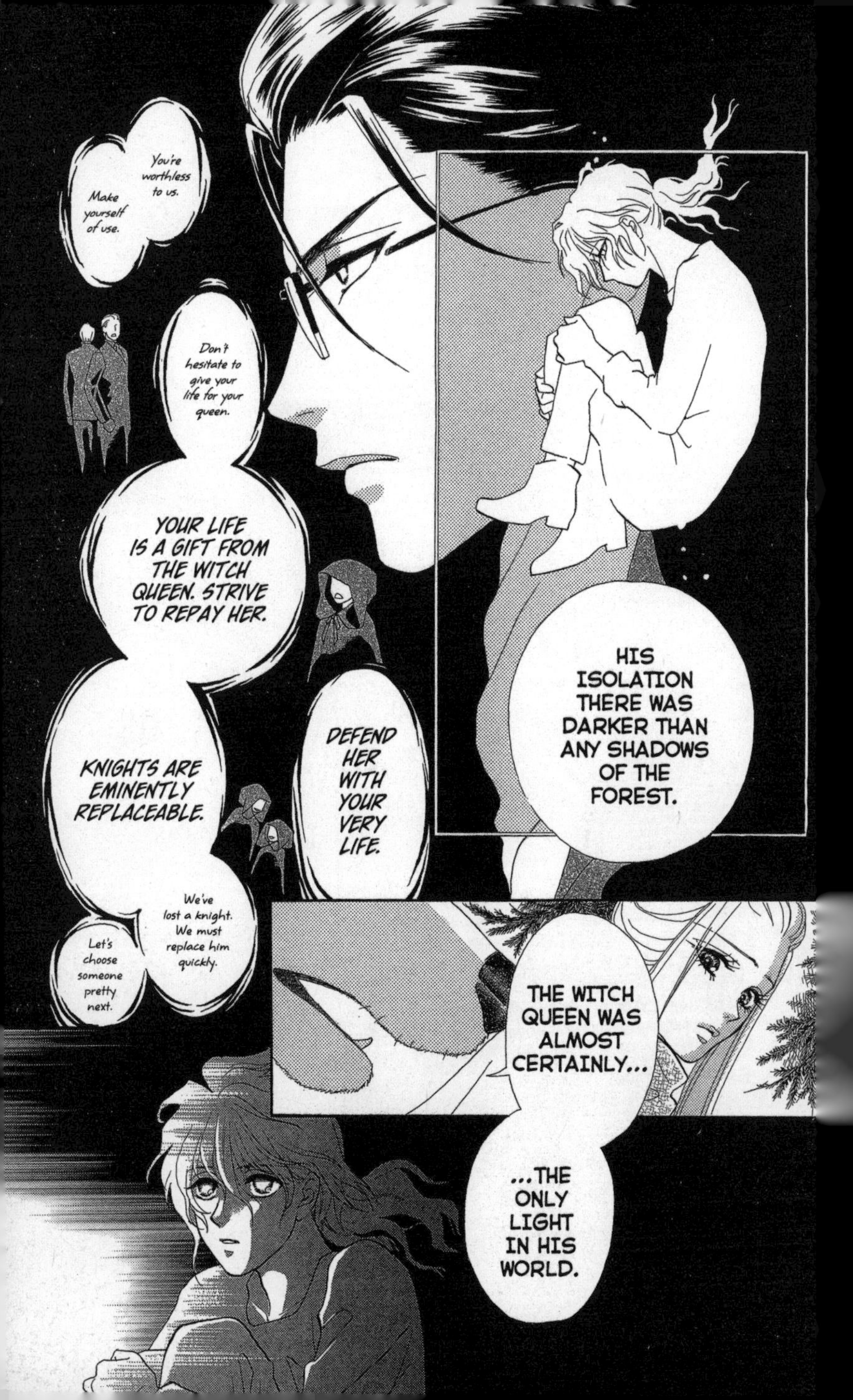
HIS ISOLATION THERE WAS DARKER THAN ANY SHADOWS OF THE FOREST.
You're worthless to us.
Make yourself of use.
Don't hesitate to give your life for your queen.
YOUR LIFE IS A GIFT FROM THE WITCH QUEEN. STRIVE TO REPAY HER.
DEFEND HER WITH YOUR VERY LIFE.
KNIGHTS ARE EMINENTLY REPLACEABLE.
We've lost a knight. We must replace him quickly.
Let's choose someone pretty next.
THE WITCH QUEEN WAS ALMOST CERTAINLY...
...THE ONLY LIGHT IN HIS WORLD.

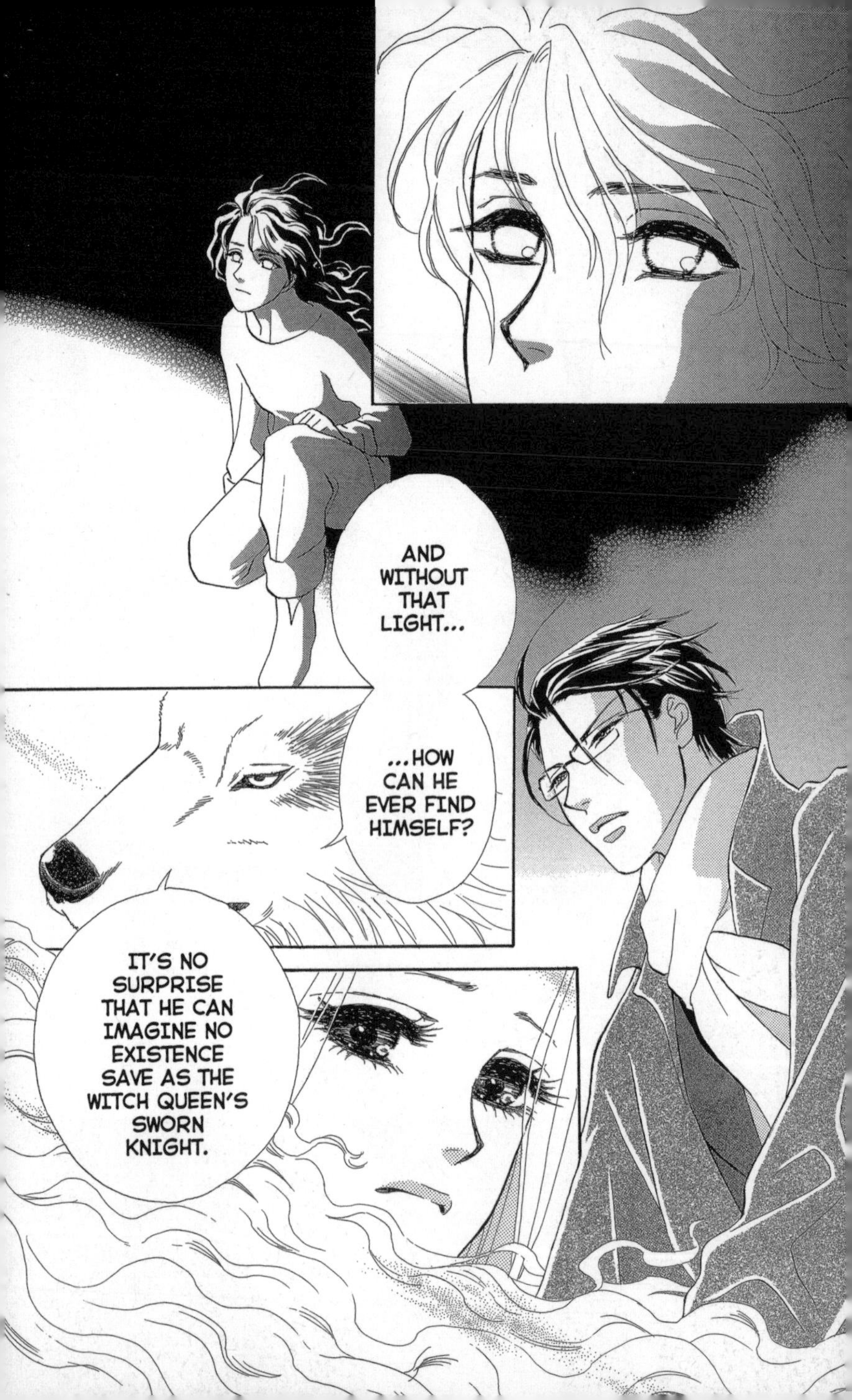
AND WITHOUT THAT LIGHT...
...HOW CAN HE EVER FIND HIMSELF?
IT'S NO SURPRISE THAT HE CAN IMAGINE NO EXISTENCE SAVE AS THE WITCH QUEEN'S SWORN KNIGHT.

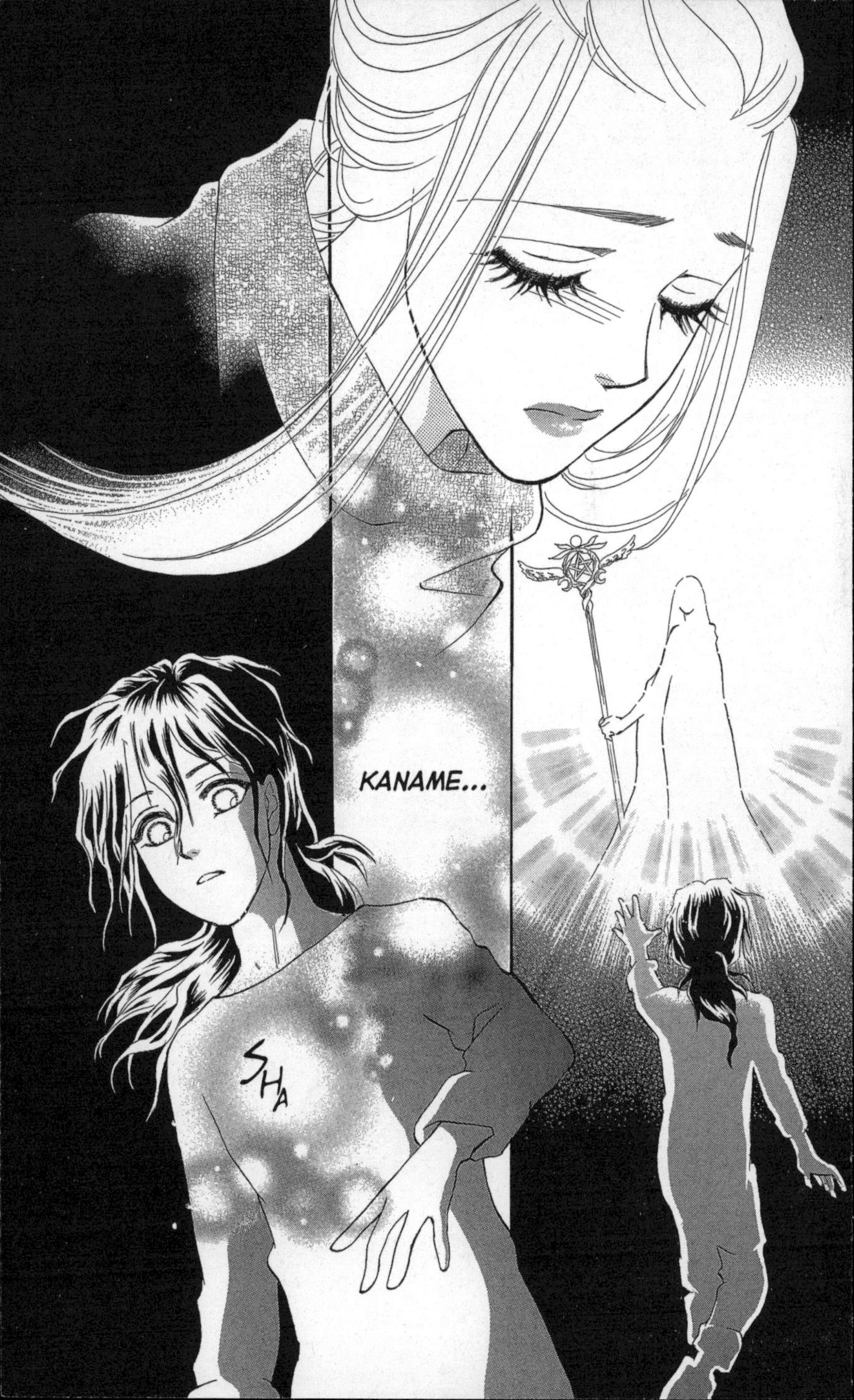
KANAME...
SHA

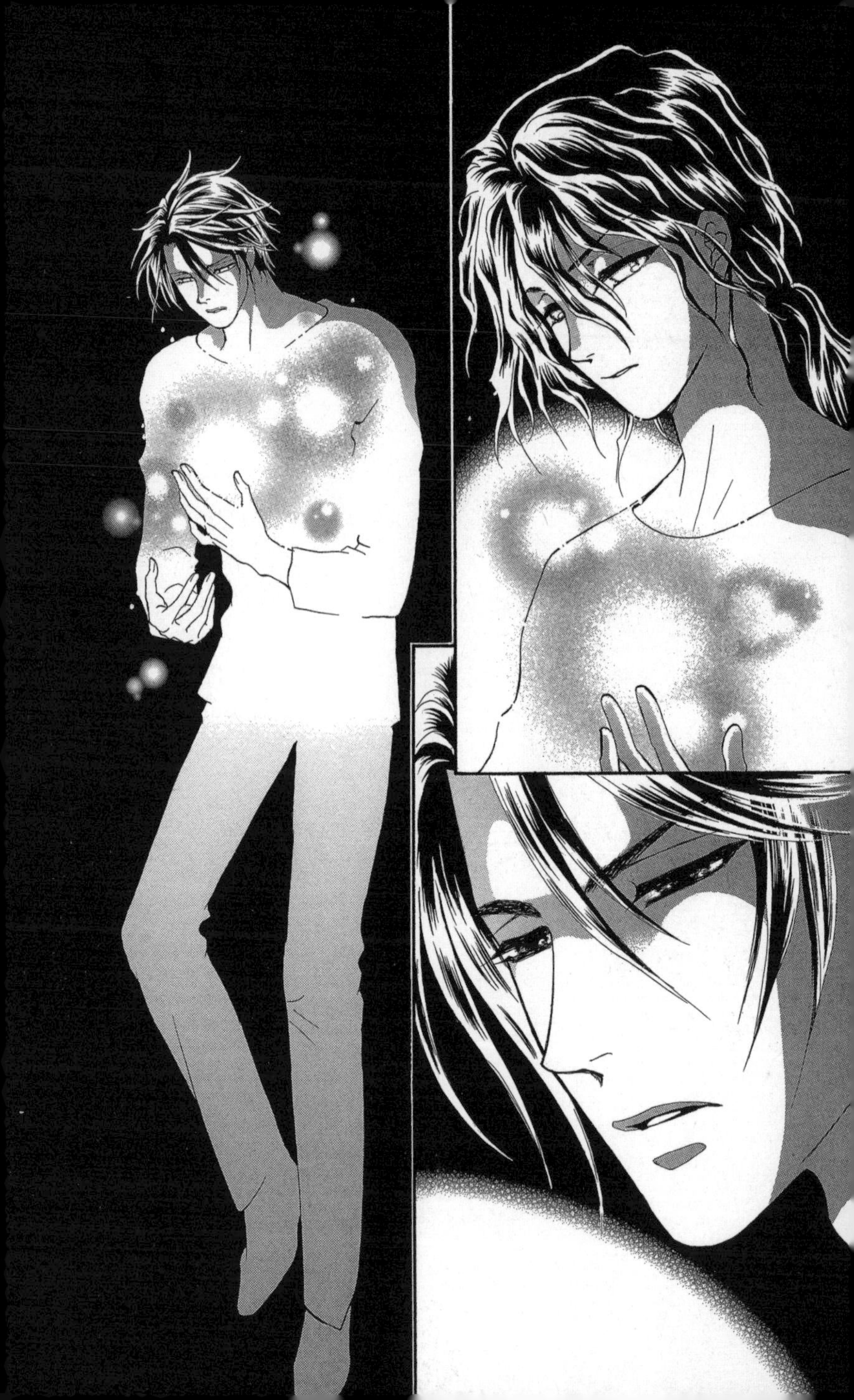

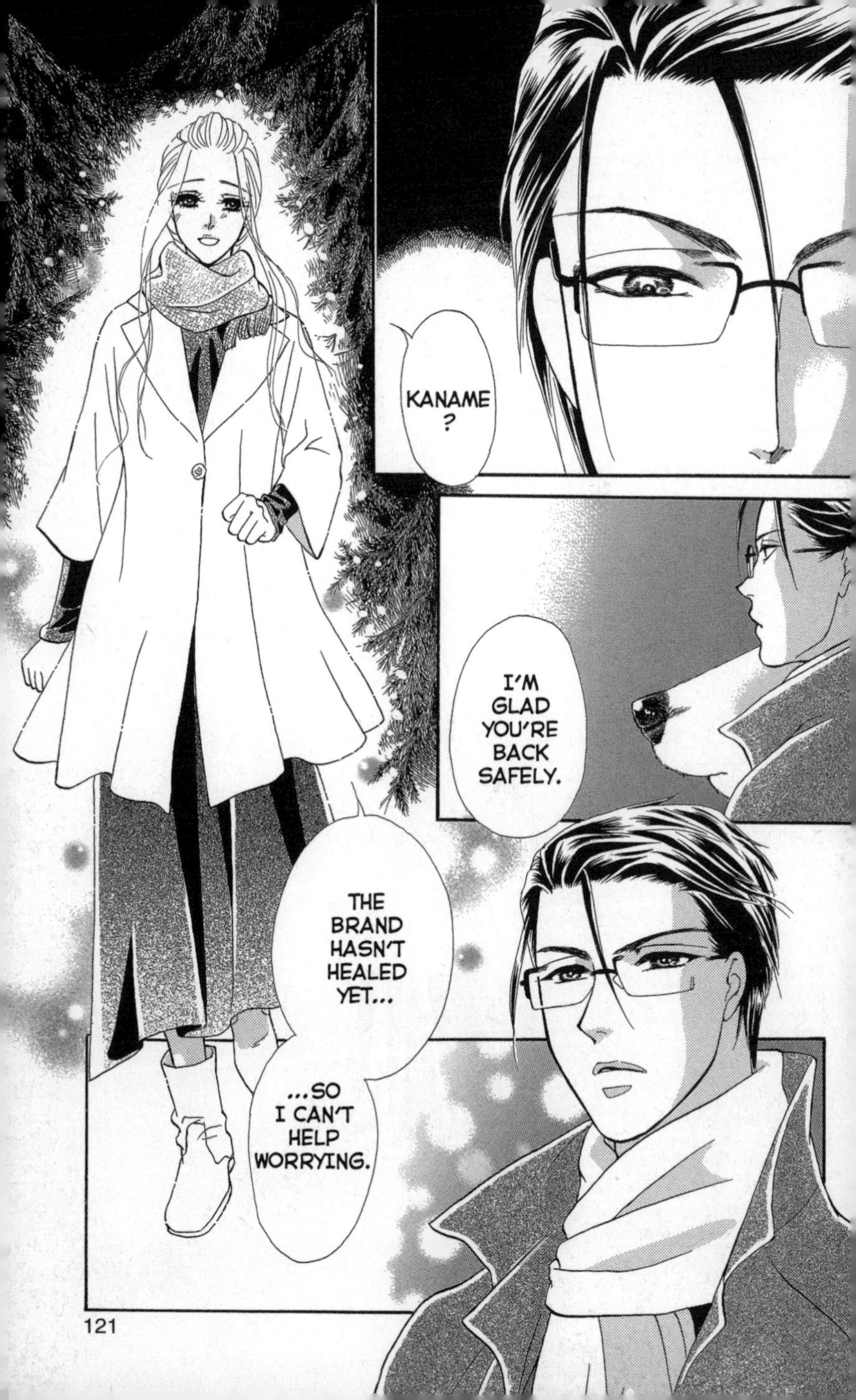
KANAME?
I'M GLAD YOU'RE BACK SAFELY.
THE BRAND HASN'T HEALED YET...
...SO I CAN'T HELP WORRYING.

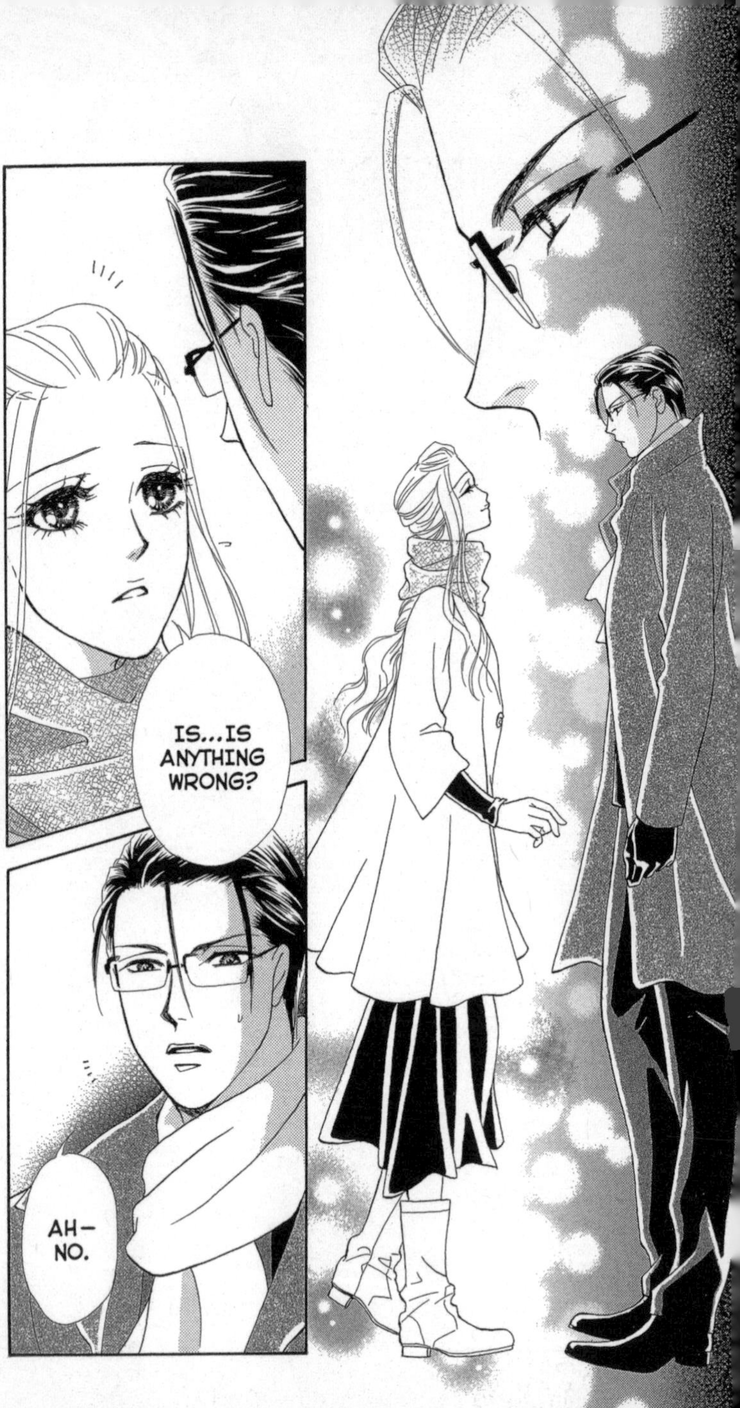
IS...IS ANYTHING WRONG?
AH— NO.

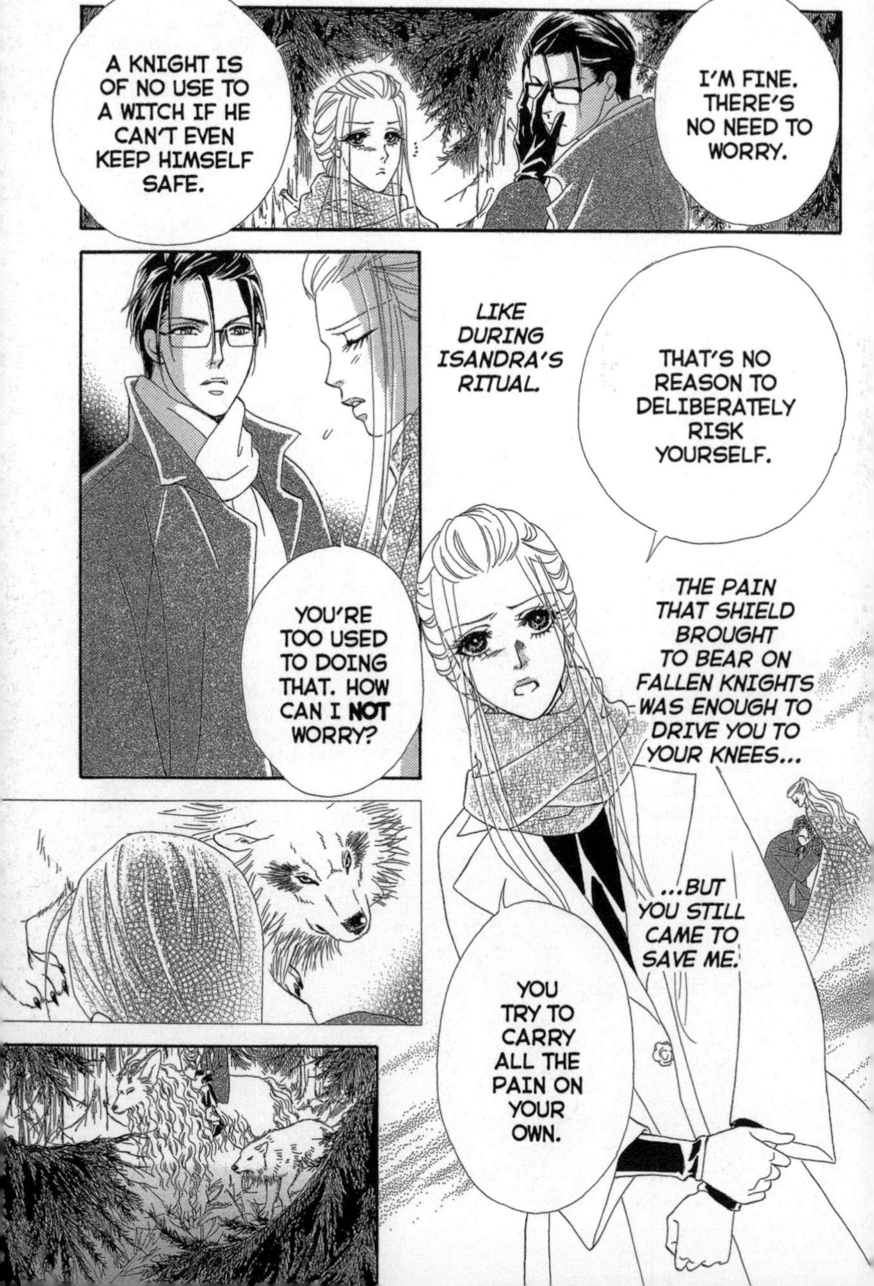
I'M FINE. THERE'S NO NEED TO WORRY.
A KNIGHT IS OF NO USE TO A WITCH IF HE CAN'T EVEN KEEP HIMSELF SAFE.
THAT'S NO REASON TO DELIBERATELY RISK YOURSELF.
LIKE DURING ISANDRA'S RITUAL.
THE PAIN THAT SHIELD BROUGHT TO BEAR ON FALLEN KNIGHTS WAS ENOUGH TO DRIVE YOU TO YOUR KNEES...
...BUT YOU STILL CAME TO SAVE ME.
YOU'RE TOO USED TO DOING THAT. HOW CAN I **NOT** WORRY?
YOU TRY TO CARRY ALL THE PAIN ON YOUR OWN.

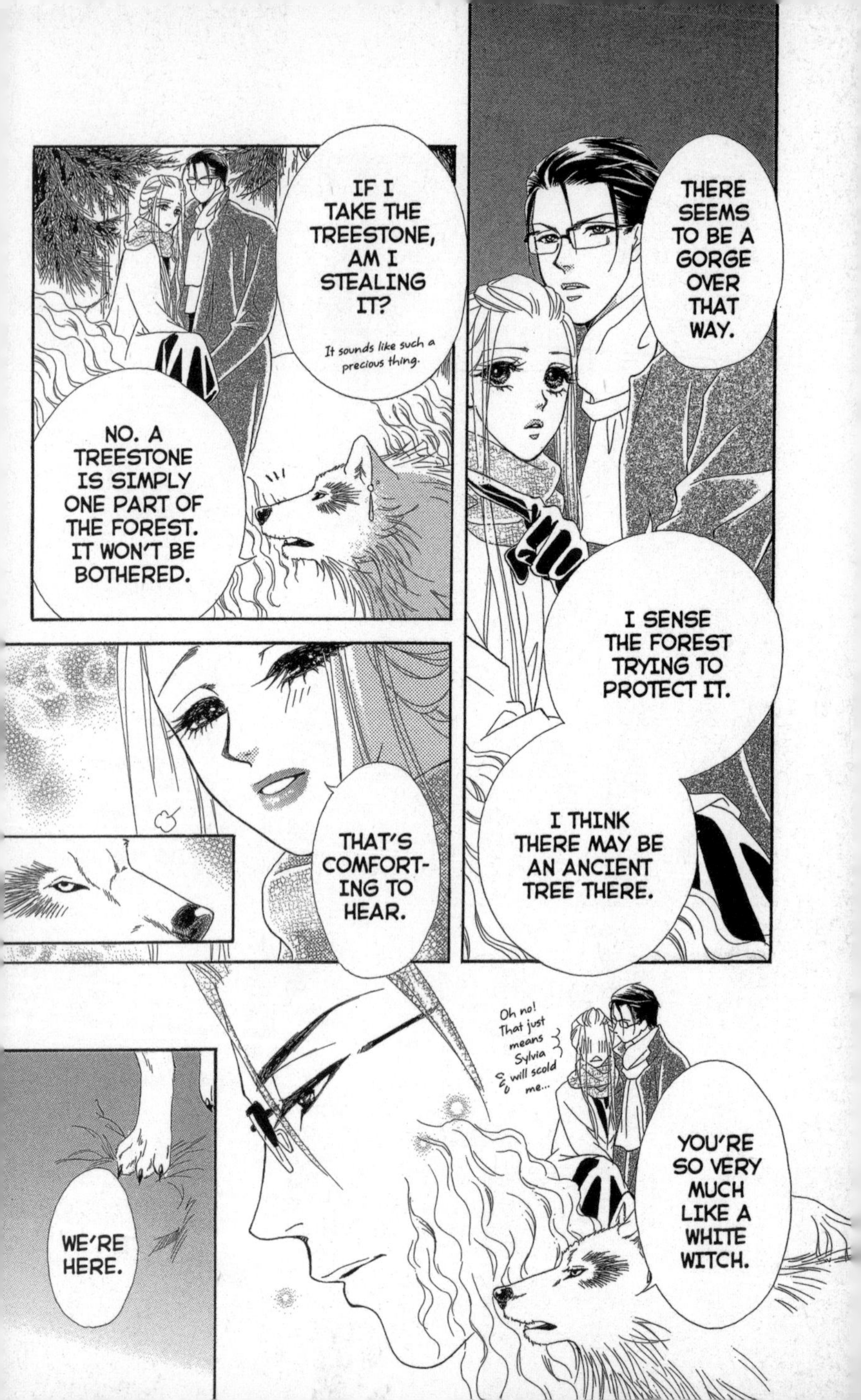
THERE SEEMS TO BE A GORGE OVER THAT WAY.
I SENSE THE FOREST TRYING TO PROTECT IT.
I THINK THERE MAY BE AN ANCIENT TREE THERE.
IF I TAKE THE TREESTONE, AM I STEALING IT?
It sounds like such a precious thing.
NO. A TREESTONE IS SIMPLY ONE PART OF THE FOREST. IT WON'T BE BOTHERED.
THAT'S COMFORT-ING TO HEAR.
Oh no! That just means Sylvia will scold me...
YOU'RE SO VERY MUCH LIKE A WHITE WITCH.
WE'RE HERE.

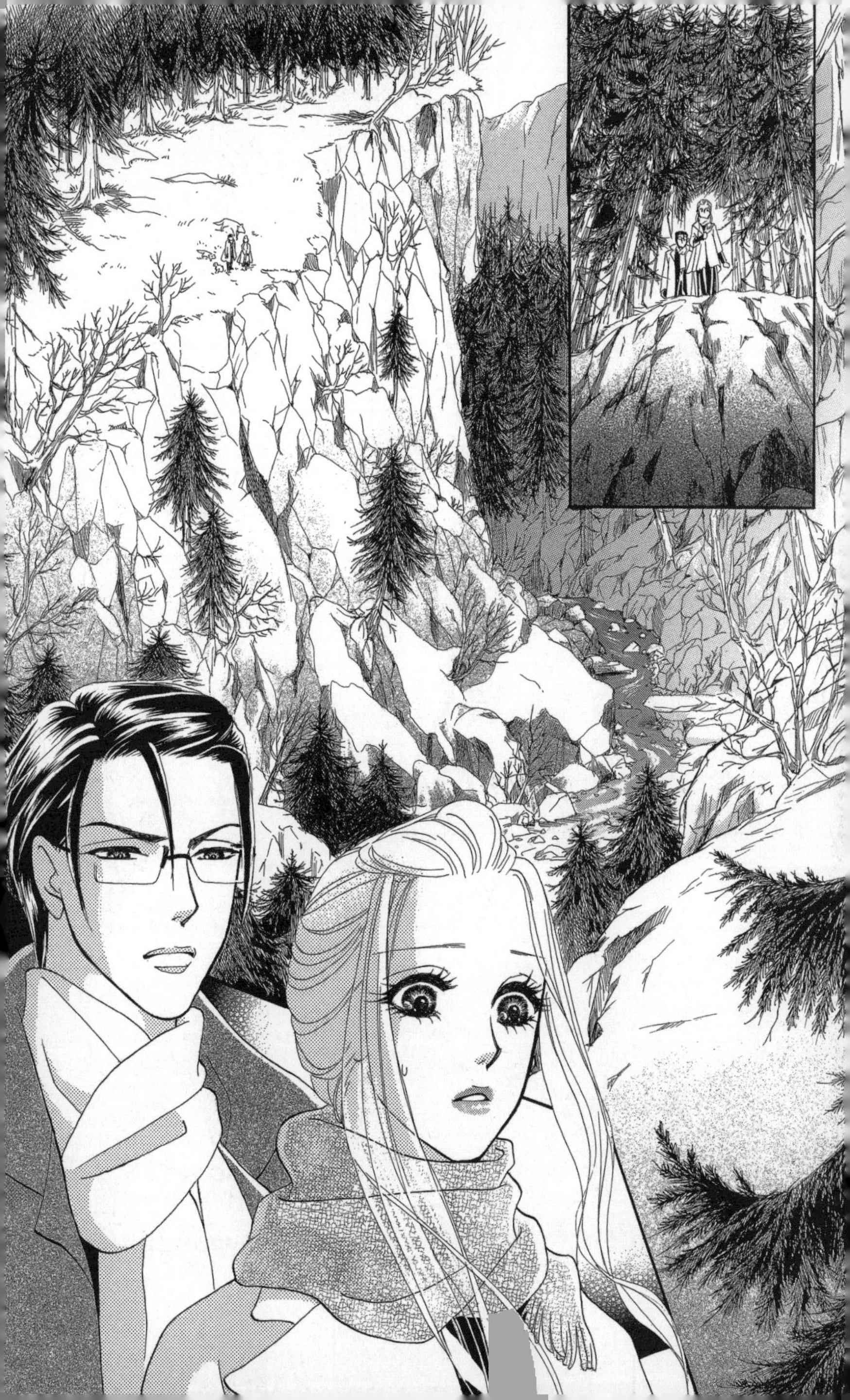

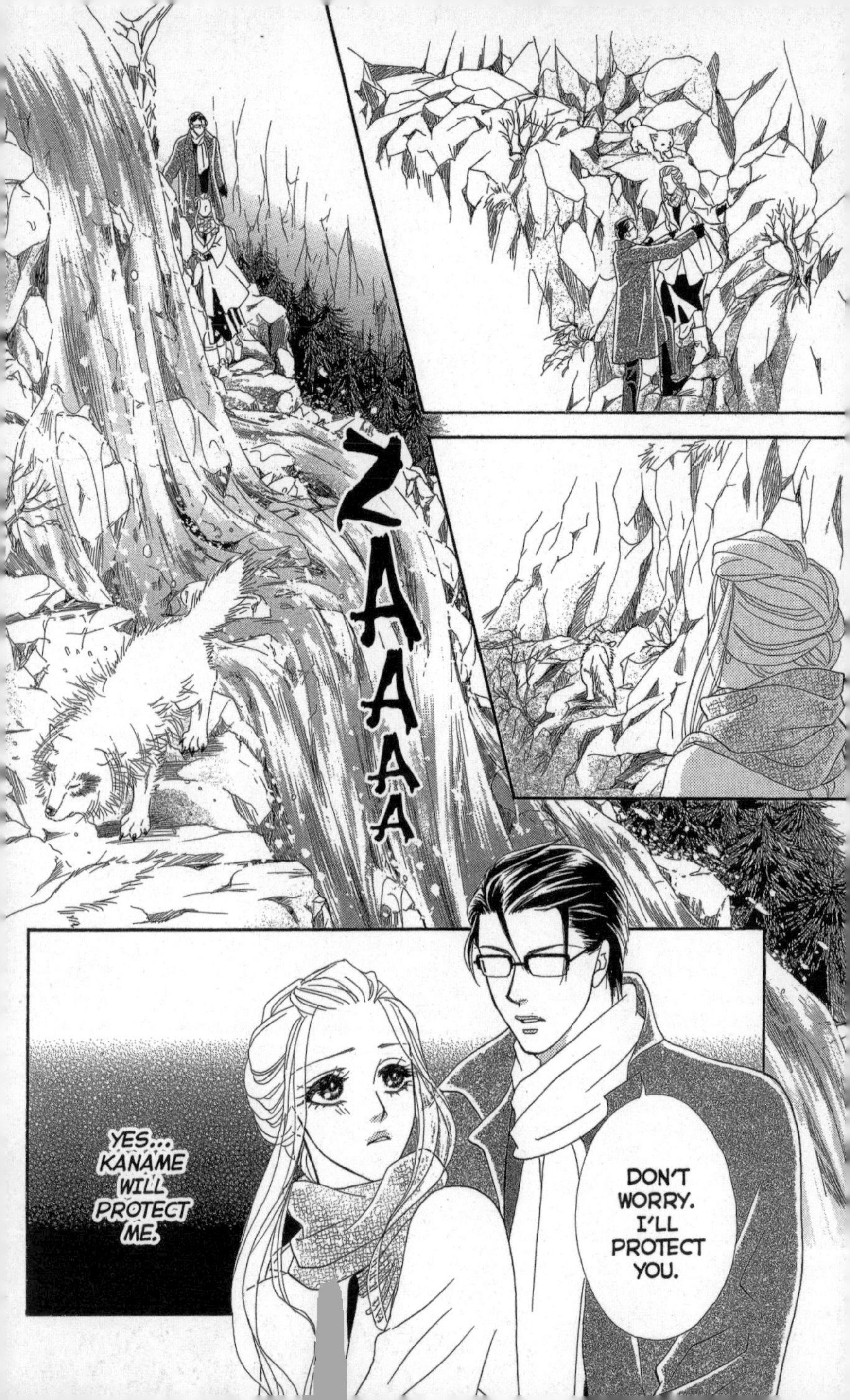
ZAAAA
DON'T WORRY. I'LL PROTECT YOU.
YES... KANAME WILL PROTECT ME.

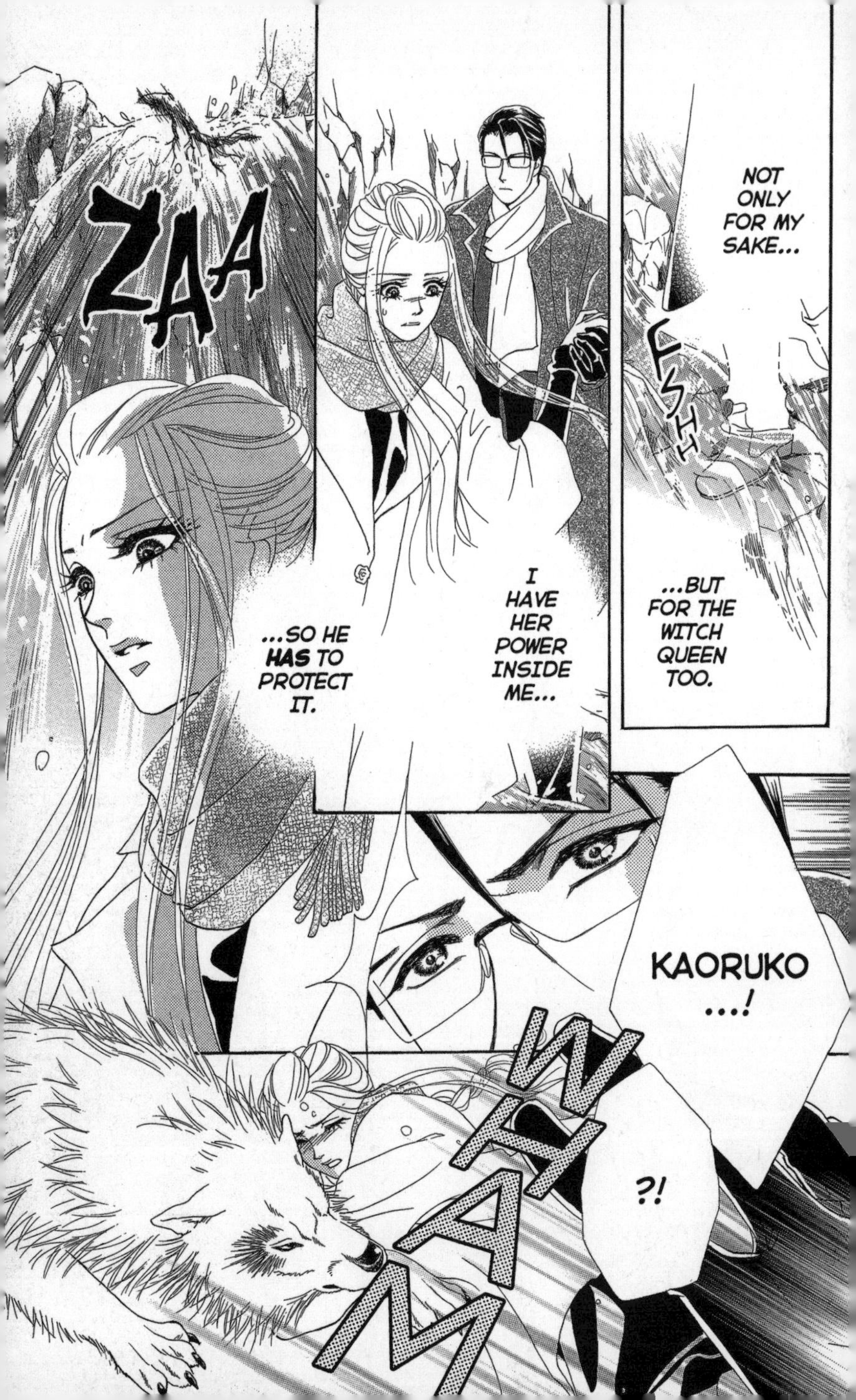
NOT ONLY FOR MY SAKE...
FSHH
...BUT FOR THE WITCH QUEEN TOO.
I HAVE HER POWER INSIDE ME...
...SO HE **HAS** TO PROTECT IT.
ZAA
KAORUKO ...!
WHAM
?!

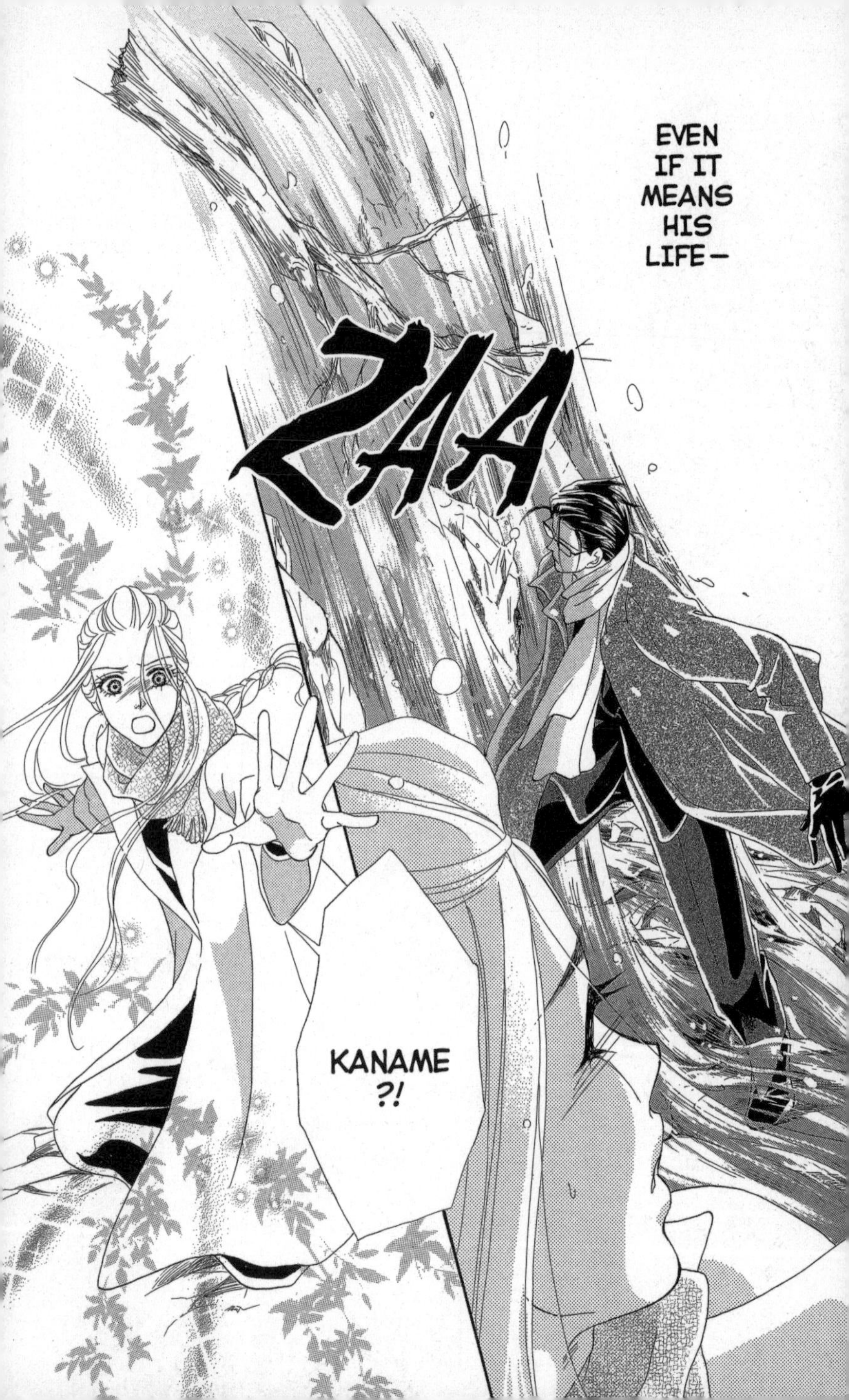
EVEN IF IT MEANS HIS LIFE—
ZAA
KANAME ?!

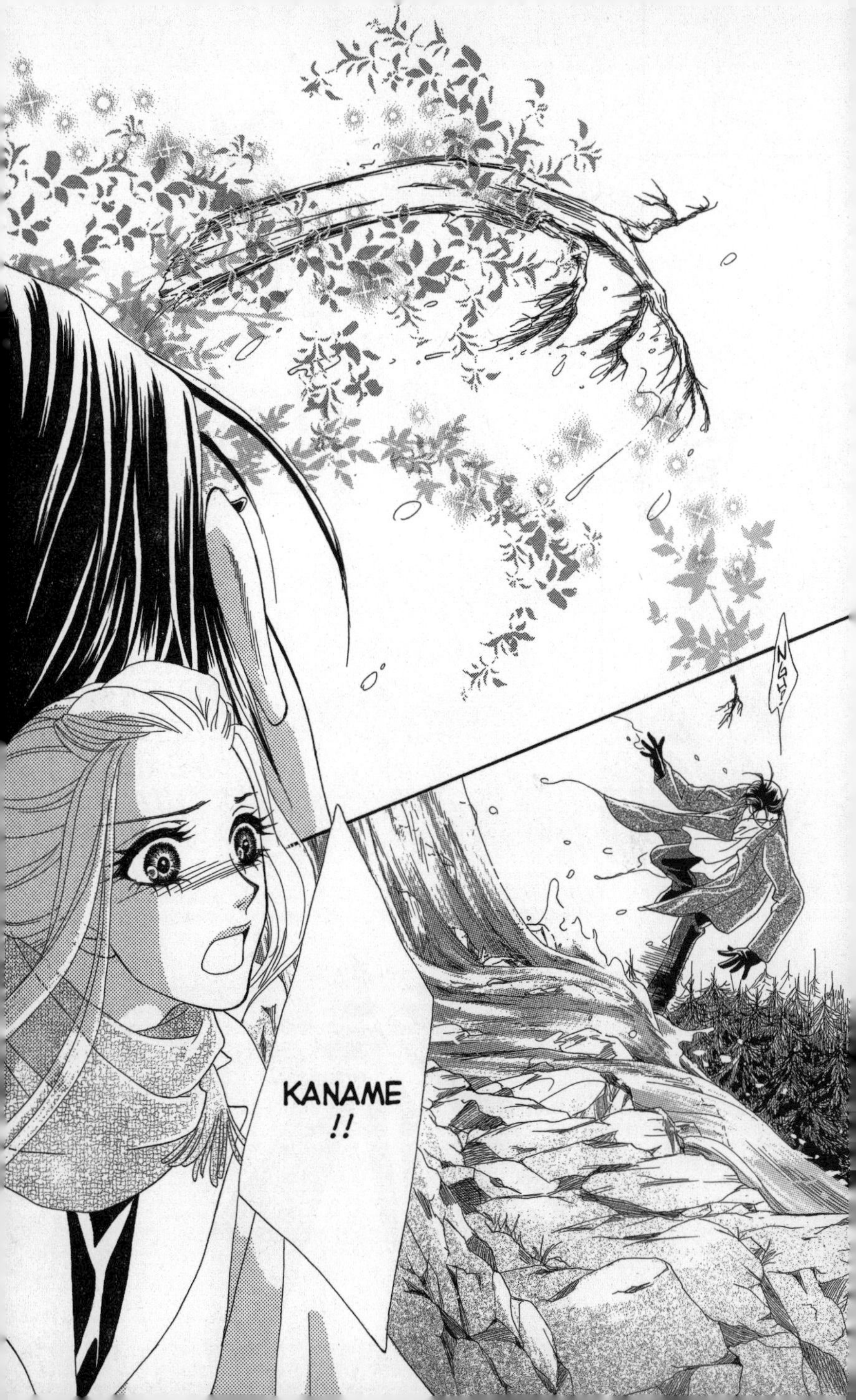
NGH!
KANAME
!!

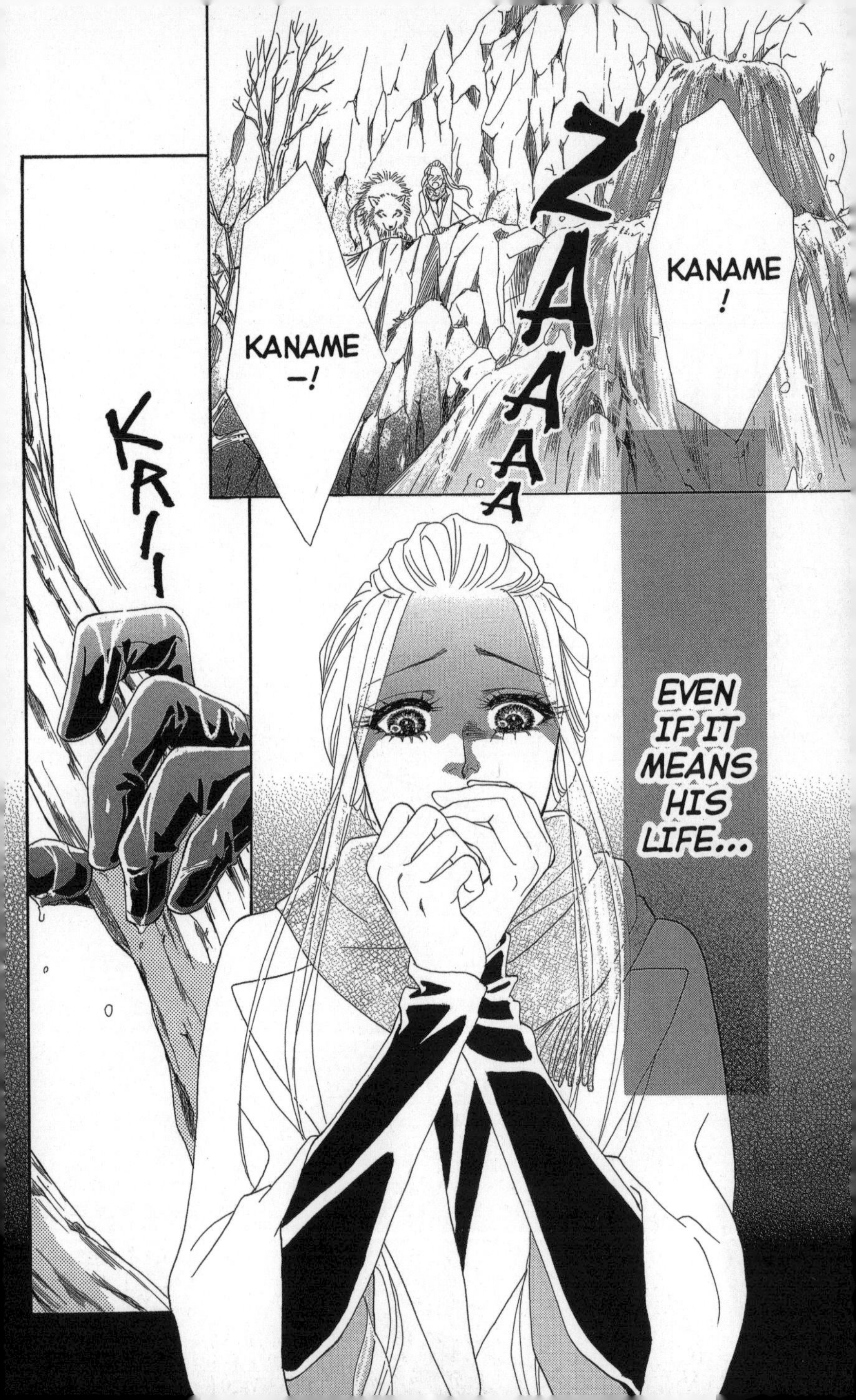
KANAME!
ZAAAAA
KANAME—!
EVEN IF IT MEANS HIS LIFE...
KRII

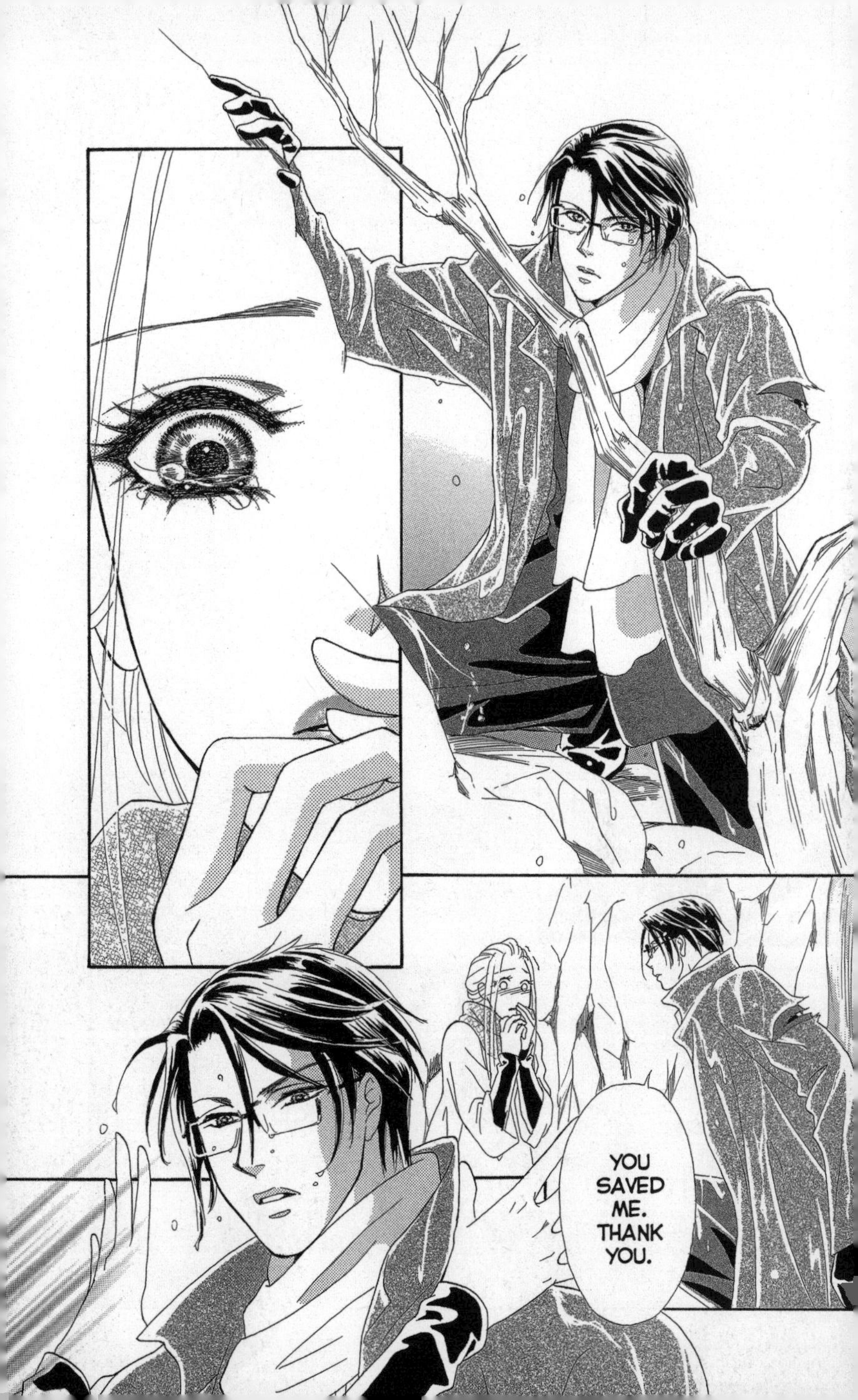
YOU SAVED ME. THANK YOU.

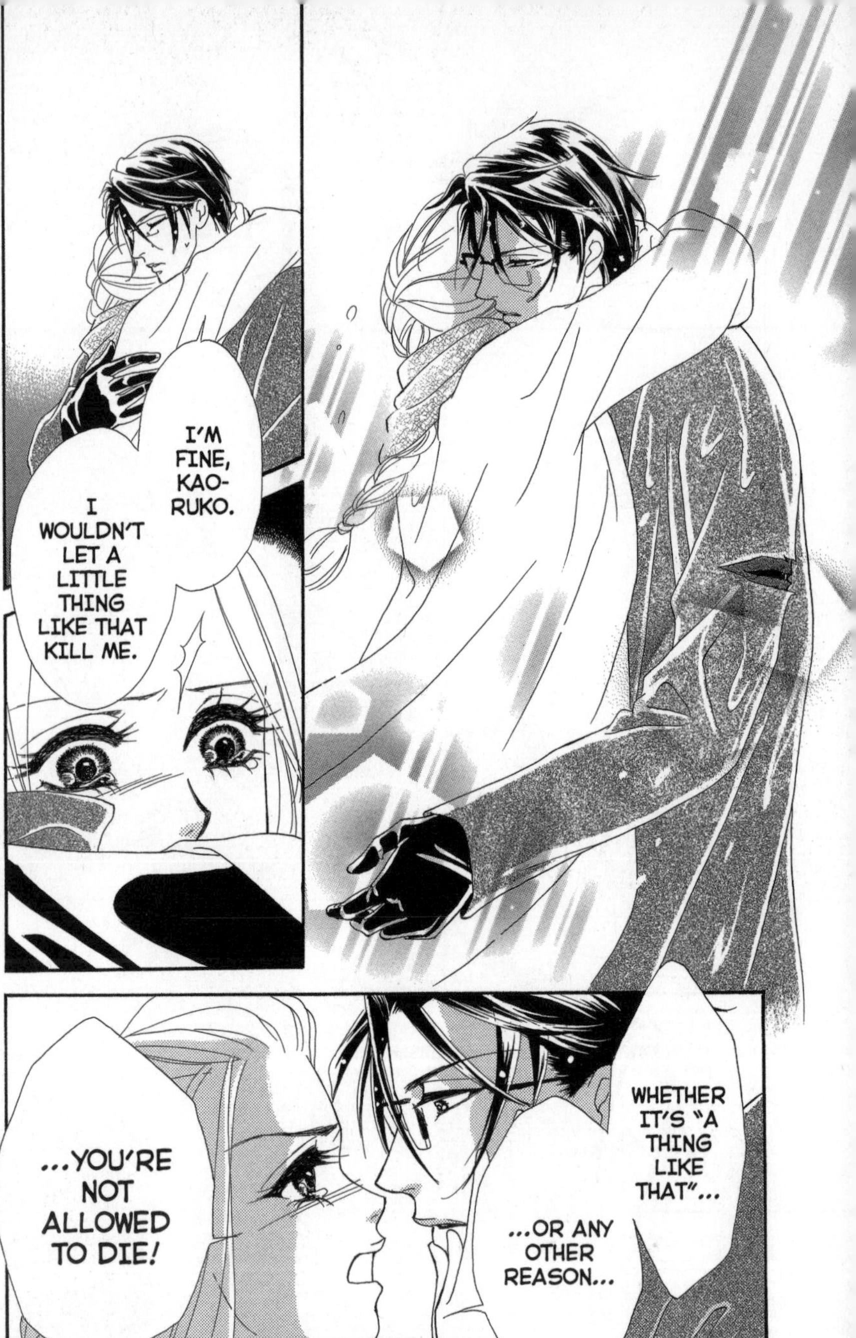
I'M FINE, KAO-RUKO.
I WOULDN'T LET A LITTLE THING LIKE THAT KILL ME.
WHETHER IT'S "A THING LIKE THAT"...
...OR ANY OTHER REASON...
...YOU'RE NOT ALLOWED TO DIE!

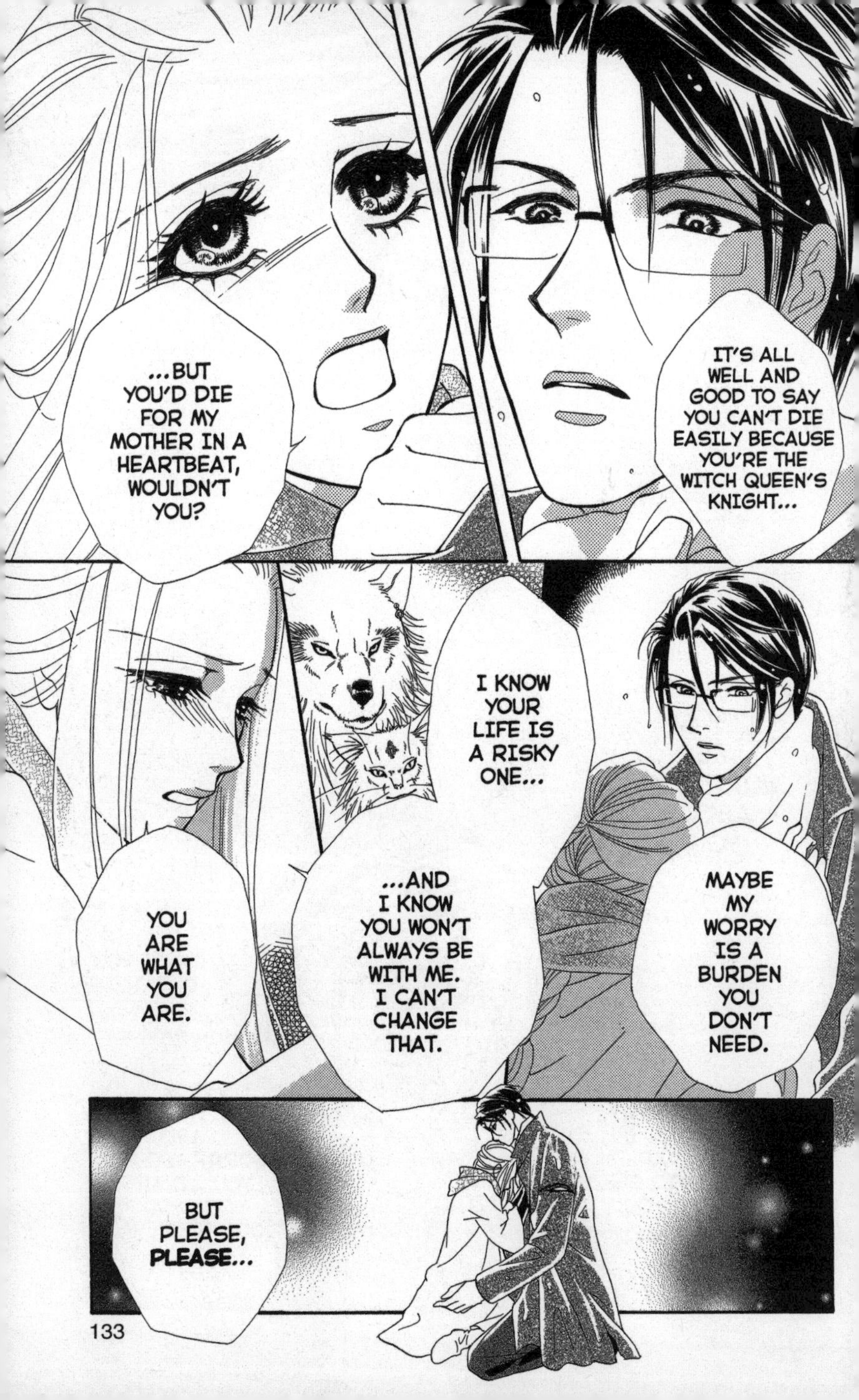
IT'S ALL WELL AND GOOD TO SAY YOU CAN'T DIE EASILY BECAUSE YOU'RE THE WITCH QUEEN'S KNIGHT...
...BUT YOU'D DIE FOR MY MOTHER IN A HEARTBEAT, WOULDN'T YOU?
I KNOW YOUR LIFE IS A RISKY ONE...
...AND I KNOW YOU WON'T ALWAYS BE WITH ME. I CAN'T CHANGE THAT.
MAYBE MY WORRY IS A BURDEN YOU DON'T NEED.
YOU ARE WHAT YOU ARE.
BUT PLEASE, **PLEASE...**

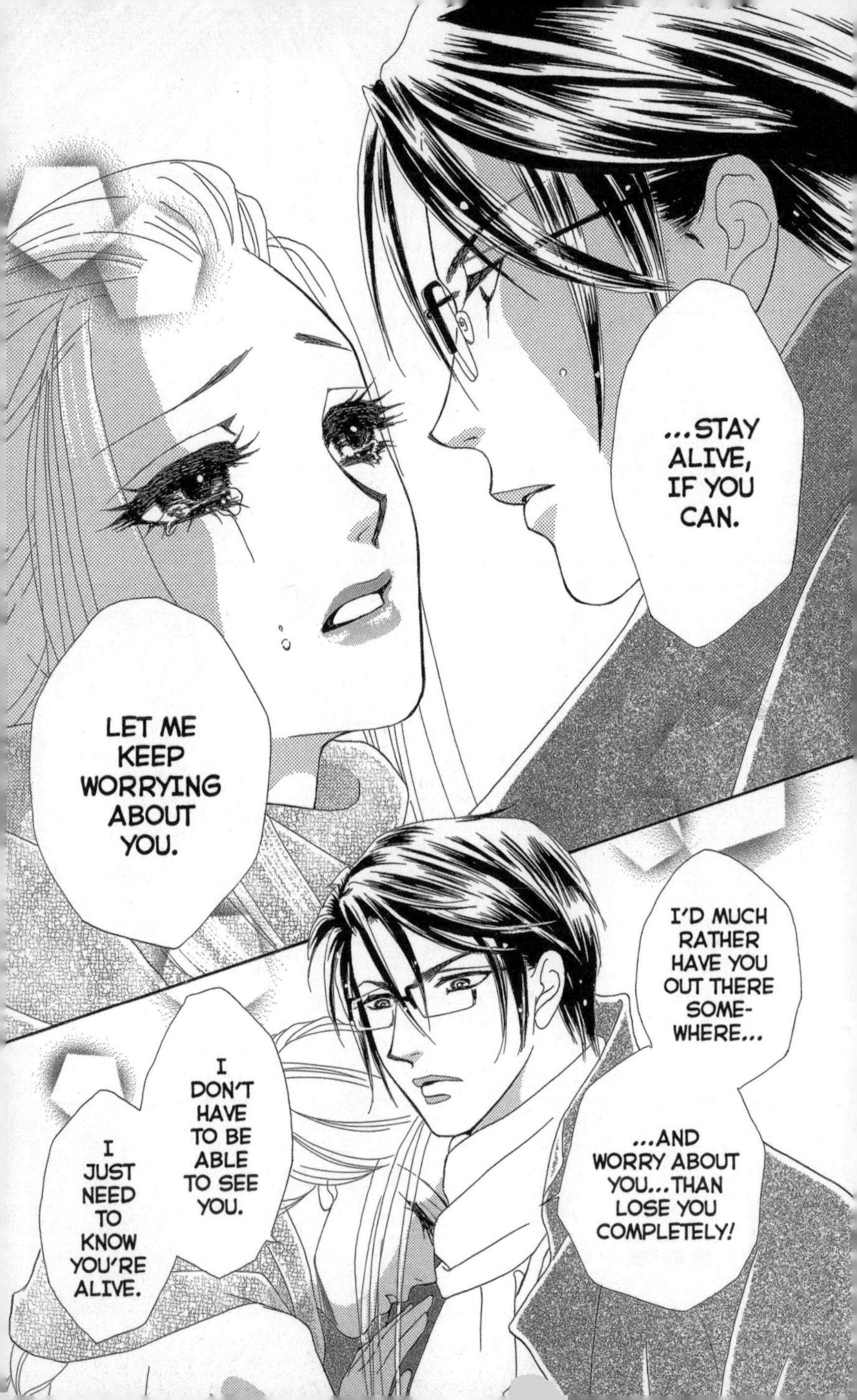
...STAY ALIVE, IF YOU CAN.
LET ME KEEP WORRYING ABOUT YOU.
I'D MUCH RATHER HAVE YOU OUT THERE SOME-WHERE...
...AND WORRY ABOUT YOU...THAN LOSE YOU COMPLETELY!
I DON'T HAVE TO BE ABLE TO SEE YOU.
I JUST NEED TO KNOW YOU'RE ALIVE.

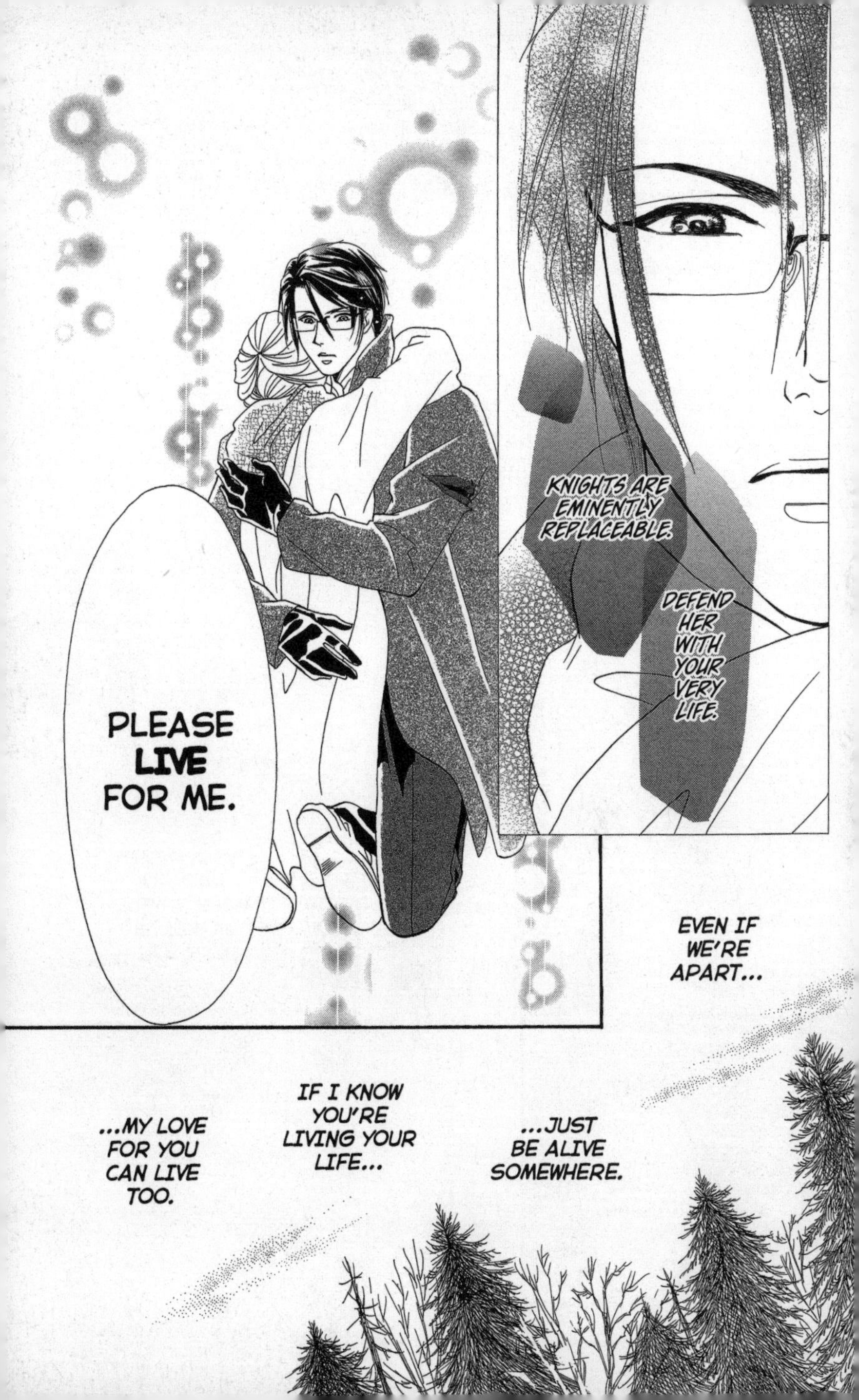
KNIGHTS ARE EMINENTLY REPLACEABLE.
DEFEND HER WITH YOUR VERY LIFE.
PLEASE **LIVE** FOR ME.
EVEN IF WE'RE APART...
...JUST BE ALIVE SOMEWHERE.
IF I KNOW YOU'RE LIVING YOUR LIFE...
...MY LOVE FOR YOU CAN LIVE TOO.

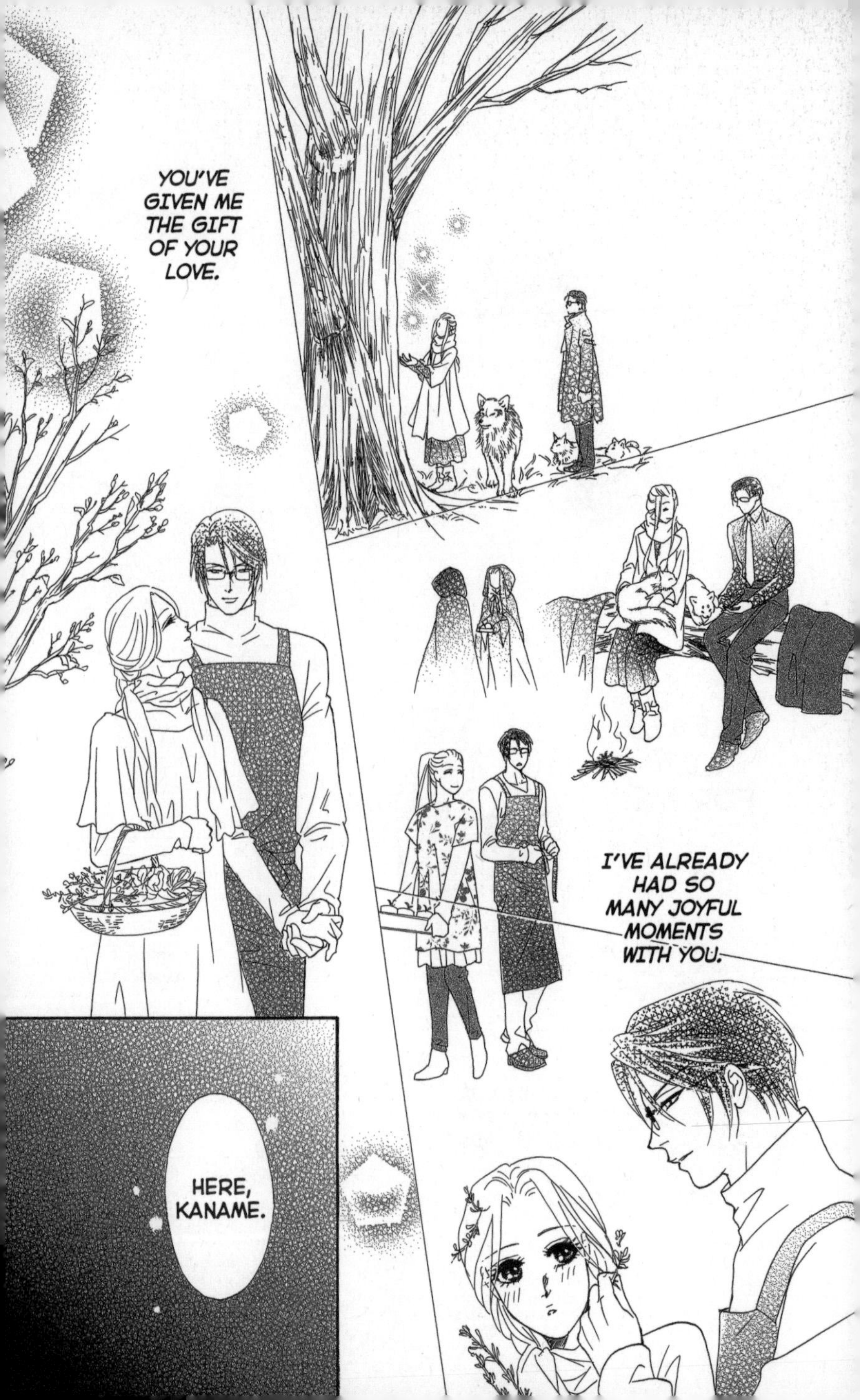
I'VE ALREADY HAD SO MANY JOYFUL MOMENTS WITH YOU.
YOU'VE GIVEN ME THE GIFT OF YOUR LOVE.
HERE, KANAME.

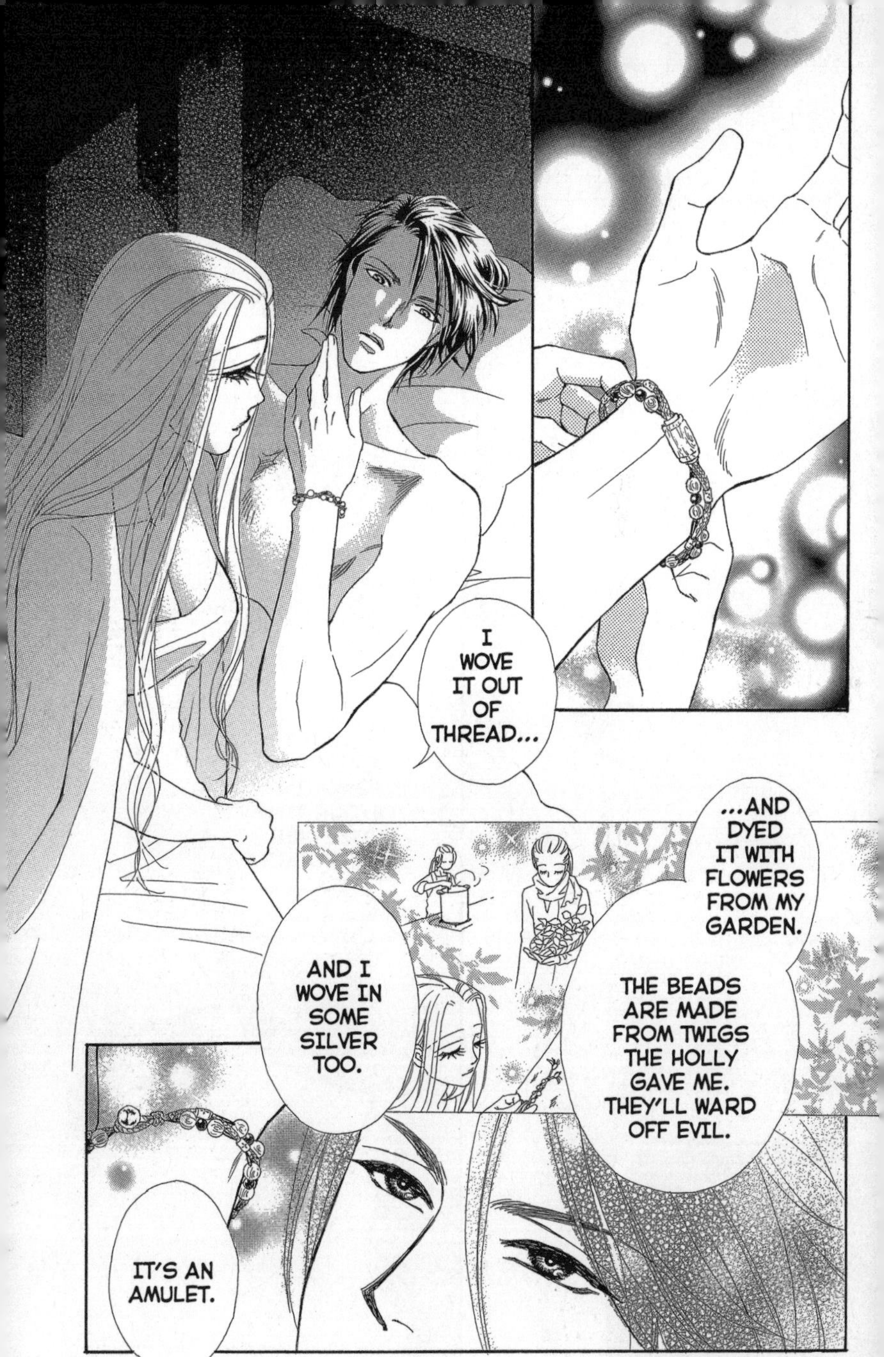
I WOVE IT OUT OF THREAD...
...AND DYED IT WITH FLOWERS FROM MY GARDEN.
THE BEADS ARE MADE FROM TWIGS THE HOLLY GAVE ME. THEY'LL WARD OFF EVIL.
AND I WOVE IN SOME SILVER TOO.
IT'S AN AMULET.

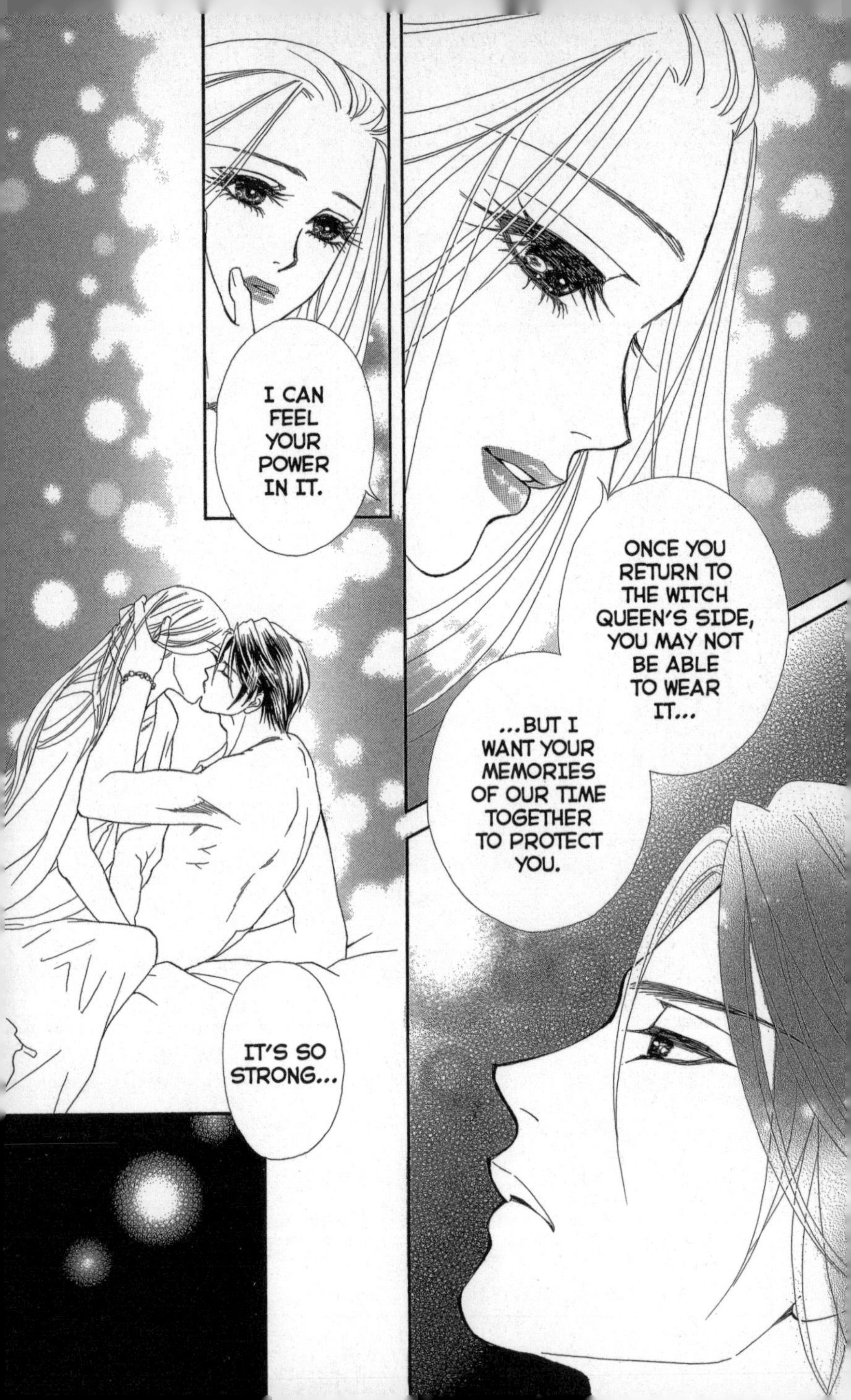
ONCE YOU RETURN TO THE WITCH QUEEN'S SIDE, YOU MAY NOT BE ABLE TO WEAR IT...
...BUT I WANT YOUR MEMORIES OF OUR TIME TOGETHER TO PROTECT YOU.
I CAN FEEL YOUR POWER IN IT.
IT'S SO STRONG...

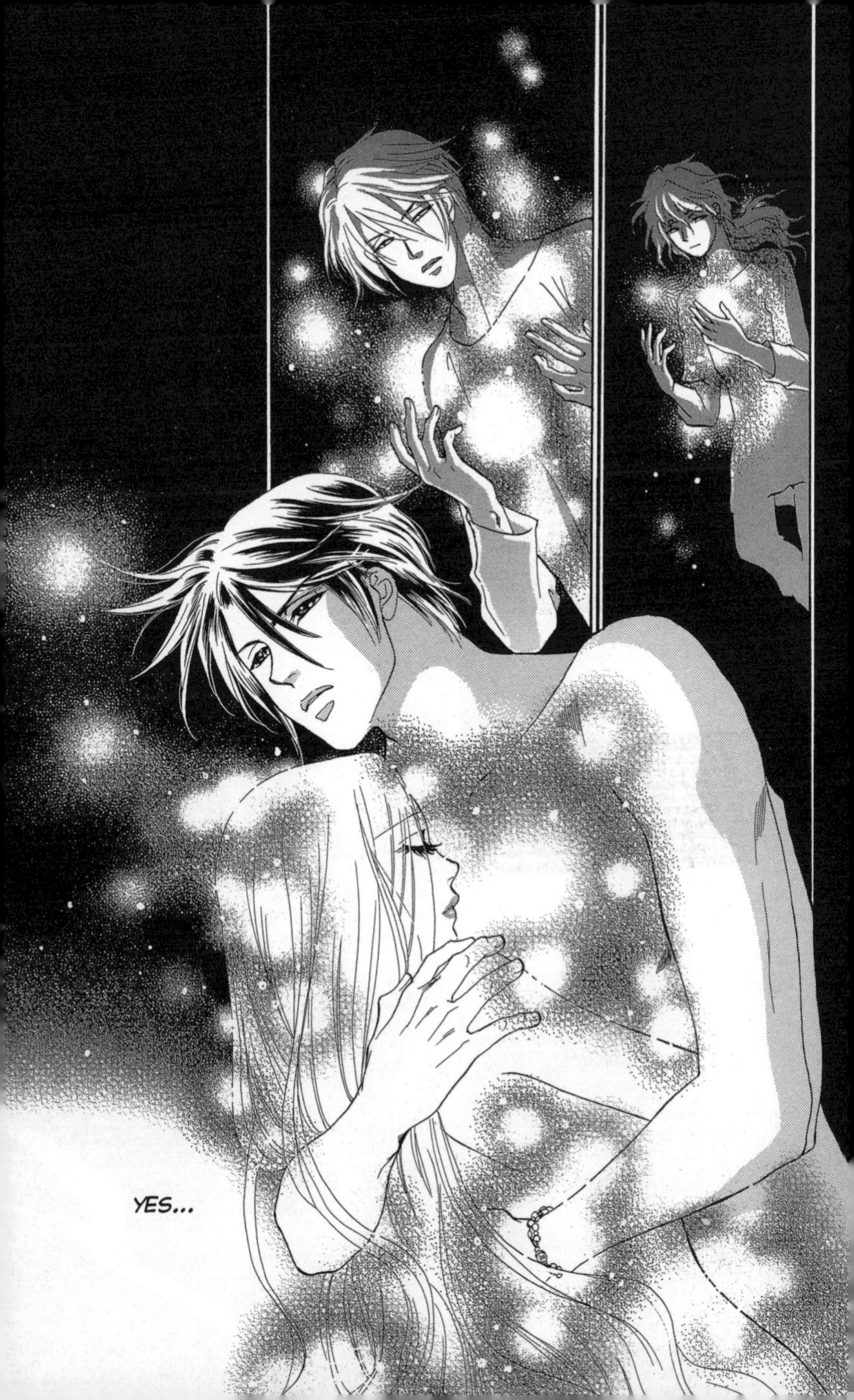
YES...

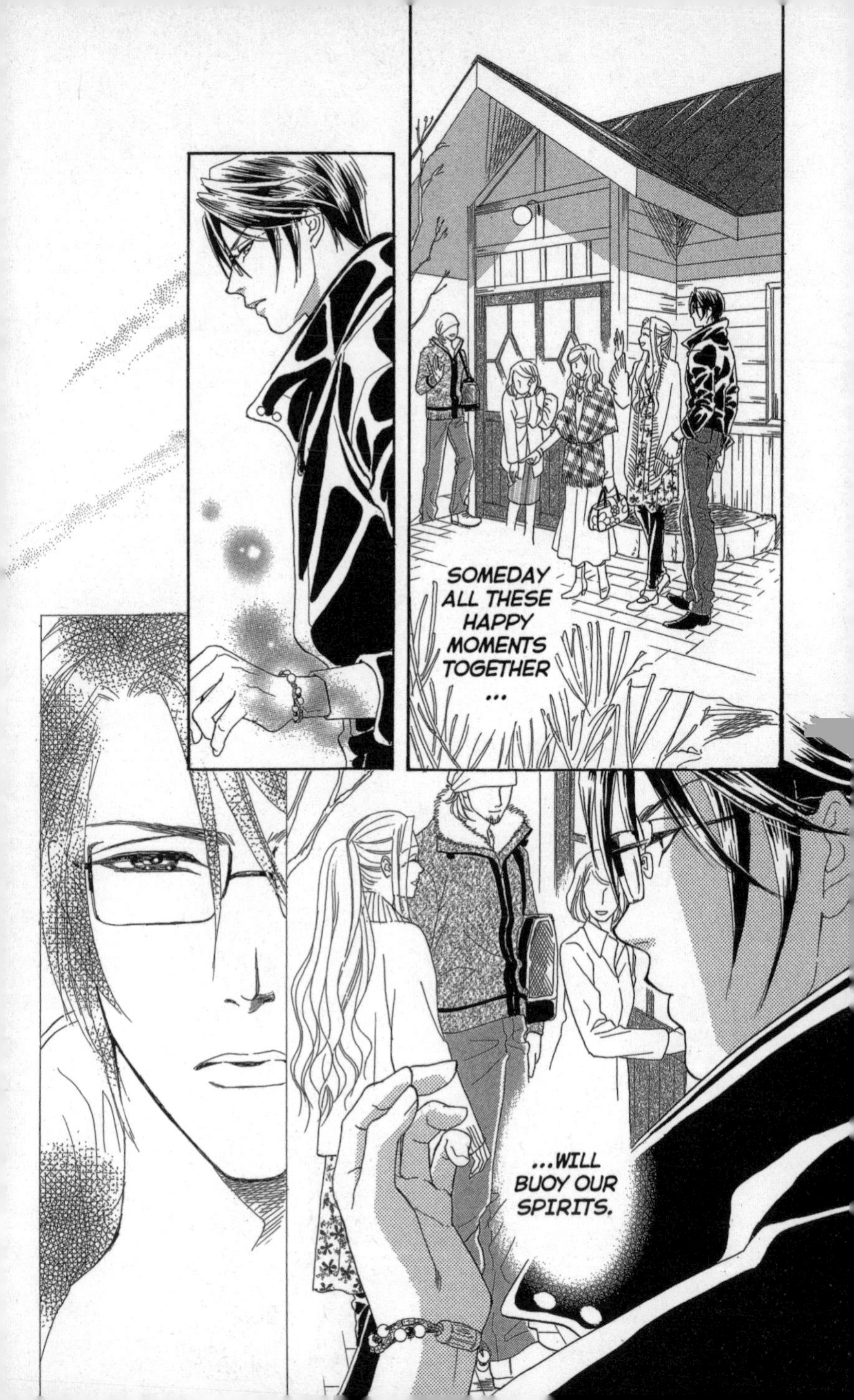
SOMEDAY ALL THESE HAPPY MOMENTS TOGETHER ...
...WILL BUOY OUR SPIRITS.

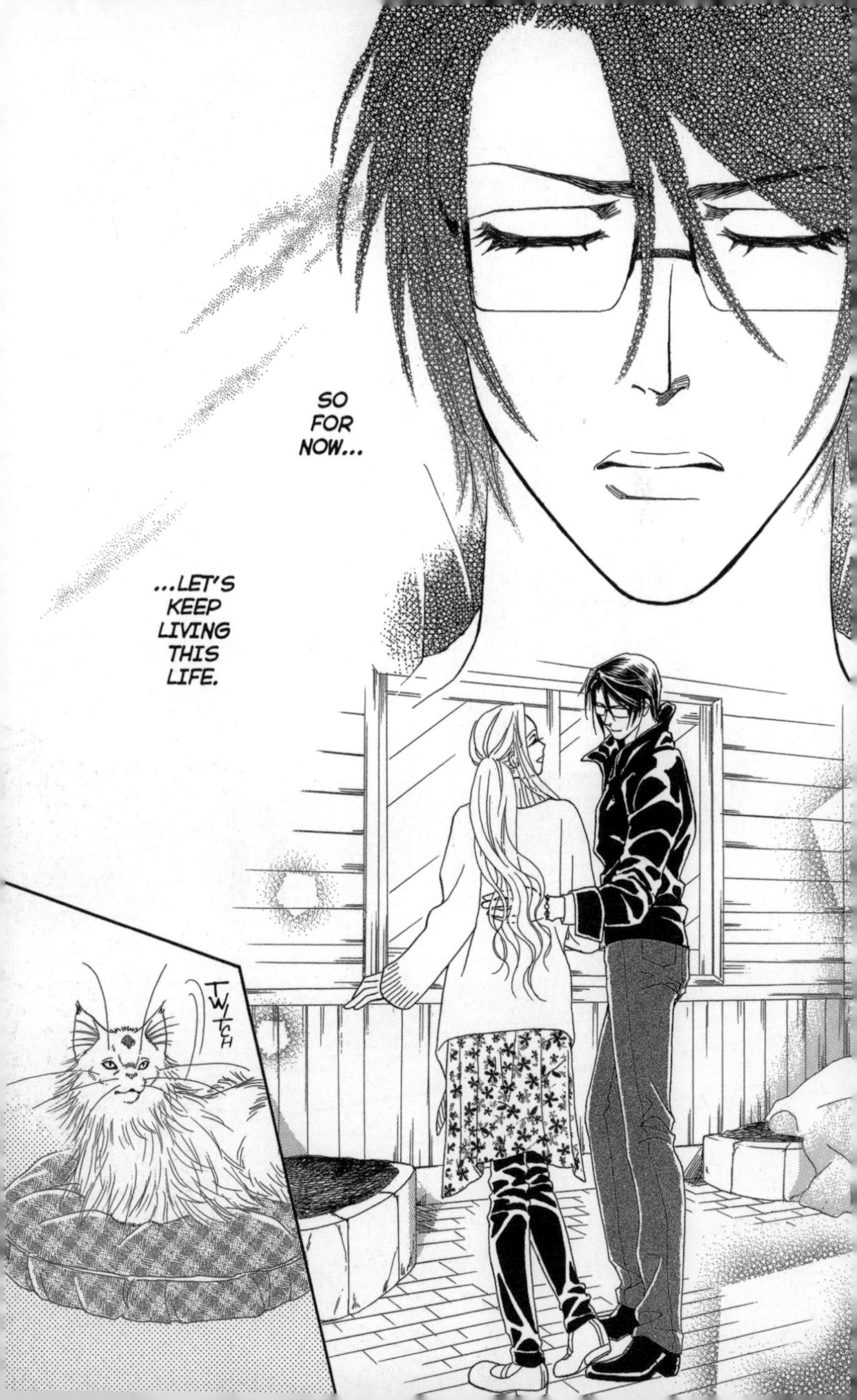
SO FOR NOW...
...LET'S KEEP LIVING THIS LIFE.
TWITCH

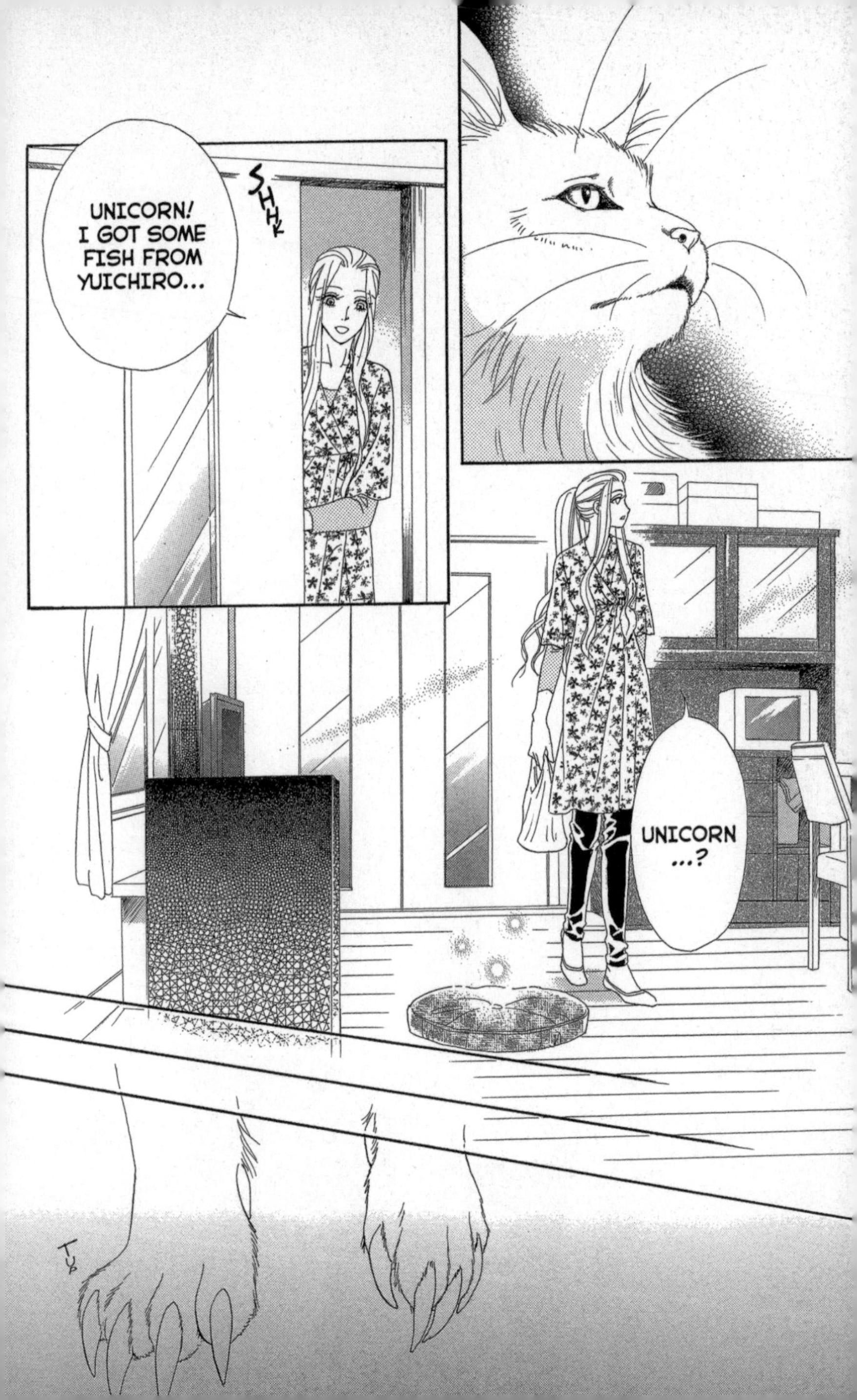
UNICORN! I GOT SOME FISH FROM YUICHIRO...
SHHK
UNICORN ...?
TUP

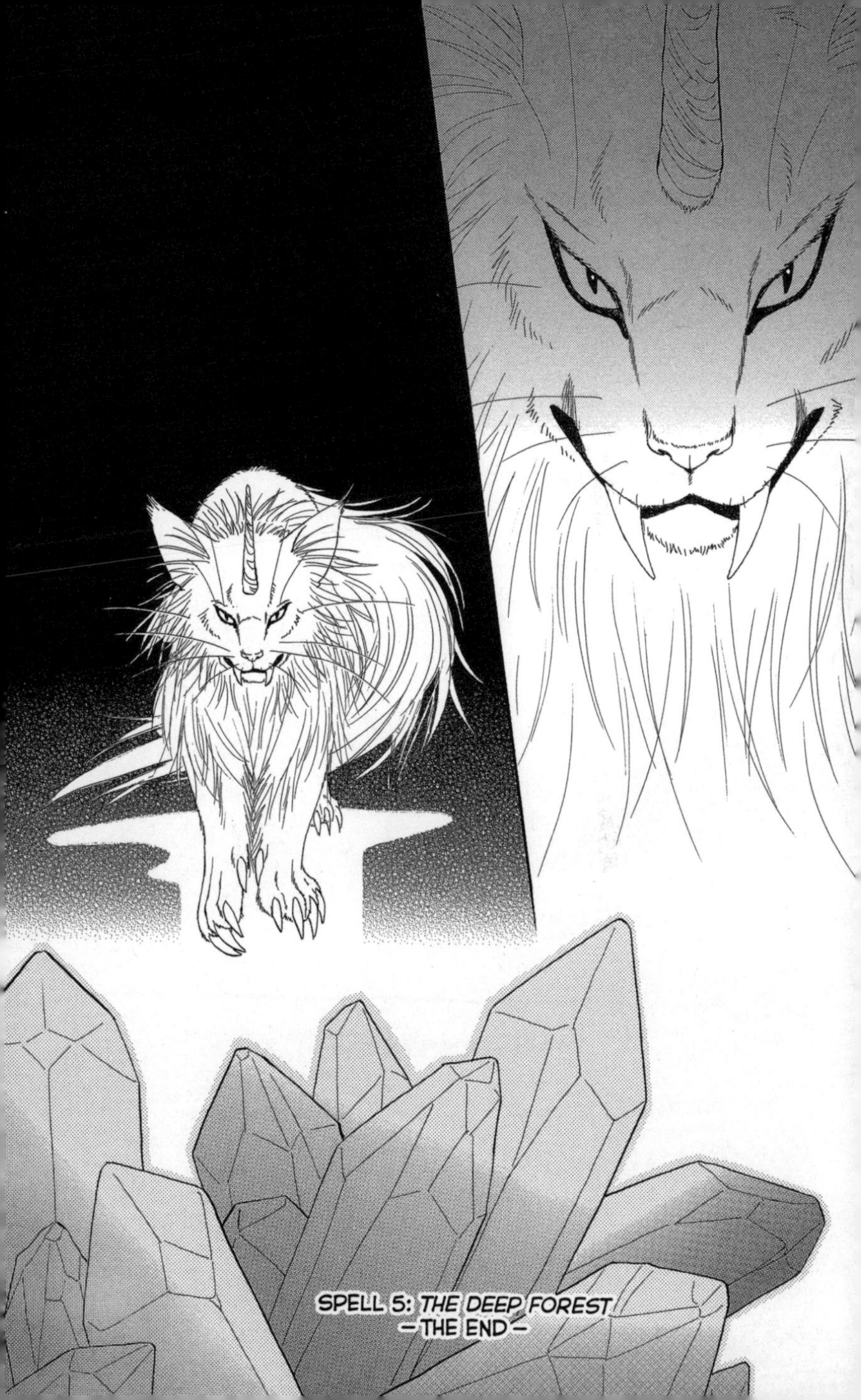
SPELL 5: THE DEEP FOREST
—THE END—

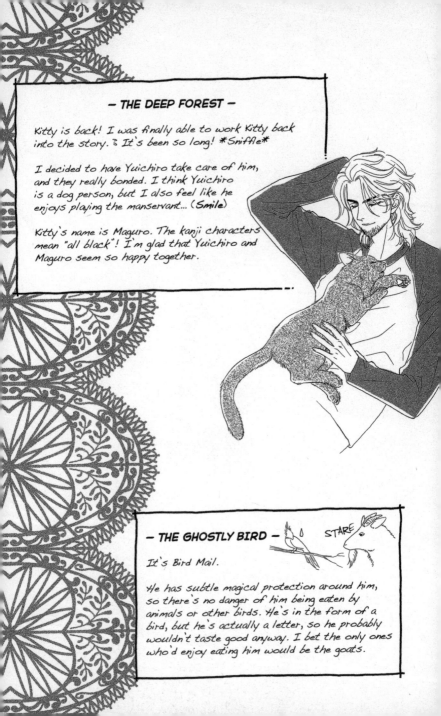

– THE DEEP FOREST –

Kitty is back! I was finally able to work Kitty back into the story. It's been so long! *Sniffle*

I decided to have Yuichiro take care of him, and they really bonded. I think Yuichiro is a dog person, but I also feel like he enjoys playing the manservant... (Smile)

Kitty's name is Maguro. The kanji characters mean "all black"! I'm glad that Yuichiro and Maguro seem so happy together.

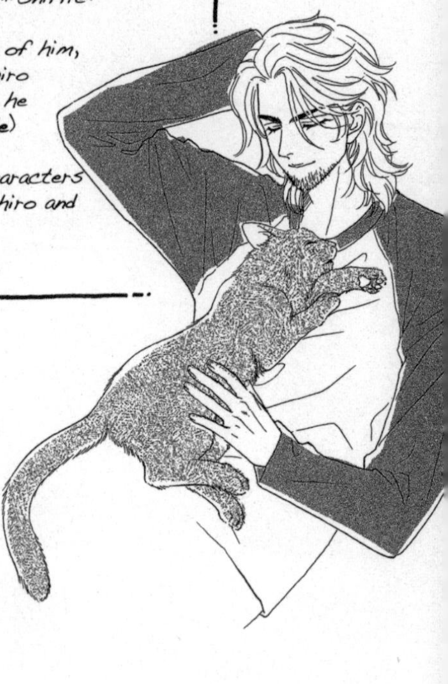

– THE GHOSTLY BIRD –

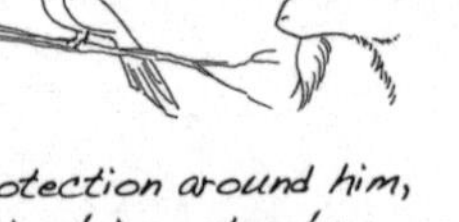
STARE

It's Bird Mail.

He has subtle magical protection around him, so there's no danger of him being eaten by animals or other birds. He's in the form of a bird, but he's actually a letter, so he probably wouldn't taste good anyway. I bet the only ones who'd enjoy eating him would be the goats.

Spell 20: The Ghostly Bird

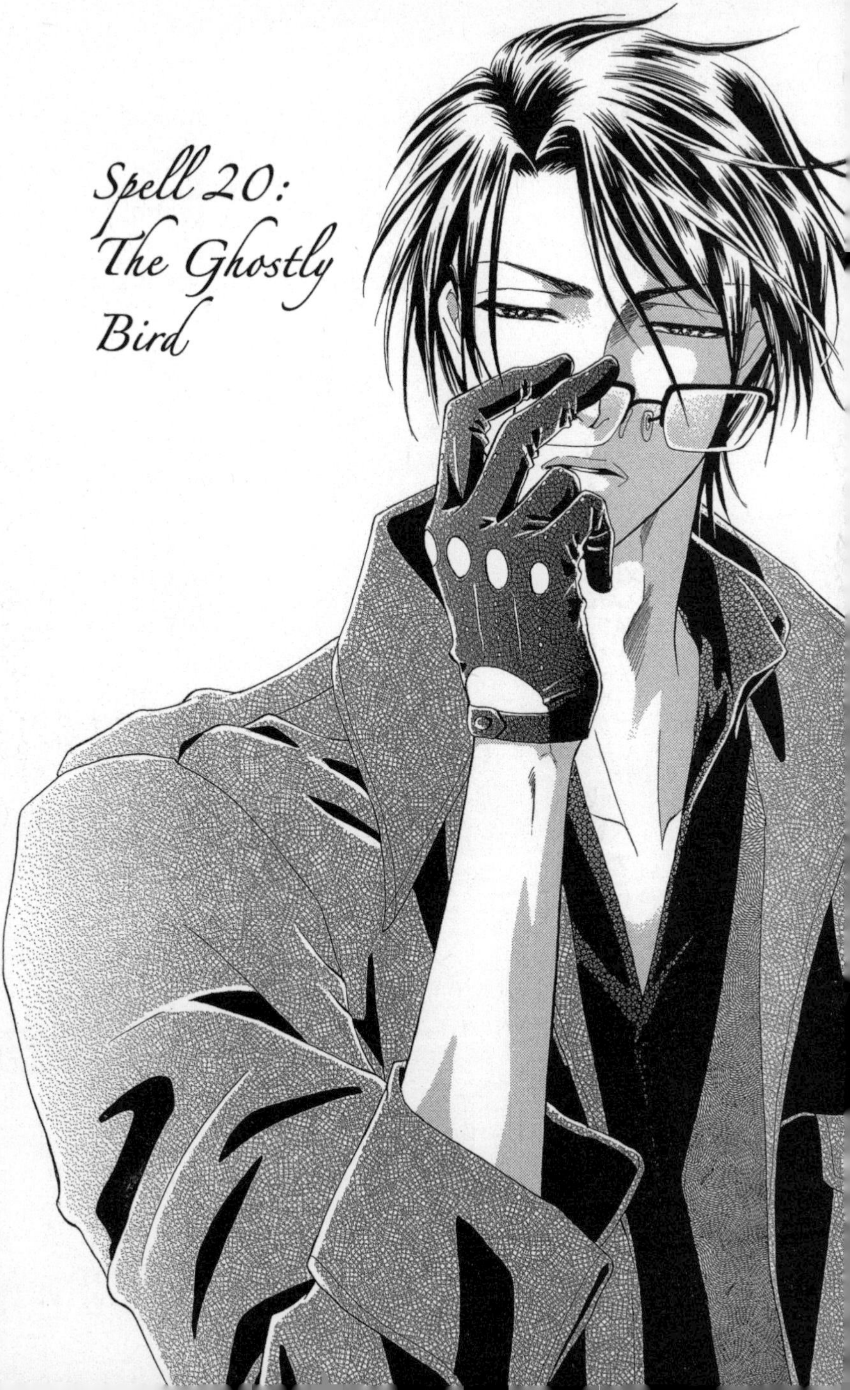

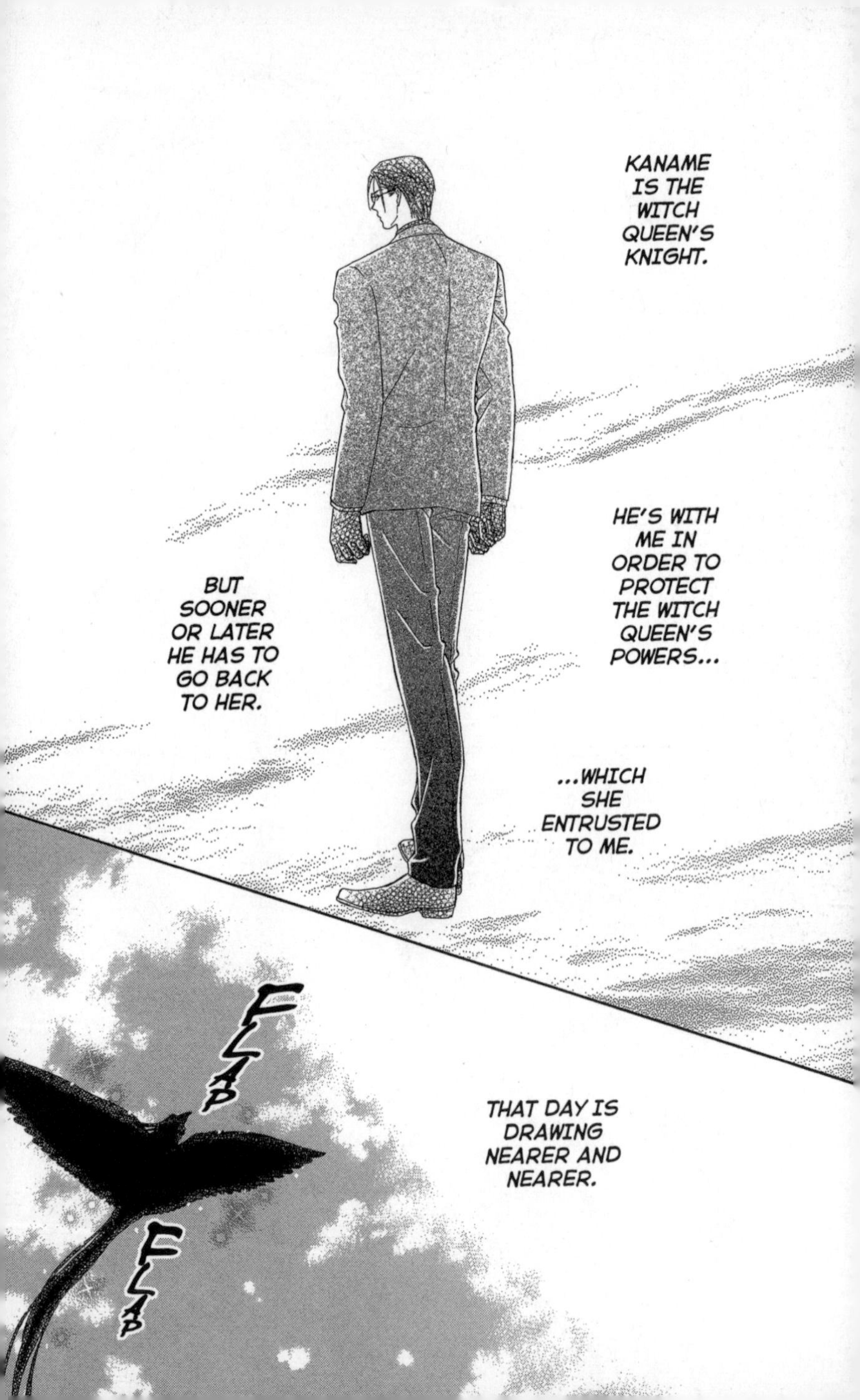
KANAME IS THE WITCH QUEEN'S KNIGHT.
HE'S WITH ME IN ORDER TO PROTECT THE WITCH QUEEN'S POWERS...
...WHICH SHE ENTRUSTED TO ME.
BUT SOONER OR LATER HE HAS TO GO BACK TO HER.
THAT DAY IS DRAWING NEARER AND NEARER.
FLAP
FLAP

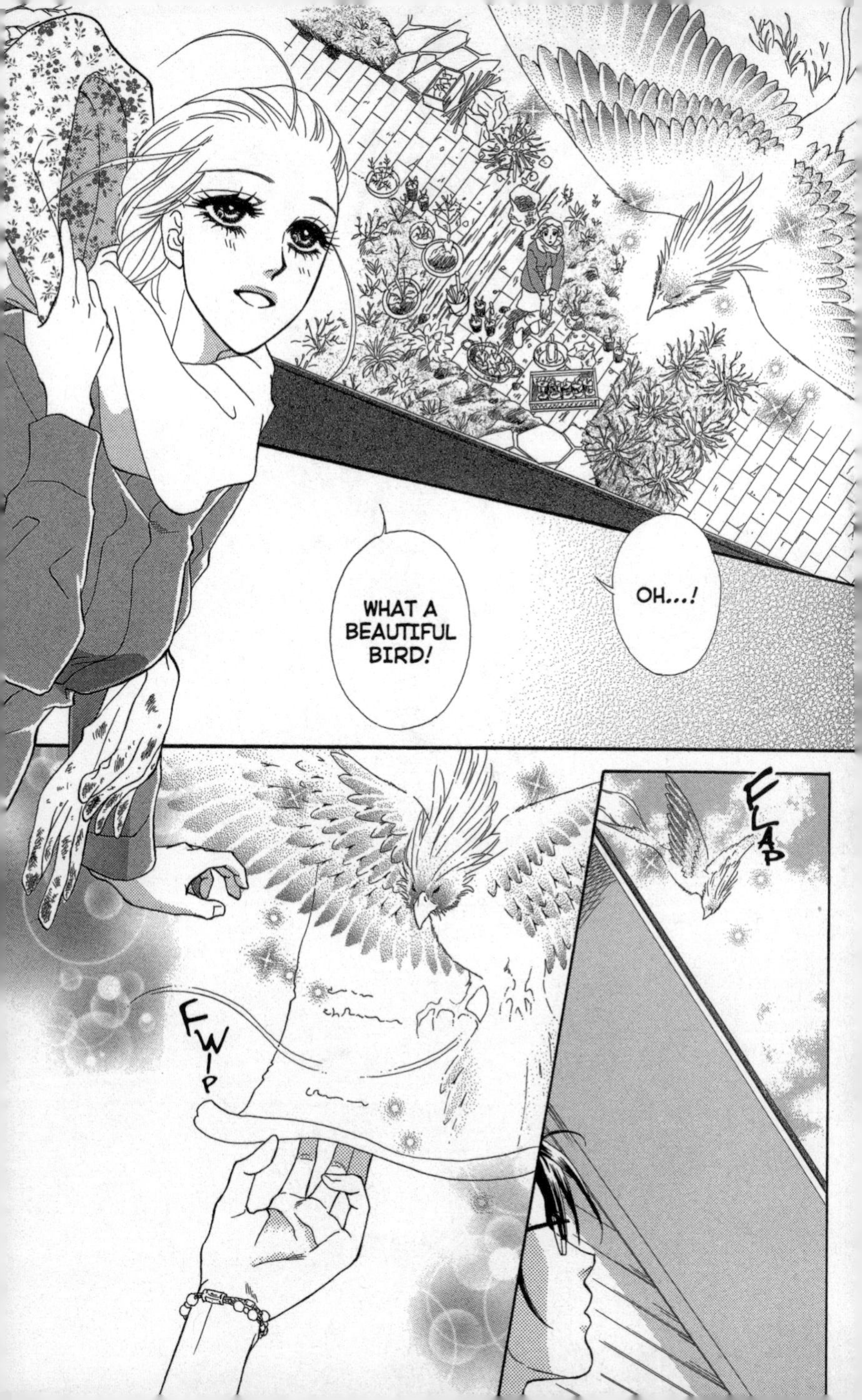
OH...!
WHAT A BEAUTIFUL BIRD!
FLAP
FWIP

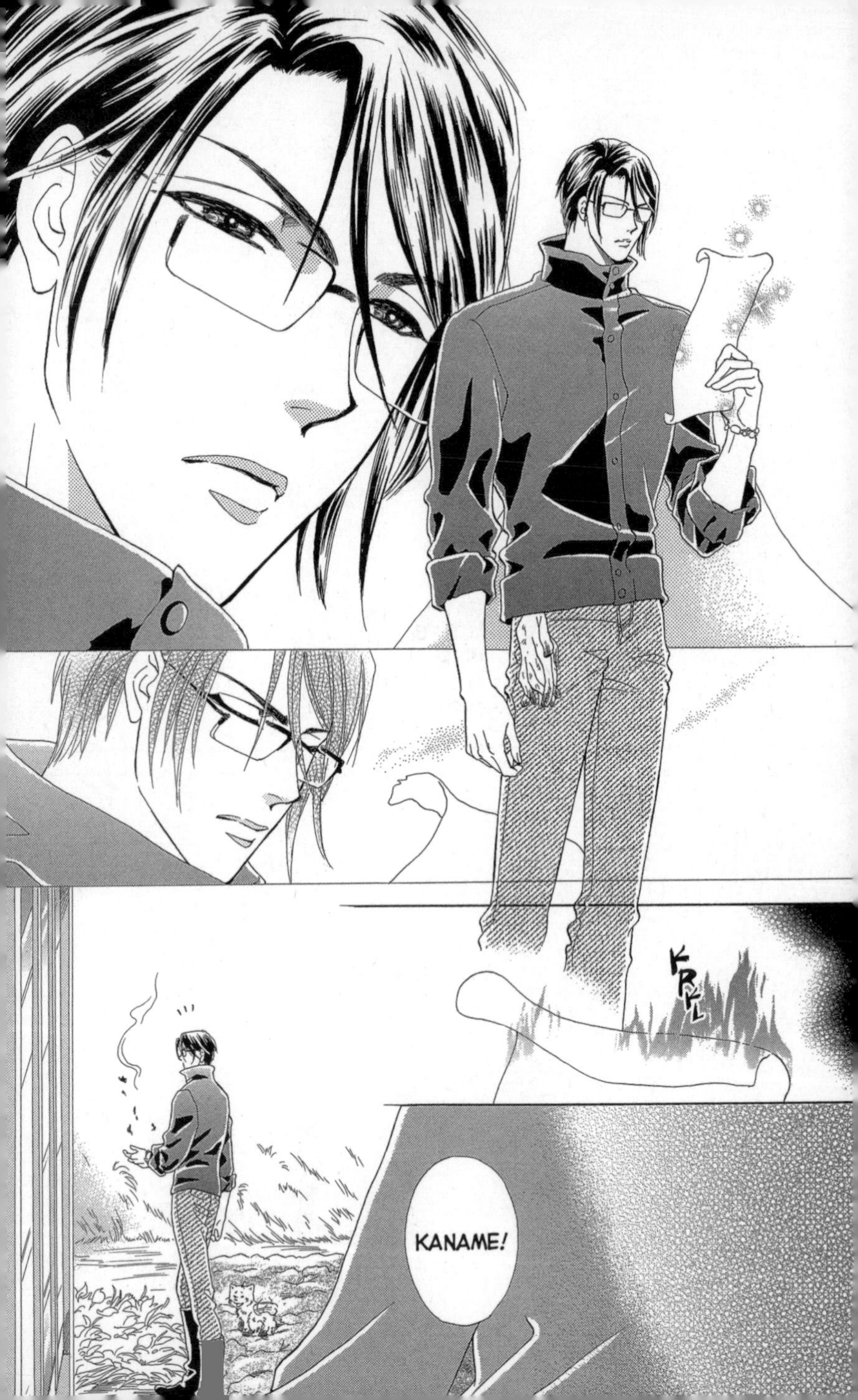
KRKL
KANAME!

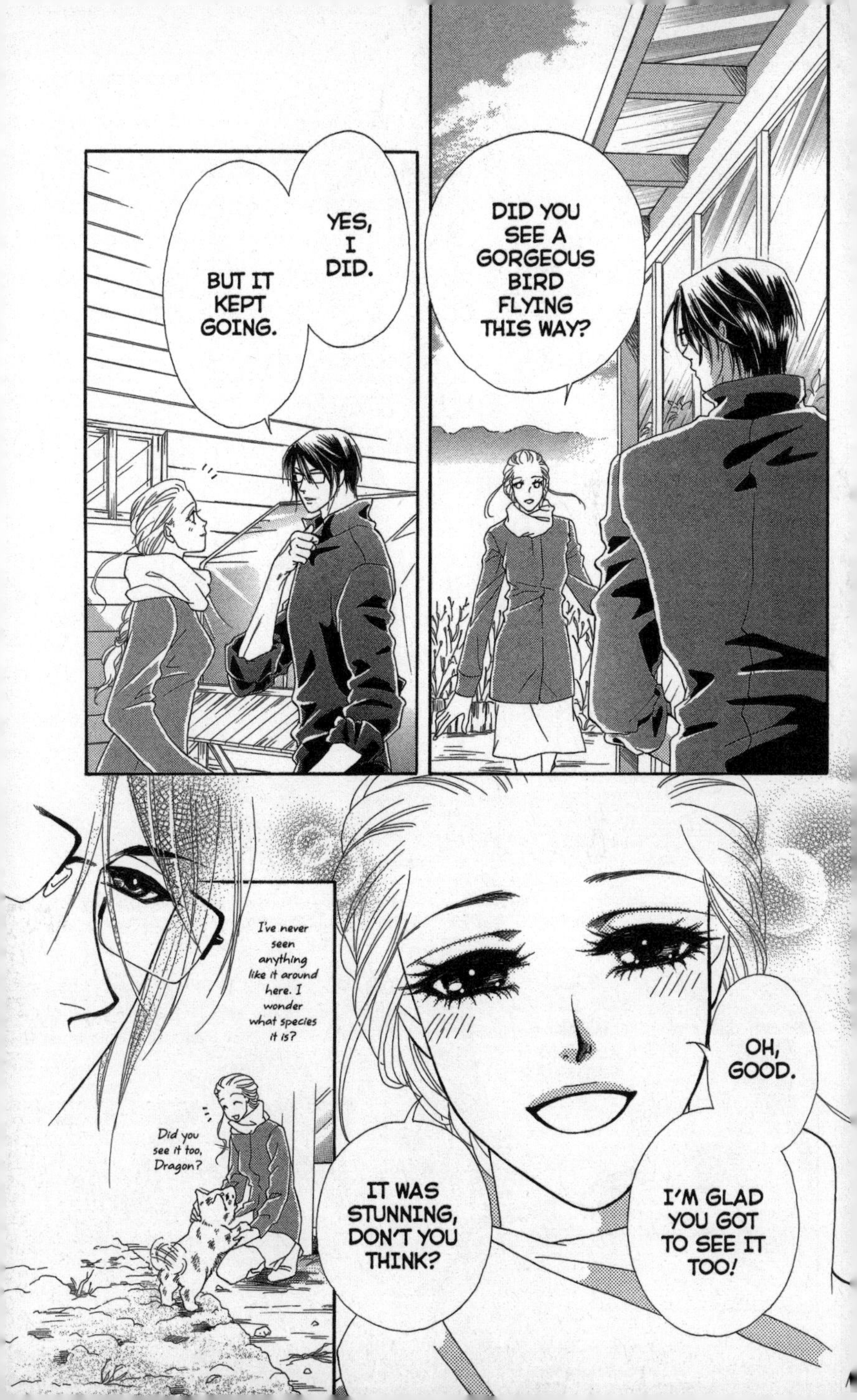
DID YOU SEE A GORGEOUS BIRD FLYING THIS WAY?
YES, I DID.
BUT IT KEPT GOING.
OH, GOOD.
I'M GLAD YOU GOT TO SEE IT TOO!
IT WAS STUNNING, DON'T YOU THINK?
I've never seen anything like it around here. I wonder what species it is?
Did you see it too, Dragon?

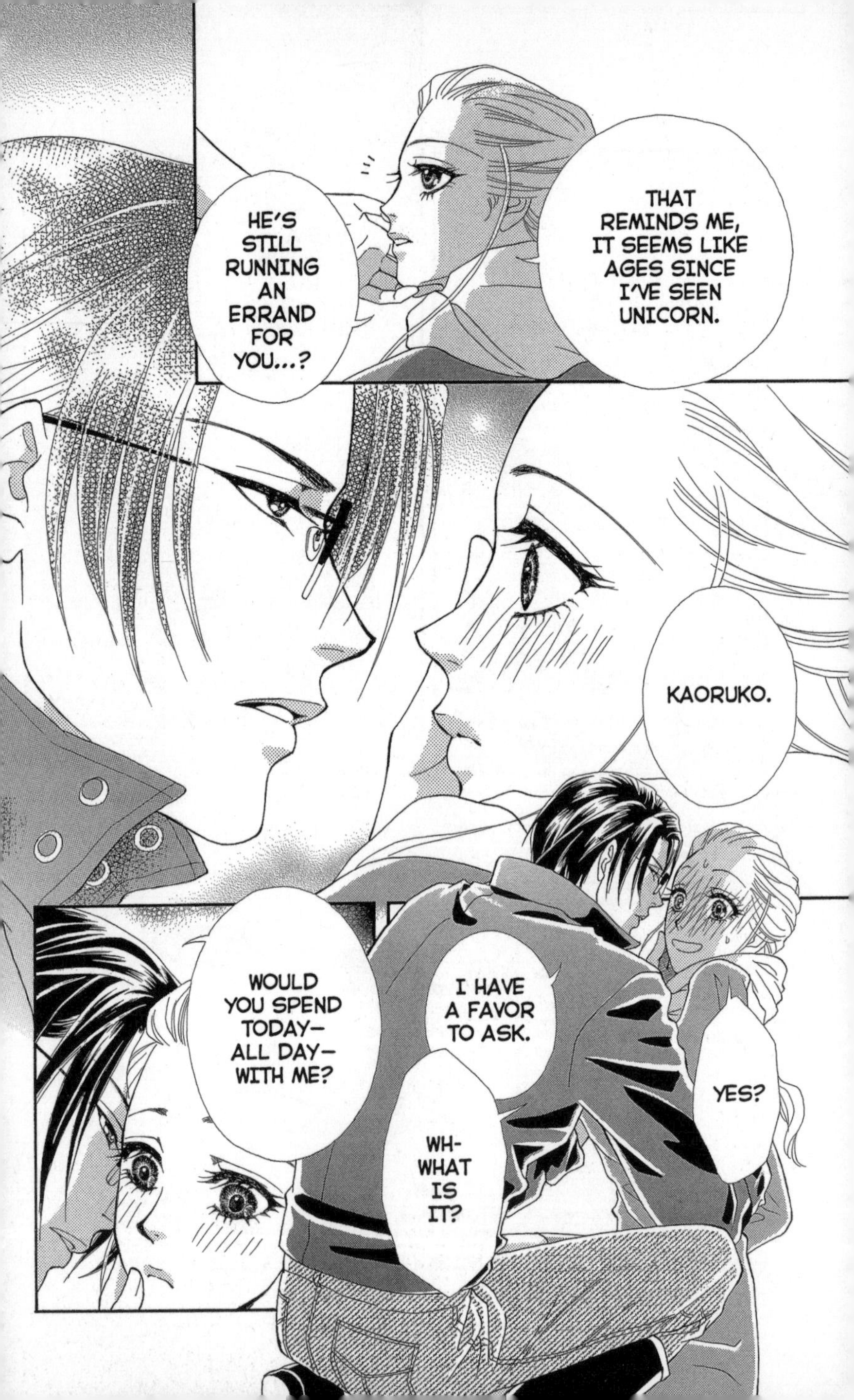
THAT REMINDS ME, IT SEEMS LIKE AGES SINCE I'VE SEEN UNICORN.
HE'S STILL RUNNING AN ERRAND FOR YOU...?
KAORUKO.
YES?
I HAVE A FAVOR TO ASK.
WH-WHAT IS IT?
WOULD YOU SPEND TODAY—ALL DAY—WITH ME?

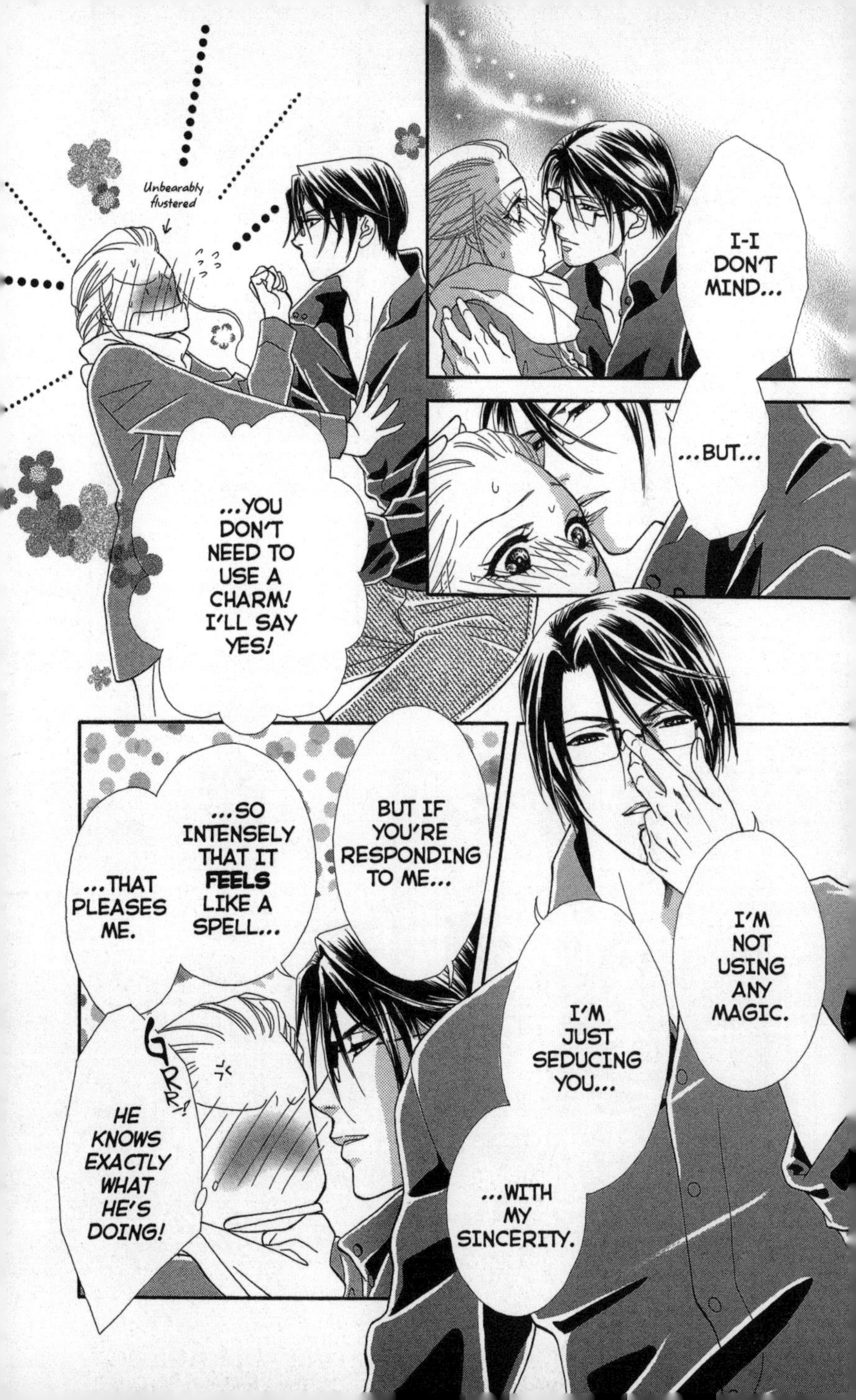
I-I DON'T MIND...
...BUT...
Unbearably flustered
...YOU DON'T NEED TO USE A CHARM! I'LL SAY YES!
I'M NOT USING ANY MAGIC.
I'M JUST SEDUCING YOU...
...WITH MY SINCERITY.
BUT IF YOU'RE RESPONDING TO ME...
...SO INTENSELY THAT IT **FEELS** LIKE A SPELL...
...THAT PLEASES ME.
GRR!
HE KNOWS EXACTLY WHAT HE'S DOING!

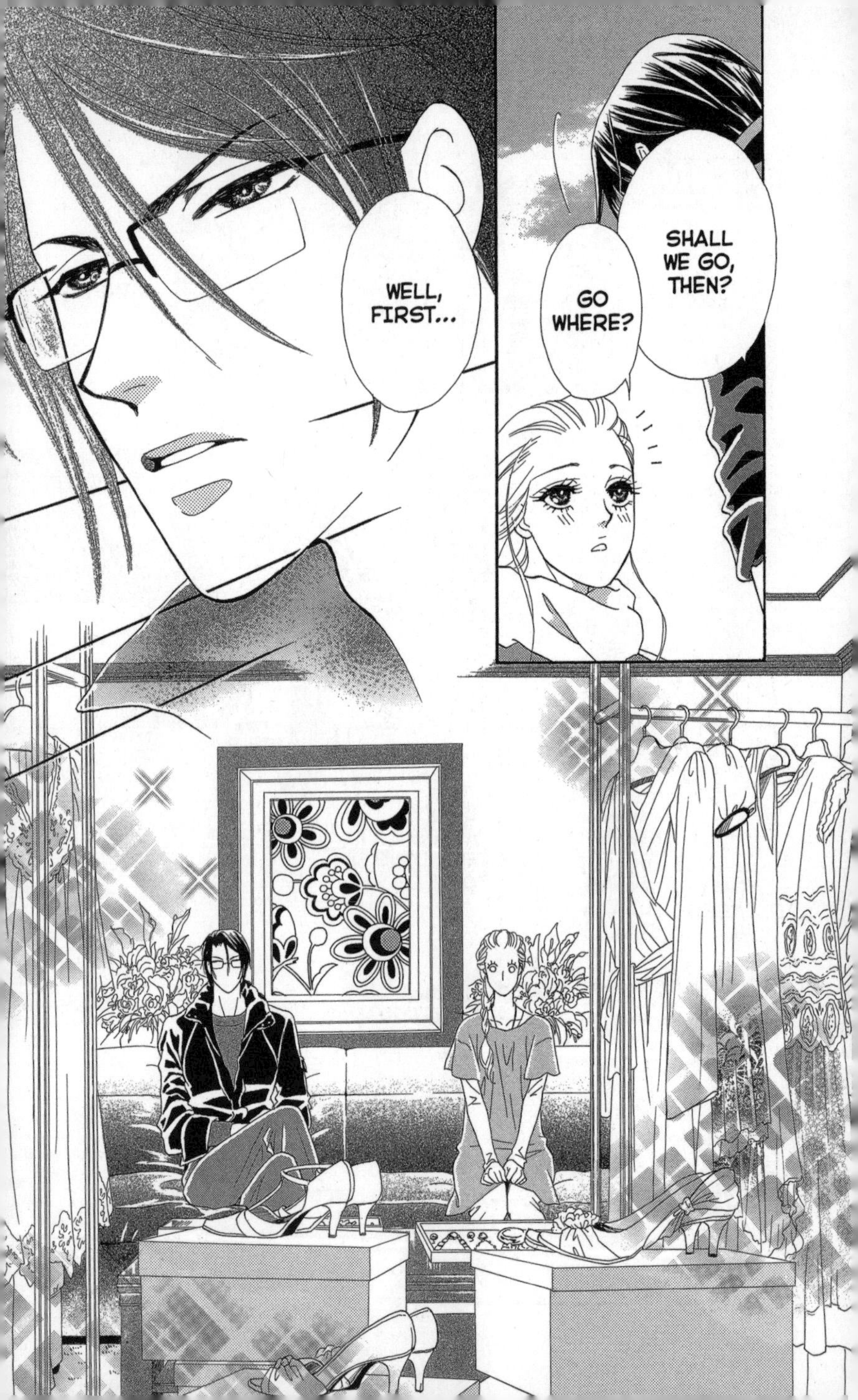
SHALL WE GO, THEN?
GO WHERE?
WELL, FIRST...

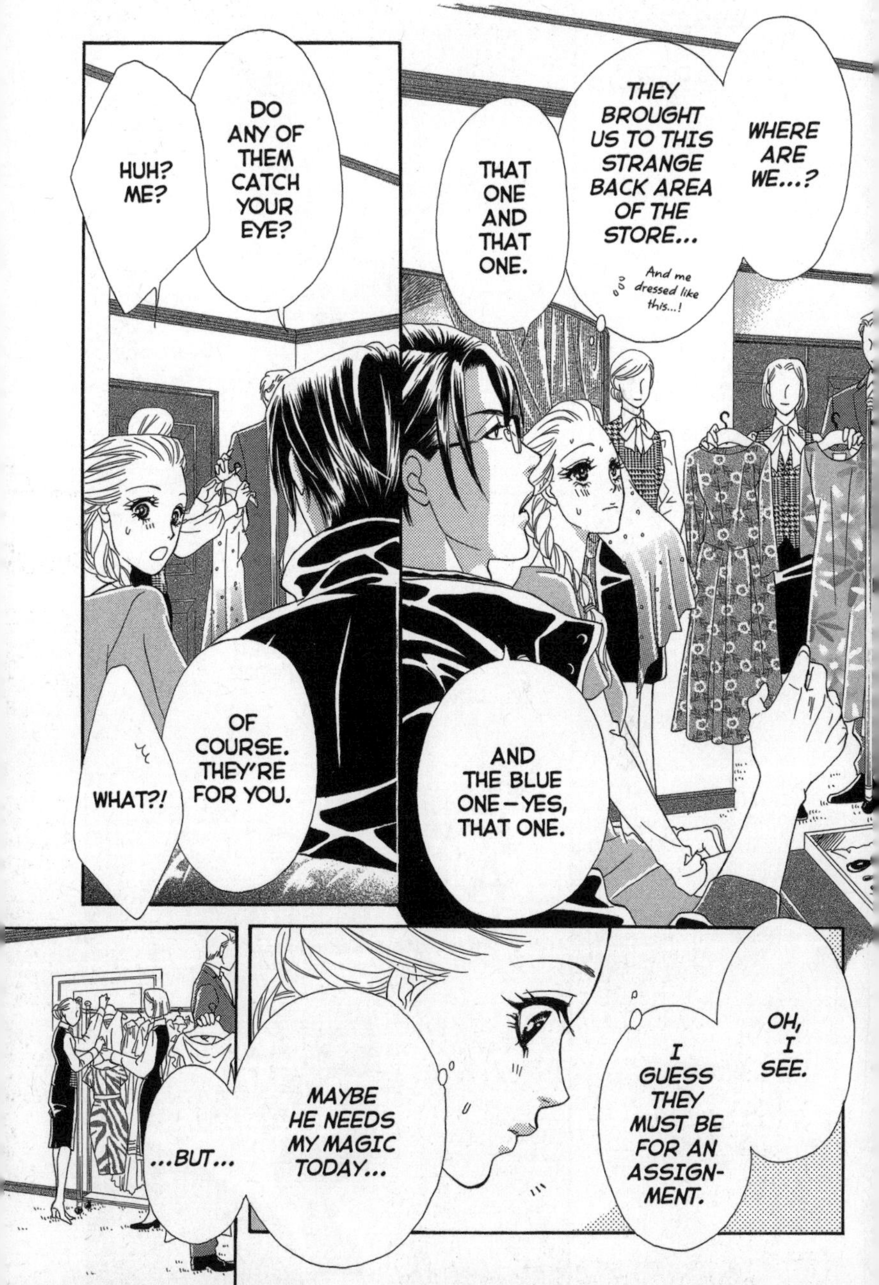
WHERE ARE WE...?
THEY BROUGHT US TO THIS STRANGE BACK AREA OF THE STORE...
And me dressed like this...!
THAT ONE AND THAT ONE.
AND THE BLUE ONE—YES, THAT ONE.
DO ANY OF THEM CATCH YOUR EYE?
HUH? ME?
OF COURSE. THEY'RE FOR YOU.
WHAT?!
OH, I SEE.
I GUESS THEY MUST BE FOR AN ASSIGNMENT.
MAYBE HE NEEDS MY MAGIC TODAY...
...BUT...

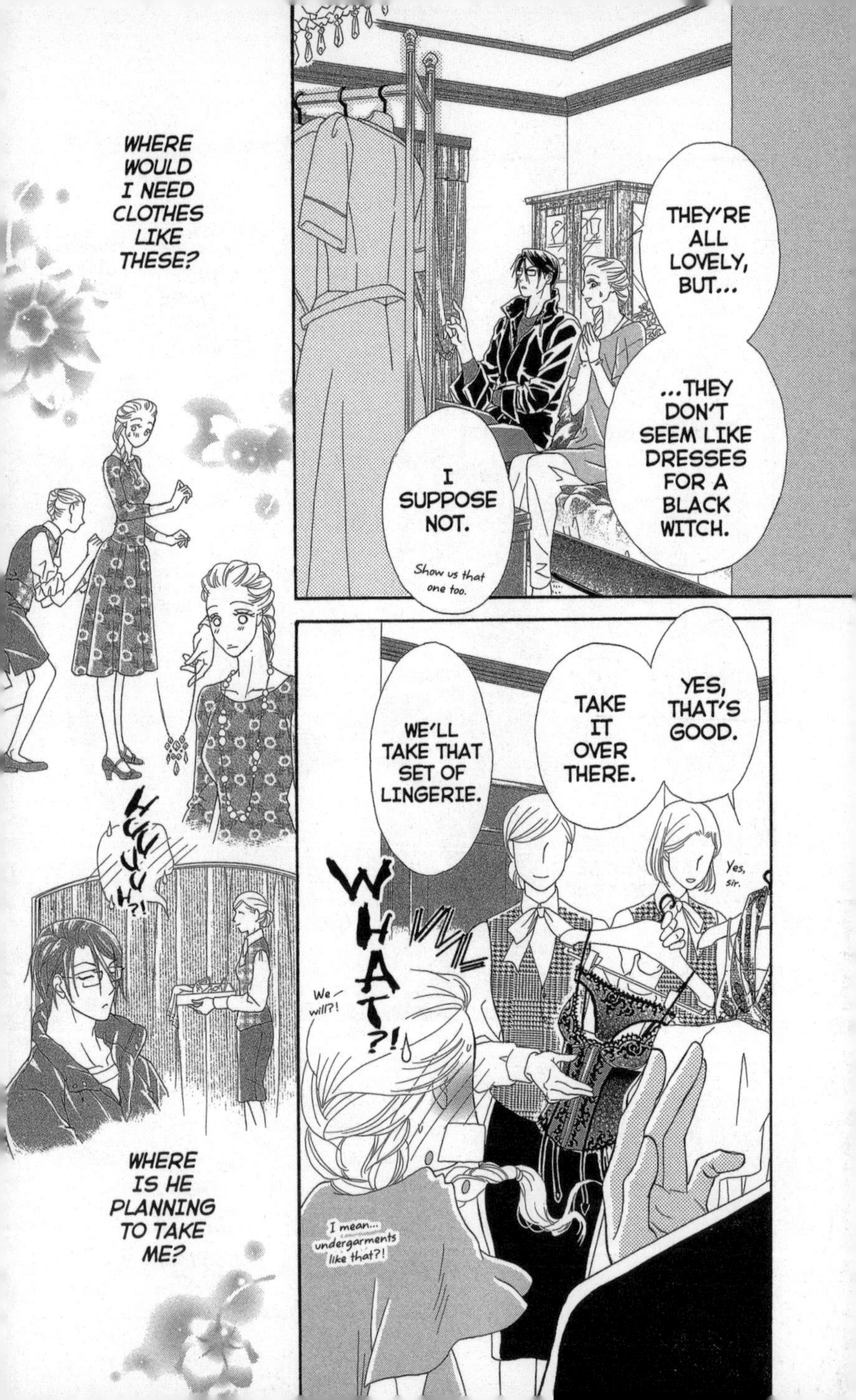
THEY'RE ALL LOVELY, BUT...
...THEY DON'T SEEM LIKE DRESSES FOR A BLACK WITCH.
I SUPPOSE NOT.
Show us that one too.
YES, THAT'S GOOD.
Yes, sir.
TAKE IT OVER THERE.
WE'LL TAKE THAT SET OF LINGERIE.
WHAT?!
We— will?!
I mean... undergarments like that?!
WHERE WOULD I NEED CLOTHES LIKE THESE?
HUUUUH?!
WHERE IS HE PLANNING TO TAKE ME?

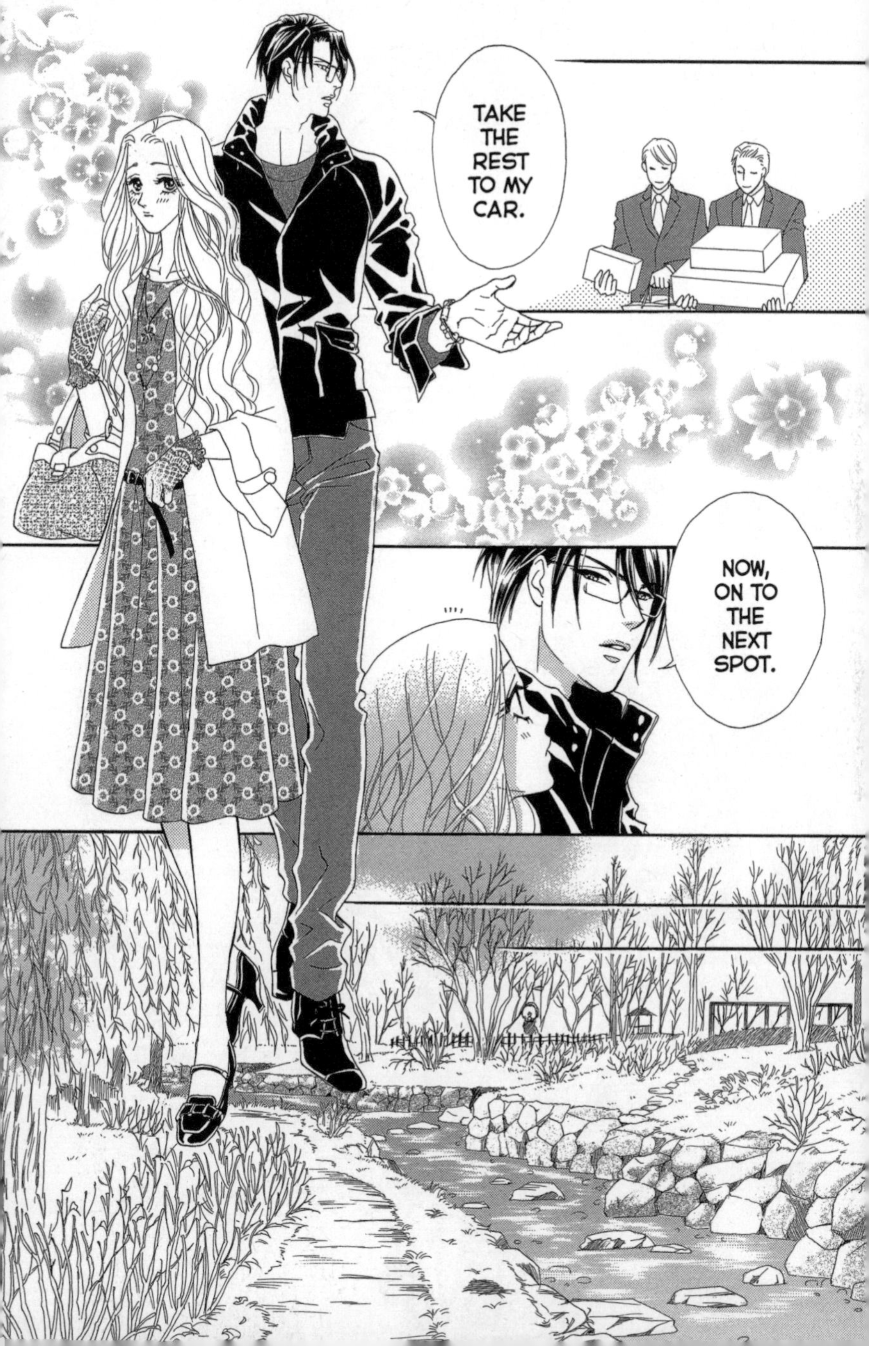
TAKE THE REST TO MY CAR.
NOW, ON TO THE NEXT SPOT.

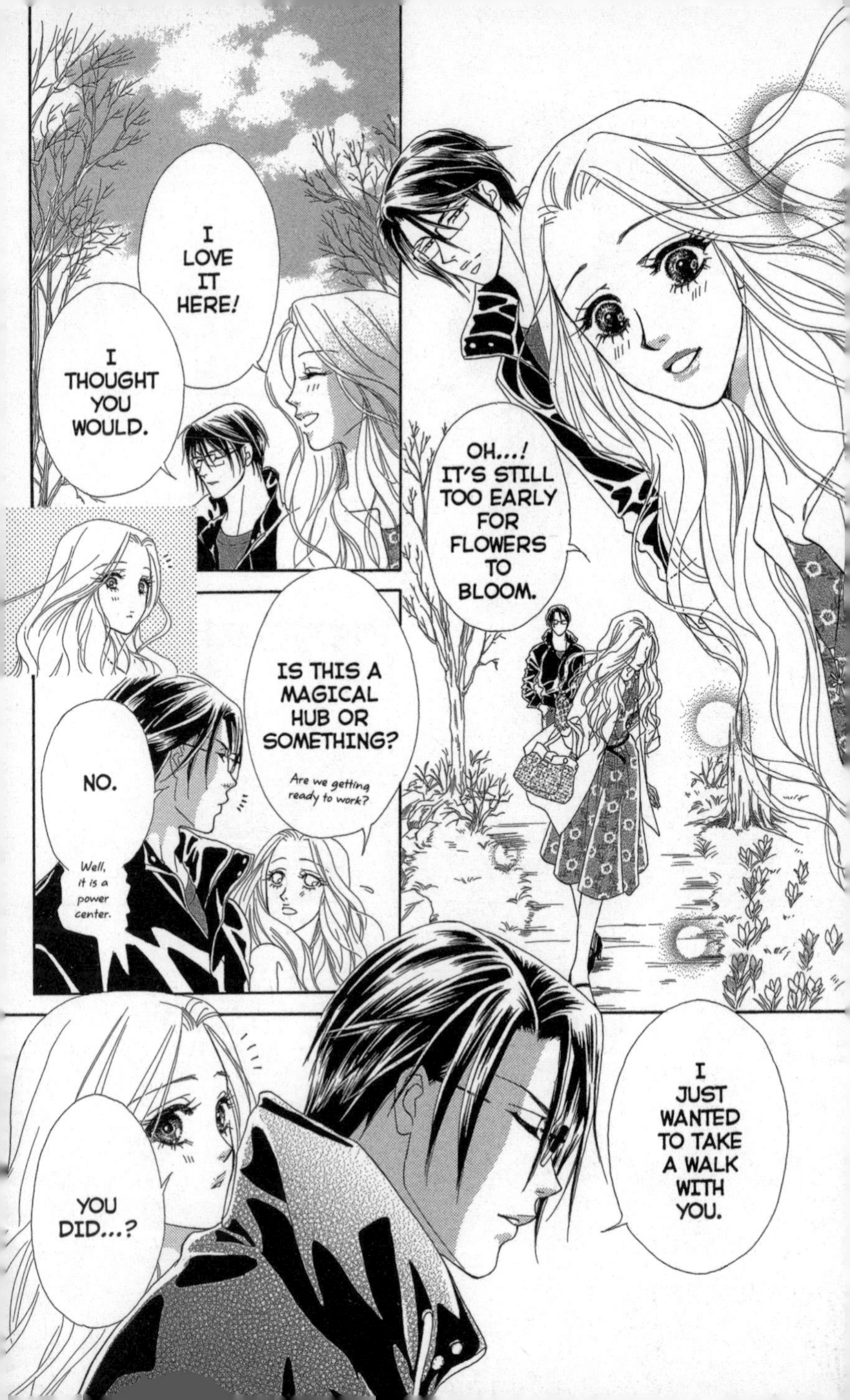
OH...! IT'S STILL TOO EARLY FOR FLOWERS TO BLOOM.
I LOVE IT HERE!
I THOUGHT YOU WOULD.
IS THIS A MAGICAL HUB OR SOMETHING?
Are we getting ready to work?
NO.
Well, it is a power center.
I JUST WANTED TO TAKE A WALK WITH YOU.
YOU DID...?

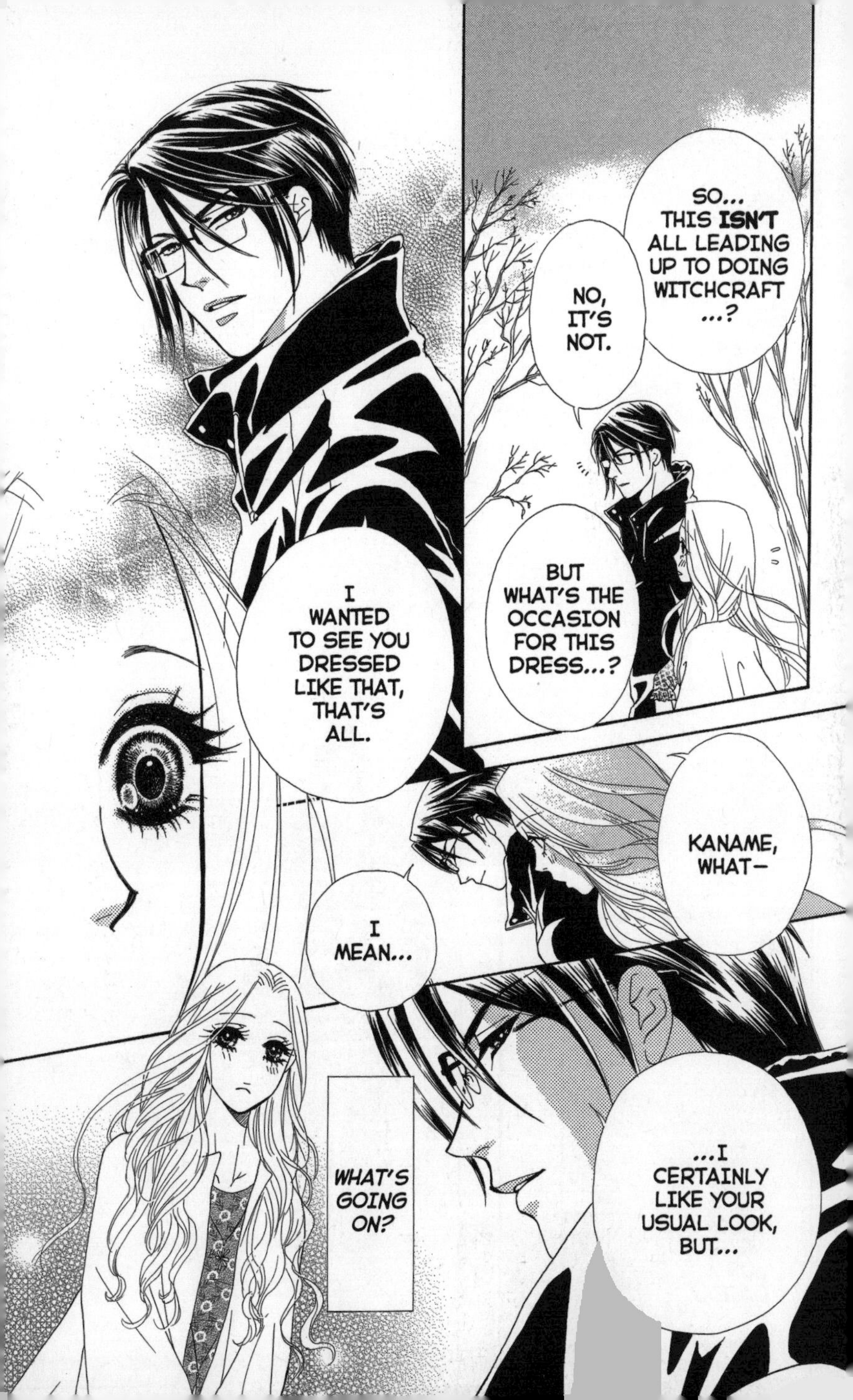
SO... THIS **ISN'T** ALL LEADING UP TO DOING WITCHCRAFT ...?
NO, IT'S NOT.
BUT WHAT'S THE OCCASION FOR THIS DRESS...?
I WANTED TO SEE YOU DRESSED LIKE THAT, THAT'S ALL.
KANAME, WHAT—
I MEAN...
...I CERTAINLY LIKE YOUR USUAL LOOK, BUT...
WHAT'S GOING ON?

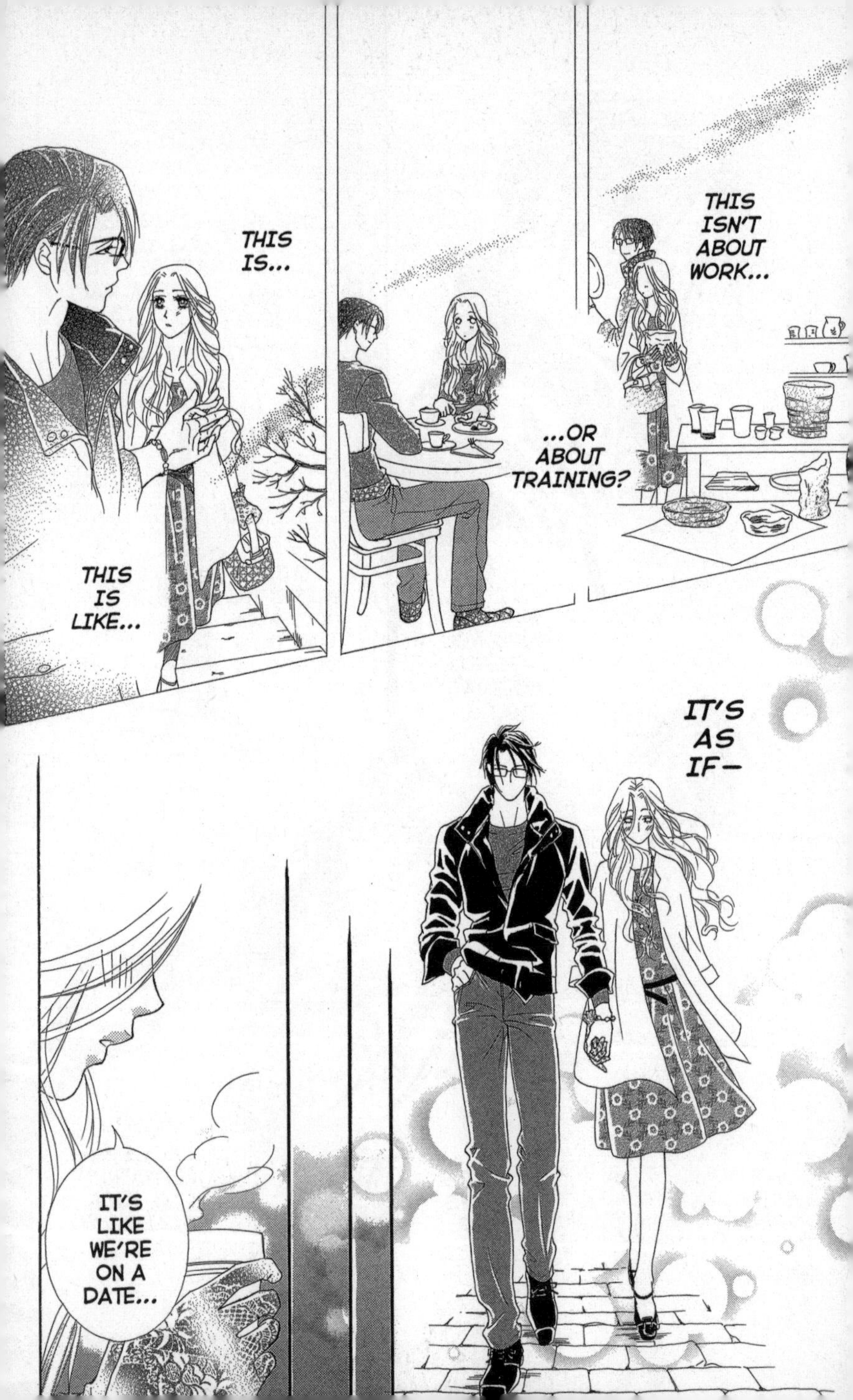
THIS ISN'T ABOUT WORK...
...OR ABOUT TRAINING?
THIS IS...
THIS IS LIKE...
IT'S AS IF—
IT'S LIKE WE'RE ON A DATE...

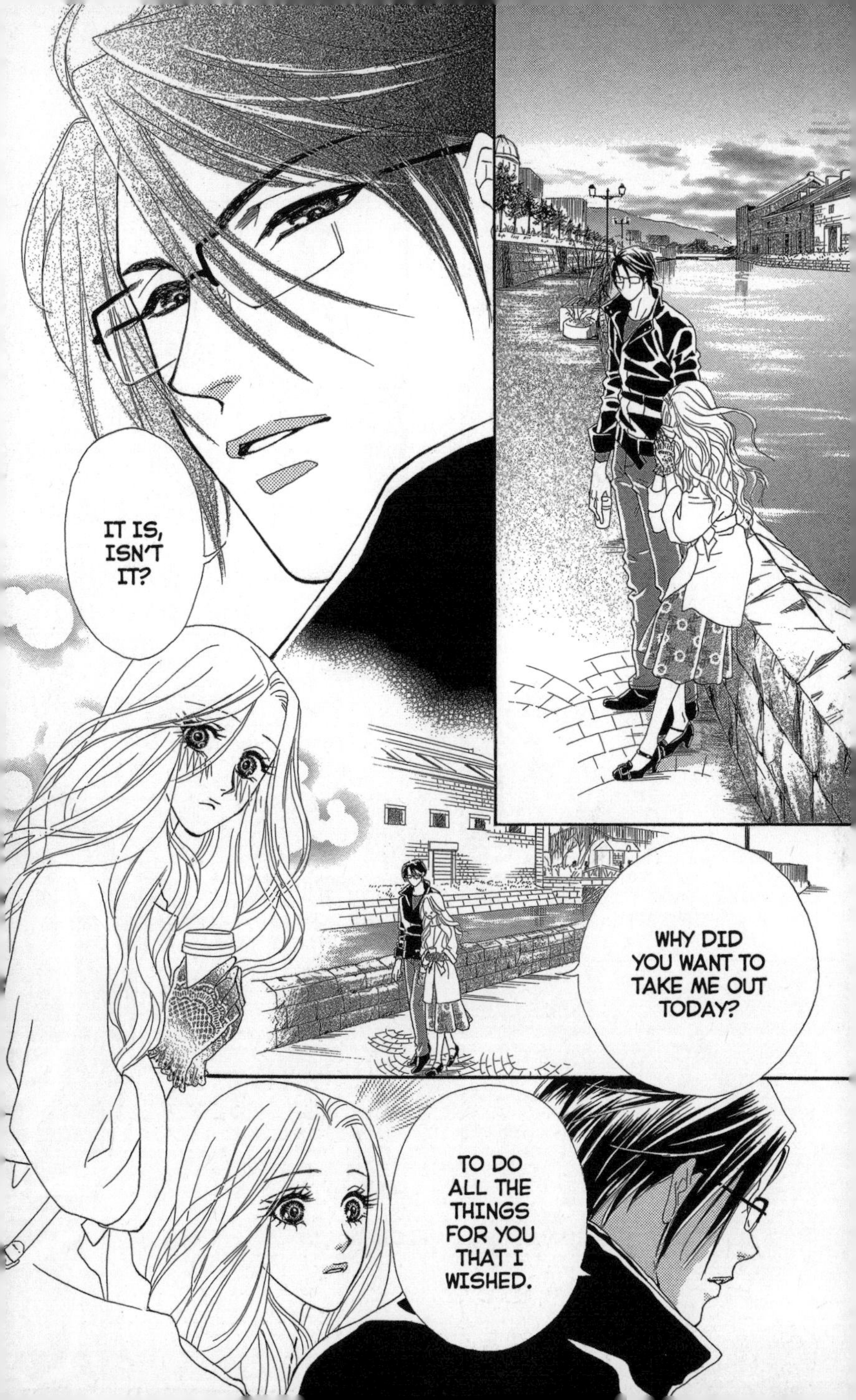
IT IS, ISN'T IT?
WHY DID YOU WANT TO TAKE ME OUT TODAY?
TO DO ALL THE THINGS FOR YOU THAT I WISHED.

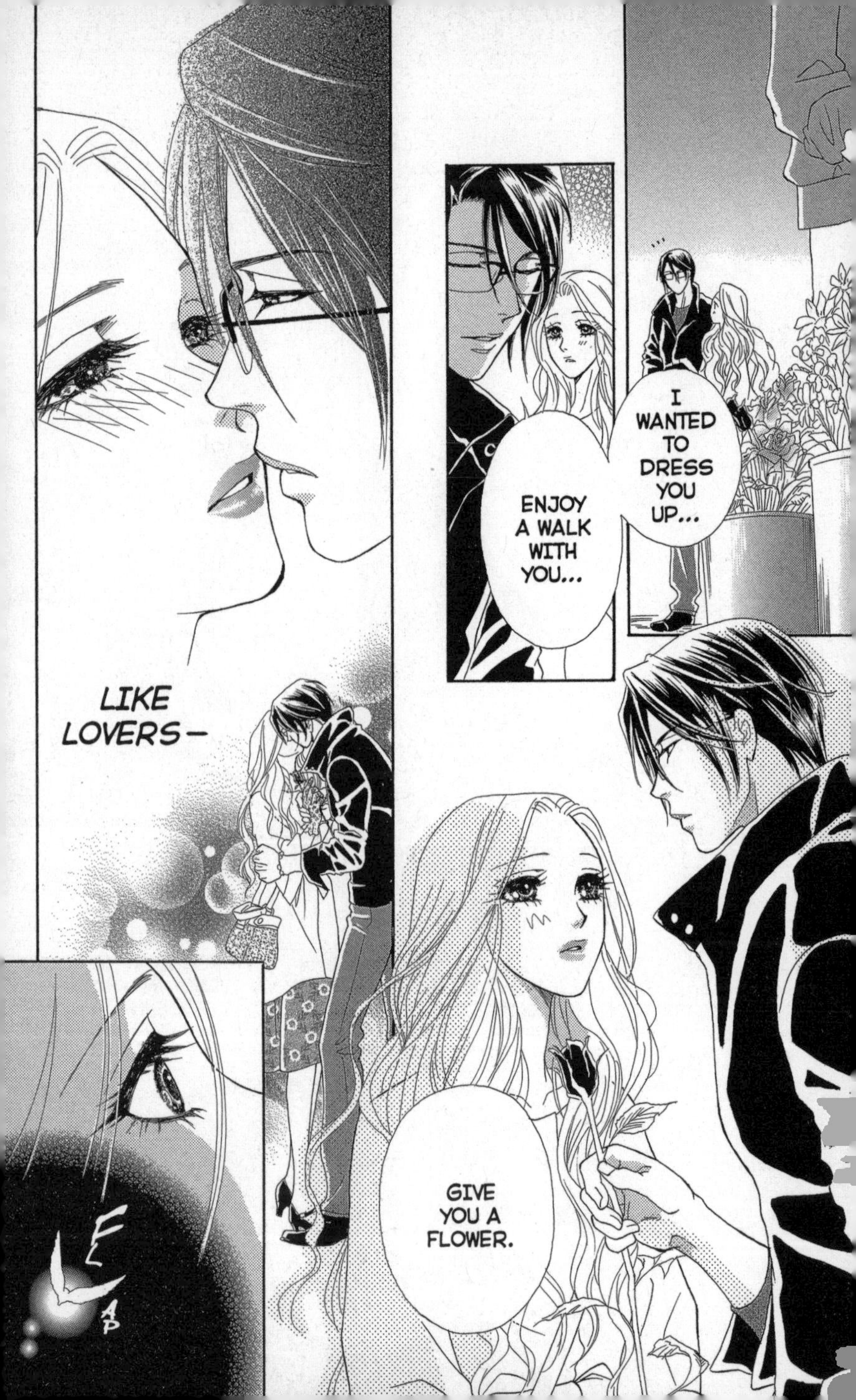
...
I WANTED TO DRESS YOU UP...
ENJOY A WALK WITH YOU...
GIVE YOU A FLOWER.
LIKE LOVERS—
FLAP

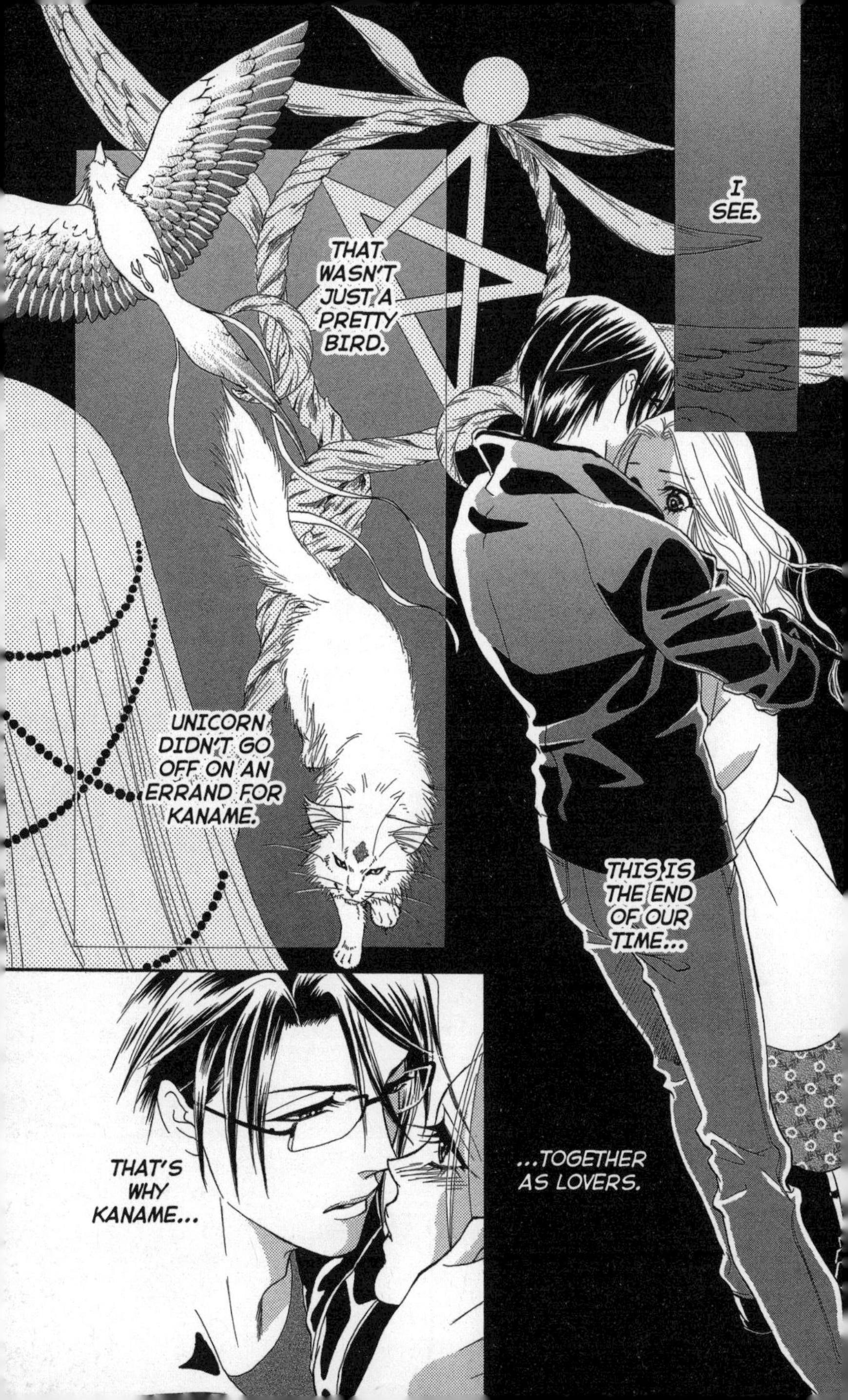
I SEE.
THAT WASN'T JUST A PRETTY BIRD.
UNICORN DIDN'T GO OFF ON AN ERRAND FOR KANAME.
THIS IS THE END OF OUR TIME...
...TOGETHER AS LOVERS.
THAT'S WHY KANAME...

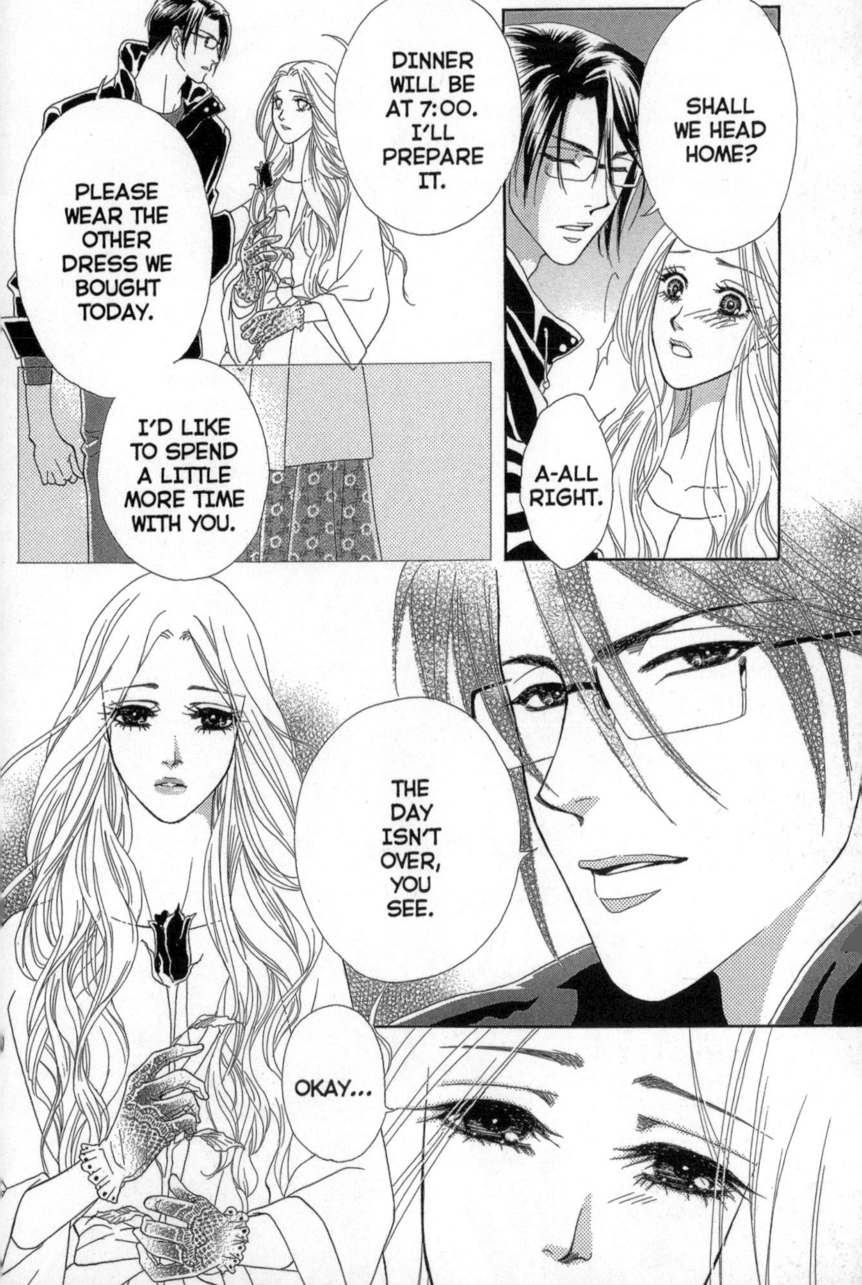
SHALL WE HEAD HOME?
A-ALL RIGHT.
DINNER WILL BE AT 7:00. I'LL PREPARE IT.
PLEASE WEAR THE OTHER DRESS WE BOUGHT TODAY.
I'D LIKE TO SPEND A LITTLE MORE TIME WITH YOU.
THE DAY ISN'T OVER, YOU SEE.
OKAY...

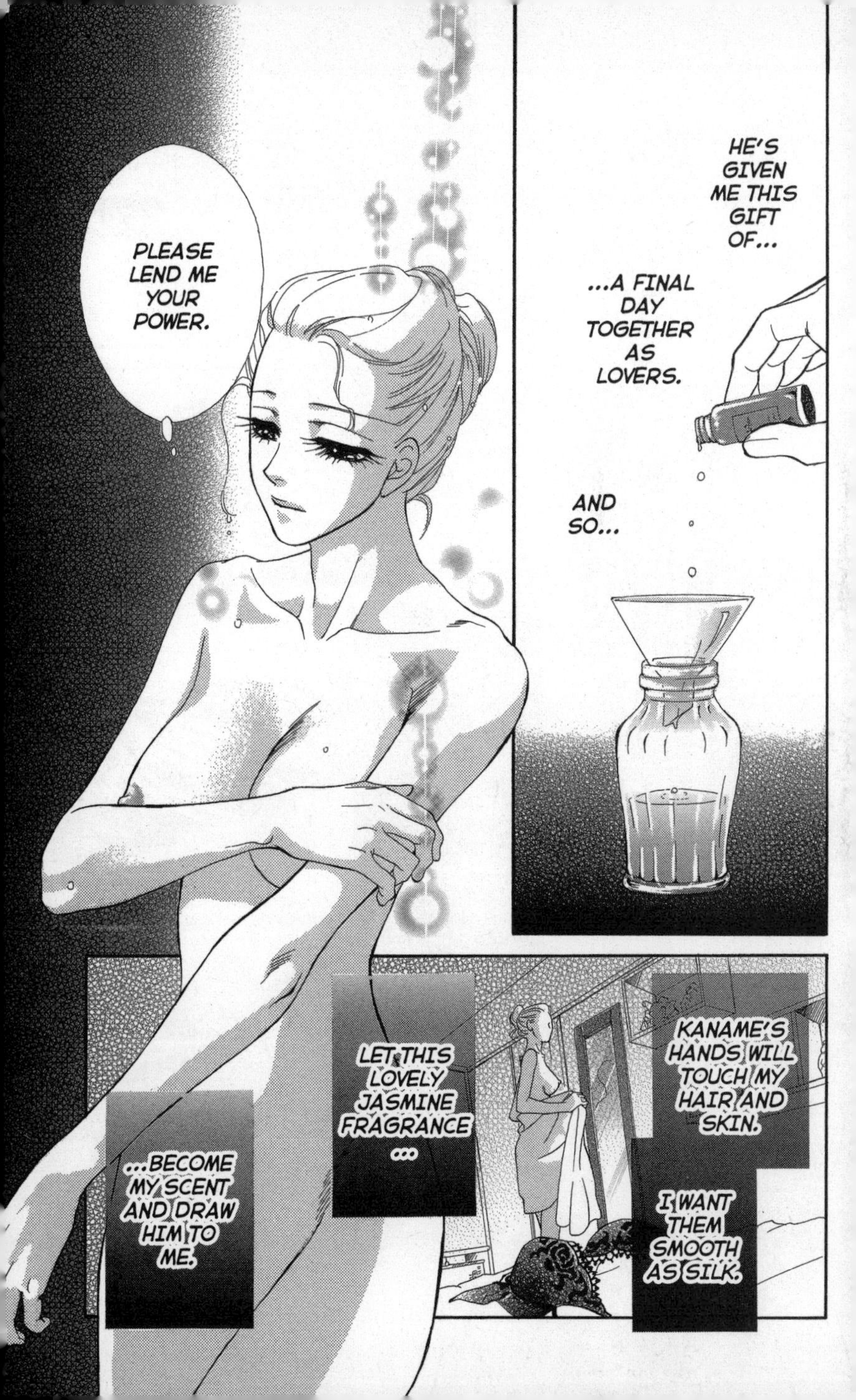
HE'S GIVEN ME THIS GIFT OF...
...A FINAL DAY TOGETHER AS LOVERS.
AND SO...
PLEASE LEND ME YOUR POWER.
KANAME'S HANDS WILL TOUCH MY HAIR AND SKIN.
I WANT THEM SMOOTH AS SILK.
LET THIS LOVELY JASMINE FRAGRANCE...
...BECOME MY SCENT AND DRAW HIM TO ME.

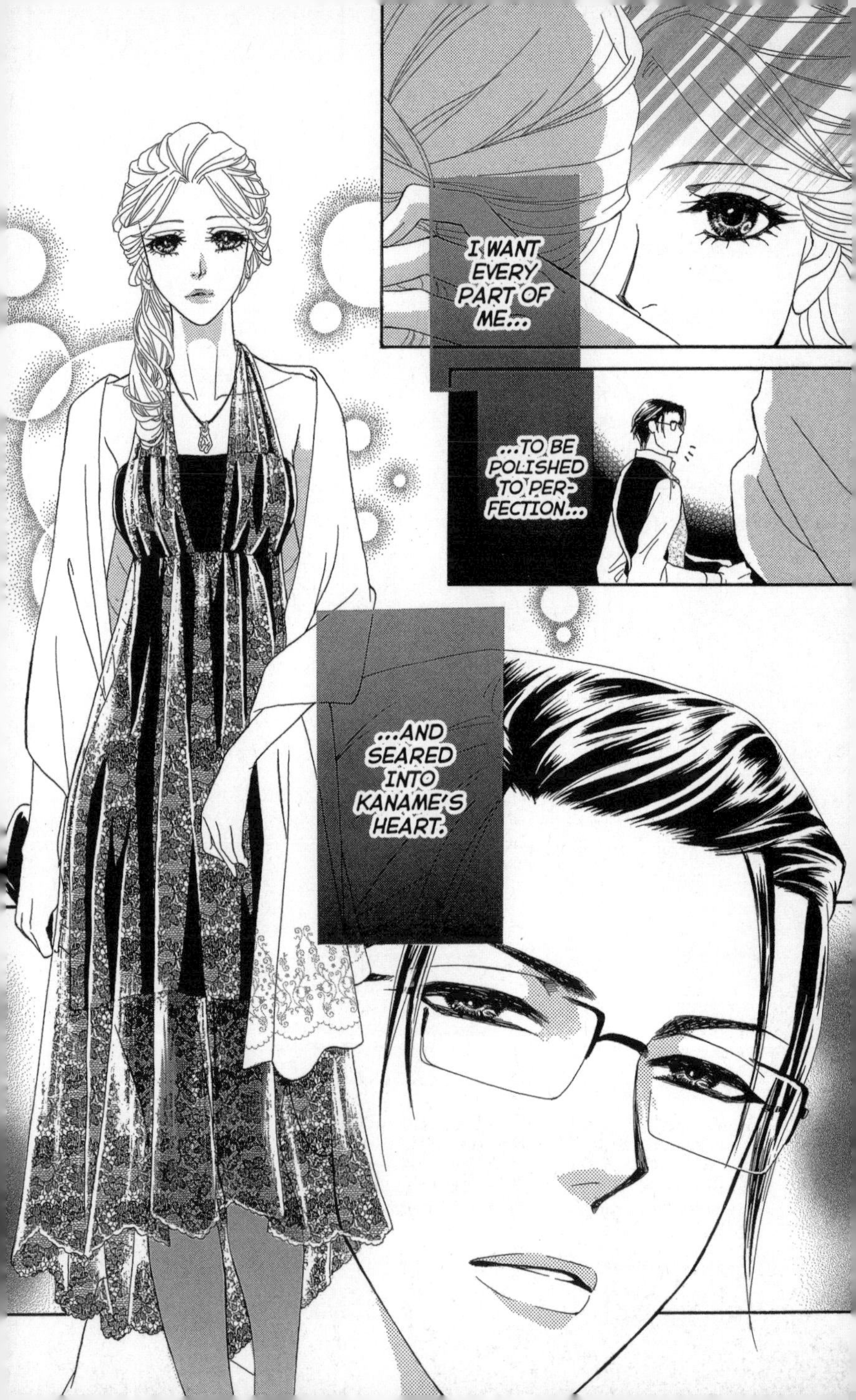
I WANT EVERY PART OF ME...
...TO BE POLISHED TO PER-FECTION...
...AND SEARED INTO KANAME'S HEART.

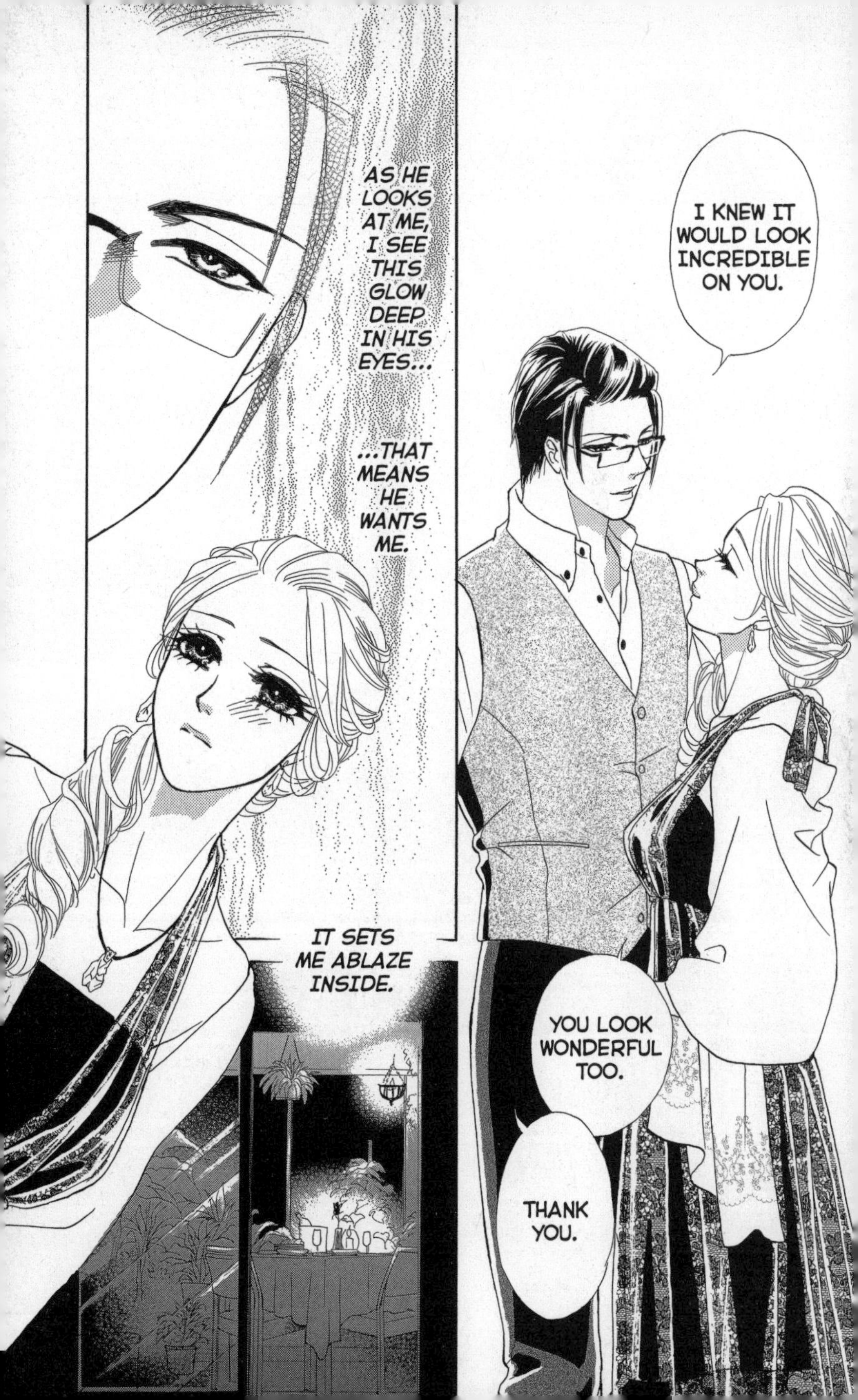
I KNEW IT WOULD LOOK INCREDIBLE ON YOU.
YOU LOOK WONDERFUL TOO.
THANK YOU.
AS HE LOOKS AT ME, I SEE THIS GLOW DEEP IN HIS EYES...
...THAT MEANS HE WANTS ME.
IT SETS ME ABLAZE INSIDE.

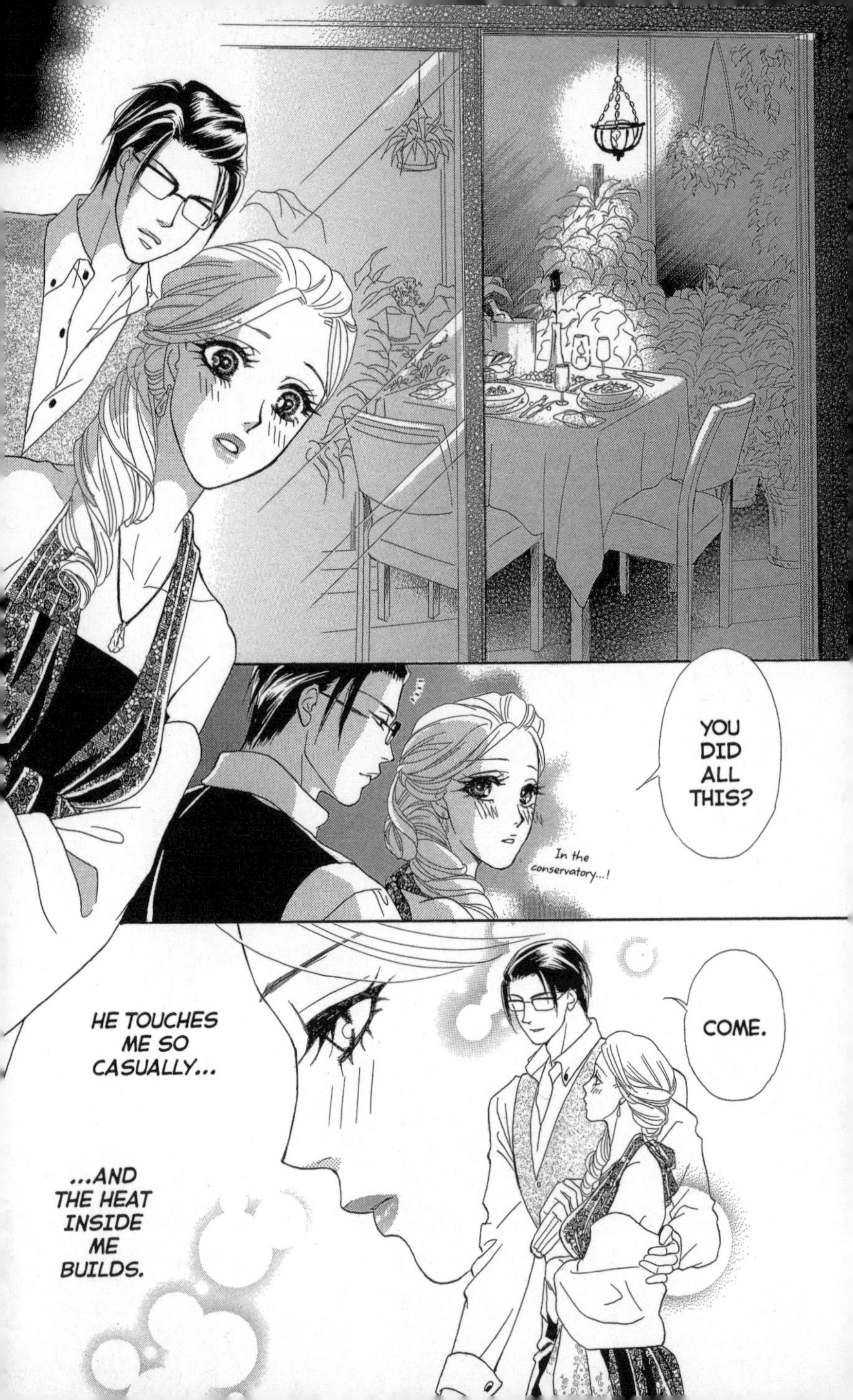
YOU DID ALL THIS?
In the conservatory...!
COME.
HE TOUCHES ME SO CASUALLY...
...AND THE HEAT INSIDE ME BUILDS.

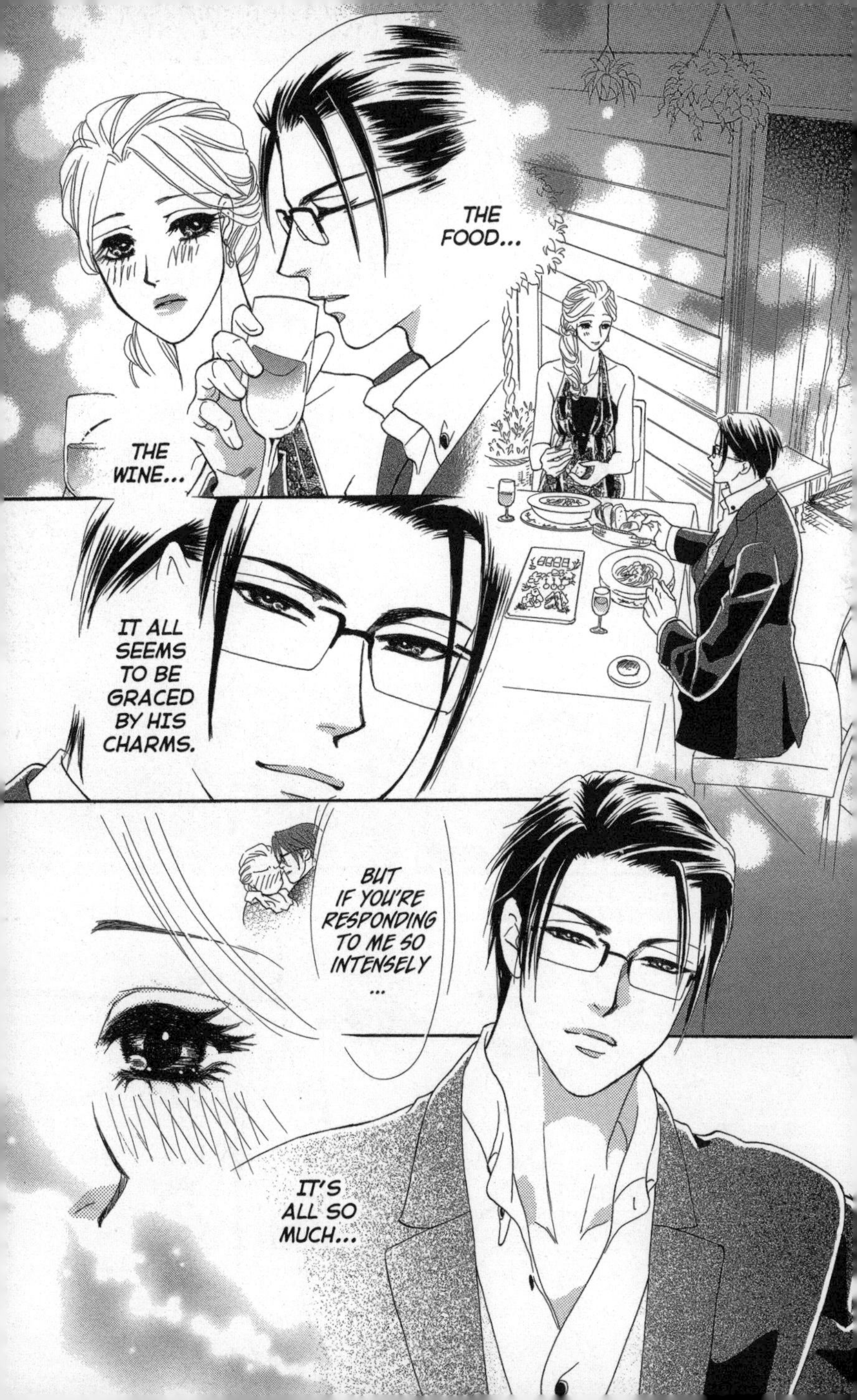
THE FOOD...
THE WINE...
IT ALL SEEMS TO BE GRACED BY HIS CHARMS.
BUT IF YOU'RE RESPONDING TO ME SO INTENSELY...
IT'S ALL SO MUCH...

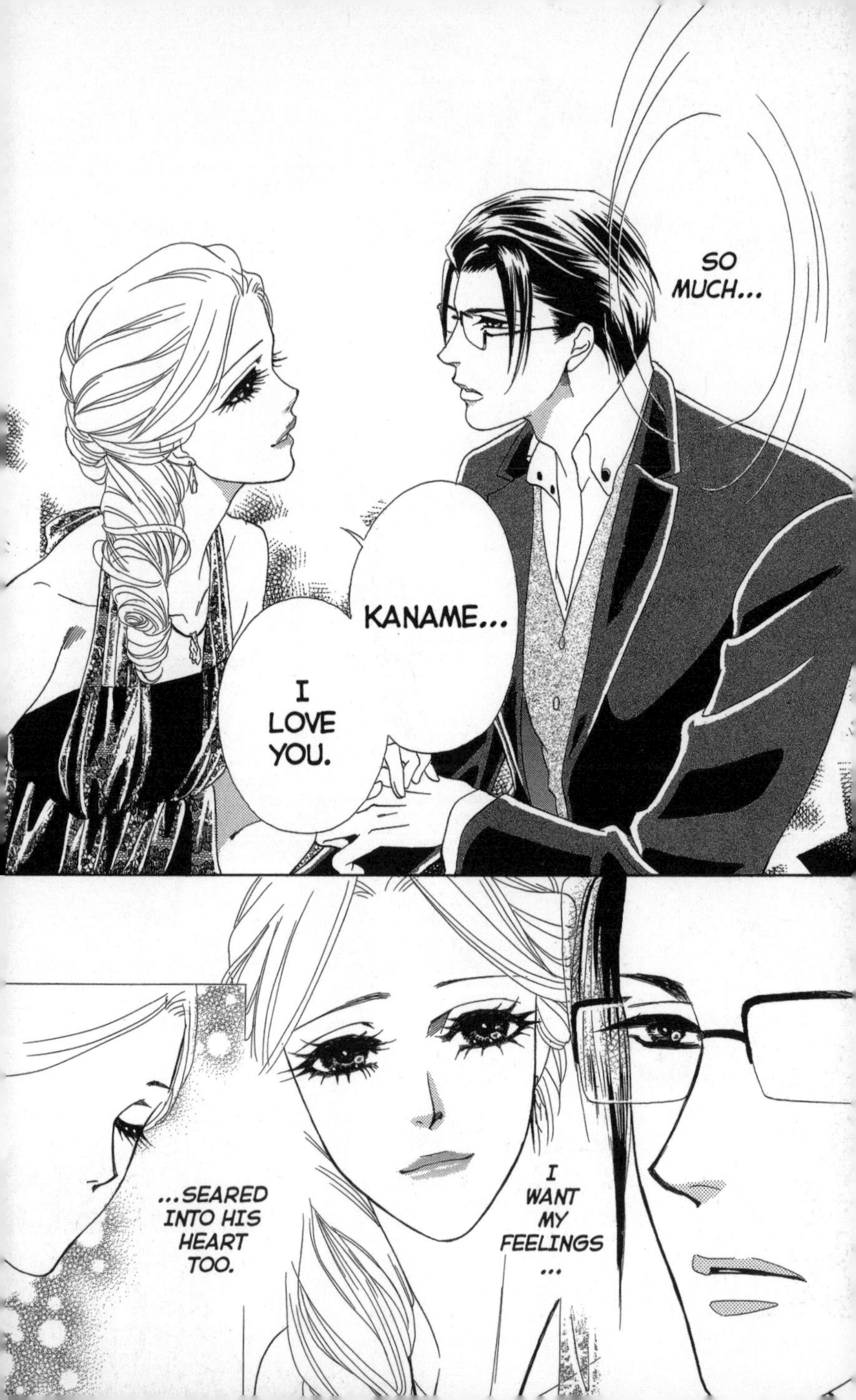
SO MUCH...
KANAME...
I LOVE YOU.
I WANT MY FEELINGS ...
...SEARED INTO HIS HEART TOO.

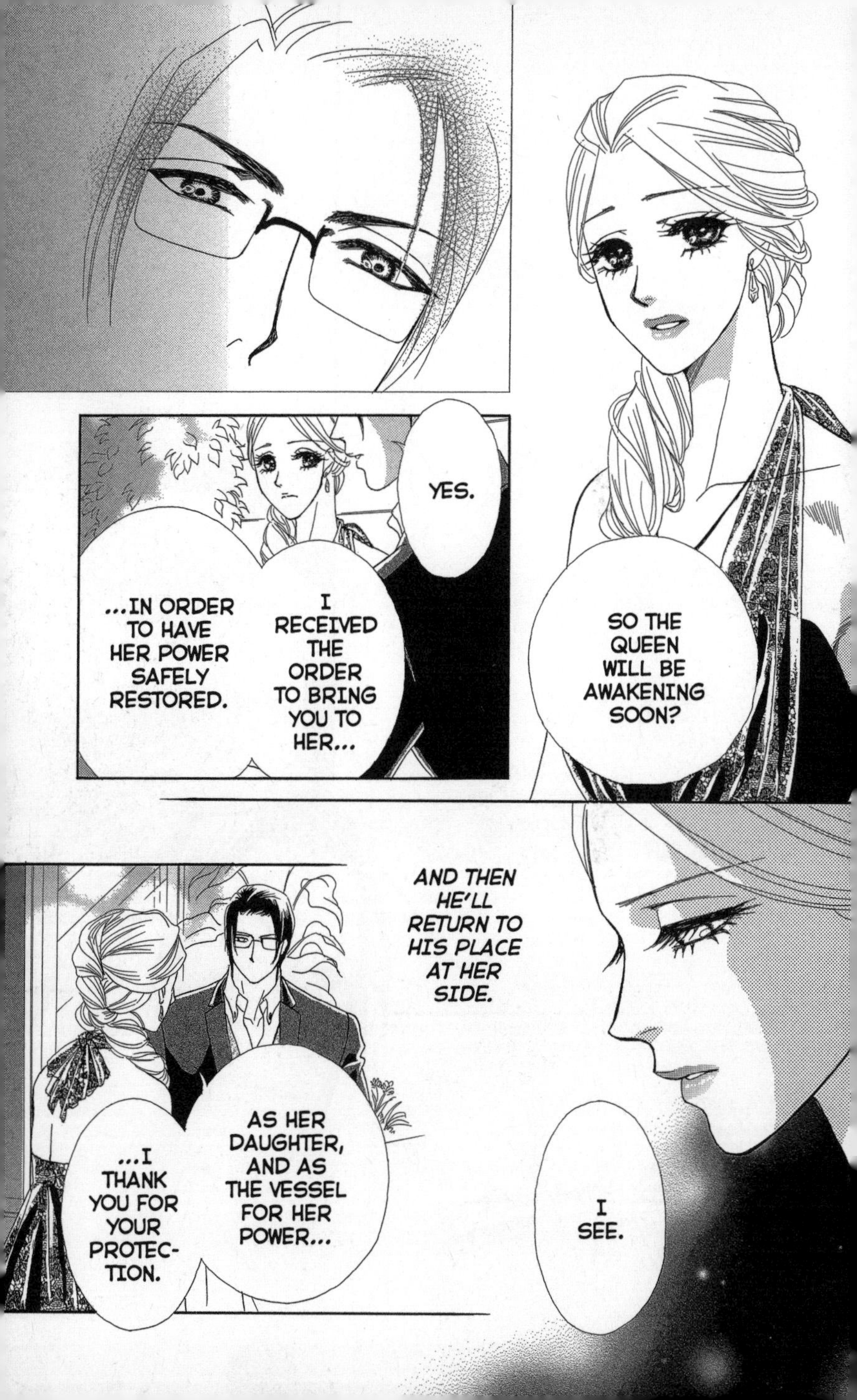
SO THE QUEEN WILL BE AWAKENING SOON?
YES.
I RECEIVED THE ORDER TO BRING YOU TO HER...
...IN ORDER TO HAVE HER POWER SAFELY RESTORED.
AND THEN HE'LL RETURN TO HIS PLACE AT HER SIDE.
I SEE.
AS HER DAUGHTER, AND AS THE VESSEL FOR HER POWER...
...I THANK YOU FOR YOUR PROTECTION.

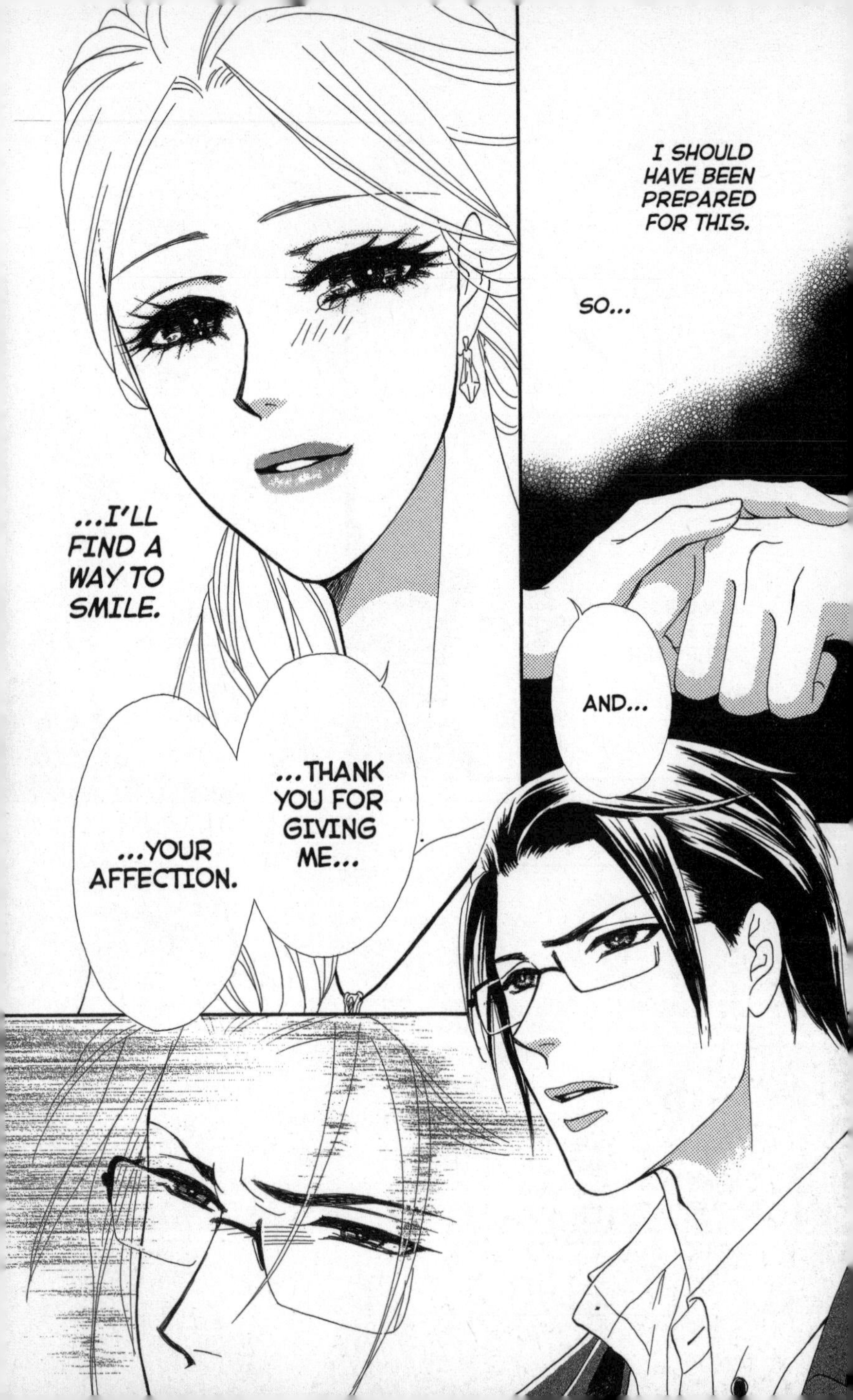
I SHOULD HAVE BEEN PREPARED FOR THIS.
SO...
AND...
...I'LL FIND A WAY TO SMILE.
...THANK YOU FOR GIVING ME...
...YOUR AFFECTION.

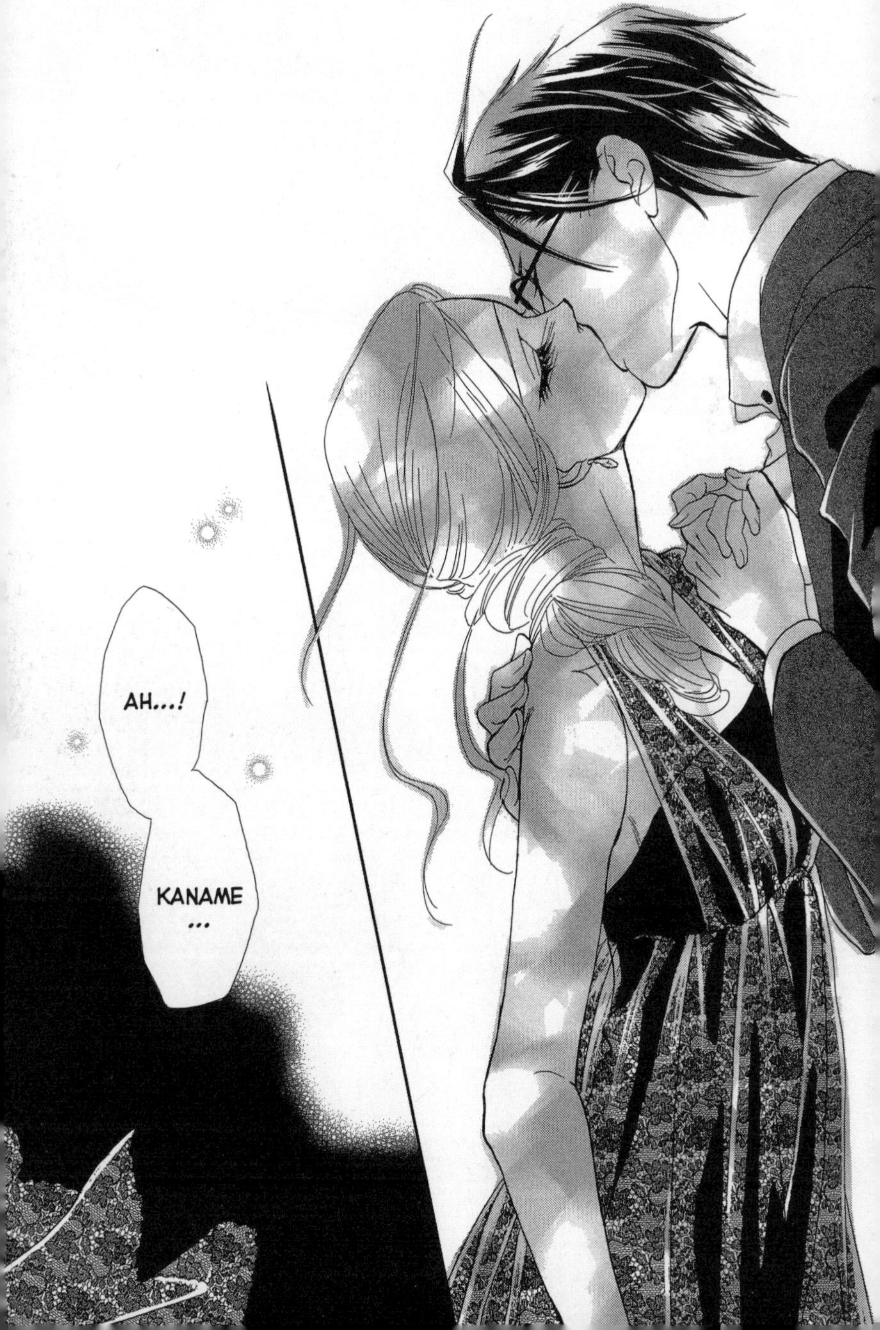
AH...!
KANAME
...

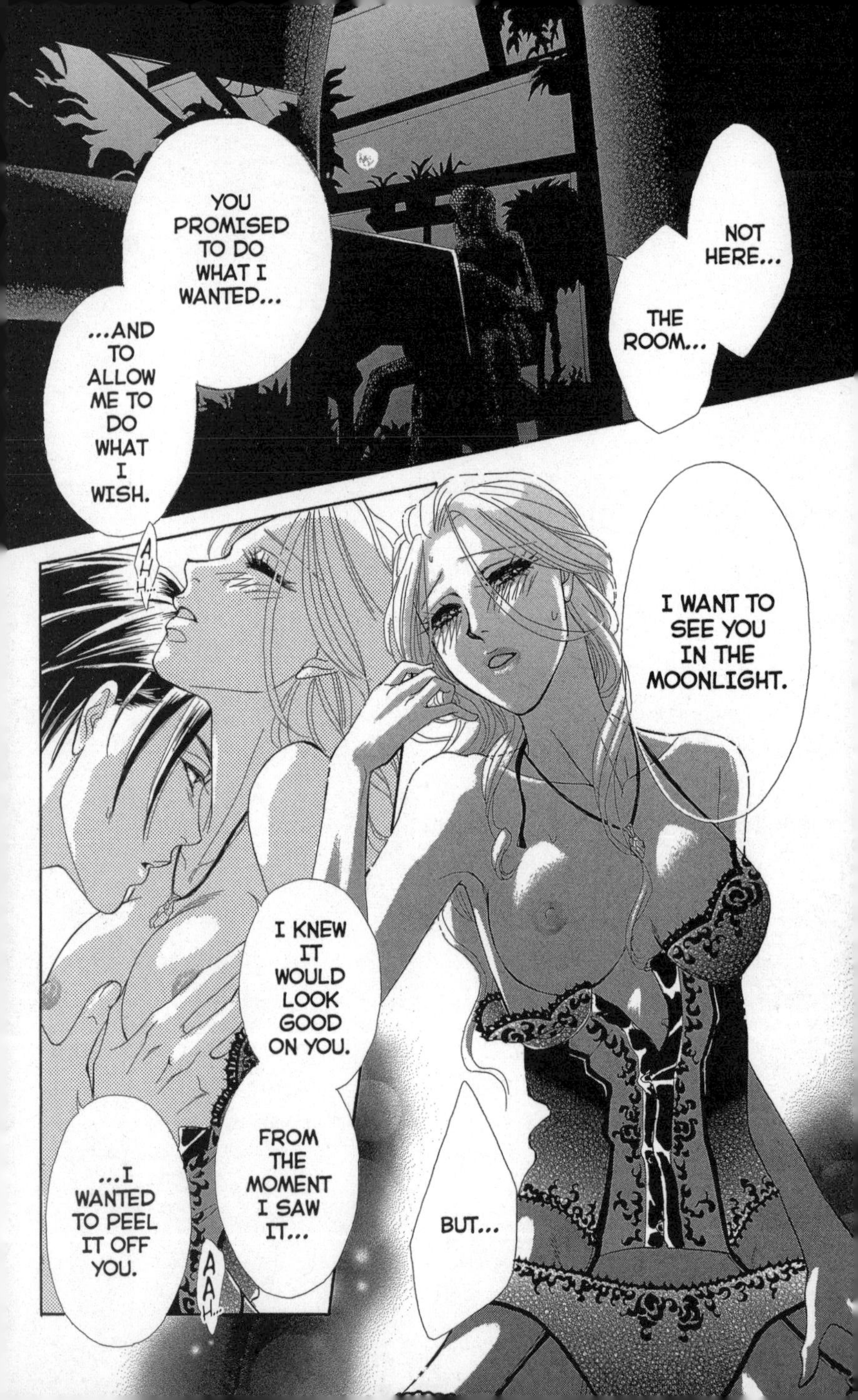
NOT HERE...
THE ROOM...
YOU PROMISED TO DO WHAT I WANTED...
...AND TO ALLOW ME TO DO WHAT I WISH.
I WANT TO SEE YOU IN THE MOONLIGHT.
AHH...
I KNEW IT WOULD LOOK GOOD ON YOU.
BUT...
FROM THE MOMENT I SAW IT...
...I WANTED TO PEEL IT OFF YOU.
AAH...

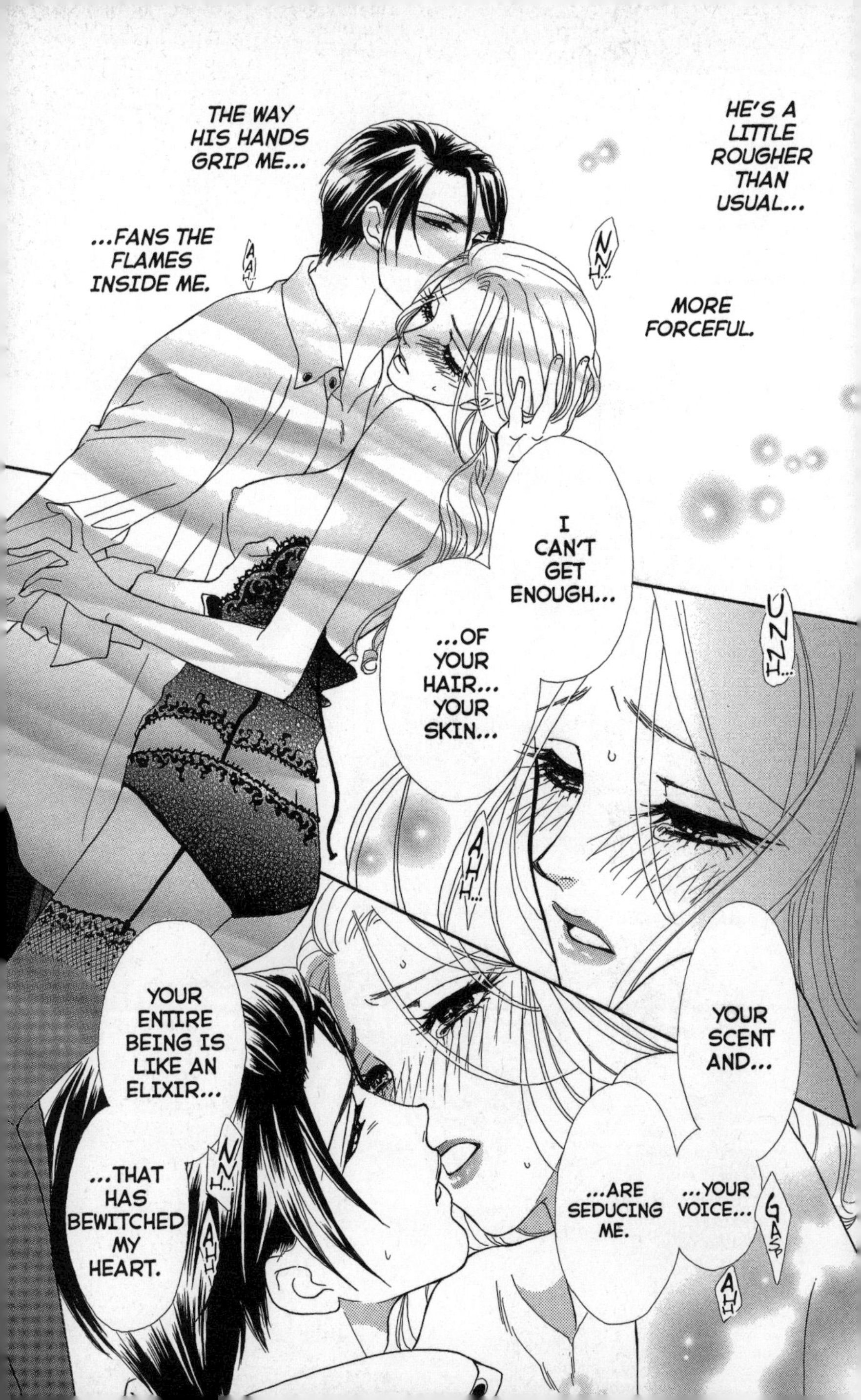
HE'S A LITTLE ROUGHER THAN USUAL...
NNH...
MORE FORCEFUL.
THE WAY HIS HANDS GRIP ME...
AH...
...FANS THE FLAMES INSIDE ME.
UNNH...
I CAN'T GET ENOUGH...
...OF YOUR HAIR... YOUR SKIN...
AHH...
YOUR SCENT AND...
GASP
...YOUR VOICE...
AHH
...ARE SEDUCING ME.
YOUR ENTIRE BEING IS LIKE AN ELIXIR...
NNH...
AHH
...THAT HAS BEWITCHED MY HEART.

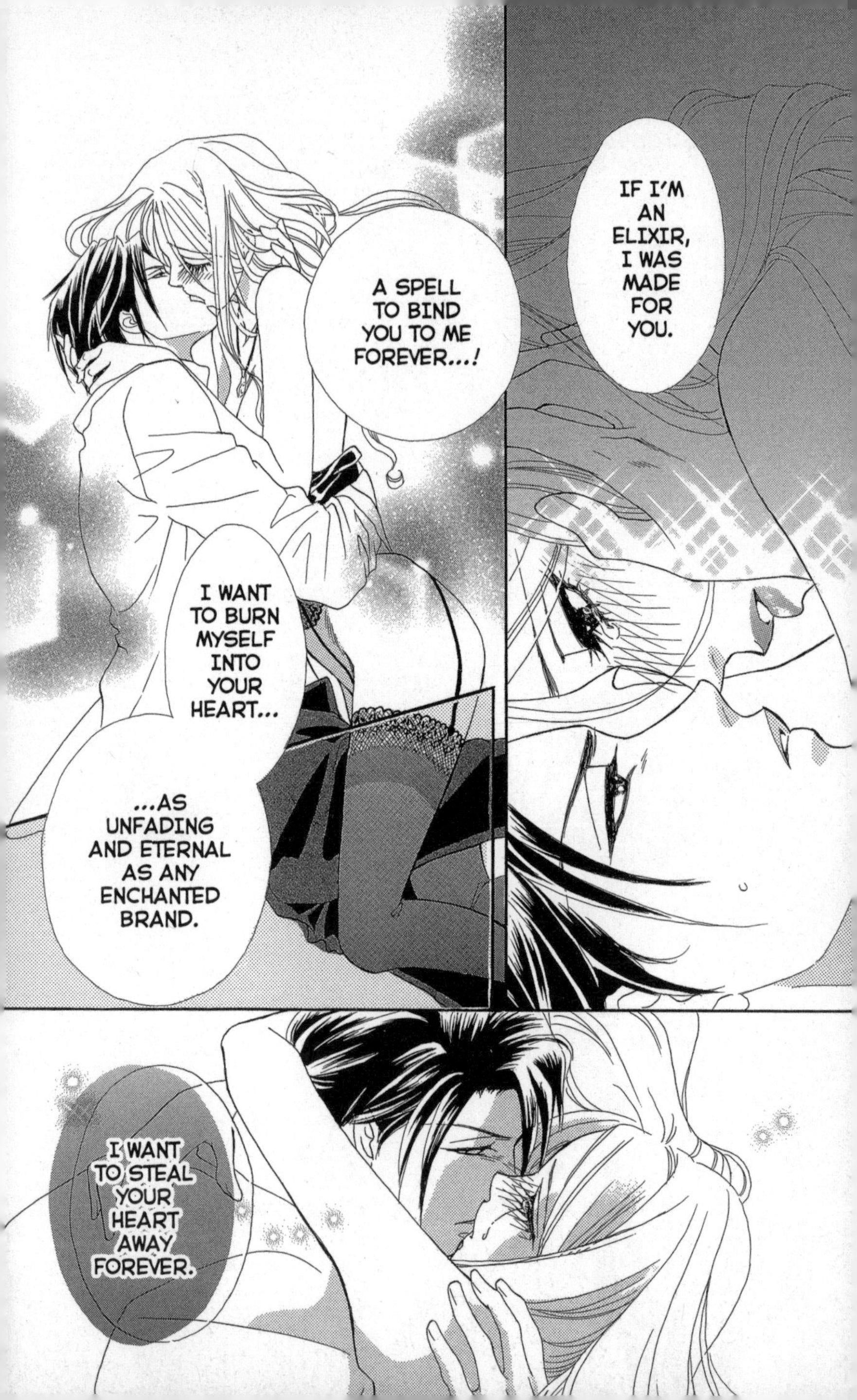
IF I'M AN ELIXIR, I WAS MADE FOR YOU.
A SPELL TO BIND YOU TO ME FOREVER...!
I WANT TO BURN MYSELF INTO YOUR HEART...
...AS UNFADING AND ETERNAL AS ANY ENCHANTED BRAND.
I WANT TO STEAL YOUR HEART AWAY FOREVER.

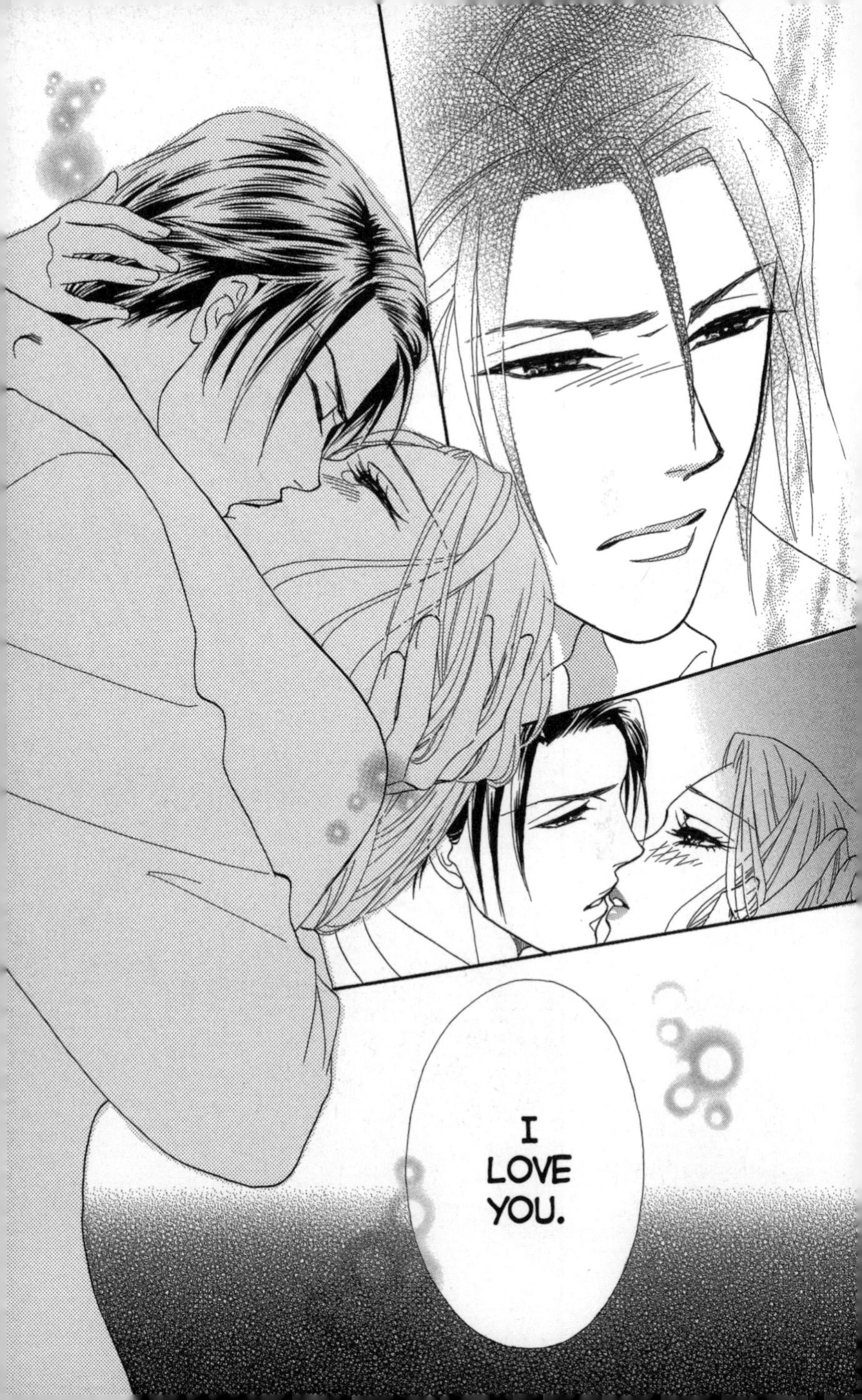
I LOVE YOU.

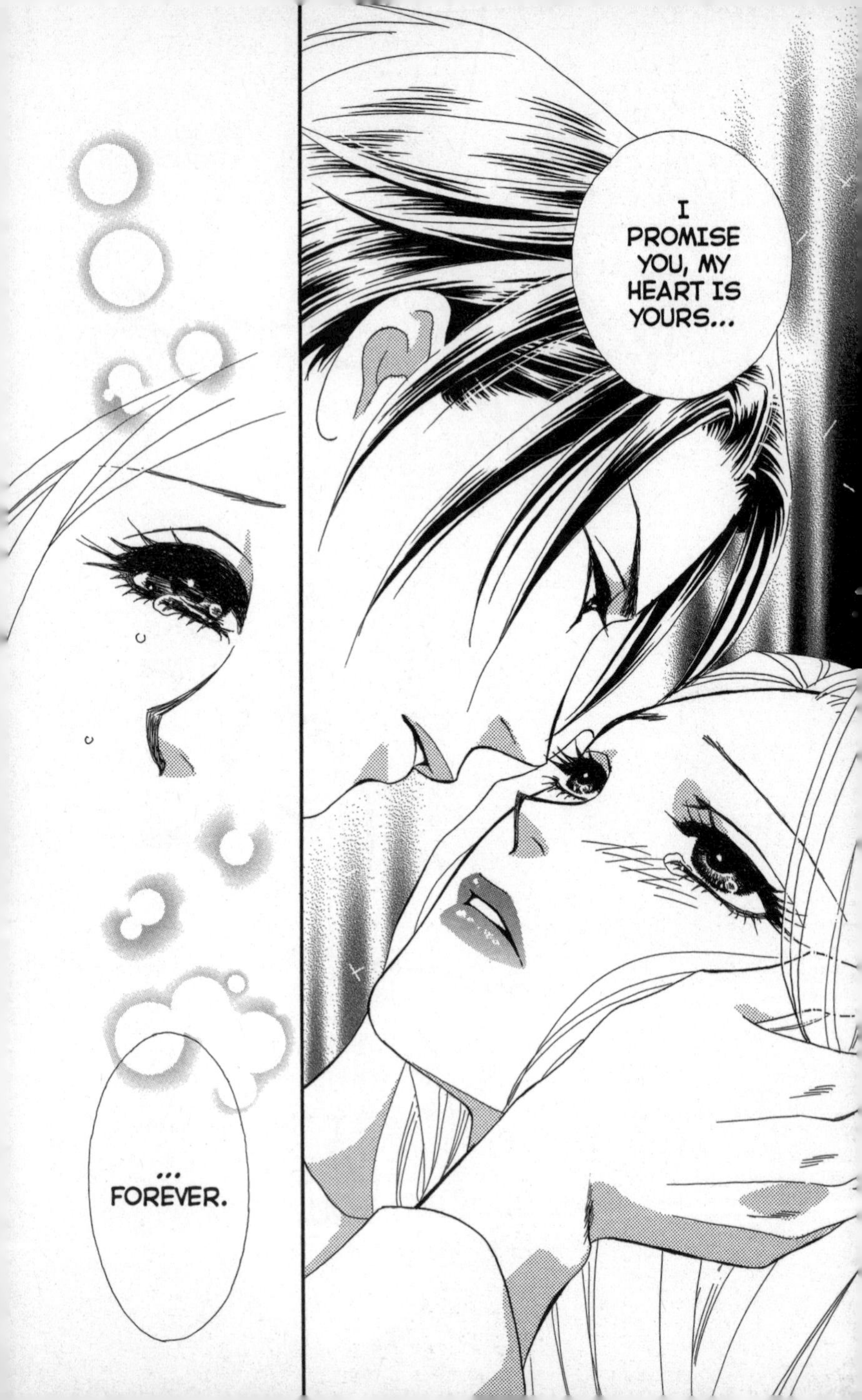
I PROMISE YOU, MY HEART IS YOURS...
...FOREVER.

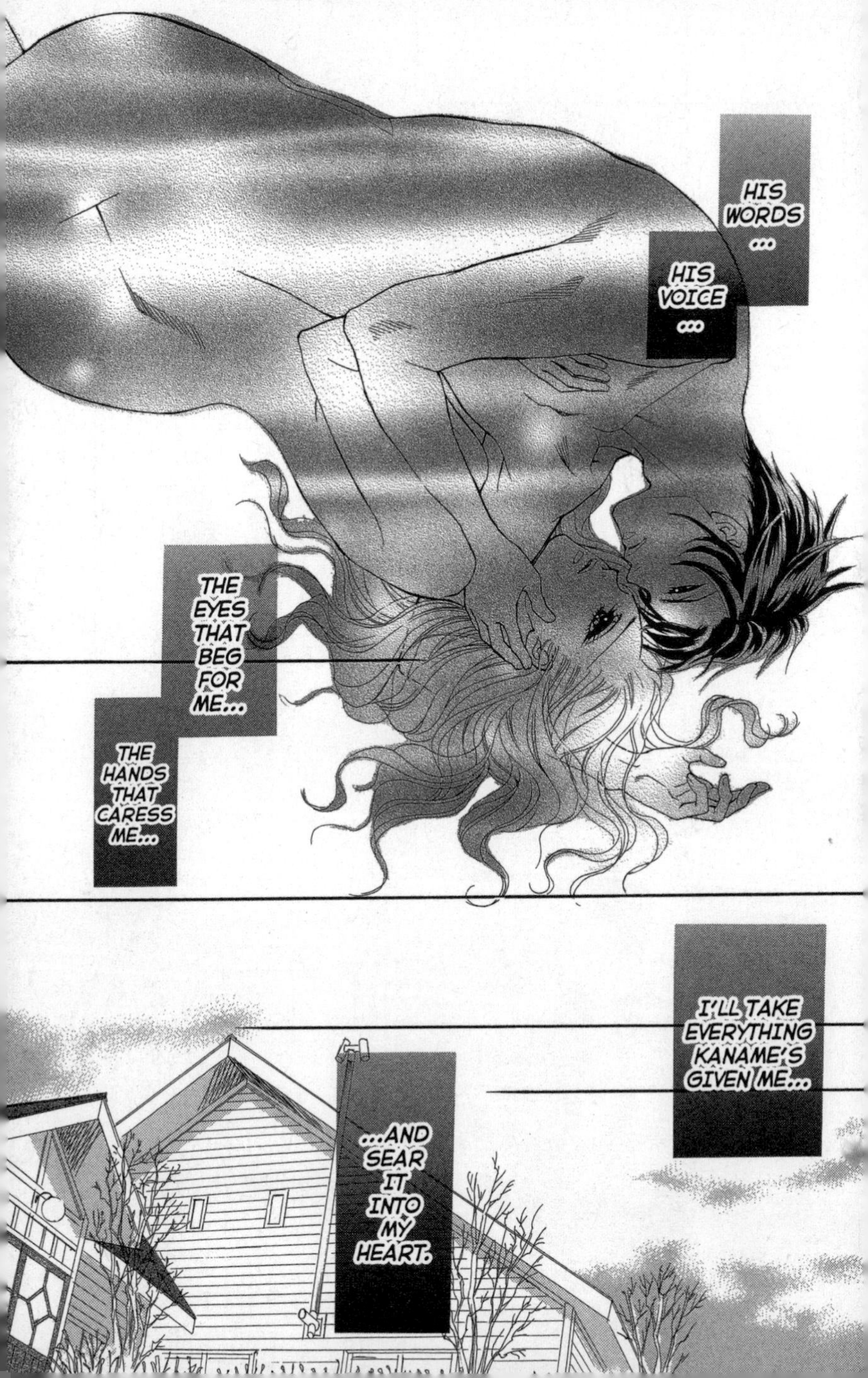
HIS WORDS...
HIS VOICE...
THE EYES THAT BEG FOR ME...
THE HANDS THAT CARESS ME...
I'LL TAKE EVERYTHING KANAME'S GIVEN ME...
...AND SEAR IT INTO MY HEART.

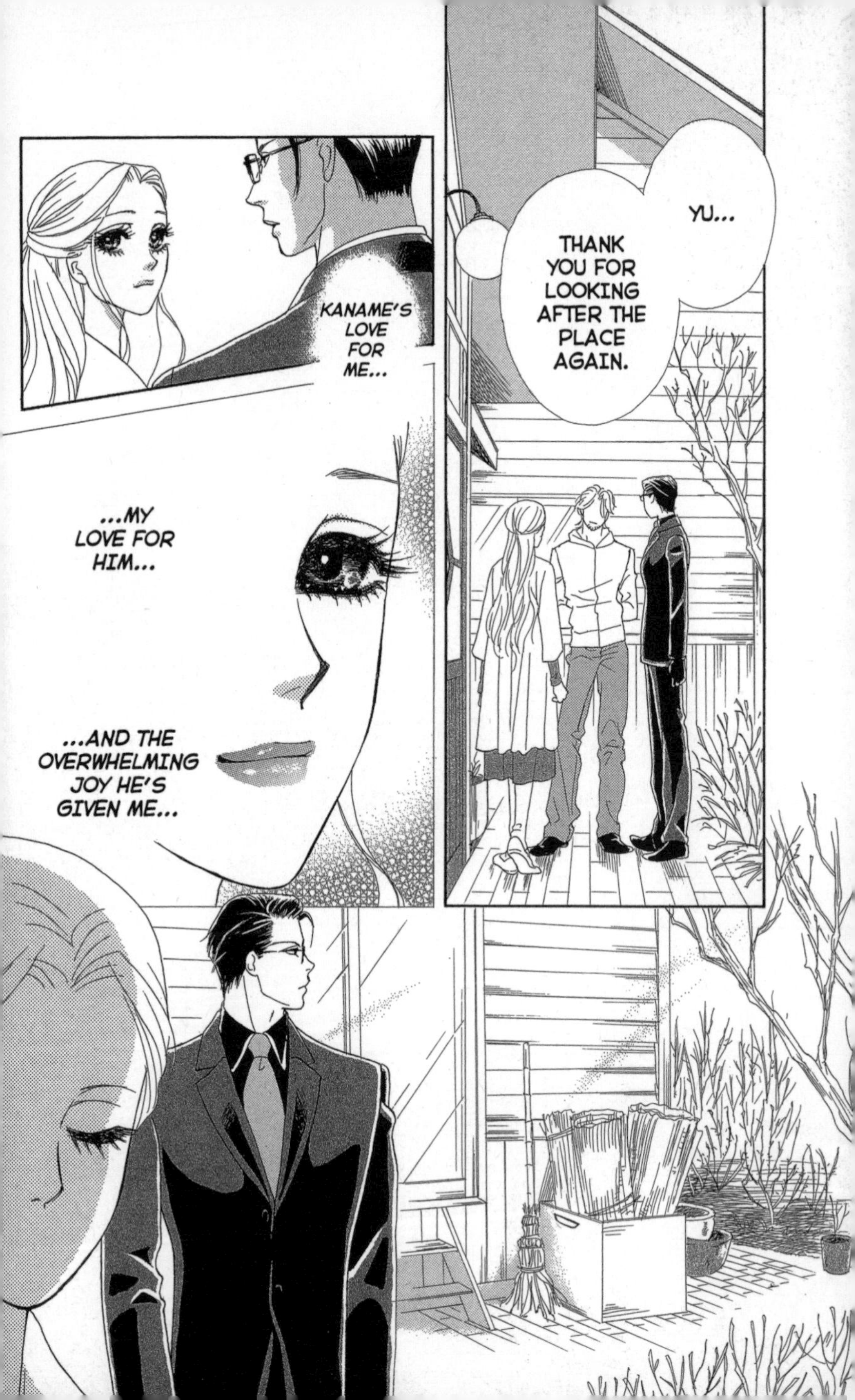
YU...
THANK YOU FOR LOOKING AFTER THE PLACE AGAIN.
KANAME'S LOVE FOR ME...
...MY LOVE FOR HIM...
...AND THE OVERWHELMING JOY HE'S GIVEN ME...

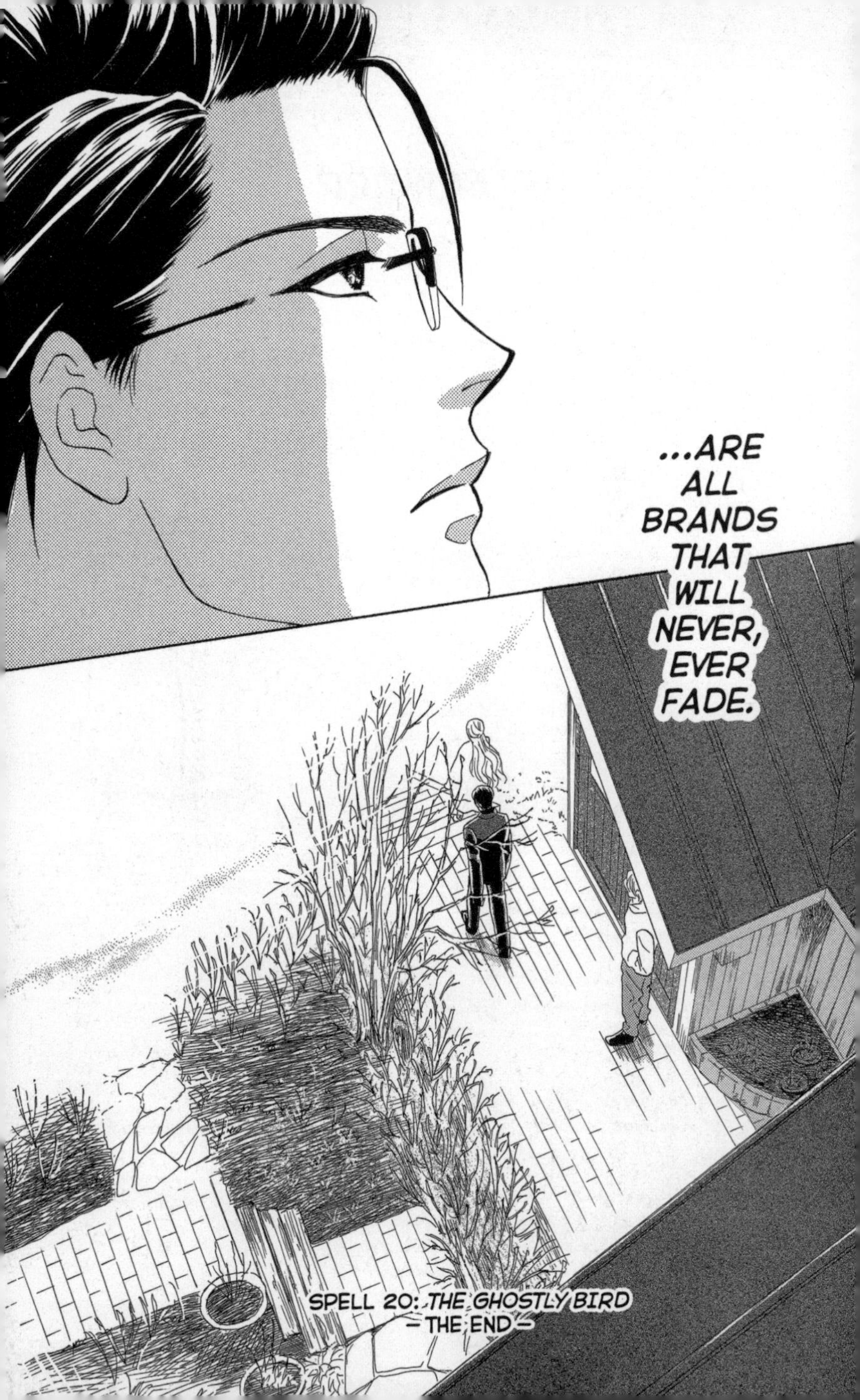
...ARE ALL BRANDS THAT WILL NEVER, EVER FADE.
SPELL 20: THE GHOSTLY BIRD
–THE END–

AFTERWORD

Hi! This is Tomu Ohmi!
I'm so glad you picked up
my 31st manga volume!

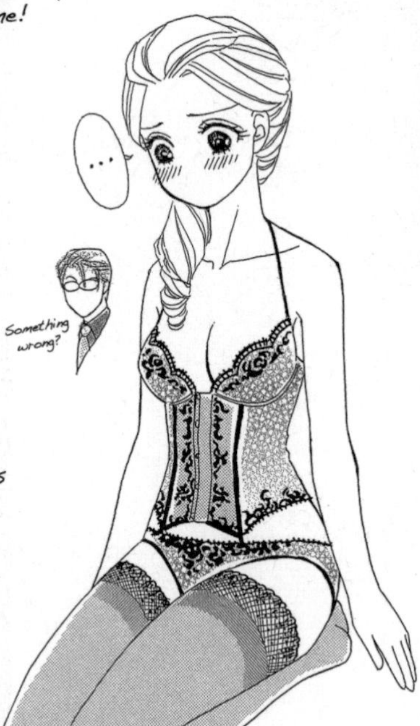
...
Something wrong?

I hope you enjoyed seeing Koko as a black witch. I had lots of fun dressing her appropriately. I'm interested to see what kind of black witch she'll become, since she's so much more like a white witch—so pure inside!

In the next volume, the Witch Queen will finally awaken. What will Koko and Kaname's fate be?! We'll finally know!

I'll look forward to seeing you in Flower Comics again!

Thank you to everyone who helped me with this manga, and to all the readers!

I may not be able to answer right away, but feel free to write to me!

Tomu Ohmi
c/o Spell of Desire Editor
Viz Media
P.O. Box 77010
San Francisco, CA 94107

You can also email your thoughts to the *Petit Comics* web address. I shouldn't say this in lieu of a reply, but I'd like to send you a New Year's greeting card, so please include your address!

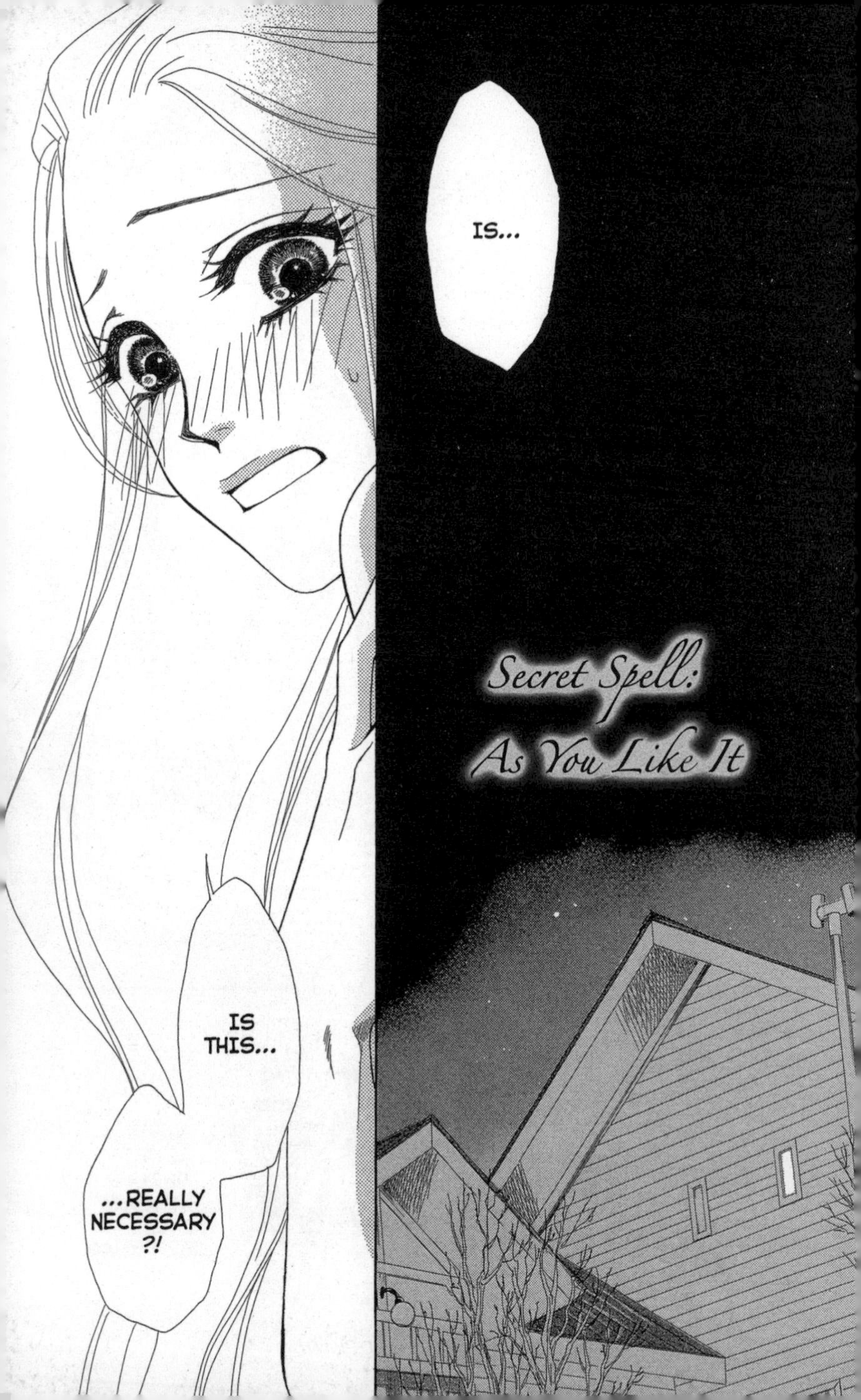
IS...
Secret Spell: As You Like It
IS THIS...
...REALLY NECESSARY ?!

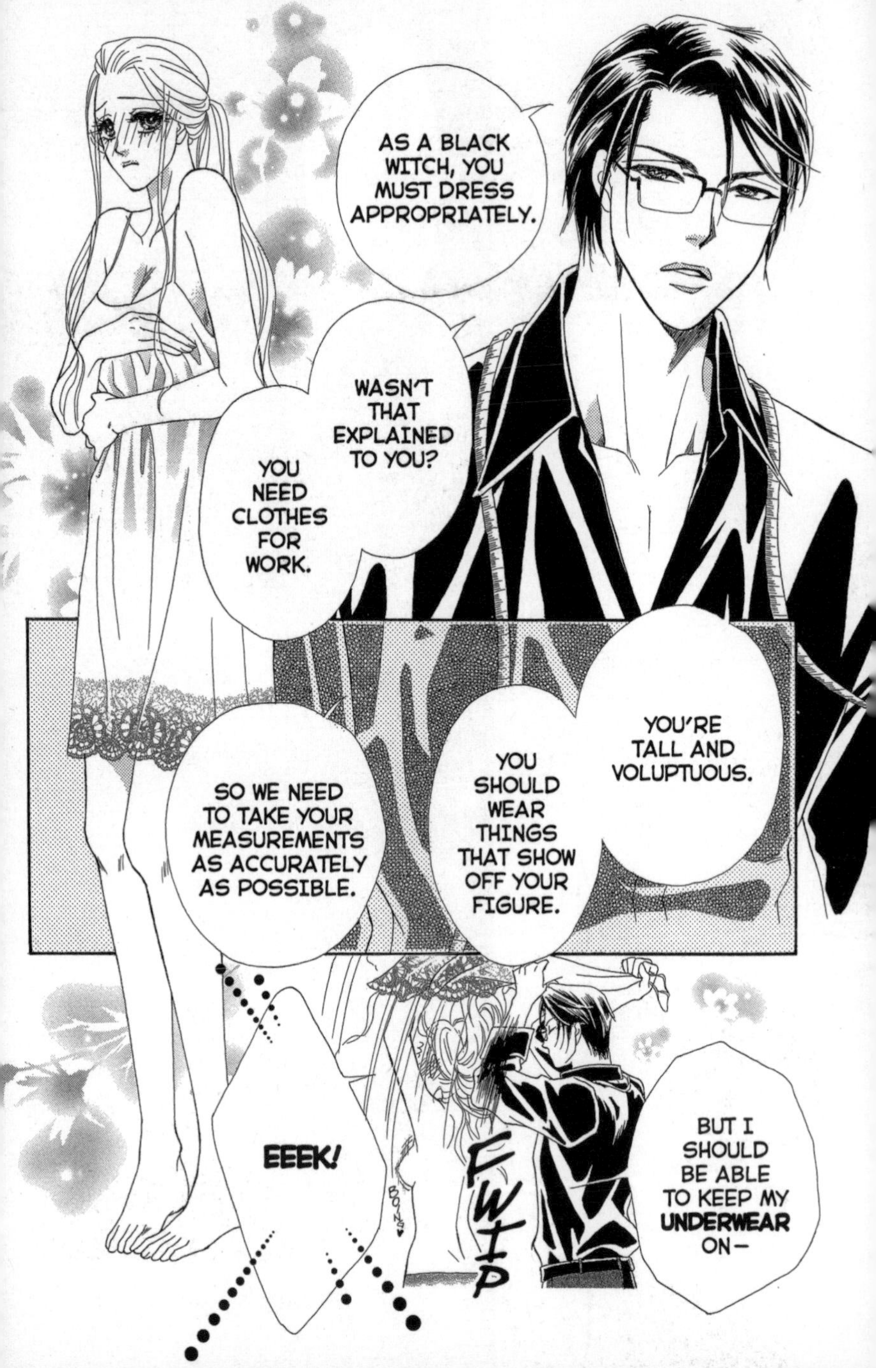

AS A BLACK WITCH, YOU MUST DRESS APPROPRIATELY.
WASN'T THAT EXPLAINED TO YOU?
YOU NEED CLOTHES FOR WORK.
YOU'RE TALL AND VOLUPTUOUS.
YOU SHOULD WEAR THINGS THAT SHOW OFF YOUR FIGURE.
SO WE NEED TO TAKE YOUR MEASUREMENTS AS ACCURATELY AS POSSIBLE.
BUT I SHOULD BE ABLE TO KEEP MY **UNDERWEAR** ON–
FWIP
BOING
EEEK!

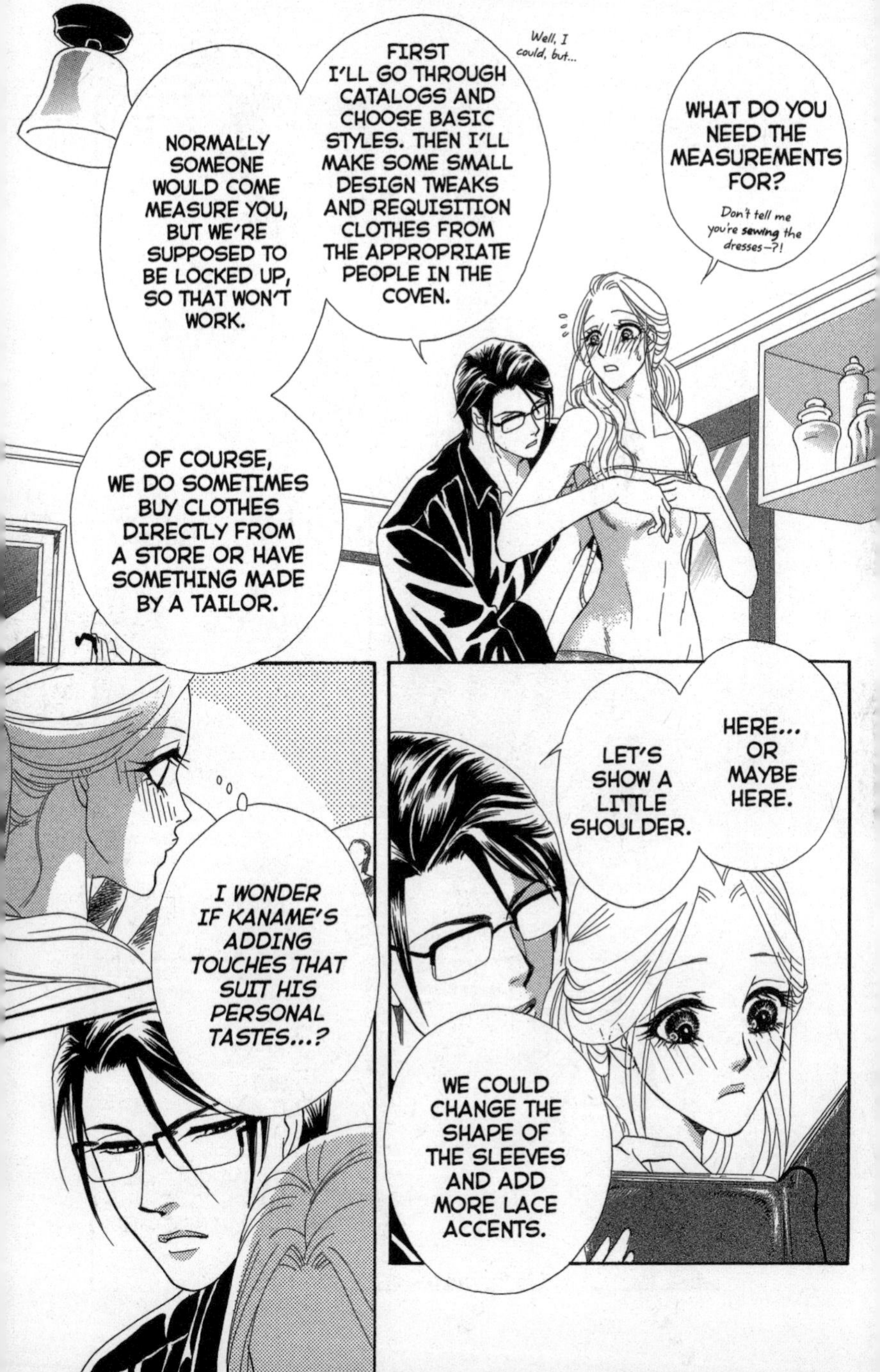
WHAT DO YOU NEED THE MEASUREMENTS FOR?
Don't tell me you're sewing the dresses—?!
Well, I could, but...
FIRST I'LL GO THROUGH CATALOGS AND CHOOSE BASIC STYLES. THEN I'LL MAKE SOME SMALL DESIGN TWEAKS AND REQUISITION CLOTHES FROM THE APPROPRIATE PEOPLE IN THE COVEN.
NORMALLY SOMEONE WOULD COME MEASURE YOU, BUT WE'RE SUPPOSED TO BE LOCKED UP, SO THAT WON'T WORK.
OF COURSE, WE DO SOMETIMES BUY CLOTHES DIRECTLY FROM A STORE OR HAVE SOMETHING MADE BY A TAILOR.
HERE... OR MAYBE HERE.
LET'S SHOW A LITTLE SHOULDER.
WE COULD CHANGE THE SHAPE OF THE SLEEVES AND ADD MORE LACE ACCENTS.
I WONDER IF KANAME'S ADDING TOUCHES THAT SUIT HIS PERSONAL TASTES...?

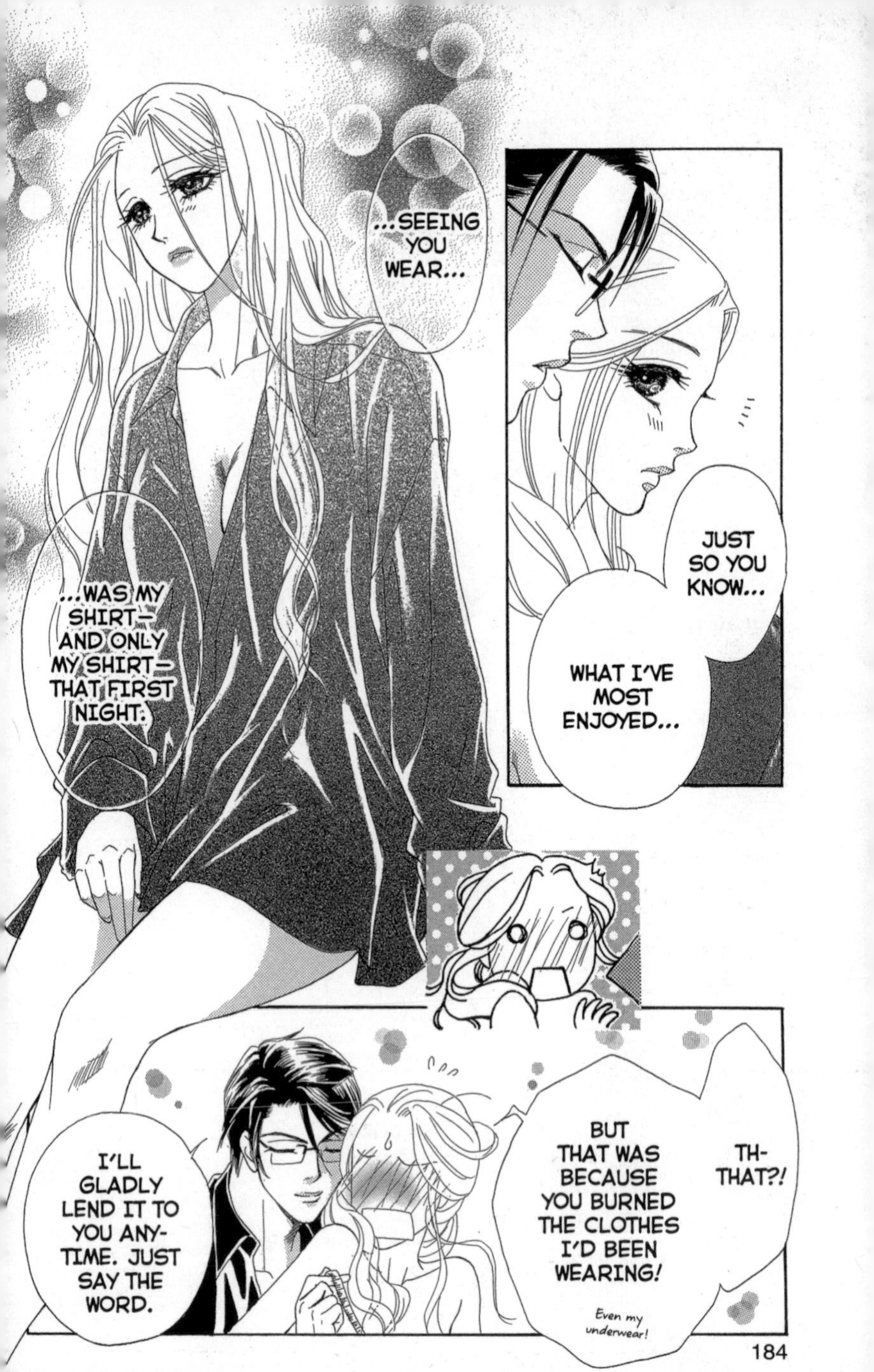
JUST SO YOU KNOW...
WHAT I'VE MOST ENJOYED...
...SEEING YOU WEAR...
...WAS MY SHIRT—AND ONLY MY SHIRT—THAT FIRST NIGHT.
TH-THAT?!
BUT THAT WAS BECAUSE YOU BURNED THE CLOTHES I'D BEEN WEARING!
Even my underwear!
I'LL GLADLY LEND IT TO YOU ANY-TIME. JUST SAY THE WORD.

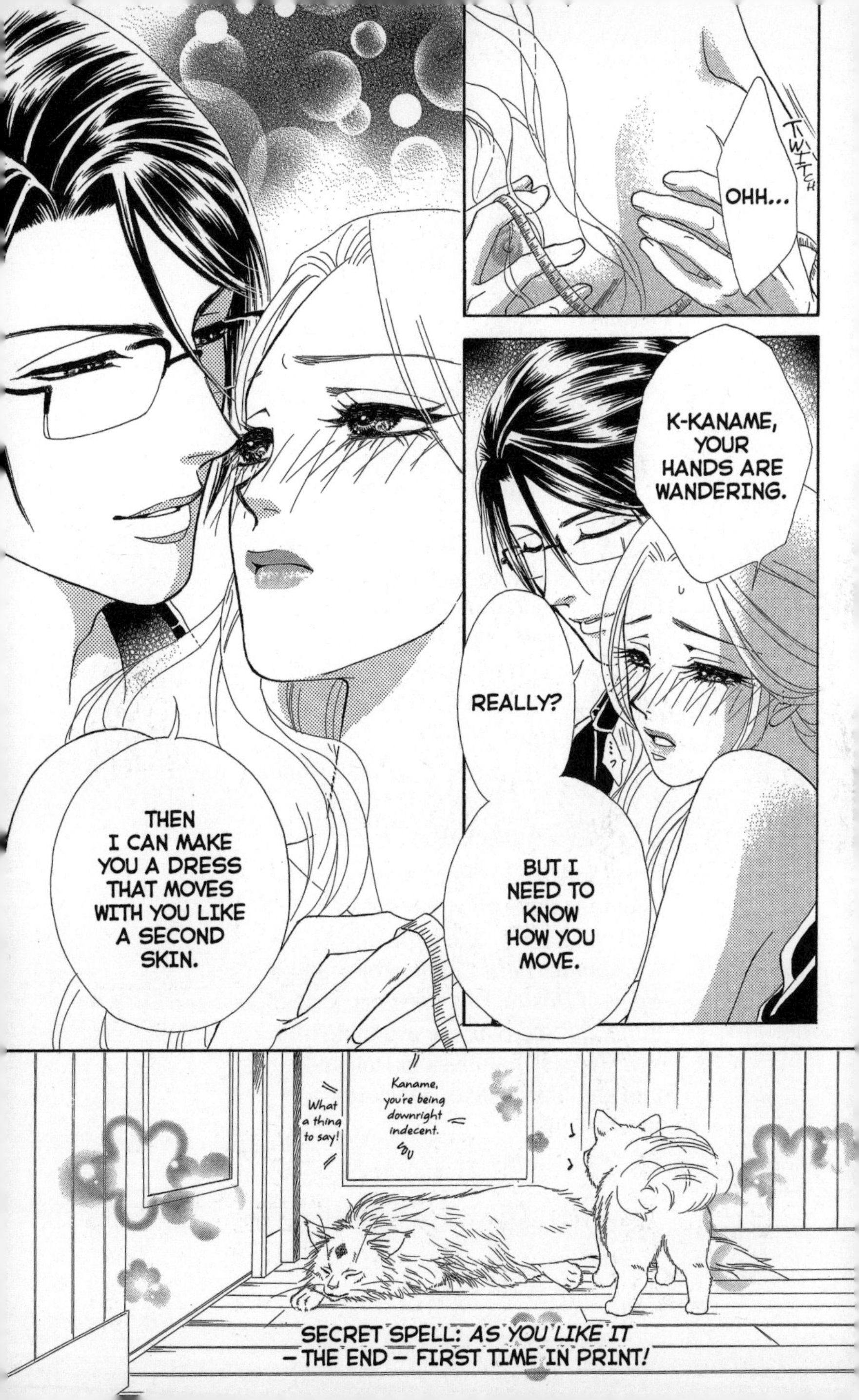
TWITCH
OHH...
K-KANAME, YOUR HANDS ARE WANDERING.
REALLY?
BUT I NEED TO KNOW HOW YOU MOVE.
THEN I CAN MAKE YOU A DRESS THAT MOVES WITH YOU LIKE A SECOND SKIN.
Kaname, you're being downright indecent.
What a thing to say!
SECRET SPELL: AS YOU LIKE IT
– THE END – FIRST TIME IN PRINT!

A WITCH'S FAMILIAR... ...IS A BLACK CAT, OF COURSE!

Yay! ♥ This is my 31st book!! Thank you very much for picking it up! In this volume, Koko begins to tap into her power as a Black Witch. I had so much fun drawing her in action! ♪ I hope it'll excite and entertain you!

–Tomu Ohmi

Author Bio

Born on May 25, Tomu Ohmi debuted with *Kindan no Koi wo Shiyoh* in 2000. She is presently working on *Petit Comic* projects like *Spell of Desire*. Her previous series, *Midnight Secretary*, is available from VIZ Media. Ohmi lives in Hokkaido, and she likes beasts, black tea and pretty women.

Spell of Desire

VOLUME 4
Shojo Beat Edition

STORY AND ART BY
TOMU OHMI

MAJO NO BIYAKU Vol. 4
by Tomu OHMI
© 2012 Tomu OHMI
All rights reserved.
Original Japanese edition published by SHOGAKUKAN.
English translation rights in the United States of America, Canada, the
United Kingdom, Ireland, Australia and New Zealand arranged with
SHOGAKUKAN.

English Adaptation/Ysabet Reinhardt MacFarlane
Translation/JN Productions
Touch-up Art & Lettering/Monalisa de Asis
Design/Izumi Evers
Editor/Amy Yu

The stories, characters and incidents mentioned in this publication
are entirely fictional.

No portion of this book may be reproduced or transmitted in any
form or by any means without written permission from the copyright
holders.

Printed in the U.S.A.

Published by VIZ Media, LLC
P.O. Box 77010
San Francisco, CA 94107

10 9 8 7 6 5 4 3 2 1
First printing, May 2015

www.viz.com

PARENTAL ADVISORY
SPELL OF DESIRE is rated M for
Mature and is recommended for ages
18 and up.
ratings.viz.com

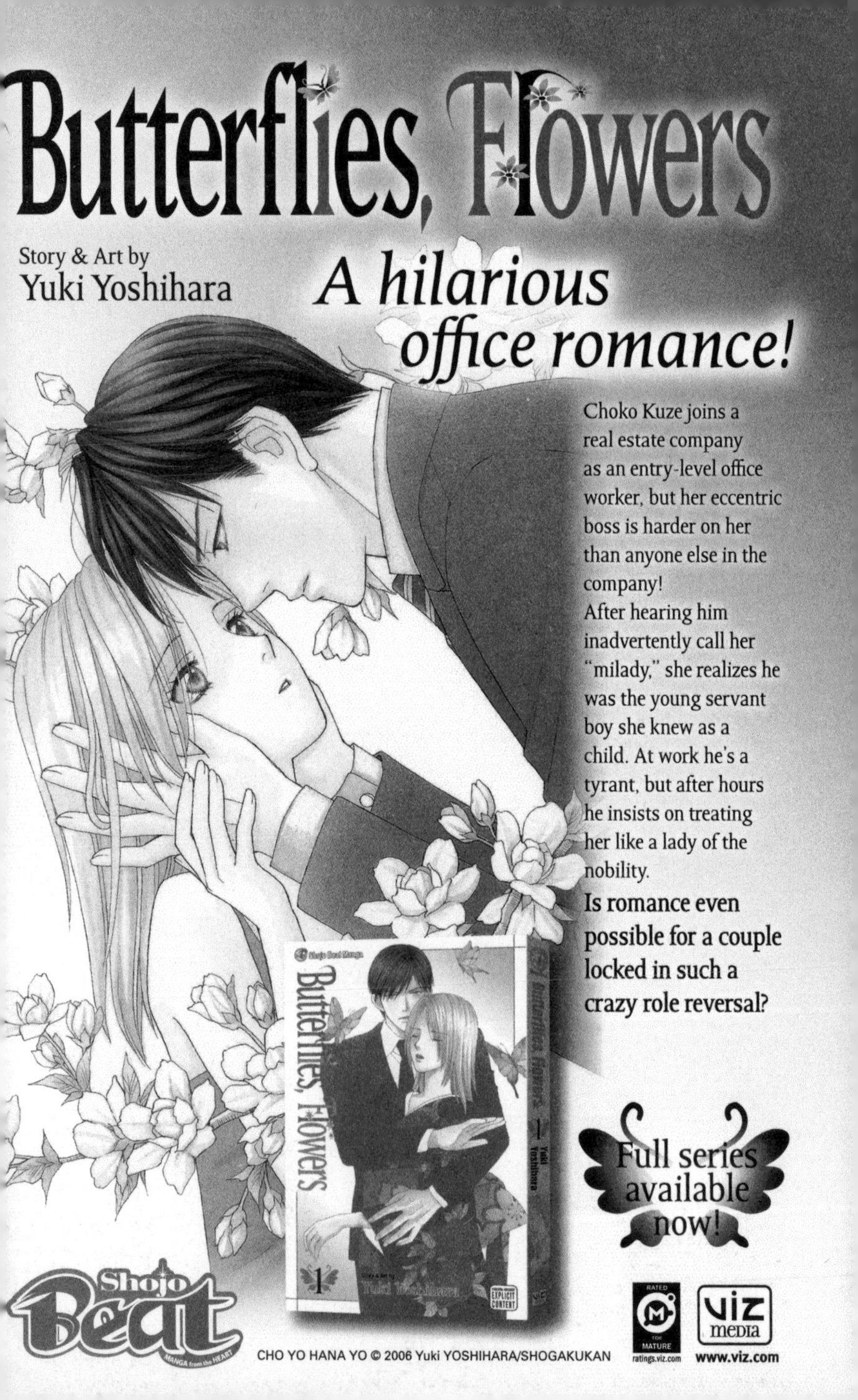

Butterflies, Flowers
Story & Art by
Yuki Yoshihara
A hilarious office romance!
Choko Kuze joins a real estate company as an entry-level office worker, but her eccentric boss is harder on her than anyone else in the company!
After hearing him inadvertently call her "milady," she realizes he was the young servant boy she knew as a child. At work he's a tyrant, but after hours he insists on treating her like a lady of the nobility.
Is romance even possible for a couple locked in such a crazy role reversal?
Shojo Beat Manga
Butterflies, Flowers
1
Yuki Yoshihara
Full series available now!
Shojo Beat
MANGA from the HEART
CHO YO HANA YO © 2006 Yuki YOSHIHARA/SHOGAKUKAN
RATED M FOR MATURE
ratings.viz.com
VIZ MEDIA
www.viz.com

Happy Marriage?!

Story & Art by Maki Enjoji

Can two strangers living together find their way to a happy marriage?!

In order to help her father, Chiwa Takanashi agrees to an arranged marriage with the company president, Hokuto Mamiya—a man she doesn't know—at the request of Hokuto's grandfather. Chiwa believes the arrangement isn't binding, but her new partner seems to think otherwise...

Start the romance today. Series available now!

RATED M FOR MATURE — ratings.viz.com

Shojo Beat

VIZ MEDIA — www.viz.com

HAPIMARI - HAPPY MARRIAGE!? - © 2009 Maki ENJOJI/SHOGAKUKAN

Honey Blood

Story & Art by Miko Mitsuki

inata can't help but be drawn
) Junya, but could it be that
e's actually a vampire?

hen a girl at her school is attacked
/ what seems to be a vampire, high
hool student Hinata Sorazono
fuses to believe that vampires
en exist. But then she meets
r new neighbor, Junya
kinaga, the author of an
credibly popular vampire
mance novel… Could it
e that Junya's actually a
mpire—and worse yet,
e culprit?!

www.shojobeat.com

www.viz.com

TSUAJI BLOOD © 2009 Miko MITSUKI/SHOGAKUKAN

Absolute Boyfriend

BY YUU WATASE

Only $8.99

Shojo Beat Manga
Absolute Boyfriend
Yuu Watase
1

Rejected way too many times by good-looking (and unattainable) guys, shy Riiko Izawa goes online and signs up for a free trial of a mysterious Nightly Lover "figure." The very next day, a cute naked guy is delivered to her door, and he wants to be her boyfriend! What gives? And...what's the catch?

MANGA SERIES ON SALE NOW

Shojo Beat
MANGA from the HEART

On sale at:
www.shojobeat.com
Also available at your local bookstore and comic store.

ZETTAI KARESHI © 2003 Yuu WATASE/Shogakukan

www.viz.co

This is the last page.

In keeping with the original Japanese comic format, this book reads from right to left—so action, sound effects, and word balloons are completely reversed. This preserves the orientation of the original artwork—plus, it's fun! Check out the diagram shown here to get the hang of things, and then turn to the other side of the book to get started!

Date: 7/29/15

GRA 741.5 SPE V.4
Ohmi, Tomu.
Spell of desire.

PALM BEACH COUNTY
LIBRARY SYSTEM
3650 Summit Boulevard
West Palm Beach, FL 33406-4198